T0294644

Membership Marketing in the Digital Age

AMERICAN ASSOCIATION FOR STATE AND LOCAL HISTORY BOOK SERIES

ABOUT THE SERIES

The American Association for State and Local History Book Series addresses issues critical to the field of state and local history through interpretive, intellectual, scholarly, and educational texts. To submit a proposal or manuscript to the series, please request proposal guidelines from AASLH headquarters: AASLH Editorial Board, 1717 Church St., Nashville, Tennessee 37203. Telephone: (615) 320-3203. Website: www.aaslh.org.

ABOUT THE ORGANIZATION

The American Association for State and Local History (AASLH) is a national history membership association headquartered in Nashville, Tennessee. AASLH provides leadership and support for its members who preserve and interpret state and local history in order to make the past more meaningful to all Americans. AASLH members are leaders in preserving, researching, and interpreting traces of the American past to connect the people, thoughts, and events of yesterday with the creative memories and abiding concerns of people, communities, and our nation today. In addition to sponsorship of this book series, AASLH publishes *History News* magazine, a newsletter, technical leaflets and reports, and other materials; confers prizes and awards in recognition of outstanding achievement in the field; supports a broad education program and other activities designed to help members work more effectively; and advocates on behalf of the discipline of history. To join AASLH, go to www.aaslh.org or contact Membership Services, AASLH, 1717 Church St., Nashville, TN 37203.

Membership Marketing in the Digital Age

A Handbook for Museums and Libraries

PATRICIA RICH, ACFRE
DANA S. HINES, CFRE
ROSIE SIEMER

ROWMAN & LITTLEFIELD
Lanham • Boulder • New York • London

Published by Rowman & Littlefield
A wholly owned subsidiary of The Rowman & Littlefield Publishing Group, Inc.
4501 Forbes Boulevard, Suite 200, Lanham, Maryland 20706
www.rowman.com

Unit A, Whitacre Mews, 26-34 Stannary Street, London SE11 4AB

British Library Cataloguing in Publication Information Available

Library of Congress Cataloging-in-Publication Data
ISBN 978-1-4422-5980-5 (hardback)
ISBN 978-1-4422-5981-2 (paperback)
ISBN 978-1-4422-5982-9 (e-book)

∞™ The paper used in this publication meets the minimum requirements of American National Standard for Information Sciences—Permanence of Paper for Printed Library Materials, ANSI/NISO Z39.48-1992.

Printed in the United States of America

We dedicate this book to everyone who works in membership in nonprofit organizations. For many nonprofits, the membership is the heart and soul of the organization. Having a strong membership program ensures that the organization can accomplish its mission. We applaud the staff and volunteers who strive to make their programs the best that they can be and, in turn, serve their communities.

Contents

Visit www.themembershipbook.com for additional resources, sample campaigns, and case studies.

Foreword

I have my roots in Rock and Roll—and baseball, and museums, and Membership! My museum training is honest—from the Cooperstown Graduate Program in Museum Studies. My baseball and rock and roll background is a result of passions developed through childhood and adolescence. My membership training was through the school of hard knocks and a chance encounter with Dana Hines and Membership Consultants back in the late 1990s.

At the time, my first position out of graduate school was a fortuitous hiring as the Membership Manager at the National Baseball Hall of Fame in Cooperstown, New York. I was fortunate that the President of the Hall of Fame shared a deep interest in building the membership base. I was invited to a seminar on Membership Marketing hosted by Membership Consultants. When I met Dana, who was a great St. Louis Cardinal Baseball fan herself, I knew that we were of one mind, and that was to significantly grow the membership of the National Baseball Hall of Fame.

Our journey of growth of the Hall of Fame's membership program began with a visit to Cooperstown for Dana, and a comprehensive membership plan that we developed together. Thanks to overall institutional commitment to membership, a healthy pool of untapped interest, and a solid plan, growth came quickly. Utilizing all sources of membership acquisition, including direct mail, a robust effort to capture memberships on-site with a well-trained team, and early adoption of email and online solicitation and communication, we were very successful. Membership growth, over a three- to four-year timeframe, exceeded 600 percent!

As my career progressed to Director of Development, overseeing membership still at the Baseball Hall of Fame, and now to the Rock & Roll Hall of Fame and Museum, membership remains one of the most powerful assets an organization can possess in fulfilling its overarching mission. Without the power and passion of the people who are members and who commit to our worthwhile endeavors, our institutions would not thrive and prosper.

I am excited that Dana Hines and her fellow authors and membership experts Patricia Rich and Rosie Siemer have created this valuable book that will lead more membership managers to success in their professions. This is the only book that focuses specifically on membership, and the emphasis on digital marketing comes at a critical time when organizations are struggling to catch up, evaluate which areas to invest limited dollars, and understand how digital efforts can support membership.

Membership Marketing in the Digital Age will help shape the next generation of membership leaders and serve to guide organizations forward, preparing them to meet the challenges of tomorrow. It will be an asset to all who seek to grow and flourish in the membership world!

Greg Harris
President and CEO
Rock & Roll Hall of Fame

Preface

In the 1800s Alexis de Tocqueville visited America, where he found that citizens were forever forming associations. As Tocqueville says, the groups can be "religious, moral, serious, futile, very general and very limited, immensely large and very minute."[1] While the landscape of membership programs still resembles Tocqueville's descriptions, the proliferation of groups to which we can belong, and the channels for joining, have grown exponentially. For those who are working in membership programs, this provides ever-increasing challenges. This book is a tool to deal with the challenges. It is a primer for anyone who is new to membership programs, interested in beginning one, or involved in growing one. As well, there is information for those who work as paid or volunteer staff in membership programs.

The philosophy behind this book is that planning the program will ensure that the organization's needs are met. We believe that a thoughtful plan is the first step in implementing a program that will meet the needs of the institution, the community, and the members. With a plan, activities are cohesive, resources are well used, and goals are met. We believe that the membership program should be integral in achieving the institution's mission. To do that well, we believe that planning is the key.

When we began writing and mentioning to colleagues that our topic was membership, we contended with questions about the church group, the hospital auxiliary, and associations. This was in addition to our fundamental work with cultural institutions and visitation-based organizations. This led us to decide to include information for all types of groups. As we started thinking about the various types of membership programs, it became clear to us that we needed a way to cope with the variety of groups. We decided to categorize them and developed a chart of types of membership programs. The many types are discussed in chapter 1. This book has information that will be helpful to all membership programs, no matter their type. That said, there is more information in this book for membership programs that are the foundation for fundraising for the institution. We do believe that for many nonprofits, the membership program should be an integrated part of the development effort.

This book provides a thorough background for those who may be new to membership, including what is involved and how membership fits into a larger nonprofit organization or is the basis for the organization itself. As well, the book gives the seasoned membership person new ideas and ways of looking at things and provides an organization considering a membership program with the information it needs to plan and develop one that is appropriate for the institution. Everyone who is involved with a membership program will find new ideas and relevant information that can be applied to help grow and sustain a program.

Throughout the book we have taken the liberty of making recommendations about a number of practices in membership programs. These recommendations are the result of our many years of working with many different types of membership programs and how they fit into the organization's development and other efforts. Not everyone will agree, but until there is more academic research on this topic, we will stand by the recommendations based on what we have experienced and the results we have seen. We hope that all membership staff, whether paid or volunteer, at least consider the suggestions. Too often we find practices in place because "we've always done it that way." Change is difficult, but as we all know, doing things the same way will produce the same results. If different results are desired, then change must occur.

In much of what is involved in membership there are multiple ways of doing things. The issue is to select the method that works for the specific organization. It is important to review the choices on a regular basis. Our fundamental belief is that the membership program must be well planned, effectively executed, and continually evaluated. Without these steps, the program will be haphazard and reactive—never reaching its full potential or producing the results needed by the organization.

We believe that a membership program offers an effective way to develop a donor base and constituency for an organization. The goal is to grow the member's relationship with the organization while at the same time growing the institution. When the relationships are developed in a thoughtful, attentive, and conscientious manner, the organization will prosper and its mission will be fulfilled.

Due to the advances in technology in recent years, we have experienced an evolution in membership. Rapid adoption of social media and mobile devices combined with intensifying media fragmentation requires new approaches and more sophisticated strategies to reach, engage, and retain members. In addition to the fundamentals of membership management, this book addresses the shift toward multichannel marketing and emphasizes opportunities to leverage digital channels such as online advertising, social media, email, mobile, and marketing automation.

Membership Marketing in the Digital Age is a book about the changing landscape of membership, and how to balance new digital channels with more traditional marketing strategies. Providing insight into the trends shaping the future of membership, this book offers a glimpse into the next generation of members, the coming technologies that will forever change how we reach and communicate with audiences, and the impact of evolving consumer behavior and expectations.

This book is intended to serve as a guide for membership, marketing, and development practitioners, leaders in the nonprofit sector, students in professional programs or continuing education courses, and those seeking to create a new membership program. Throughout the book we have included samples, guidelines, and case studies to provide additional context. Additional resources, sample campaigns, and case studies can be found at www.themembershipbook.com.

NOTE

1. Alexis de Tocqueville, *Democracy in America*, trans. G. Lawrence (New York: Harper & Row, 1966), 485.

Acknowledgments

We doubt that anyone writes a book in a vacuum. We certainly couldn't and didn't. We want to thank many of our colleagues in the nonprofit sector who have been helpful during this process. They have been helpful in sending materials, providing information, and clarifying our thoughts. This book belongs as much to them as it does to us. It is our fondest hope, however, that this book will belong to everyone involved in membership in the nonprofit sector.

We would like to thank Tabetha Debo of Membership Consultants for being our "Master of the Manuscript," shepherding chapters, charts, corrections, and changes to the documents and for keeping us all on task. Without her help, this book would not be in print yet! We would also like to thank Kathryn Rich Davis, who provided all of the computer graphics for the book and did it carefully and cheerfully. It is a special pleasure for a mother to be able to work with her daughter. Special thanks go to Agnes Garino, membership volunteer, who read the entire book while in process and made the kinds of comments that are so important for clarifying information and making certain that relevant questions and topics are covered.

And thanks, too, to many in the membership and nonprofit world who answered questions and generously provided information during the past year while we were writing and researching. This list is in alphabetical order by organization, mentioning only the affiliation of each; we could think of no other way to do it other than writing a short essay on what each contributed, which would have been yet another book. Our colleagues include Phyllis Maynerich Evans, The Abraham Lincoln Presidential Library Foundation; Halee Lynch and Beverly Duzik, Desert Botanical Garden; Tyler J. Szymczak, Faegre Baker Daniels, LLP; Liz Walker and Madelyn Harris, Friends of the Kirkwood Library; Corinna Fisk, Friends of the National Zoo; Scott Staub, formerly Friends of the San Francisco Public Library; Donna McGinnis, Missouri Botanical Garden; Angela Brink and Heather Calvin, Museum of Science, Boston; Ken Meifert, National Baseball Hall of Fame and Museum; Greg Harris, Rock & Roll Hall of Fame and Museum; Carl Hamm, Jennifer Thomas, and Kate Gleason, Saint Louis Art Museum; Debbie Podgorski, St. Louis County Library Foundation; and Kimberly Roberson, Santa Barbara Zoo. This wonderful group gave us information ranging from legal issues to benchmarking. We could not have had as complete a look at membership without the help of each and every one of them.

We also want to thank Karen Mariani, Karen Meyer, Deborah Nelson, Doris Plummer, and Diane Wallace from the staff of Membership Consultants for their help. Putting it all together would not have been possible without them.

Last but not least, we would like to acknowledge our families, friends, and other colleagues who have put up with our piles, our questions, and our lack of time for them while we were writing. We want all of them to know how much we have appreciated their patience and great good humor while we have been writing away.

Pat Rich
Dana Hines
Rosie Siemer

1

The Meaning of Membership

I don't want to belong to any club that will accept me as a member.

—Groucho Marx, American Comedian and Film Star

FOREVER FORMING ASSOCIATIONS

Groucho was in the minority. Wanting to belong is a very strong trait for most of us. We want to belong to a family, to a group of friends, to associations where we feel comfortable. From our schools to scouts to our church, we often want to join and be a part of a group. As Alexis de Tocqueville wrote in 1840 in *Democracy in America*, "Americans of all ages, all stations of life, and all types of disposition are forever forming associations. There are not only commercial and industrial associations in which all take part, but others of a thousand different types—religious, moral, serious, futile, very general and very limited, immensely large and very minute. . . . Nothing, in my view, more deserves attention than the intellectual and moral associations in America."[1]

As Tocqueville says, associations come in many different types; in belonging to them we become members.

THE EVOLVING NATURE OF MEMBERSHIP PROGRAMS

Just what is membership? Membership is a fluid concept, defined by each individual group. It can mean writing a check, providing volunteer service, professing faith, increasing self-development, advocating for an issue, attending events, or supporting a mission. It can mean one or all of these and more. Tocqueville's observation about "forever forming associations" is, perhaps, even truer today than in the 1830s when he was visiting America.

Astonishing growth has been seen in many types of membership programs. Cultural institution programs are expanding in numbers of members, and in the services the programs provide. One can now be an online member of the Metropolitan Museum of Art and never personally enter the galleries. Someone can become a Friend of the Library, even though the primary services of the library are free to all. Public issue organizations have grown with their issues. AARP, whose job it is "to help people see the real possibilities that lie ahead," is now America's largest nonreligious membership organization with more than thirty seven million members. Environmental groups have grown along with public interest in conservation and endangered species. Organizations like the World Wildlife Fund are international. Individuals interested in a rare disease have found each other, exchanged information, and raised funds. Affinity groups are now available from A to Z—from the Azalea Society of America to the Z Car Club Association. If there is an interest, there is a group.

The nature of what people want to belong to has also changed. This poses challenges for membership programs. Robert Putnam, in *Bowling Alone: The Collapse and Revival of American Community*, has chronicled what has happened to membership organizations across the country. Growth is occurring in organizations like AARP, environmental groups, and self-help groups like hobby clubs and book discussion groups. At the same time, he notes the loss of membership in many traditional organizations, such as parent-teacher associations (PTAs), labor unions, fraternal organizations such as the Lions and Elks, and in women's groups like the League of Women Voters and the Federation of Women's Clubs. Numbers of volunteers have also dropped in groups like the Boy Scouts and the Red Cross.[2]

Another shift in recent years has been the rapid adoption of social media, growth in online forums, and increases in digital subscription models. There is increased competition for time, attention, and dollars. Moreover, the next generation of members comes with greater expectations for personalization, responsiveness, and digital interaction. And, these younger audiences have exhibited the tendency to be more focused on supporting "causes," rather than a specific organization at any given time.

So what does this mean for membership? First, it is important to remember that people still want to belong. Many membership programs are flourishing. Why do some flourish while others lose members? There are certainly external factors over which a membership program has no control. Putnam discusses women entering the workforce; urban sprawl; technology, which includes television, computers, and the Internet; and, in particular, generational change.[3] The membership programs that will flourish are those that recognize what is happening in the world and how it affects them as well as those that understand their niche and appeal and how to reach people with similar values and interests.

This book is based on the concept that developing a plan of action for the membership program is the best way to ensure that the membership program will thrive. Developing a plan means that the organization takes a look at both the external and internal environments in which it exists, defines a clear purpose, and develops realistic goals. In doing this, the organization can determine where it wants to go and how to get there. A plan assures that the program can meet the goals it has set and make wise use of resources in so doing. Planning is the essential step in the program effort and the plan becomes a valuable tool in implementation.

A crucial point before beginning to plan is understanding the type of membership program involved, the characteristics of members who join, and the reasons why they join. When membership is mentioned, most people name a variety of associations to which they belong. Belonging to a church, a professional organization, a museum, a country club, or the American Automobile Association (AAA) serve very different purposes. The reasons to join are different, the people who join are different, and the benefits involved are different.

Purpose of the Membership Program

The purpose is the primary reason for the membership program. If this reason didn't exist or changed, the program would have to reinvent itself. In reality, all membership programs have more than one purpose. It is important, however, to determine which purpose is the most important. If constituency is important, then a plan will concern itself with growth. If volunteer workers are most important, then the planning issue becomes finding members who have the time and interest to volunteer, or changing the nature of the volunteer jobs to interest potential members. The issue is not just increasing the number of members. In professional associations, the plan will reflect goals that lead to promoting the profession and developing benefits to encourage those in it to join.

Most programs will have multiple goals. For many, income will be an essential one. Income will come from dues and by integrating the membership program into the development efforts. Additional income will come from sales of a variety of products and services. If the programs did not bring in any income, would they exist? Yes and no. For some institutions the membership is a large part of the budget; for others, it is very small. For some, covering costs is enough; for others, generating large amounts of income is important. This, of course, must be considered along with dues structuring, benefits, staffing, and other program issues.

Reason to Join

Above all, the prospective member must have an interest in the organization's mission and activities. If there is no interest in the mission, there is no reason for the person to join. There will be multiple reasons why people join, and it is important to know as many as possible; however, there is usually one reason that is the driving force. For visitation-based institutions, membership is a good value for the money spent when free or discounted admission is involved; in volunteer organizations, the member wants to make a difference, to be useful, or has friends involved. For some membership programs, as in cultural institutions, the reason to join may continue for a lifetime. In others, membership may be linked to another factor, as is the case with many professional organizations where membership may end when the person retires. As well, there will be people who join only because they believe in what the organization does—benefits or other incentives are irrelevant. Knowing these reasons becomes essential in order to position and market the program effectively.

Criteria for Membership

These are the criteria imposed by the institution in order for someone to join. Some criteria are strict requirements, as in professional associations where one must be employed in the profession. Participant-based organizations may have a time requirement. Alumni and shared experience organizations always have a prior experience that is a prerequisite in order to join. For example, to join an alumni association, one must have attended the school.

Dues Structure

This is a fundamental issue. Virtually all membership organizations have dues. There are a few that are free (the National Nova Association), some ask for a small amount (AARP is $16 per year), and some, especially professional associations, require a large amount. There are some programs with a sliding scale, and this arrangement can occur on both ends of the spectrum. An organization that wants to attract a diverse membership might base its fee on what the person can afford or offer subsidies or scholarships for membership. A professional association or organization that has income level as a criterion for membership would charge more as the person's income increases.

Dues have two main structures: flat dues are the same for everyone; whereas graduated dues have different levels at which people can join. Another important issue relates to how dues are collected. Annual dues are collected once a year for the entire organization; anniversary dues are collected on the anniversary date of the member's enrollment. How dues are structured is one of the first things that needs to be decided when beginning a program.

PROGRAM TYPES

The types of membership programs that are in existence defy easy definition. There are a variety of types and purposes for membership programs just as there are a variety of nonprofit institutions and organizations.

The actual name of the program type reflects the defining characteristics for the membership program. For example, "visitation-based" institutions are different from "public issue" organizations, even though both have a goal of developing constituencies. Having a place to visit is a defining characteristic that makes visitation-based institutions different from all others. While hospitals are places that can be visited, the membership programs (usually hospital auxiliaries) are not based on visitation, but rather on attracting volunteer workers. Knowing and understanding this defining characteristic is crucial in developing a membership program.

The defining characteristic is the main issue that affects a membership program; however, a program may change over time in any of the categories. Many membership programs could fit into more than one category. For example, a visitation-based institution might also take on public issues, have affinity groups, and use volunteer workers. The defining characteristic and its primary purpose are the first consideration when planning the membership program. Table 1.1 provides an overview of the various types of membership programs.

Visitation-Based Programs

A visitation-based program is one that is a part of or related to a museum, library, zoo, botanical garden, historic house, park, or other institution that

Table 1.1 Types of Membership Programs for Individuals

PROGRAM TYPE	Visitation-Based	Public Issue	Participant	Volunteer	Faith-Based
Purpose	Building a Constituency	Building a Constituency	Gain Active Participants	Attract Volunteers for the Organization	Gain Participants and Volunteers
Reason to Join	Interest, Good Value	Support the Cause	Self Development	Be Useful	Serve Others in Faith Context
Criteria for Membership	Interest	Interest	Time to Participate	Time to Volunteer	Belief in the Faith
Dues Structure	Graduated	Flat or Graduated	Flat	Flat	Flat
Location of Members	Local to International	Local to International	Local Activity, National/International Network or Organization	Local to International	Local to International
Types of Organizations	Cultural Institutions Libraries	Issue Groups, Public Radio and Television	Youth Groups, Civic Groups, Self-Help Groups	Auxiliaries, Guilds, Friends Linked to an Organization	Religious Congregations and Faith-Based Charities
Examples	Rock and Roll Hall of Fame, Tulsa Botanic Garden, St. Louis County Library	League of Women Voters, Mothers Against Drunk Driving (MADD), Wisconsin Public Television	Girl and Boy Scouts, Junior League, Rotary	Heard Museum Guild Organization (Phoenix), Barnes-Jewish St. Peters Hospital Auxiliary (St. Louis)	Knights of Columbus, United Methodist Women

continued...

PROGRAM TYPE	**Shared Experience**	**Affinity**	**Professional**	**Social**	**Brand Loyalty**
Purpose	Strengthen Relationships	Promote Interest in Subject Area	Promote the Profession	Social Ties	Retain Customers
Reason to Join	Continue Relationship	Education	Professional Development	Social Life and Standing	Value
Criteria for Membership	Prior Relationship	Interest	Professional Requirements	Social Relationships	Customer or Client
Dues Structure	Flat	Flat	Flat or Based on Criteria	Flat	Often "Free," Dependent on Being Customer or Client
Location of Members	National to International	Local to International	International, Local Chapters	Local, non-resident members	International
Types of Organizations	Alumni Associations, Fraternities and Sororities	Subject Related Clubs and Organizations, Book Clubs	Professional Associations and Related Groups	Golf, Country and Eating Clubs	Credit Card, Frequent Flyer
Examples	University of Michigan Alumni Association, Delta Sigma Theta, Veterans of Foreign Wars	Local Garden Club, Local Investment Club, Z Car Club	Association of Fundraising Professionals (AFP), American Medical Association (AMA)	University Clubs	American Express, Delta Sky Miles Program, American Automobile Association (AAA)

attracts visitors or patrons. These institutions are interested in developing a constituency for attendance, contributed and earned income, education, community support, advocacy where appropriate, and volunteers. The membership program is often integrated with the institution's development program. The membership becomes the donor base for fundraising efforts. It also becomes the way the institution relates to its donors. There are no real criteria for membership, though members usually have an interest in the subject matter or events at the institution. Dues tend to be graduated and many join at the "basic" level because it is a good value—offering free or discounted admission, a discount at the gift shop, subscription services, or invitations to special events.

These institutions tend to be local, although there are some with national and international recognition. Those that are local will have, for the most part, a local membership. Those institutions that are well known are able to have nonresident membership programs as well as a local base. The Metropolitan Museum of Art is in this category. With technology, institutions with specialized collections are able to offer online memberships with benefits suited to that particular audience. The Metropolitan Museum of Art offers Met Net and The Art Institute of Chicago offers an E-Member level.

Libraries are "free" institutions in that their services (i.e., circulation of books, music, movies) are offered at no charge to the public, and yet people feel such a connection to these institutions that they want to join a Friends of the Library group to provide additional services or offerings. Literacy programs, author lectures, book clubs, summer reading programs, and bookmobiles for classrooms or senior facilities are all added services that a Friends support group can help make possible through added funding. These added services may be available to the public, even though they are privately supported.

The distinguishing characteristic of the visitation-based program is that there is a place to visit and, most often, a major member benefit relates to admission. With a membership, the admission is offered free, at a reduced cost, or for a certain number of visits. In addition to libraries there are other visitation-based institutions that are free to the public. When this is the case, the admission benefit is related to special exhibits or presentations that have an admission charge, access to increased hours for admission, or free parking. The Saint Louis Science Center, for example, has free admission, but tickets to the OMNIMAX® Theater are a member benefit.

The Smithsonian Institution, comprised of numerous museums including the National Zoo, has both a local and national membership program even though all of the museums and the zoo are free to the public. The major benefit is its publication *Smithsonian Magazine*, which is another way for an institution with free admission to offer a desirable benefit. In addition, many of the separate museums and the zoo each have a membership program, with its own list of benefits.

For visitation-based institutions where there is no fundraising, such as those supported by public funds or an endowment, membership is still a desirable program in order to develop a constituency and find volunteers. There are very few institutions that do no fundraising at all. Of those that are heavily supported by public or endowment funds, many have also found a need to raise private funds as a supplement for operations or for special exhibits and programs.

Public Issue Programs

Organizations formed around issues often offer membership programs. The major purpose is to develop a constituency. These programs are centered on one or several related public issues. Groups devoted to a neighborhood issue, the environment, women's issues, senior issues, education, and so forth are all a part of this category. Members join because they want to make a difference in the local, regional, national, or international community. For those who are active in the organization, there is the added benefit of working with like-minded people. The organization's prerequisite is that a member is interested in the issue, and it is hoped that the member will help work on it. Some of these organizations have enormous political clout due to the numbers of members and the members' level of activity. AARP and the National Rifle Association (NRA) are organizations that have used their numbers to press their case.

The members may be called upon to help educate the public, the media, legislators, and government officials about the issue and all of its ramifications. For example, Mothers Against Drunk Driving (MADD) has as its mission "to stop drunk driving, support the victims of this violent crime, and prevent underage drinking." There may also be other programs associated with the organization's mission, such as MADD's support services for victims of impaired driving, public awareness campaigns, and a variety of youth programs. These groups can be local, regional, national, or international. Some, like MADD, are national with local chapters.

Many members are happy to write a check to support the work of others, because they do not have the time to help on a sustained basis. Putnam's interest in *Bowling Alone* is in the amount of social capital created by organizations. Social capital is—on a very basic level—the connectedness between and among people and the community. For example, the League of Women Voters (the League), a group that is organized on a grassroots level with face-to-face meetings, discussion, and volunteer service, adds much to social capital, while Greenpeace members need only write the check. The public issue groups that do not require social capital are showing enormous increases in membership while groups like the League have been losing members during the past three decades.[4]

While both of these organizations clearly focus on public interest issues, the way they approach the issues is very different. In planning for their varied futures, they must take into consideration what is happening in the world around them.

Participant Programs

For some programs, active participation is a condition of membership. These programs want the member's time and efforts. In fact, that is the prerequisite for joining and remaining a member. Scout organizations, for example, expect that their members will be active Scouts; otherwise, there is no reason to join. Junior Leagues and service leagues also often have a participation requirement. The reason to join these programs is to participate in the organization's projects. This participation may include self-development, a chance to give back to the community, and a way to meet new people and network.

These programs will also develop a constituency, raise funds, and educate their members, but participation is the main purpose of membership and the reason to belong. Dues vary from very little money (e.g., $5 annually) to significantly high dues (several hundred dollars annually) and the dues structure is often flat. Many of these groups will also have fundraising activities that members will support.

Volunteer Programs

Much like participant-based programs, volunteer programs expect a level of personal involvement. The difference is that these organizations exist to serve a larger institution or organization rather than their own. The involvement is in service to the institution to which the organization is attached.

The organization and the volunteer group may work together to decide which projects the group will undertake and which volunteer positions its members will fill. The hospital auxiliary that runs the gift shop, the opera guild that raises funds, and the theater backers who provide actors with meals are all examples of these programs.

Dues are usually modest, though many require that the participant first be a member of the institution itself. Time is always a requirement.

Faith-Based Programs

More than anything else, people join religious organizations.[5] These are places of worship as well as related organizations. Belief in the work of the faith (not necessarily the faith itself) is the requirement for membership. With their diverse programming, religious organizations offer many choices for their members. There are religious programs that are active locally, regionally, nationally, and internationally. Many denominations have programs throughout the country.

Belonging to a faith-based institution may include dues and other fundraising activities. For some, the concept of tithing is an integral part of the financial obligation; for others a simple dues commitment or an annual gift. For as long as Giving USA has been charting philanthropic donations, giving to faith-based institutions has always been the largest segment.

Virtually every religious institution has a core of workers, those for whom faith is translated into volunteer service. For some of these institutions, this volunteer commitment is a requirement. Some institutions also have membership programs within their structure, such as a Jewish temple's sisterhood, a group of women from the congregation, or a men's club that conducts activities of particular interest to the congregation's men. Many of these organizations also take on community issues, providing food pantries, homeless shelters, and programs to alleviate addictions. The Salvation Army is certainly one of the best known for community volunteer work. It is a faith-based membership organization with many of its activities run by the officers of the Army.

Faith-based institutions also become involved in public policy issues in a variety of ways. Some of the most contentious issues in our society (pro-choice vs. pro-life; prayer in school) are based on belief. There are institutions on all sides of such issues; they often call on their membership to help make their positions known.

Alumni and Shared Experience Programs

Once a member, always a member might be the motto of these organizations. Alumni groups of all sorts fit into this category. All levels of education now have alumni groups, from elementary through graduate and professional training. Other shared experience groups include sororities and fraternities, Veterans of Foreign Wars, and any other organization for which the membership requirement is having been a past member or participant. The purpose of these programs is to stay in touch with the members and keep the relationship between the member and the organization vital and strong. With our mobile population, members may live anywhere in the world. Fundraising is one of the reasons to keep effective ties, but the need for a constituency is also important for the times when issues arise. In alumni associations, the alumni program itself often does not include the fundraising campaigns, but the closer the alumni feel toward the school because of alumni association information and activities, the easier the fundraising calls will be for the development department. Dues for these types of programs tend to be flat with other fundraising done in a variety of ways.

Affinity Programs

If there is an interest, there is a group. Rather than having an issue as the major focus, these membership programs are formed around a subject. People join these groups to further their interest and education in the subject, whatever it might be. This is an opportunity to meet people with the same interests and to participate in activities with them. Membership appeals to those who have an interest in the subject matter. The groups range from the Azalea Society of America to local ski groups to book clubs to the Z Car Clubs (all about Datsun/Nissan Z-cars) around the world.

The requirement for membership in these groups is an interest and usually a small membership fee to cover the cost of mailings and meetings. Members come and go depending on their level of interest in the subject. There may be attendant issues that the group becomes involved in and there may be some fundraising, but it is the interest in the subject that is at the heart of the membership. Some of these organizations meet virtually, though most continue to meet in person, produce publications, and hold events. There is usually no need for other fundraising; events tend to be self-supporting.

Professional Associations

Just as there is a club for every interest group, there is an association for every profession—and then some. The criteria for membership in a professional association are set by each organization. They may include educational criteria as well as actually holding a position in a particular field. Advancing the profession is the foundation for these organizations, but they also have a multitude of other activities. Professional education is usually essential, ethics for the profession are frequently developed, and advocacy for the profession and related issues is often important. Members join for the educational activities, networking within the profession, and, in general, to be a part of how the profession develops. Unions are another type of professional association with differences that may include job-related mandatory membership with the benefit of being represented in bargaining.

There are also groups in this category that are subsets or multidisciplinary. For example, there are major associations such as the American Medical Association and then subsets that focus on specialization within the field (American Academy of Family Physicians) or on cross-disciplinary interests (American Medical Women's Association). In addition, there are local groups defined by position that would fall into this category, such as a local group of women in business or consultants.

There are also associations that are not professionally focused, but rather focused on avocations. These tend to include collectors' clubs or recreation-related clubs. These clubs do offer a connection between like-minded people, and offer a forum for the exchange of ideas and expertise or just sharing the passion for a certain pastime. The International Mountain Bicycling Association or National Association of Watch and Clock Collectors are examples of this type of organization. Such associations often supply a combination of individual benefits while also making a better environment for the proliferation of the interest served (building better biking trails or connecting owners or collectors of watches or clocks).

Social Organizations

On a very personal level, many people want to join social groups—golf clubs, luncheon clubs, and other "elite" groups. These groups need members to exist. They provide for the member the sense of belonging, status, and prestige, and, often, networking opportunities for social, business, and community involvement. The membership core usually focuses on business relationships or on social relationships. Often social organizations offer programming of interest to spouses, couples, or families.

Typically these organizations have a membership procedure and often require a new member to be sponsored by other members. When these organizations see a drop in membership, they react much as any membership program by developing acquisition and retention strategies that are appropriate to the group. Dues and other financial requirements make some of these memberships the most expensive of the membership programs. Monies given to these organizations are not tax deductible.

Brand-Loyalty Programs

The interest in and compelling nature of the concept of membership is also used in the world of commerce. With the idea of membership well accepted among a variety of institutions, the notion has also been used by the for-profit sector, particularly as a marketing device. The American Express card tells its owner that he or she has been a "member since" the card's acquisition date. All of the airline frequent flyer programs call their customers "members." AAA (American Automobile Association) began as a nonprofit representing "the interests of motorists and other travelers." It is still a nonprofit, but now perhaps is best known for its member services of emergency road service along with insurance, travel, and financial services, and numerous other related activities and its sponsorship of school safety patrols.

Many of these groups have events for members, newsletters, websites, and a great number of the trappings of a traditional nonprofit membership program. For the most part, brand-loyalty programs are free, though open only to clients and customers of the company involved. These programs are, above all, testimony to the strength of the notion of membership.

THE ROLE OF INCOME

Building a constituency, promoting professions and interests, finding volunteers and participants, and keeping relationships are the primary purposes of a membership program. However, the one issue that all programs grapple with is that of income. For many organizations, income is a significant reason to have a membership program. A membership program should be designed to earn income for the organization. An institution should not subsidize a membership program. Of course, there are exceptions. One exception would be organizations like the Scouts where the membership fee is minimal and various additional kinds of fundraising support the activities.

For the most part, however, the dues, at a minimum, should fully cover expenses. This is true for many affinity groups for whom out-of-pocket expenditures are really the only funds spent. It is also true for some of the volunteer groups such as hospital auxiliaries with very small token dues and for some arts institution guilds where the member must first be a member of the organization and then pay an extra fee to belong to the guild. For most other organizations, funds come to the institution through dues; using the membership as the donor base for fundraising; offering products; providing food service options; using the membership base as an incentive for sponsorships and advertising; and by members raising money for the institution through events and other fundraisers.

Income is an integral component of membership programs. Deciding the role that it plays in any one program is an important decision before planning or changing the program.

Dues

Membership dues will range from a major portion to a very small part of the institution's budget, depending on the size of the overall budget, the amount of the dues, and the number of members. But in almost all organizations, this funding is important. In addition to its potential size, membership money is important because it is unrestricted funds that can be used where the need is greatest in the institution. More importantly, with a well-run membership program, renewals bring in money annually. The lifetime giving of a member can be substantial. Because this funding is monthly or annual, it is also predictable and, thus, an excellent source of the base of a funding program.

Development

The membership is the donor base for many institutions with membership programs. This base can be used for numerous other development programs. The possibilities include a second annual gift, special project giving, major and capital gifts, and planned giving.

Marketing

The membership base becomes the database for direct marketing. The institution can market directly for attendance at new exhibits, education programs, and lectures, for sales in the gift shop, earned income projects, special events, and a variety of other opportunities. Having the database for a direct marketing program is also very appealing to some corporate sponsors who are interested in marketing their products to the organization's members.

Earned Income

Offering products to members is another way to increase income. In institutions with visitation there is the possibility of gift shops and food service. For all organizations, there is a variety of possibilities ranging from logo merchandise to insurance products to affinity credit cards (credit cards marketed through the organization with the organization's logo) to publications. Not all members will be interested, but if the member base is sufficiently large, enough members will have an interest to make the offer worthwhile for both the member and the organization.

It is important for an institution that charges admission to understand that as the membership grows there may be an adverse effect on income from the turnstile. This is due to a frequent visitor becoming a member and no longer paying admission. However, the ongoing renewal, upgrading, other fundraising activities, and earned income generated often bring more to the institution than admission alone. In addition, some who become members will never visit the institution, but join to show support for the work that is being done.

Gift Memberships

The membership is the group to solicit for additional memberships. This is particularly appropriate for institutions with visitation or widespread popular appeal. There are a variety of memberships that can be offered. Gift memberships, especially for the holidays, are popular. Gift memberships at other times during the year can also be made available. For example, gift memberships are popular for gift-giving times such as Mother's and Father's Days, Administrative Assistant's Week, and Valentine's Day.

Corporate Sponsorships

To provide sponsorship funding, a corporation is often interested in an organization's demographic profile. Who visits? Who is a member? The demographic profile is the information about the age, income, residency, and other such traits of the membership. A large membership with a demographic profile that matches the corporation's target audience can be helpful when recruiting sponsors for programs, projects, and exhibits.

THE APPEAL OF MEMBERSHIP

Who Joins?

The characteristics that define one organization's members and those that define another's can be very different. While they are different across membership types, there are similarities within types. The person who joins one museum may well join another; the person who joins an environmental group may well join another; the person who volunteers at one activity in the community may volunteer at another. This is very important to remember when selecting a target market for potential members. Familiarity does not breed contempt; it breeds more members.

Motivations for Joining

Why do people want to become members? The characteristics of joiners are very different, and so are their motivations for joining. There are two sets of benefits that motivate and appeal to members, tangible and intangible. The tangible ones are those that are physical or real, many of which have a financial implication. The intangible benefits are those feelings that a member gets from the organization.

Tangible Benefits

The tangible benefits include everything from a membership card to a discount in a shop to free admission to an invitation to a lecture. They include the mug or tote bag that is offered as an incentive to join. Virtually all membership programs include tangible benefits. But we also know that, in many cases, the tangible benefits do not equal the cost of the membership.

In fact, a study by Bhattacharya, Glynn, and Rao found that at least at one major museum, "In describing their visiting behavior, nearly all (90 percent) of the respondents had visited the museum at least once in the last twelve months; however, less than one-fifth (19.2 percent) visited 6 or more times, the approximate point at which the member begins to realize economic gains from the free admission benefit of membership."[6] While it is not at all scientific to generalize from one study, anecdotal information supports this finding. There is a small core group of members who will visit frequently; most will not come enough times to realize the economic advantage. Additionally, there are large memberships at visitation-based institutions where there is no admission fee at all.

Intangible Benefits

What are the intangible benefits that motivate people to join? There are many. The basic motivation for many may be the idea of belonging, particularly to those organizations that we believe are doing something meaningful. In beginning psychology, most of us learned about Abraham Maslow's theory of motivation, described in his book, *Motivation and Personality*. He portrays people as having five levels of needs that are fulfilled in a hierarchical order. The first two levels describe the need for basic survival efforts: food, water, safety, and shelter. The third level has to do with belonging. Belonging is a very strong sense for people including the need for acceptance, relationships, and being a part of a group. The last two levels deal with esteem and fulfilling one's potential. Many membership organizations provide the activities and forum for a member to receive respect and admiration, and provide challenges for members to "reach their potential."[7]

Members, however, rarely describe why they want to join in these terms. When a member is asked why he or she joined a group, the tangible benefits and those that relate to family, community, personal interests, and supporting a worthwhile organization are the ones that are cited. While members rarely speak in terms like Maslow's, those programs that make members feel like they belong, they are valued, and that their membership makes a difference are the ones that are very successful. A membership brochure from the Chicago Botanical Garden quotes a longtime member as saying, "This is my garden. I have a sense of belonging."

There are a number of reasons that people give for joining an organization. It is important to know how people feel about joining a group because when a group can meet significant needs, those are the issues that become important in marketing the program. For example, members of a program may believe that having a membership is a good value, a way to meet new people, a network for business, or an educational opportunity. Those beliefs, in turn, can be used in marketing the program to potential members.

Reasons for Joining

Value

For members, particularly of visitation-based institutions, value is the initial motivation to join. Members who join at the basic levels of these institutions are "value members." These are members who are interested in benefits such as free or discounted admissions, free or reduced parking, and discounts. As discussed earlier, many of these members do not pass the economic point of paying for their membership with use. These benefits, however, are important because they are the starting point for the member to become involved in the organization.

Pursuing a Personal Interest

All of the membership programs have some basis in a personal interest. Whether it is a hobby, the environment, our faith, or our career, the membership organizations that relate to our interests have appeal. The organization that makes members feel like they belong and provides a way to meet these personal interests will be able to hold on to its members. The level of interest will vary among members. The successful organization will have a set of programs and information for those with a casual interest in the subject matter and another those for who are interested in depth.

When the members lose interest, the membership tends to disappear. To keep the interest high it is incumbent on the membership program to provide programs and information in a format and on an interest level that is appealing. The membership program cannot afford to become stagnant. With visitation-based institutions, this manifests itself in having new programs, new exhibits, and new attractions. The museum with nothing added will soon lose its appeal. The library that does not offer educational lectures or discussions will not be able to sustain its membership program in the long term. Public issue organizations need to stay on top of the most current and relevant information, legislation, and regulations in their area. The same is true of professional associations.

Making a Difference

Members with this inclination want to provide direct service to individuals or volunteer for or support groups that make a difference in others' lives or for society. These members feel good about what they are doing and have a real sense of self-satisfaction. Many types of membership programs offer these opportunities. In a professional association an experienced member might be a mentor to a new professional; in a faith-based organization a member may be involved in services for the poor; and in a volunteer organization a member might give direct service through a hospital auxiliary. Many join public issue groups because they believe that their membership will support work that will make a difference for the issue at hand, such as better government, the environment, or health care. The challenge for these organizations is to make sure that their members know that they are making a difference whether through volunteer work or support for the cause.

Giving Back

For some, joining a group by making contributions of time and money is a way of giving back to an institution or to the community. Belonging to an arts or cultural organization, because it is important for the community to have these facilities, fulfills this need. This may be the reason behind longtime memberships in visitation-based organizations, where the members do not join just for the economic value. On a more personal level, a member of a hospital auxiliary may be giving back because a family member received exceptional care when ill.

Many join alumni associations or keep active with their fraternities and sororities because they feel that the education, the relationships, and the networking that they have gained from that prior experience is worth supporting. While contributions to faith-based institutions are always the largest segment of gifts given during a year (31 percent), gifts to educational institutions are the next largest (16 percent), followed by social service (12 percent).[8] People feel very strongly about the important role of education in their lives and want to give back. As discussed in the work by Putnam, education is the one predictor of joining. This accounts for, at least in part, the strength of alumni programs of all kinds.

Pride

Many people want to be associated with what they consider a worthwhile organization. People join civic organizations and cultural institutions to show pride in their community. Rotarians wear their lapel pins as a sign of pride in their organization. Many alumni are proud of the schools they attended and join the alumni association. Members of hobby clubs who are proud of their particular interest or craft are willing to work in their organization to continue the programs. Most of all, members in participant and volunteer organizations who contribute their valuable time are very proud of what they and their organizations do. Pride is one of the factors that encourages their participation and why they are stalwart supporters.

Being with Similar People

The faith-based, professional, and social organizations all provide the member with a group with which he or she will be comfortable. With a common bond, whether it is experience, faith, profession, or lifestyle, the members immediately feel a sense of belonging. One of the attractions of joining a social organization is the sense of belonging that the organization confers. All relationship programs are based on this premise. Veterans' groups provide a place for people who have shared similar experiences. This can be a very strong stimulus for membership. Family and friends have not gone through the same experience and can't discuss it in the same way that another soldier can.

Networking

Although some consider networking to be an overused term, there is no doubt that many membership organizations offer the potential for the members to network. Networking is defined as "the exchange of ideas and information among people who share interests and causes."[9] It is particularly important in professional associations and in affinity groups for serious hobbyists. In professional associations, networking is often cited as a member benefit by the association and a reason for joining by members. The offer of an organization in which members can share information, acquire education, and develop a network of colleagues with the same interest is of great value. Of course, there is some networking in all groups. Many join social clubs, business-related organizations, and similar groups to be in a place where networking may set the stage for working together.

Status and Prestige

Rarely admitted, but certainly an important motivation, is status and prestige. Some organizations confer status and prestige because other important people are involved. This is particularly true for some educational and cultural institutions. It is certainly also true for social clubs (country clubs, luncheon clubs), for those organizations for which a level of accomplishment is a necessary prerequisite (exclusive professional groups), and for those groups for which a certain position is a necessary prerequisite (civic groups based on position in employment). Often endorsements or recommendations are necessary in order to be considered for membership in these organizations. There is also status and prestige in relationship organizations, particularly when the school, sorority, fraternity, or other organization is considered a status organization.

SUMMARY

The meaning of membership is different for each member, for each organization. This can be seen in the multidimensionality of programs, the members they attract, and the members' motivations for joining. All of these differences underscore the individuality and unique bases for individual membership programs. There are, however, commonalities among the decisions that need to be made in planning, structuring, and implementing a membership program. The meaning of membership is defined by how the organization or institution develops its program. Further, the rapid adoption of technology, shifting attitudes among younger members, and increased competition for attention will greatly impact the growth and sustainability of many membership programs in the coming years.

NOTES

1. Alexis de Tocqueville, *Democracy in America*, trans. G. Lawrence (New York: Harper & Row, 1966), 485–88.

2. Richard D. Putnam, *Bowling Alone: The Collapse and Revival of American Community* (New York: Simon & Schuster, 2000), 48–64.

3. Ibid., 277–84.

4. Ibid., 155–56.

5. Ibid., chapter 4.

6. C. Bhattacharya, M. A. Glynn, and H. Rao, "Membership in Museums: A Study of Customers of Cultural Non-Profit Institutions," in *Conference Proceedings of ARNOVA*, Session H8, October 1994, 414.

7. Abraham H. Maslow, *Motivation and Personality* (New York: Harper & Row, 1954–1970), 35–48.

8. Lilly Family School of Philanthropy, *Giving USA 2014: Highlights* (The Giving Institute, Indiana University, 2014), 1.

9. *The AFP Fundraising Dictionary* (Association of Fundraising Professionals, 1996–2003), 86, accessed June 8, 2015, http://www.afpnet.org.

2

Planning for Membership

It takes as much energy to wish as it does to plan.

—*Eleanor Roosevelt, First Lady*

PLANNING AS THE FOUNDATION

The foundation of a nonprofit organization is its mission. The mission statement defines why the nonprofit exists. The organization's plan is its map of activities for fulfilling that mission. Planning is a systematic way to make certain that the organization's goals are relevant to the mission, and that its various activities will accomplish the goals. Nonprofit strategy consultant David La Piana defines a strategic plan as "a coordinated set of actions aimed at creating and sustaining a competitive advantage in carrying out the nonprofit mission."[1] And, as author John Bryson notes in *Strategic Planning for Public and Nonprofit Organizations: A Guide to Strengthening and Sustaining Organizational Achievement*, increased uncertainty, competition, and interconnectedness require a "fivefold response" to ensure sustainability.[2] Bryson describes this multifaceted response as follows:

1. Organizations must think and learn strategically as never before.
2. Organizations must translate insights into effective strategies to cope with changing circumstances.
3. Organizations must develop the rationales necessary to lay the groundwork for the adoption and implementation of new strategies.

4. Organizations must build coalitions that are large enough and strong enough to adopt desirable strategies.
5. Organizations must build capacity for ongoing implementation, learning, and strategic change.

For membership programs that are their own organization and not part of a larger institution, there is a need to develop a plan for the organization with membership as an integral part. For the membership program that is a part of a larger institution, the membership should be designed to fit into the larger overall institutional plan and to help fulfill the organization's mission. The membership program is one of the major outreach programs of an institution and endows the organization with a base of people who can become involved and invested. Even in an institution that does not have a plan, planning for the membership program is still advised and will be helpful to all involved.

Planning is the basic first step in developing a membership program. Peter Drucker, the management guru who is credited with inventing the concept of management,[3] says, "for the non-profit organization . . . you need four things. You need a plan. You need marketing. You need people. And you need money."[4] All four are as important for the membership program as they are for the organization as a whole. And the plan is first. The other three are covered later in this book. Why bother to spend the time to plan? As Yogi Berra, Hall of Fame catcher for the New York Yankees and linguistic gymnast, once said, "We're lost, but we're making great time." For Drucker, the plan leads a nonprofit into "converting good intentions into results."[5] There are clear organizational reasons to plan.

First, it gives the membership program a way to deal with limited resources. No matter the size of the membership program, there is never enough time, staff, volunteers, or money to do everything. Planning gives a way to allocate all of the resources in a rational manner. Having the plan gives staff and volunteers the reason to say "no" to projects that would take resources and take the program in a nonproductive direction.

Second, planning gives everyone involved in the program a unified vision of the future. This becomes the basis for cohesiveness in implementing the program; everyone understands what is happening. It gives everyone involved the opportunity to understand the direction of the program, the desired results, and the reasons for myriad tasks. The planning helps everyone to be on the same page.

Third, the plan is also a communications tool both internally and externally. Planning offers the opportunity to include others in the organization that have an impact on membership in the planning process. When the plan is complete it can be shared with everyone, so they understand the direction of membership. When all departments within an organization develop a plan, it allows everyone to see how his or her piece of the puzzle supports the whole, reduces isolation among those working in the institution, and brings about the feeling of everyone working together. The plan communicates the organization's direction to all of the external audiences for the organization such as volunteers, board members, and other related groups.

Fourth, using the plan as a base, there is a sense of accomplishment for everyone involved as the work is completed. Membership staff need to know that they are making progress and that projects are moving in the right direction. Having measurable steps along the way gives this guidance and that sense of accomplishment felt when a task has been completed. For supervisory personnel, goals and objectives are one way that employee performance can be measured.

The plan provides a method to evaluate the work. If the goal for the membership program is "to have a successful program," everyone will have a different idea of what success looks like. During planning, it is essential to reach agreement on questions such as, how many new members equal successful acquisition? During the evaluation time, the question becomes, did we meet our goal? The same is true for each part of the program. Successful projects can be celebrated and repeated. Those that were not as successful can be changed. As someone once said, repeating things that don't work will bring the same results. Having measures in the plan provide a way to know how successful, or not, the program and its projects are.

Last, but not least, is the message the plan sends to the entire organization that the membership program is well run and thoughtfully managed. For an objective evaluation, there is no better basis than having a good plan. For the membership department in a large organization, sending the message about good management is also crucial. The program needs to be respected if it is to attract increased resources, be seen as an important part of community outreach, and understood as a means for furthering the organization's mission. Having a plan and meeting its goals and objectives is one of the ways to do this.

Having a plan is also a message for external constituents. A plan can increase the possibility of finding funding for membership program activities.

There are sometimes funders who are willing to help a local membership program, understanding that it is the basis for the organization's fundraising programs. This may happen on the national level as well. Funders are almost always interested in seeing a plan before committing funds. In addition, organizations that are working to become accredited in their field may need plans for all of their activities, including membership. The plan is a clear signal that the program is being conducted in a professional manner.

THE PLANNING PROCESS

Strategic, Long-Range, and Operational Planning

When people talk about planning, it is first important to distinguish between and among the different terms. Do not become distressed over the terms. Strategic and long-range are terms that are often used interchangeably. The terminology is not as important as what needs to be accomplished.

Long-range planning takes current activities and plans for them into the future. There may be some change in what is done, but actions are predicated on "existing conditions."[6] If the membership program is working well for the organization, with no major issues at hand, putting this framework around planning is fitting.

Strategic planning takes a deliberate look at the environment and the impact it may have on the program. If the planning group for a membership program understands that business as usual will bring the same results and that isn't what the group wants, then strategic planning is desirable. Strategic planning may result in major changes in direction, in approach, or in desired results. For example, a membership program that has reached a plateau and isn't growing, when growth is desirable, will want to make its planning strategic in nature.

Operational planning is developing the work plan for the year. It is derived from the long-range or the strategic plan. This is the plan that details the objectives and action plans that everyone follows to make certain that the tasks are accomplished. There should be an operational plan every year. This is the plan on which the budget and the work calendar are based.

The Planning Pyramid

There are many planning methods, systems, and strategies. Any method will work as long as it is followed. The method suggested here is easy to use and based on "management by objective" (MBO), which was first described by Peter Drucker.[7] His management concept is that a plan will have objectives by which performance is measured. Objectives flow from the goals. In a nonprofit, all of this derives from and serves the mission of the organization. The issue is to have a way to ensure that good intentions are converted into results. If a different method is used, make certain that there are parts of the plan that are measureable so that evaluation can take place.

Planning begins with determining the strategy for the program, followed by goals to achieve the strategy, objectives designed to bring about the goals, and action plans that include all the activities to support the objectives. This is graphically presented in figure 2.1, the Planning Pyramid. The planning process itself involves discussion of the strategy, goals, objectives and action plans and documenting the plan. The document, particularly the objectives and action

FIGURE 2.1
The Planning Pyramid

plans (e.g., operational plan), becomes the basis for the budget and the yearly calendar. It provides the objectives against which the work is measured. In order to develop the plan, it is first necessary to organize for the planning process.

The process presented here is a general outline for actually doing the planning for a membership program. It is important to organize the facets of the planning before beginning so that the process moves along smoothly and in a timely manner. There are a number of decisions about the planning process that need to be made before starting.

Length of Time

How long should planning take? There is no absolute answer to this question. Because of the time needed to discuss and come to decisions about strategy, strategic planning will take more time than long-range planning. In strategic planning, time is also spent detailing the strengths, weaknesses, opportunities, and threats, known as a "SWOT" analysis, that face the program. Long-range planning assumes that conditions stay the same, thus alleviating the need for this step.

While the planning should not be prolonged forever, neither should it be consigned to one two-hour meeting. It is important for the planning leadership to think through the process to develop a reasonable time line. Having an external deadline (e.g., the budget process) is one way to contain the time spent. The other major issue in timing is the approval factor. The greater the number of people who must approve the plan, the longer it will take from inception to adoption.

The Forces Driving the Planning

There are several forces that drive planning. A membership program may experience one or more of them. The specific impetus for an operational plan is often the budget process. In fact, many programs use the budget process as the planning tool. Take this year's program, add for inflation, maybe add a program, and, voilà, a budget for the coming year. This is short-term planning and does not encourage a serious look at the program as a whole. Drucker addresses this way of planning, stating that "The budget is the document in which balance decisions find final expression; but the decisions themselves require judgment; and the judgment will be sound only if it is based on sound analysis."[8] Planning by budgeting is a reactive method rather than proactive, which has some efficiency in the short run, but little to offer in the long run.

A frequent impetus for planning is a symptom, usually negative—the membership is declining, no one is attending events, or volunteers have disappeared. This calls for a strategic planning effort to identify the causes and then to develop a plan that addresses the issues. The new plan may involve small changes or a major redesign of the entire program. On the reverse side, the symptoms are sometimes positive—incredible increases in members, events that have grown too large, not enough projects for volunteers. In this case, the issues become more operational. Planning will help answer these questions. Be happy with these problems even though they may cause turmoil. Organizations coping with the negative symptoms must spend time discussing the environmental issues, how to cope with them, and whether the membership program can do anything about them.

In a large organization, the organization's planning may be the driving force. The membership planning, then, is a part of the organization's planning. The challenge for those involved in membership is to make certain that the membership program is a part of the overall plan. If the development or marketing department is doing planning and the membership is a part of that department, the membership planning may be a part of that department's work.

Yet another driving force is the arrival of a new leader for the program. A new membership manager will want to understand the program as it exists and then he or she will undertake planning as a management activity if it is a part of his or her job description. The caveat is that the direction of the program should not be changed on an annual basis unless there is a major problem. This can be an issue in a volunteer organization where the membership chair is a new person each year or in an organization with recurrent staff turnover. There needs to be consistency in how the program works.

Time Frame

Is this a plan for two years? Three? If the program is new, the plan should have goals for two or three years. Where would the organization like to be in three years with the membership program? There should be strategic goals that reflect the vision for the future. Then a one-year detailed operational plan can be developed for the first year. Depending on the first year, the second year may be different than imagined. For an established program with a solid history, consider a three-year plan. If major changes are being made, it may take three years to implement the changes, but there need to be some short-term benchmarks along the way to make certain that the changes are working. If not, contingency plans can be implemented.

Often, institutional events may dictate membership planning. An upcoming anniversary or the opening of a new building, for example, may present a significant milestone in the institution's history that creates an opportunity for membership to reach a new peak. Whatever the reason that drives membership planning, the result will be a more strategically run program.

PLANNING STEPS

The planning steps are easy to follow and will provide a substantial plan for the membership program (see exhibit 2.1). This process can be used by a volunteer organization, by a small nonprofit with one staff, or by a big institution with a large staff in the membership department. If, in reality, one person is going to sit down and write the plan, then that one person should still follow the basic process. This should be considered a way to make the work easier in the long run, because once the plan is in place, the direction is clear, and it becomes much easier to stay on track and reach the goals. Otherwise, the membership effort, as Yogi might say, may be making good time, but it may be lost. For a sample plan and additional planning resources, visit www.themembershipbook.com.

1. Select the Planning Leader

Who will design and manage the process? Who will lead the meetings? Who will document the discussion and decisions? Who will write the plan? This can be done in-house or with an outside facilitator. If the decision is to do this in-house, then the responsibility to take the leadership role and keep the process moving must be assigned to a staff person or volunteer. The lead

1. Select the Planning Leader
2. Gain Participation
3. Provide Information Base
4. SWOT Analysis
5. Agree on Strategy
6. Develop Goals
7. Establish Objectives
8. Create Action Plans
9. Write the Plan
10. Prepare the Budget
11. Construct a Calendar
12. Gain approval
13. Work the plan
14. Evaluate

EXHIBIT 2.1
Planning Steps

person needs to be a good group facilitator, listener, and writer. The person should also spend some time learning the program if it is not his or her main responsibility. The advantage to using someone in-house is that there is no additional cost. The disadvantage is the time it takes from other duties.

If it is at all possible, the recommendation is to use an outside facilitator. A facilitator is particularly helpful if those involved do not have the time or experience to manage and lead the process, if there may be very conflicting ideas that have to be reconciled by a neutral outsider, or if someone with membership experience will bring an added dimension—and knowledge—to the process. A facilitator can ask the questions that an in-house person might be uncomfortable asking and bring up issues and ideas from his or her experience that might not be available otherwise. Using a facilitator also makes it possible for the staff and volunteers to participate fully, something that is not possible for the person who is leading the meeting.

The facilitator's role is to plan the process, manage it, conduct the meetings, and, in the end, document the plan. Facilitators are usually paid, but it is sometimes possible to find someone with the right skills who will do the work on a pro bono basis. Look for a pro bono facilitator at nonprofit management resource centers (sometimes a part of the local United Way), at organizations like the Junior League that may offer the service, at the business school of a local university, or at a consulting firm that may have a board member as a client. It is important to interview possible facilitators before hiring them, whether it is for a fee or pro bono. A facilitator whose personality does not fit with those working closest with him or her will not provide a good experience. It is also important to check references to make certain that facilitator is the right person for the group.

2. Gain Participation

Asking the potential participants to become involved is the first step in gaining participation. With everyone's busy calendars, scheduling the planning meeting is often the most difficult part of the process. If the organization has staff, then both staff and volunteers might participate. If membership is a part of the development or marketing department, then the director of that department should be included. Also consider including the support staff. The staff that enter data and answer phone calls often have very good ideas about how and when to structure membership campaigns. These staff members are the people closest to members on a daily basis and often the most in touch with the day-to-day operations of the program.

Is there a volunteer component to the program? If so, include the volunteers who are most involved in helping recruit and keep members. Are there board members who would be good additions to the planning group? If the staff is small, the executive director might also be involved. In a larger organization it is helpful to include other staff that have a role in membership. One of the key values in planning is coordination among departments, and this is the time to do it. For example, if the special events staff works on the membership events, include someone from that area. It may also be helpful to meet with program, education, publications, and other staff whose work has some relationship with the membership program and the members. If another department staffs the front of the house sales staff, include these team members in the planning.

Often in a small organization the same person is executive, development, and membership director. While this scenario makes it easy to have all positions in the room at the same time, there is much to be gained from having a larger group. If this is the case, work to find others who might have relevant ideas. If the organization is mainly or totally volunteer driven, then all who are involved in membership and related activities should be included in the planning.

Planning groups have the best discussion when there are seven to twelve participants involved. If there are many more than this, it will take much longer to plan. For every person added to the group, the time needed expands exponentially. Then why not have just one person? This is certainly the fastest way to plan; however, it also produces the least in terms of results. With more people more ideas are generated, more creativity stimulated, and, most importantly, more people have "buy-in" and a commitment to the final plan. To work the plan takes both personal and financial commitment, so the more people who are involved and who have a stake in the outcome, the better the results.

Potential participants will ask, "How long will this take?" There is never a good time and there is never enough time to meet or plan. But if it is agreed that planning is important, a group will make time for it. This is one of the benefits of taking time to develop a real plan—everyone is required to consider the facets of the plan and document his or her thoughts.

There are a number of variables for the time it will take. First is the current state of the program—less time for a well-established program, more time for a brand-new program. More time is needed for a program experiencing difficulties than one that has few issues to confront. It will take longer if the organizer (e.g., the membership manager) has a multitude of other activities that also take time. Perhaps the most difficult part of planning is making and taking the time to do it; however, once done, the time needed to implement is always shorter.

If possible, have at least two planning meetings. It may be that the work can be done in one lengthy session (four to six hours), but if there are two sessions, there will be time for the participants to think things through between the meetings. Sometimes an idea that seems brilliant at first glance gathers doubts over time. If there are major issues involved, it may be helpful to have more than two meetings.

In the real world, the time available may be too little. Ways to shorten the time needed might include having the committee react to parts of a plan (perhaps developed by small sub-committees) rather than trying to create them; presenting the background material in written form ahead of time so that no time is taken at the planning meeting going over it; or having several very short meetings, each focused on an issue, so that committee members can fit them into their schedules.

3. Provide Information Base

Everyone involved in the planning should have a base of information from which to discuss the issues. This might include the history of the program, current staffing pattern, statistics on acquisition, renewals and upgrades, and the relationship of the membership program with the fundraising program. Materials can be assembled and sent to planning committee members ahead of time. There should be a review of the materials and the meaning of the information at the beginning of the planning session. Questions for clarification should be answered, but this is not yet the discussion time. The program should also be put into the context of the organization so that planning participants understand how the program fits into the overall organization and what it means to the organization. The planning leader should not assume that the participants are all well versed in the program.

4. SWOT Analysis

A SWOT analysis is a listing of the Strengths, Weaknesses, Opportunities, and Threats for the membership program. This discussion provides a basis and the information for the issues that need to be addressed. For the SWOT analysis, the facilitator leads the group in a listing of the SWOTs. Then they are discussed to select those that are the most important.

Strengths and weaknesses relate to internal issues. An attribute can be both a strength and a weakness; the issue for the organization is how to manage it. For example, a strength might be rapid growth in the membership program; however, it might also be a weakness because the membership department staff has become overburdened and are not able to service the increased numbers properly. When the planning group discusses membership growth, membership staffing, then, becomes one of the planning issues in order to determine how to provide the appropriate level of service. The same is true of opportunities and threats—the opportunity for more members might also be viewed as the threat (or challenge) of not being able to provide the service. The opportunities and threats are external issues. Is membership down because a new museum opened and is drawing the members away? What strategies can the planning committee develop to address this?

5. Identify Issues and Strategies

Once the informational foundation is set and the SWOT completed, the group discusses the strategic issues and what strategies might address them. Is acquisition a problem? Renewals? Events? Processing? Discuss each issue and determine the strategy needed to deal with it. For example, if membership numbers are dropping, how best to change the situation? By more aggressive acquisition? A more deliberate renewal and retention program? For each strategy, at least one goal should be created.

6. Develop Goals

On the most basic level, the two fundamental issues for every membership program are acquisition and renewal. If a program is not acquiring new members, it will die simply by attrition—by not replacing those who do not renew. Acquisition is necessary even if the organization wants to maintain and not increase its membership numbers. Without a renewal program, there is loss of ongoing income and a dependency on acquisition efforts, which can be expensive and are almost always more expensive than renewal efforts. There must be a goal for acquisition and one for renewals in every membership plan. For each of these goals, as well as for all the others, it is necessary to determine the strategy. For example, in acquisition, the strategy could be increased direct mail, stronger on-site sales, or an email campaign. The same is true for renewals. The planning group decides what the strategy should be.

After acquisition and renewal, there should be three to five other goals that relate to strategic issues, at least one goal for each issue. Those issues can come from the institution itself or from within the membership program. They will, most likely, have been discussed in some manner during the SWOT discussion. If there is a strategic plan for the institution as whole, the membership program needs to look at these goals with an eye to supporting them. For example, if an institution wants to attract family visitation, the membership program should consider benefits and/or events that appeal to families. Other goals might address upgrades, events, a strong social media presence, technology, or record keeping. These goals depend on institutional goals, the status of the current program, budget, and other resource needs such as staffing and volunteer help. Goals are written as the major accomplishments for the program.

7. Establish Objectives

After goals, objectives are written. The system is called management by objective because the objectives provide the basis for managing the program. Objectives are measurable activities that will help you reach the goals. Objectives are written for each goal, and every goal must have at least two objectives. Many talk about objectives being SMART—specific, measureable, assignable, realistic, and time-bound (i.e., deadline). From a practical point of view, the objectives are the work that must be done to accomplish the goals. Saying that it is important to acquire a certain number of members is one thing, figuring out how to do it is quite another. The objectives are really the heart of the plan.

The committee then works on the objectives. How will a particular goal be accomplished? Ideas should be generated, with the group agreeing to two or three of those that seem most realistic. While discussing the goals and objectives, it is imperative to have the leader keep the budget in mind. For example, if the committee wants to conduct a direct-mail campaign, the leader needs to know whether this is realistic. It is not time well spent to have the committee concentrate on an activity that may be impossible. For the institution that wants to attract family visitation, one objective might be "to develop a membership brochure that appeals to families by February, with the membership manager responsible." Another might be "to develop a direct-mail campaign targeted to families that increases net family membership by 300 members by June, with the membership manager responsible." And yet a third might be "to add three events during the year that appeal to family members by December, with the volunteer committee responsible." It is essential to understand that what is measured is what will happen. The above objectives will produce a membership brochure appealing to families, a direct-mail campaign to net 300 family members, and three family-oriented events.

8. Create Action Plans

For each objective, there is an action plan: How will the objective be accomplished? If there is membership staff, developing action plans are often assigned to the staff. If volunteer involvement is necessary for the plans to come to fruition, it will be helpful to have them involved in the discussion to decide what is possible and to gain their commitment. If the organization is a volunteer one, everyone who needs to participate should be involved in the action plan discussion. The action plans for the first objective, "to develop a membership brochure that appeals to families," might include a focus group of current young family members to determine what is appealing; a review of current membership materials to determine if they have the appropriate messages; and speaking engagements at groups with younger members that include an incentive to attend events designed to appeal to this group with on-site sales during these events to add members. For this planning it would be helpful to include the staff responsible for marketing, admissions, and/or visitor services. Each of these action steps would have a date and assigned responsibility.

9. Write the Plan

After each goal and its objectives and action plans are developed and agreed to, the plan must be documented. The planning leader or the facilitator writes the plan. Once written, it should be presented to the planning committee to make certain that the plan is recorded as discussed and that everyone agrees. Most often the document itself will also have an introduction, discussion of the current state of the program, dialogue about the critical issues facing the program, and the worksheets that actually document what will be done. See Appendixes A–E for sample planning worksheets, and visit www.themembershipbook.com for additional planning resources.

10. Prepare the Budget

The budget is then developed. In *Strategic Planning for Public and Nonprofit Organizations: A Guide to Strengthening and Sustaining Organizational Achievement*, author John Bryson notes that implementation of a strategic plan requires "developing a useful strategic management system, including linking budgeting, performance measurement, and performance management, and allowing desirable changes in ends and means to emerge over time."[9] The budget should include all membership activities, not just those that are discussed in the plan. For the plan review, the budget should show the magnitude of expenditures and increases in income. In many cases, additional financial resources are not available. If an acquisition or stronger renewal program looks promising, there may be the possibility of the institution taking the up-front risk knowing that there will be net income in the end. With each program component there needs to be a cost and the projected revenue or impact attached to it. All involved need to know the ramifications of adding or deleting that item from the membership plan. Along with the budget, developing cash flow and membership total projections is very helpful, and for many institutions necessary for the acquisition and renewal part of the plan.

With a plan in hand, it is sometimes possible to find outside funding and in-kind donations to help with the program. Some funders are willing to fund infrastructure issues such as a membership program. For example, a local corporation or foundation might be convinced, on the basis of the revenue projections from the budget, to help with acquisitions because it will leverage ongoing operating support for the organization. If it is decided that a telemarketing campaign would be most effective to regain lapsed members, perhaps a real estate office would donate space and phones for an evening. If additional funding is not possible, then it will be necessary to decide how to shift and reallocate resources. It may be more important to the institution to have the family members than to conduct several of the usual member events, thus requiring changing the focus of some of the current events. Or the organization may be willing to mail fewer pieces in the regular direct-mail program in order to be able to mail to the family segment. These are all issues to discuss during the planning process.

To determine budget magnitudes, it is necessary to have a good idea of the cost of activities. Reviewing past history and adding for inflation can accomplish much of the estimating process. With new programs, cost estimates will take research. This is also the time to assess staffing issues. If a major drive for new members is planned, are there enough support staff to enter data? Or is it possible to use temporary help? If there is not extra help, what will be the ramifications? For example, if it will take four weeks to process a membership application instead of two, can anything be done to alleviate the situation—knowing that many people will call asking for their membership cards? In a volunteer organization it is particularly important to know if there is enough volunteer help to accomplish what is proposed. A sample budget is available at www.thememberhipbook.com.

11. Construct a Calendar

The calendar should be attached to show when the work will be accomplished; it can be designed in written or chart format. Examples of calendars in both formats are available at www.thememberhipbook.com. The calendar should include all the activities of the membership program, not just the new ones in the plan. When developing the calendar it is important to consider the length of time for many of the projects. A direct-mail campaign takes about twelve weeks from design to the mailbox and another eight to twelve weeks to bring in the income. An event can take several months to plan and implement; very large ones may take a year. It is imperative to remember these time lines when developing the calendar.

Other institutional events must be factored into the calendar. These might include events implemented by other departments or communications to the membership from other areas. On-site sales should be coordinated with large institutional events and high visitation times. It is also essential to consider the real-life calendar. If the institution attracts children, remember the school calendar. Campaigns can be tied to holidays such as Valentine's Day or Mother's Day. Events should not be scheduled on major religious holidays (check with local religious organizations for dates). It is difficult, if not impossible, to find many volunteers (and sometimes staff) to help during the winter and spring holiday seasons. A sample calendar and other planning resources are available at www.themembershipbook.com.

12. Gain Approval

The written plan is then submitted to whoever needs to review and approve it. This may be the director of the department where membership is located, it may include the volunteer group associated with the program, and it may be the executive director of the organization. The issue is to make certain that everyone is on board with the plan. If necessary, rework those items that do not receive approval. Once approved along with the budget, the plan can be worked.

When the entire plan, calendar, and financials are reviewed at one time, omissions, conflicts, and unrealistic expectations can be identified and corrected. All staff and volunteers on whom the plan might have an impact should be included at this point for review. This is particularly important in large organizations, where the effect on a particular department's plan may not always be apparent. For example, the communications department may be considering a speakers' bureau and the membership interest in speaking to groups with family members might affect both departments' plans.

13. Work the Plan

Now it is time to get to work. The calendar provides direction on what needs to be done each week; the budget and revenue projections are an evaluation tool to use monthly to make certain that the program is on target. As Drucker famously remarked, "plans are only good intentions unless they immediately degenerate into hard work."

14. Evaluate

Evaluation is the means by which the organization knows whether the plan is working, and, more importantly, that the program is achieving what it set out to do. Evaluation on a regular basis is also the way in which the membership manager makes certain that the plan is used and not put in a drawer or on the shelf until the next planning process is announced.

Monthly review of the financial projections is the fastest way to determine whether the plan is working. If something is not working as expected, corrections should be made. If the acquisition numbers are not where they should be, perhaps an extra campaign can be added or a planned one augmented. Perhaps research is needed to make certain that the acquisition marketing program is appropriate for the audience. Whatever the case, the periodic measurement against the plan is an important evaluation method. At the end of the year, a complete evaluation should be conducted to prepare for the next year's planning.

The plan contains objectives that are the basis for evaluation. The objectives should be reviewed monthly. The evaluation of the objectives against the plan should be in writing and discussed with whoever is the ultimate supervisor of the membership program. This may be the board in a volunteer or very small organization. It may be the development director in a large organization.

A WORD ABOUT FLEXIBILITY

The plan is finished. The budget is approved. The cash flow projections look good. An opportunity arises that has no relevance to the plan whatsoever. The plan is an objective way to say "no" to a well-meaning, but inappropriate, suggestion. But what if the opportunity does make sense? Never pass up an opportunity that will benefit the institution and that truly makes sense for the membership program. When this happens, it is time to see how the opportunity will fit into the plan. It may be necessary to postpone another activity for a few months, or until the next year. Depending on the circumstances, maybe it can be added without many changes to the original plan. Whatever the case, make certain that all involved understand the ramifications. The issue for planning is to maintain the integrity of the program while remaining flexible. Sometimes opportunities really are too good to ignore. The planning process should be willing to embrace them. Good plans are flexible plans.

SUMMARY

Planning is an integral part of a well-functioning membership program. As Jeanne Bell, Jan Masaoka, and Steve Zimmerman emphasize in *Nonprofit Sustainability: Making Strategic Decisions for Financial Viability*, the leaders of today's nonprofit organizations are "expected to run successful hybrid businesses—to be facile at acquiring and maintaining an array of earned and contributed funding streams."[10] Planning will help ensure that all parties are in agreement about direction, that the actions to be taken are funded, and that the future is not based just on wishful thinking. Programs that plan have a greater chance to be successful.

NOTES

1. David La Piana, *The Nonprofit Strategy Revolution* (New York: Fieldstone Alliance, 2008), 31.

2. John M. Bryson, *Strategic Planning for Public and Nonprofit Organizations*, 4th ed. (San Francisco: Wiley, 2011), 1.

3. Jack Beatty, *The World According to Peter Drucker* (New York: Free Press, 1998), 101.

4. Peter F. Drucker, *Managing the Nonprofit Organization* (New York: HarperCollins, 1990), 53.

5. Drucker, *Managing the Nonprofit Organization*, 38.

6. *The AFP Fundraising Dictionary* (Association of Fundraising Professionals, 1996–2003), 76, accessed June 8, 2015, http://www.afpnet.org.

7. Peter F. Drucker, *The Practice of Management* (New York: Harper & Row, 1954), chapter 7.

8. Ibid., 87.

9. Bryson, *Strategic Planning*, 27.

10. Jeanne Bell, Jan Masaoka, and Steve Zimmerman, *Nonprofit Sustainability: Making Strategic Decisions for Financial Viability* (San Francisco: Jossey-Bass, 2010), 175.

3

Membership and Fundraising

We make a living by what we get. We make a life by what we give.

—*Winston Churchill, World Leader and British Prime Minister*

MEMBERS GIVE

They give and they give to more than the membership program. No matter the multitude of purposes for having a membership program, bringing in revenue is always an important factor. Depending on the funding structure of the organization, the membership program may provide either a small part or a substantial portion of the organization's total operating budget. For an organization funded wholly by membership, the financial consideration is obvious. For institutions with various sources of financial support, the financial consideration can be less clear.

Why does a nonprofit decide to have a membership program? Why wouldn't a public issue organization just ask for donations to support the cause? Why don't visitation-based institutions just market for attendance and then ask for annual gifts? Why don't hospitals and museums advertise for volunteers rather than having auxiliaries and guilds? How does a nonprofit make this choice?

MEMBERSHIP OR ANNUAL GIVING?

Many fundraisers equate having a membership program as equivalent to annual giving. There is a difference. While annual giving generates gift support, a membership program is equally as interested in generating a constituency and developing a relationship with the donor. A membership program assumes an equal relationship between the member and the institution. The donor is not just making a gift, but rather there is an implied relationship. That relationship is based on the exchange of money for benefits, both tangible and intangible. At the basic levels, the benefits and the dues have some relationship. People who join an organization because of the economic value they perceive in membership are known as "value members." In programs with graduated dues, benefits become increasingly intangible at the higher levels, and the dues are more and more of a contribution. People who join at the higher levels are known as "support members" or "philanthropic members" of the organization.

Annual giving is a gift "ask." Membership is a gift ask with a program that encompasses it. Membership is more marketing oriented and promotional in its appeal. Members have expectations that there will be benefits, member service, activities, communication, and recognition, all of which is designed to increase the interest and involvement in the organization. It is that sense of belonging and of solidifying the relationship between the member and the organization that is so important.

WHY MEMBERSHIP

Why should an organization consider a membership program when sending an annual gift solicitation seems so much easier? A number of reasons affect all organizations, and some reasons depend on the type of organization. For all organizations, there are the benefits of constituency, education, public financial support, corporate marketing support, public relations, cash flow, and dependability, consistency, and predictability. Visitation-based and public issue organizations have the additional reasons of attendance and cause-related support.

Building a Constituency

With the implied relationship that a membership brings, there is the opportunity to build the support group for the organization. The constituency supports the institution not only financially, but in other ways in addition. From time to time, all organizations need public support, even if the organization is not a public interest group. This support may be for a cause. A zoo might enlist the support of its members to help bring the message about an endangered species to those who make decisions about it. The support may also be asked because of an issue that arises. A botanical garden enlisted the support of its members when a new highway building project threatened its grounds. An association with a large membership will have more lobbying muscle when making their case to policy makers in Washington.

Education

Most organizations have education as a part of their mission. Having a membership group with which to communicate on an ongoing basis through publications, visitation, events, activities, networking, and classes is significant. The membership group has a basic interest in the subject matter and, by self-selection, is a group ready, willing, and interested in learning more about it.

Public Financial Support

The membership may be helpful in seeking and obtaining public funding. For example, a school may be seeking public (e.g., government-related) funding for capital expansion and ask alumni association members to endorse the project. A museum may be seeking direct tax support and members may be willing to be a part of the campaign to win it. A library may want support for a bond issue. In all cases involving public support, having a significant membership program is one way to demonstrate that the organization has support in the community.

Corporate Support

Much as with public financing, corporate marketing support becomes more of a possibility with a substantial membership program. A company that is interested in marketing to a certain group of people is very interested in an organization that has members who meet that market profile. For example, one outdoors-related organization has corporate support from a company that manufactures outdoors sporting goods equipment. It is a mutually beneficial relationship. The membership receives information about the newest products (a service for the members who like to be up to date in this area) and the company reaches potential customers. The organization also sends the membership other information and educational materials, and calls on the membership to help support environmental issues that affect outdoor programs. For organizations that attract a wider variety of people such as museums and libraries, it is important for them to learn who their audiences are.

When these institutions can quantify the demographics of their members, the information is there to use with marketing proposals to corporations.

Public Relations

The most effective public relations is always word of mouth and, more recently, the attendant social media. When people are members of an organization, they often will talk about it, share information with others, often through social media, and, hopefully, persuade others to join. Being a member, for most people, is year-round and constant, not a single annual gift. This encourages them to talk about the organization. The membership also becomes a marketing tool for the institution. At a visitation-based institution, a new exhibit is marketed to the members, who, in turn, tell their families, friends, and neighbors. Members can be encouraged to bring others to exhibits and special activities. For an issue organization, having the membership spread the word about good work, upcoming events, and important concerns is invaluable. A library with a membership program may use that membership base to promote an author's event. Every membership organization should consider its membership as a means of public relations for the organization and use it as such.

Cash Flow

Organizations with annual giving programs tend to ask for the annual gift at one time during the year. Organizations with significant membership programs are acquiring members all year long. Anniversary dues, which are paid on the anniversary of joining, are the most effective for cash and work flow purposes. Thus renewals take place throughout the year, ensuring cash flow throughout the year. If it is helpful to smooth out the cash flow during the year for staffing or other reasons, at some point extra months can be offered as an incentive for renewing or upgrading, thus moving the renewal into a different month when the cash flow is weaker.

Dependability, Consistency, and Predictability

Membership is an implied year-round and ongoing commitment, as opposed to a single gift. Not everyone will renew, but the new member understands that this can be a long-term relationship if he or she finds it beneficial. If the membership program is well planned and executed, the renewal rate should be significant. This means that the income from the program is dependable, consistent, and predictable—always a positive situation in a nonprofit organization. Annual giving doesn't imply the ongoing commitment or year-round belonging that a membership program does.

Some institutions take advantage of special exhibits or controversial issues for acquisition and they need to factor that type of acquisition into the predictability equation. There will be those who join just based on that unusual event and may not be interested in a continued relationship. The issue for the organization is to make the first-year experience so good that the new members will want to continue.

Visitation

In a visitation-based institution, the membership is a keystone for attendance. Having a membership gives the organization a target audience for its exhibits, programs, and events. Direct marketing to this group will bring a base of visitors to the institution. For those organizations that attract large numbers of tourists, the tourists typically come in certain seasons. A zoo in the north will have many tourists in the summer, few in the winter. This may be exactly the opposite for a zoo in the southwest where northerners winter. The membership base provides a group that the organization can encourage to attend during those slow times. The membership program can increase its activities during the non-tourist times to increase visitation among members to offset the lower number of tourists.

Public Issues

Public issue organizations with a membership base validate their message: "Join our cause." Substantial numbers of members prove to the public that the cause is not just that of a few, but that it enjoys widespread support. A substantial number can be fifty neighbors in an area fighting a landfill or can be hundreds of thousands—or millions—supporting either side of the gun control issue. If one side of a controversial issue has significant membership, then the opposing side will find itself trying to attract equal or greater numbers. Again, the concept of membership implies an ongoing commitment to the issue, not a one-time appeal.

MAKING THE MEMBERSHIP DECISION

To have or not to have a membership program is a question that a new organization or one that is redesigning its development program should ask.

Membership is a development strategy that many organizations can use if there is an interest in doing so. There are differences between membership and annual giving from both the potential member or donor and the organization's perspectives.

Membership

There are certain expectations from the potential member's perspective. The member is entering into a relationship that, by definition, lasts for a year or more. In a membership program, the member will expect benefits, regular and consistent activities and communication, and special treatment, whether it be from someone answering the telephone or when attending an exhibit. The member will expect a membership card and invitations to events. The member will expect attention on a year-round basis. In exchange, the member will seriously consider renewing support on an annual basis. The member may become very involved in the organization, make more and generous gifts, volunteer, publicly support the cause, or do other things that reflect his or her sense of belonging.

For many members, the membership gift is the annual gift. They can be approached for a number of different types of gifts during the year, and many will give. But for most, this will be the one gift. Most interesting from the fundraising viewpoint is that longtime, value-level members will be the donors of a high proportion of planned gifts.

When an organization creates a membership program, it is making a public statement about the relationship between the members and the institution. This includes providing the benefits, service, activities, communication, and recognition on a consistent basis, making the organization a worthwhile one for people to join. A good part of this value is increasing that feeling of belonging that members expect. An organization of any size can do this as long as there is a commitment to making it happen.

The member's expectations from a small, local organization will be different than from one that is large and national. There would not be an expectation that a local organization's newsletter would rival the *Smithsonian Magazine*. There would be, however, an expectation that there would be regular and consistent communication in either case.

Acquisition and renewal of members are based on a marketing approach, emphasizing the exchange between the member and the organization. The solicitation pieces tout tangible benefits in addition to the intangible ones.

Once members have been members for a few years, an upgrading process can begin in those organizations with graduated dues, and in all organizations, additional gifts can be solicited during the year.

Annual Giving

From the donor's perspective, annual giving is just that, an annual once-a-year gift. A gift the second year is not necessarily a renewal, but rather another annual gift based on the solicitation that is made. There is not an expectation of tangible benefits and solicitations are generally based on the intangible benefits such as feeling good about the work that the organization is doing, giving back to the community, or personal interest. There is usually no expectation of activities or special services. Most donors do expect to hear from the organization during the year, not just at annual giving time; that can be accomplished with a newsletter.

From the organization's perspective, annual giving is one of the several ways in which donors are solicited. In addition, an annual giving solicitation is not the direct marketing exchange that is used in membership. The solicitation is based on the intangible benefits that the donor receives from meeting the needs of the organization's clients. Some annual giving programs give tangible benefits (e.g., address labels, note cards, etc.), but usually not to the extent that membership programs give them. In organizations with a long history, this means of fundraising is predictable based on history, just as membership. The major difference for the organization is that there is no necessity for the program elements associated with membership; there is no need for a membership card, for developing significant tangible benefits, for member service or activities. It is, however, incumbent on any strong fundraising program to develop those activities that bring donors closer to the institution.

The Decision

The essential question for an organization considering a membership program is "why membership?" as opposed to annual giving. The critical reason why organizations have membership programs is that membership in some way supports the mission of the organization. These organizations have needs in addition to income. For some organizations, membership is what is necessary; the need for income is minimal. As mentioned earlier, having a membership program does not preclude going back to the membership for other gifts. Membership is not an either-or proposition.

Tradition also plays a part. Cultural institutions almost always have a membership program in order to develop their constituency and encourage visitation in addition to creating income. For those who patronize cultural institutions, a museum without a membership program would seem unusual indeed. And what would we think if public radio and television gave up their pledge drives for new members?

Organizations such as some museum guilds, hospital auxiliaries, and faith-based programs have traditionally used membership as a method of building their volunteer programs. Participant programs and some public issue groups need the numbers and the volunteers for their activities that a membership program brings. The raison d'être for shared experience organizations like alumni associations and fraternities and sororities isn't necessarily raising funds; it is keeping the ties that bind strong and current.

How does an organization make the decision? Those working on the project should ask themselves the following questions:

- Would a membership program support our mission?
- Do we need and want members?
- Do we have tangible benefits that make sense and correspond to the dues we are asking?
- Are we able to distribute and provide the benefits in a timely manner?
- Are we able to solicit members during the year for other projects if income is important?
- Are we able to provide member service?
- Do we have a consistent communication program?
- Are there activities or programs that we can provide, if appropriate?
- Do we offer recognition for members including a membership card?
- Do we have the human and financial resources to keep the membership program going?

If the reason for having members is clear, and the answer to most of these questions is "yes," then implementing a membership program is the right decision. If the answers are not so clear, an annual giving program may be a better choice. In many cases, the public understands membership more than giving without the expectation of getting something in return (benefits). Membership can be a training ground for other types of giving.

MEMBERSHIP STRATEGY

Once the membership choice is made, then the organization is able to begin planning and implementing the program. The next choice is what the membership strategy will be. The strategy can be based on growth in numbers, growth in income, or stability. Each of these strategies has numerous ways to approach it.

Growth in Membership Numbers

The growth in numbers strategy says that the number of members is the most important goal. With this approach, resources are put toward acquisition and renewal and they are aggressive, whether using direct mail, personal solicitation, or other techniques. This strategy makes sense in local areas where the program is new, or the population is growing, or where there are audiences that might be interested in the organization, but haven't been approached. It also makes sense for an organization with a current stirring issue or a museum with a new exciting exhibit. When growth is the goal, it is also important to make certain that the renewal process is in place and well executed. Acquiring new members is a waste of resources if they are not renewed at acceptable rates. In fact, developing a strong renewal program may be the most efficient and cost-effective way for an organization to increase its numbers.

For a beginning program there is no doubt that the first effort is to find a critical mass. That critical mass might be 10, 100, 1,000 members, or more. It needs to be a number of members for whom, with dues, it makes sense to provide the benefits and other parts of the membership program. A book club might need a critical mass of twenty to have enough people to attend regularly and join in the conversation. A new aquarium might want a beginning membership of 20,000 to make the membership program possible. Making the membership program interesting is particularly crucial for new organizations because the renewals will be critical to building the base of members.

This strategy is sensible in growing areas of the country, if the additional population is in the age range to which the organization appeals. The organization needs to find ways to reach the new people in the area and to make its presence known. For institutions that have a significant share of the people who meet their member profile, one way to increase the numbers is to find audiences that might be interested in the organization but haven't been approached. For cultural institutions and libraries, this may mean finding ways to appeal to a younger audience or to minority audiences. In either case, it will take an effort by the institution to find the benefits and activities that are attractive to the group they want to reach.

Organizations with exciting issues or exhibits can often use those events as a spur to gain new members. It is very important to make the first-year membership as enticing as possible, so that renewals will be high. Some organizations find that members who join just to see a certain exhibit or support the current cause will not stay with the organization. This is why that entire first-year experience is critical. The one issue or exhibit is not enough. For some issue organizations, just having significant numbers is the key to success.

One question that always comes up is how big should or could a membership program be. The answer is different for different types of programs. For brand-loyalty programs and professional associations, the pool of prospective members can usually be counted and the issue becomes one of marketing in ways that will appeal to the greatest numbers. For other organizations, there is no easy way to know. One way is to compare the current membership numbers with similar organizations. If the organization has a member profile, through census and other information it is possible to find out how many people in the area fit that profile to gauge the potential for growth.

If growth in numbers is important, and it appears that there are potential members, but the program seems to have hit a plateau, consider other approaches. Market research can provide information about the appeal or lack of appeal of the benefits, the program, and other attendant issues. If the organization wants to appeal to new segments of the population, the research can discover what might entice them. Another consideration would be to change or enhance acquisition or renewal methods. The issue might really be a problem with renewals rather than acquisition.

A certain amount of energy and resources is necessary to keep a program growing. The larger the program becomes, the more time and money it takes. Staffing becomes an issue; larger and larger direct-mail campaigns become an issue; servicing the members becomes an issue. There is a cost for growth, but for many the cost for no growth is greater. Understand that once a membership program is up and growing, acquisition and renewals must always continue at a high level just to stay even. If the organization is not willing at least to keep the numbers stable, the program will die from attrition.

Growth in Membership Income

For programs where membership income plays a vital role in the organization, growth in income may be more important than growth in numbers. There are several ways to increase income. Growing the number of members through acquisition and renewal is just one of them. The others include changing the dues structure, increasing the dues, changing the tangible benefits, implementing an upgrade program, and increasing efficiency.

Changing the dues structure, increasing the dues, and changing the tangible benefits will get an immediate reaction from current members. When doing any of them, inform the members that this will happen at a certain date. Offer early renewals to keep the current rates and benefits for the next year before making the change. The organization will lose some members, depending on the size of the change. If it involves a few dollars, nothing may happen. If it involves perceived large changes, be prepared to answer questions and talk to unhappy members. The real test is what happens over the course of a year. If there is a significant loss of membership, the institution may have to reconsider the changes.

Knowing that there will be some attrition due to the changes, it is important to make the changes so that the organization will still increase income if there is a drop in membership. For example, if the dues are going to increase from A to B, and the assumption is made that there will be a 10 percent drop in membership, then B must be more than the current total from 90 percent of the members. Know that some members are very vocal. It is their organization. If the program has a large membership and the calls are few, do not worry. Try to calm the unhappy members as much as possible. People do understand that prices rise. One organization raised rates and noticed in the first two months that a large number of members downgraded to a lower level rather than increase their membership. The organization decided to offer an incentive to members who remained at their current level at the new increased dues fee. Downgrading immediately stopped and total income increased. In most cases, with modest dues increases a minimal drop-off will be noticed—3 percent or less.

It is sometimes more difficult to change benefits than to change the cost of membership. Membership has its privileges and when those are removed there can be a lot of unhappiness. If members are typically invited to an event that will no longer be held, tell them why in a small note in the newsletter. If the event is cancelled because it is not very popular, just let it fade away. If there are particular people who were very vested in the event, make certain to let them know what is happening. If there is an overall restructuring of the program—changes in the benefits and dues structure simultaneously—it may be helpful to send a letter to members explaining the changes, and letting them renew with the current structure for a short time; then proceed with restructuring. Usually, the comments and complaints will last a year or less. No organization wants to do this often, but sometimes, particularly when restructuring the program, it must be done. Small price increases every two to three years is the recommended strategy. By doing this, a major price increase won't be necessary because a program has waited too long to increase dues.

Upgrade campaigns for membership programs with graduated dues are very effective in increasing income. This strategy for increased income does need resources put toward it. The resources may be financial to support offering an incentive to upgrade. This may include anything from a product with the institution's logo to an additional two months of membership if the member upgrades. What is offered depends on the organization.

Another upgrade campaign that can produce increased income is a personal solicitation campaign to add members at support levels. This can be done as a fundraising campaign, with a committee and an organized way to solicit lists of potential upper-level support members.

Stability

Growth in numbers or income may not be the goal for the program; the goal may be stability. The membership program is important, but in organizations where the membership program is part of the larger institution, the institution's goals are paramount. It may be that the organization's priority is a capital campaign and that is where the resources need to be invested. In that case, the issue will be to keep the membership numbers and income at about the same level rather than trying to increase them. Even with a strategy of stability, there is a need for acquisition and renewal. Without acquisition and renewal, the program will begin to fade. Attrition must always be countered. In the natural order of things, there will always be some attrition due to people moving, life circumstances changing, or priorities shifting.

It may also be that an institution does not want to add resources to the membership program. This is a suitable decision as long as there are enough resources to make certain that the program doesn't die from attrition. If resources are diminished, there must be an attempt to make certain that renewal and acquisition efforts are not totally reduced. In addition, an organization serving a limited geographic area will be constrained in membership size by the size of the community. If the community is not growing or is declining, the membership program may reflect this reality if it already has as many members as the community will sustain.

Another reason for stability may be that the organization has reached its limit of being able to service the membership. In some participant and volunteer programs there just aren't enough projects or volunteer opportunities to take care of the number of members. When this is the case, the organization may want to limit its numbers until it has more ways to make use of the members' time. Asking people to volunteer and then having nothing for them to do is a certain way to ensure discontent. For more information and resources regarding volunteers, visit www.themembershipbook.com.

THE MEMBERSHIP RELATIONSHIP

Even if a membership program generates only a small portion of the organization's total budget, whether that is 5, 10, or 15 percent, that amount may be the important difference in giving the organization some financial stability and flexibility. Remember that membership money is unrestricted, and unrestricted funds are always the most difficult to raise. With unrestricted funds, an organization may pay the utility bills, salaries, or other unexciting (to most donors) but absolutely necessary expenses. It may also provide seed money to fund a new program or buy needed equipment. No matter how it is spent, it has significant value because the organization can make the decision to spend the money where the funds are most needed.

A well-designed membership program can be powerful in increasing the relationship with the members and turning them into donors. People who join a membership program have an interest in the organization and they may become even larger donors over time. Strong fundraising programs are often based on a relationship being developed between the member and the organization. This relationship is based on the member's interest and involvement in the organization. Thus, the membership program should be designed and developed as the foundation of giving for the organization. The membership becomes the donor base for the institution and it should be regarded as such.

Membership's Place in the Organization

Membership programs can be found in a variety of departments in organizations—development, marketing, visitor services—or as a stand-alone department. To use the membership as the foundation of an institution's fundraising program, the membership program belongs, more often than not, in the development department. If there is any question about where membership belongs, choose development.

Membership in the Development Department

When the membership program is a part of the development office, it is, by definition, an integral part of the fundraising program of the institution or organization. With the opportunities for integration with the development program, membership fits well in this department. A single database is easily used for all projects and the driving force for all concerned is raising more funds for the organization.

Membership in the Marketing Department

In a large organization, with separate development and marketing departments, there may be a reason to include the membership program in the marketing department. There is often the feeling that membership is more of a marketing function than a philanthropic one. Because the basic membership program begins with a marketing exchange, it would seem logical to include it with other marketing ventures. Members are profiled, surveyed, and targeted. A variety of marketing techniques is used to appeal to a prospective member. Membership has all the markings of marketing. Thus, the decision is made that it must be a marketing function.

Organizations that have high admission fees frequently place membership in the marketing department to try to circumvent the competition between membership and admissions that seems to occur when one person's budget is affected by the success of the other. Membership can depend heavily on the admissions staff for its on-site sales success. Thus in some organizations it may make sense to have membership and visitor services under one administrator.

Some zoos and aquaria have membership programs that are placed in the marketing department. With high gate fees and the perception of a ticket package comparable to a theme park or similar venue, this placement may make sense. Also, historically many zoos had membership programs long before they had development departments.

With the rise in social and digital media, there is a necessity for membership to have access to these tools, whose management is usually housed in marketing. This situation may predicate that membership and marketing be housed together. If this is the case, the membership and fundraising must be carefully coordinated and work together. The membership manager must have a good working knowledge of development issues, and be certain that once a member joins, he or she receives communication that underlines how important his or her support is for the institution. The worst-case scenario is when there is competition between the marketing department and the development department or between development and a separate membership department. Competition within the institution works to the distinct disadvantage of the organization as a whole.

Membership in a Department with Visitor Services

An increasingly frequent situation is the inclusion of membership in the same department with visitor services. Because of the connection and reliance on the front-of-the-house staff to be involved in membership on-site sales and to circumvent the usual competition between those functions, membership and visitor services may be housed together. Such arrangements can work to maximize on-site sales.

Donated Income

With a membership program that functions as the donor base for the organization, there are numerous possibilities for increasing contributed and earned income. In some organizations, membership and development keep separate databases. This is also counterproductive. If it is at all possible, the institution should have only one database. That database should, of course, have coding to enable the selection of segments of the membership so that it can be used in a variety of ways. For most organizations, to have separate databases makes it difficult, if not impossible, to use the list for multiple or cross-cultivation and solicitation efforts. In an institution with a natural constituency, like a university, the alumni association would use the school's database to solicit members rather than the school using the alumni association list. This one-way cross-cultivation is a different situation and, as necessary, should be coordinated to suit the needs of both the development and alumni offices. In some cases, alumni may be more likely to report a change of address to the alumni association than to the school's development office. Thus, the alumni association can become an excellent source of updated contact information. With one database for both entities to share, successful two-way cultivation would be easier.

Membership Giving Cycle

For organizations without a natural constituency, such as a museum or civic group, offering a membership program becomes an important method for discovering who has an interest and who might become involved. The membership program is a prospecting tool, a cultivation mechanism and the donor base from which to solicit the additional donations. There is a giving cycle for a membership program much as there is for any fundraising program. Figure 3.1 shows the Membership Giving Cycle.

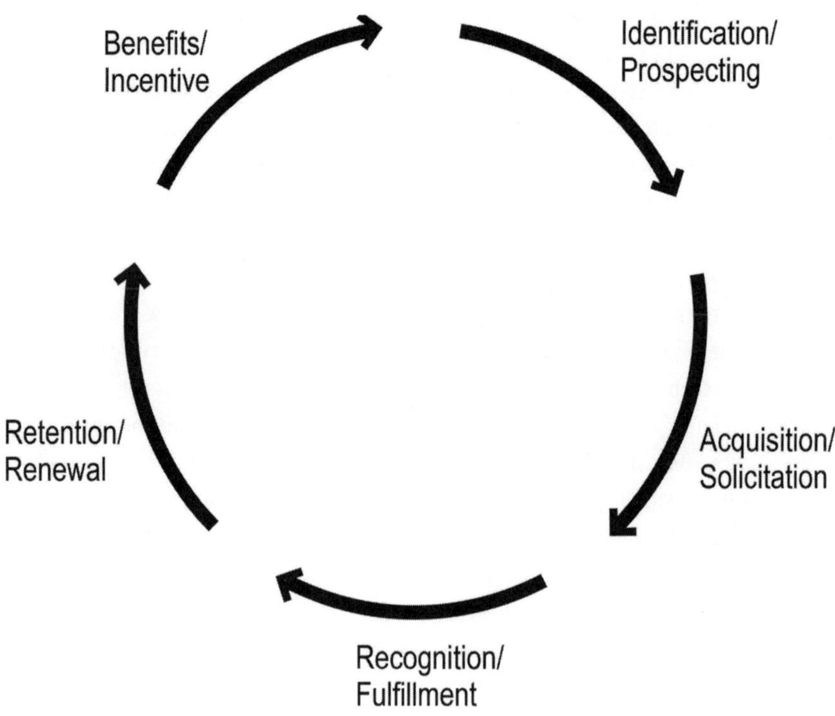

FIGURE 3.1
Membership Giving Cycle

Benefits and Incentives

The case for a fundraising program is "the reasons why an organization both needs and merits philanthropic support."[1] The case for a membership program is foremost its benefits, which underscore the merit of supporting the institution. The benefits or any incentive for joining will make no difference if the potential member has no interest in the organization or its work.

Along with the package that includes the benefits and any incentive to join, there also needs to be a case made for the organization itself. The potential member will be interested in the organization, but at the value levels of membership, the benefits and the incentive to join are the real focus of the appeal and the major interest of most of the prospective members. That offer is the "hook" that encourages the potential member to look further. If the offer is not one that is appealing to the prospect, then the relationship will end before it begins.

For organizations that are working to appeal to more than one market, the acquisition effort might emphasize different benefits for different groups. A museum that can identify those interested in activities for kids might use the benefit of access to free children's programs while marketing lectures and publications to another audience.

Identification and Prospecting

Organizations continually need to increase and broaden their constituency base. Some members will leave: they will find a new or different cause; they will move out of town; their personal situation will change and they will no longer be able to contribute or participate. If new members are not found, in the long term, the program will die from attrition. Having a membership program gives a very appealing way to add to the base of support. Because the basic frame of reference for a membership program is a marketing exchange—that is, money for benefits—the appeal is broad and direct.

Finding new members to add to the base is straightforward. Potential members are often called "suspects" and "prospects." A suspect is a potential donor whose linkage to the organization, ability to give, and interest are unknown.[2] There are, however, demographic or psychographic characteristics that enable an organization to select a suspect pool. Places to look include magazine or catalog lists from those publications that have a relevance to the organization's work. For example, an environmental group might consider using a mailing list from a magazine with a focus on natural areas or a catalog mailing list from a company that sells camping or mountain-climbing equipment. Those lists can be purchased on a zip code basis and are often targeted by such specifics as household makeup and income.

A prospect is identified as having "linkage, giving ability and some interest."[3] To reach prospects, the possibility of exchanging lists with like-minded organizations should be considered. For example, museums can exchange lists for prospecting, remove duplications ("deduping"), and use the cleaned list. These potential members are prospects; they have, for the most part, the interest and ability to join. Those who join one organization will often join others that are similar. With a membership program, the organization has the possibility of offering something of value to attract the member. Once a member joins, the organization then has the opportunity to bring that member closer to the organization, increase the linkage, and involve the member with the institution.

In 2014, the "Patron Loyalty Study: Loyalty by the Numbers," conducted by the Greater Philadelphia Cultural Alliance and TRG Arts, analyzed the overall impact of list sharing and collaboration. Using data provided by seventeen arts and cultural institutions in the Philadelphia area, the study found that list sharing benefited the participating organizations while also building a more supportive giving community in general. According to the report, "Collaboration and sharing of data holds the potential to increase overall engagement while simultaneously increasing loyalty efforts for individual groups. The more a patron becomes involved across the community the more likely they are to increase their commitment to their most favored organizations. Greater sharing of data, collaborative marketing efforts and cross promotion strategies hold the potential to benefit everyone. This is probably one of the most compelling findings in the study."[4]

Acquisition and Solicitation

Acquisition is the successful art of solicitation for the membership program. When the new member returns the membership form that was included in the mailing, or purchases a membership on-site or online, the solicitation has taken place. In membership solicitation where the program has graduated levels, the first several tiers are straightforward. The benefits and incentive have encouraged the person to join. It is an immediate transaction.

Recognition and Fulfillment

Recognition in a membership program begins immediately with the fulfillment of the offer made in the acquisition effort. If the member does not receive a timely thank you, his or her membership card, information about programs, and the incentive that was offered, then the membership program will suffer in the long run. This is a part of the retention effort and, because it is the first real communication with the member as a member, it is extremely important. First impressions do count and they are remembered. Any other recognition also needs to be timely (e.g., listing in a newsletter) and correct.

Retention and Renewal

A retention plan is the cultivation program for a membership program. It is the way that an organization "engages and maintains the interest and involvement of a donor."[5] A membership program is a built-in way to encourage members to become more significant donors to the institution. A strong effort will have a series of programs designed to engage and maintain the interest of the members. These programs are often marketed as some of the benefits of membership. Invitations to members-only events (e.g., a special lecture on a topic related to the institution), VIP treatment at public events (e.g., a member line to enter an exhibit), or special publications at a free or reduced cost are some of the possible opportunities.

"Special" is the operative word when describing how an organization wants its members to feel. All programs and events should be designed to encourage that feeling. If the members feel like part of the institution's family, then the membership program and the cultivation are successful. This translates into strong support for the institution through renewed membership and increased and more frequent gifts. Feeling special also encourages the member to spread the word, advocate for the cause, and encourage others to add their support.

Pyramids of Giving

The Donor Pyramid of Giving (figure 3.2) graphically represents the development process.[6] The membership program is the pyramid's foundation for many institutions and organizations. The premise of the pyramid is that the more people become interested and involved in the organization, the more likely they are to make major and planned gifts. Some donors self-select and move from annual giving into major giving in the pyramid, while others enter at a major gift level. The challenge, however, is to involve the donors more closely in the organization. A membership program can provide the framework for that effort.

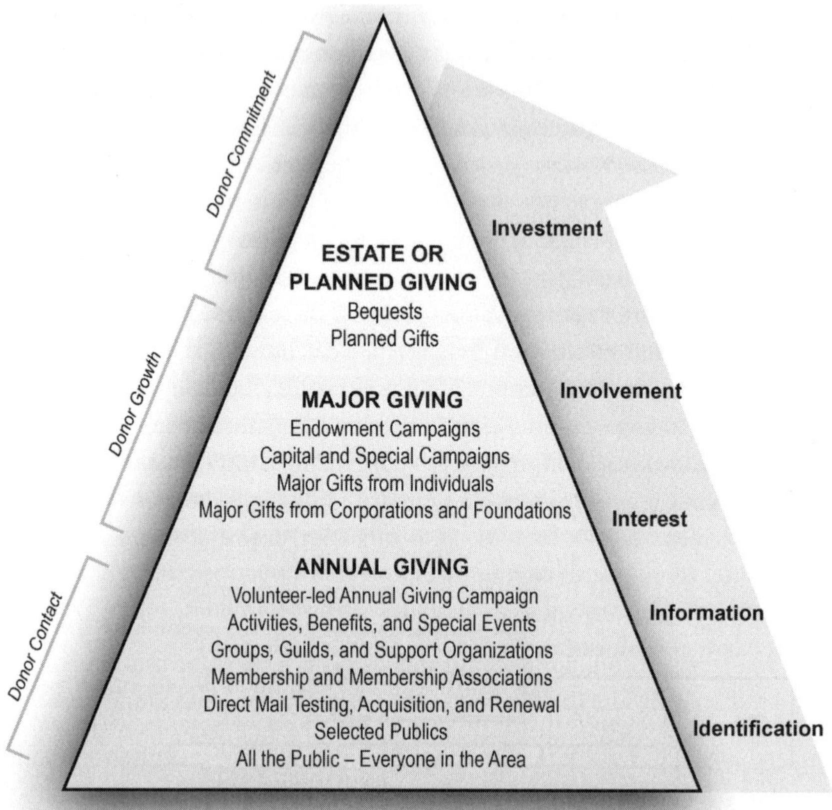

FIGURE 3.2
Donor Pyramid of Giving
Source: James M. Greenfield. *Fund Raising*, Copyright © 1999, John Wiley & Sons, Inc. Reprinted by permission of John Wiley & Sons, Inc.

The Membership Pyramid of Giving (see figure 3.3) shows how the membership program in an organization with graduated dues becomes the way to develop the fundraising program.

Value Members and Support Members

An annual giving program is almost always the base for a fundraising program. Many people consider their yearly membership gift to an institution as their annual gift—and for many it is. Having an ongoing renewed membership from this group is tantamount to annual giving. The technical difference is that an annual gift is often an unrestricted donation, with the

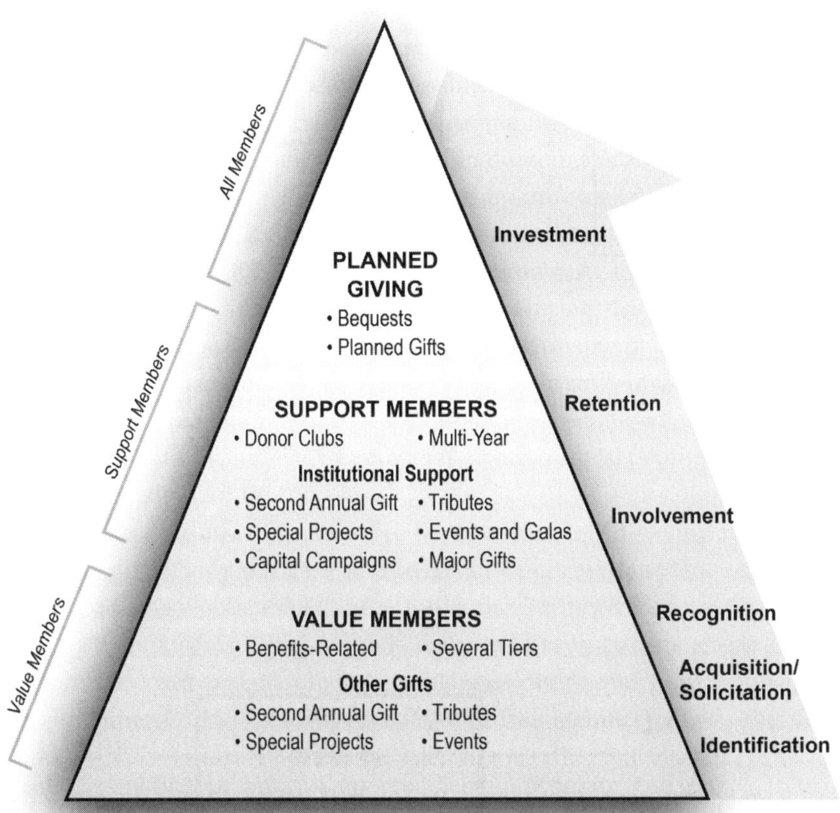

FIGURE 3.3
Membership Pyramid of Giving—Graduated Dues

donor receiving nothing in return, while the membership gift, also usually unrestricted, is based on a marketing exchange of money for something of value (membership benefits). That something of value can be free admission, an incentive gift, or an array of other benefits with value.

The member whose membership gift is dependent on the benefits is a value member or one who makes the gift because it is a good value. That good value, for example, might be free admission to a museum that the member frequents—it is money saving to buy the membership rather than paying the admission price each time. Entire membership programs may be value programs. Many high-ticket-priced admission programs, such as those for aquaria, tend to be more heavily value member based. Because the decision to join is based so strongly on the immediate benefit, gaining long-term organizational commitments and donations may be difficult.

Some members at the value membership level ask not to receive the items of value and, in this case, the gift is truly a donation. For those who do avail themselves of the membership benefits, they may still equate their membership gift with an annual donation. The important thing about the membership program is that, with anniversary renewal dates (yearly renewal on the anniversary date of joining), the annual giving from members becomes systematic. A member who has renewed for several years will often continue this giving for many, many years. This predictability of this income stream underlies the importance of membership funding. The lifetime giving of a renewing member can be substantial.

Even value members can be asked for other gifts. Value members are good prospects for a second annual gift, special projects, tributes, and events. Special projects can even include capital projects that can be accomplished with a small (for a capital campaign) amount such as a brick program that asks members to buy bricks in a patio to support a building campaign.

Some members, however, become support members, moving beyond value member status to higher steps on the pyramid. Support members are those who make a membership gift at a level where benefits are no longer the only reason for giving. Where this is for an institution depends on the benefit structure. Support members make a larger gift, make additional gifts, and, in some cases, become major donors to the institution.

Finding Support Members

Upgrades

Periodically it's important to ask members to upgrade, or to increase the amount of their annual membership. Some members will self-select and give at a higher level without being asked, but asking will increase the number who do give more. Not asking is a major reason why people don't give and one of the reasons why they don't give more. The higher the gift, usually the less bearing the membership benefits have on the donor—and the gift is more of an outright unrestricted donation.

Donor Clubs

The higher member giving levels become donor clubs. Donor clubs usually begin at a level considered to be a major gift. In some organizations this is $100, in others $1,000, and in yet others a much higher level. Donor clubs usually have a name, (e.g., "The President's Club"), and make special offers to the donor. These offers are often events or opportunities designed to bring the donor closer to the institution and increase their involvement and interest or provide recognition of their generosity. Opportunities might include events such as a tour with the institution's director, dinner with other club donors, a name on a plaque in the reception area of the organization's building, or a periodic "insider" newsletter. According to the "Burk Donor Survey," donors ranked recognition events as the most meaningful recognition.[7]

These member/donors receive a special renewal. The renewal can be a personalized letter or a personal call or visit from a board member or the chief staff officer. These donors do receive the typical member benefits such as free admission, the publication, and discounts. Some, but not all, of these donors will opt out of taking the tangible member benefits. These donors do consider themselves members, and a number of them will have originally joined the organization at a value level of giving.

When a new donor makes a gift to the organization at a support level, it is appropriate to make that person a member at the level of his or her giving. This ensures that the donor will be on the regular mailing list and, importantly, will be in the system to be re-solicited on the anniversary date of the first gift. In addition, the new donors will also be invited to events that will bring them closer to the institution and encourage them to become more involved.

ASKING MEMBERS

Other Requests

Other funds from members come from a variety of requests in addition to the yearly membership renewal. Members, because of their belief in the organization and personal involvement, should always be considered as one of the groups to ask for donations for special projects. The "Burk Donor Survey" states, "Membership is not a deterrent to other forms of giving; two out of three members reporting that they also make charitable gifts to those same nonprofits, membership appears to be a conduit to giving philanthropically."[8] They are the ones closest to the institution and the ones with the greatest stake in it. In addition, the membership is the perfect audience for earned income opportunities.

A successful membership program provides the opportunity for successful fundraising of contributed and earned income. This successful fundraising is the foundation of support for an institution or organization. There are a number of possibilities for raising funds through other requests, as described below.

Matching Gifts

Many corporations have matching gift programs. These programs are corporation specific, with different criteria for the types of gifts that can be matched and different ratios at which they are matched. Some corporations will match gifts for membership. It is important to include asking for matching gifts on the membership enrollment form. If a matching gift is made, give the member the increased membership level.

Second Gift

It is possible to solicit what might be called an annual gift or, in this case, a second gift. Many institutions have an annual giving fund in addition to the membership program. It needs to be very clear that this is not a membership solicitation; it is a request for another gift. This gift may be for general purposes or tied to a specific program. Often the program is one that the organization presents regularly (an education program, for example) and the organization is looking for new and additional ways to fund it.

Some members will be confused about being asked for a second gift. This confusion should not keep the institution from asking for a second gift. Wording on the second gift solicitation should be clear. For example, one institution's director writes to his members, "I realize that your membership is also due for renewal at this time, and I am truly grateful for your consideration of this request." Or at the bottom of the response slip, "I understand this is not a renewal of my current membership." If a member calls about this confusion and wants to make a gift but is uncertain about the difference, the member service staff should explain the differences and help the member select the option that he or she is interested in. Confusion for some members should not be used to eliminate this additional program.

Gift Memberships

There is no one better to purchase a gift membership than a current member. The gift can be for any holiday. Membership programs can promote the gift membership idea as a way to acquire new members, and this campaign is most effective with current members. Gift memberships can be publicized for the holiday season, Valentine's Day, Mother's Day, Father's Day, and so forth. The membership manager should select those commemorative days that have some connection to the institution or that can be marketed in a productive way—a Baseball Hall of Fame with its online publications is a natural for Father's Day, a botanical garden for Mother's Day, or the Smithsonian for the holidays for someone interested in its magazine. The organization must consider the extent to which it can market the gift memberships. Even if the organization does not have the resources to publicize gift memberships, it should make them available to anyone who requests one.

Tributes

Many organizations have a tribute fund. A tribute fund allows people to make a gift in honor or in memory of someone. It has become quite common for those who have a special birthday or anniversary to ask friends to make a donation to a charity of choice rather than send a gift. When people die, many families ask for donations in lieu of flowers. When these requests are made, and it is for a charity of the donor's choice, it is important for members to have a way to select the organization to which they want to contribute. A tribute envelope is a useful way for organizations to make certain that their members have the information and the convenience of making this type of gift.

There are at least two ways to make tribute envelopes available to members. The first is to include one with the member's information packet. This can be one of the items sent to all members. One envelope can be sent each year if the tribute program is large or every second or third year if the program is small. Many cultural institutions and hospital groups have particularly well-developed tribute programs. The second way to promote this program is to do a mailing once a year, at a time that is appropriate for the institution. Botanical gardens may find that this is in the spring, while a friends group at a library might want to mail closer to the winter holiday season.

Special Projects

Seeking funding for a specific project is a great opportunity to solicit the membership. Members who have been receiving information from the organization will know about many of the programs and facilities. When there a special project, members like to know about it and some will be willing to support it.

Over time, it will become possible to identify members who have special interests and provide them more information about their favorite areas of interest.

Capital Campaigns

Capital campaigns are also an opportunity to solicit the membership. Members who are in the support-level donor clubs will, of course, be solicited at levels appropriate for the campaign. When the campaign is in its public stage, seeking a broad range of smaller gifts, value members should be solicited for various projects. Some organizations take this opportunity to relate a special project to the membership; for example, a room may become a members' room in a new facility, or a new endowment fund for a special program might be named for members. Significant amounts of money can be raised from a large pool of value-level members.

Planned Giving

Planned giving programs are appropriate for members of long standing. This is the donor base to which planned gifts can be marketed. There are many anecdotal stories about large bequests coming from value-level members. According to Timothy Sharpe of Robert F. Sharpe & Company, the planned giving specialists, "A major misconception is the belief that most large planned gifts are made by people of great wealth. While stories abound of six- and seven-figure bequests coming from the estates of persons who had made very modest gifts during life, these cases are often treated as amazing exceptions. As it turns out, these gifts are more the rule than the exception."

Bequests come from members who have known the institution for a long time and believe in it. From Robert Sharpe on bequests, "There appears to be no pattern to the gifts made prior to death other than the fact that most bequests appear to come from relatively long-term donors." They have an interest, have been involved through their membership, and are ready to make an investment through their bequests or other planned gifts. Length of time of association with an organization is a significant attribute of planned givers.

Special Events

Members also provide a good pool for prospects for special events. Members are those who support your organization regularly and when there is a fund-raising event many may want to participate. If it is an event with a modest to moderate ticket price, the entire membership may be solicited. If, however, it is a high-ticket price event such as a black-tie gala, it may make sense to send invitations only to the support-level members. For those who come to an event with a high-ticket price, the organization may choose to make that person a member at the appropriate level. Many people come to events because a friend invites them. When this is the case, the allegiance is to the friend, not to the institution. While making the person a member guarantees that he or she will be on the mailing list and receive information and invitations, the likelihood of renewing the person is slight. This doesn't mean that it shouldn't be done, but the expectation of renewal should not be high. If the event is a success, some people will return to annual events while never responding to other appeals.

Special Interest Groups

For some institutions, members provide the base from which to solicit membership in special interest groups. For example, many art museums will have member groups dedicated to a certain kind of art. Groups might include one for contemporary arts, one for decorative arts, and another for classical arts. The Denver Art Museum offers seven themed support groups ranging from the Friends of Painting & Sculpture to the Asian Art Association. There are benefits associated with these subgroups, and they are also a way to further cultivate members and increase their giving. Special interest groups can also be found in organizations such as environmental or hobby-related groups. For example, an environmental group might offer subgroups relating to rare plants or to endangered animals with each providing specialized communications and events relevant to the participant's interests. Often, to belong to a specialty membership group, it is necessary, first, to join the regular membership group; for most programs this should be required.

Travel Programs

Membership programs may offer travel options. University and college alumni associations, museums, environmental groups, and others occasionally organize trips related to their mission. Lectures, knowledgeable guides, and special events are all a part of these tours. In addition to the cost of the trip, organizations will often include an expected donation to the organization, which is tax deductible. This extra donation can be a noteworthy addition to an organization's budget. Of course, many of these trips are advertised and available to members only. In addition, when a staff member accompanies the group, there is the opportunity for the members and staff to forge a relationship that carries on long after the trip is over. This relationship can be a strong motivator for further interest and involvement in the organization by the member.

Products

Logo merchandise (the caps, shirts, and mugs, with the institution's logo) can be very popular. Offering these items to the membership is one way to encourage sales and to promote the use of items that bring visibility to the organization. Art museums have taken this to great levels with four-color catalogs of items based on their collections. Alumni groups make use of this with school logo merchandise; fraternities and sororities do the same.

Publications (print and electronic), insurance, and affinity credit cards are examples of other products that can also be offered to the membership.

Facility Rental

For visitation-based institutions, a member benefit can be a discount on or first priority for facility rental. Rentals include space for meetings, conferences, weddings, and parties of all sorts. These institutions can be very desirable and in demand. If an institution is building its facility rental program, a mailing to the membership is one of the ways to make this service known.

Frequency of Requests

Overall, a member should be solicited during the year. How often can a member be asked? There are no hard and fast rules about the number of requests that can be sent to a member. There seem to be different perceptions about the kinds of "asks" to make. For example, a request for matching gifts solicited on the membership enrollment form is not really perceived as a second request. Sending tribute information can be viewed as a service; many people choose to honor or memorialize someone in this manner. Events provide ways to involve members and different types of events appeal to different types of members. Those who want to attend will respond to those of interest. These are perceived as requests but not in the same vein as those for contributions without participation.

Special interest groups and travel choices are both services and opportunities for members for involvement and education, should they decide to participate. These are very positive ways for the institution to interact with members—and members view them in that way. These opportunities, when done well, are popular and perceived as real benefits for being a member.

Those asks that are perceived as additional requests are the requests for a second gift, for special projects and for capital campaigns. Again, interested members will give support. For those who are not interested, the request is a form of communication, letting the members know what is happening in the organization. Planned giving information is just that, information and another way to communicate with the membership.

Requests or information of any type should be considered a part of the communication package. Requests should not constitute the greatest number of pieces of mail that a member receives. A small organization might send two or three additional solicitations during the year, while a large one might send four or more in addition to the yearly membership renewal. Additional solicitations might be for a second annual gift, the tribute fund, a special project, a special event, and one to buy gift memberships. A member might also receive an invitation to a planned giving seminar. If the organization is involved in a capital campaign, members might be phoned for a gift in addition to the mail requests.

There are members who do not want to be solicited for anything but their membership. They will let the organization know who they are and that they do not want to be solicited for other efforts. The wishes of these members should be honored; they should be taken off the mailing list for those fundraising campaigns. Many organizations worry about asking for a gift too often. Most organizations err on the side of not asking often enough. Always honor a person's request not to be solicited, but don't allow a few complaints to dictate the fundraising strategy.

COUNTING THE MONEY

There may be times when there is disagreement about which department takes credit for certain revenue; the issue should really be the overall "bottom line." This is typically an issue in organizations with staff. How the money is counted can be any way the organization wants to, following generally accepted accounting procedures, but the overriding issue should be how much is raised overall. There should be cooperation among staff to provide the best and most fundraising for the organization as a whole. No fundraising program should lead to turf wars. It is the work of the leader of the program to make certain that this doesn't happen. Everyone needs to be working cooperatively toward the same end: more resources for the institution.

In an organization where membership is in the development department, the money that comes in for membership is a part of the development revenue. Some organizations recognize membership income as earned income rather than contributed income. In museums, membership income is often considered earned income instead of contributed income due to the value proposition of benefits. Museums may want to refer to the American Alliance of Museums for the most appropriate way to do this for their organization.

For other organizations this may complicate the issue, particularly since it's known that not all members use the benefits offered and most do not use all of them (e.g., if an incentive needs to be picked up, usually one-half or fewer members actually claim them). Members believe that they have joined in order to support the organization. If possible and appropriate, count all the funds as contributed.

Membership begins with many small gifts. In fundraising, it is almost always more expensive to raise small gifts than large ones. This is because direct mail, events, and the other ways that small gifts are solicited cost money. Often a volunteer with a personal solicitation and little expense will secure a major gift. These gifts, however, are typically based on a long relationship with the organization (or the solicitor) and are backed by staff efforts. The question then is, why spend time on small gifts if they are more expensive to raise? There are several answers.

First, if an organization attracts only a small number of donors, it is putting "all its eggs in one basket." A strong donor base is built on a large, broad donor base to give a solid foundation. With it, the loss of a major donor is difficult, but not threatening. Second, for visitation-based institutions, the organization also wants a broad base to attend. Having a membership program with its events and activities is a significant way to build attendance at the institution. For other organizations, the broad base gives a core group to approach for volunteer work, educational messages, and programs. Third, if there is a planned giving program, many of these gifts will come from supporters who are not major donors.

In visitation-based organizations, it is also short sighted for the organization as a whole to consider members attending and enjoying free admission as revenue forgone and charge the membership department for it. If this happens, it is counterproductive and there is no incentive or reason to have a membership program, at least not one that offers any type of admission as a benefit. The concept of revenue forgone is not concrete. If a person were not a member, would he or she come as often? Anecdotal information suggests not.

Further, the member who comes frequently may eat more often in the restaurant, may shop more frequently in the gift shop, and, as a result, provide a higher level of earned income. Those who come frequently may also tend to be those who provide other support to the institution, whether in direct financial support, planned gifts, volunteer time, or all three.

SUMMARY

When designing the fundraising program for an organization, if there are reasons in addition to or other than income involved, membership will be a good foundation for the program. In those programs where other fundraising also occurs, the membership program should be the base for much if not all the activity. Membership draws individuals closer to the organization's mission, and provides opportunities for volunteering, education, and a sense of belonging. The deeper an individual's involvement, the greater is the likelihood for increased giving. For example, the Fidelity® Charitable Gift Fund found that on average, "those who have volunteered in the last 12 months donate ten times more money to charities than non-volunteers ($2,593/yr vs. $230/yr)."[9] Membership programs can provide a solid structure for fundraising.

NOTES

1. *The AFP Fundraising Dictionary* (Association of Fundraising Professionals, 2003), 21, accessed June 8, 2015, http://www.afpnet.org/files/ContentDocuments/AFP_Dictionary_A-Z_final_6-9-03.pdf.

2. Ibid., 162.

3. Ibid., 140.

4. Greater Philadelphia Cultural Alliance and TRG Arts, "Patron Loyalty Study: Loyalty by the Numbers," December 11, 2014, 15, accessed March 10, 2015, http://www.philaculture.org/sites/default/files/2014_patron_loyalty_white_paper_-_final.pdf.

5. AFP, *Fundraising*, 44.

6. James M. Greenfield, *Fund Raising*, 2nd ed. (New York: John Wiley & Sons, Inc., 1999).

7. Cygnus Applied Research, "Burk Donor Survey," 2013, 12.

8. Ibid., 77.

9. Fidelity® Charitable Gift Fund, "Volunteerism and Charitable Giving," 2009, 2.

4

The Membership Program

Nothing will work unless you do.

—Maya Angelou, Poet

VARIETY IN MEMBERSHIP

There is great variety in membership programs. It would be impossible to find two that are exactly alike. There are differences in structures for the programs, differences in benefits, differences in markets. This occurs because of the different types of nonprofits that develop them; nonprofits have different purposes, geography, and competition. There can also be packages within a membership program for different kinds of members.

MEMBERSHIP PACKAGES

All membership programs have a basic membership package. For those with dues levels, such as the ones offered by most visitation-based and issue organizations, there may be several packages from which the potential member can choose.

Variety in Offerings

The basic package for a visitation-based organization might include admission benefits for two adults and two children less than twelve years of age, a newsletter, a discount on merchandise and programs, and invitations to events. There may be different price points for this package for individuals, students, seniors, grandparents, or nannies, though the benefits would be close to the same. As the levels of membership increase, so do the benefits, including more admissions tickets, tickets for special exhibits, free parking, discounts for gift shops or food service, invitations to more exclusive events, and so forth.

Nonresident Program

For institutions where visitation is a primary benefit, a program can be designed for those who live 100 to 200 miles or more from the institution. This works for institutions that are tourist attractions and that have special shows or exhibits that will attract visitors from a certain distance. Most often there is one level for this, although some institutions have two—one for value members and the other for support members. The Friends of the National Zoo (FONZ) offers one level for those who live at least 200 miles from the zoo, while the Abraham Lincoln Presidential Library Foundation offers a National level for those who live at least 100 miles from Springfield, Illinois.

Online Membership

Some organizations offer online memberships. Often, these memberships are a way for people who have little likelihood of visiting to stay in touch with an organization. The program at the Metropolitan Museum of Art offers Met Net members benefits, including screen savers, online audio features, and special members-only offers in the online Met store. With an online membership, all benefits are delivered virtually.

Special Interest Groups

Many museums develop special membership groups that one may join if already a member of the institution. In particular, art museums have designed these groups to take advantage of their collections and the interests of museum goers and curators. These groups offer special lectures, educational opportunities, and travel experiences. There is often a second membership fee for these groups. Examples of special interest groups include decorative arts groups, young professional groups, collector's groups, and film or photography groups, among others. Often these groups allow for members with similar interests to have a deeper, more involved experience with the organization and its mission.

Guilds, Auxiliaries, and Friends Boards

Guilds and auxiliaries are typically volunteer organizations that exist to provide programs and volunteers for an institution. At the Heard Museum in Phoenix, the 800 volunteers join the guild after joining the museum. For those who want to be involved with the institution, this is the way to do it. Some institutions may also require membership before it is possible to volunteer. Friends boards are popular within some library friends organizations. Boards offer a leadership component to the most engaged members. It is important to ensure that the focus of the friends board is aligned with the mission and direction of the organizations that it serves.

Voting Programs

There are also membership programs with voting privileges attached. At the Ohio History Connection, members are allowed one vote per membership in the annual trustees election. Increasingly, programs with voting privileges are disappearing from the membership landscape. Decision-making roles are reserved for board members and trustees of the organization, not dues-paying members.

Other Programs

Botanical gardens often have a category for garden clubs and plant societies. This category can be tied into special privileges for their members, meeting space for the club/society, or the group's ability to stage flower shows at the garden. Yet another type of membership program relates to planned giving. Institutions with planned giving programs will often have a "Heritage Society" or "Legacy Circle" for those who have designated a planned gift. This designation is usually the requirement of membership and benefits may include special events at the institution, certificates, and other recognition efforts.

A very popular type of membership that has grown recently is the young friends group (also known as "young professionals"). This membership is designed to appeal to those from twenty to forty years of age. These groups typically plan events that attract this age range and often, but not always, are geared to singles. For visitation-based institutions, this is seen as a way to build engagement among an audience younger than most members. Social media often facilitates connection to this group and is important in engaging and recognizing member participation.

VARIETY IN DUES

There is variety in dues as well as in programs. Most programs will have value levels and support levels. There are, however, other dues levels that programs sometimes offer. Make certain that dues levels are kept simple.

Annual, Multi-Year, or Automatic Renewal Memberships

Dues are the financial part of the membership equation. If possible, dues should be annual. This gives the organization the opportunity to upgrade the member on a yearly basis. Some organizations offer two- and three-year memberships. The strength of this option is internal; the renewal process is eliminated for one or more years. If the institution's staff is very small, this may help. The other positive aspect of this membership is for organizations that depend on blockbuster exhibits or programs that may only be scheduled every other year. The two-year option, if enough people take advantage of it, might help level out the membership numbers rather than having spikes every other year. Such a dues structure would also keep these members on the rolls for other fundraising rather than losing them in the year when no major program offerings are scheduled.

The negative aspect of multi-year memberships is that there is usually a discount for the second and third year. Unfortunately, costs rise and multi-year dues do not take this into consideration. In the long run, the financial aspects of such a structure make multi-year dues less attractive than annual dues for most organizations.

One of the growing trends in membership programs is the offering of automatic renewal programs or monthly billing options for membership dues payment. These payment options are designed to take the nonrenewal option away while providing ease of payment for the member. Following the popularity of the monthly payment option used by public radio and television station memberships, membership dues are paid in twelve monthly payments via credit card or electronic funds transfer from a checking account. Some organizations offer this option at all membership levels, while others offer this option only for higher-level memberships.

Automatic renewals of a different variety include an annual automatic charge to a member's credit card at the time of the expiration date for the full amount of the membership. The Museum of Science, Boston offers such a program. Typically, members are offered this automatic option while interacting with Visitor Service personnel at the time of a museum visit. Approximately

50 percent of Museum of Science, Boston members have selected this option, offering the museum a head start on the renewal rates.

The challenge with both the monthly payment option and the auto-renew programs is the ability to deal with credit card expiration dates and to manage this process and still comply with Payment Card Industry (PCI) Data Security Standards for credit card security. PCI Security Standards require that organizations not maintain members' credit card information without encryption. Database managers must rely on their software providers for encryption services or outsourced credit card donation processors like CaringHabits.com. Another issue that has surfaced is that when a corporation has a breach in its security and many (i.e., thousands of) credit cards are compromised, this can effect monthly giving since many cards will be canceled and new ones issued.

Flat or Graduated

For organizations where membership is not a fundraising issue, an alumni association or a hospital auxiliary, for example, a flat structure is possible. In this case, there is one level of dues. In the school example, the school conducts the fundraising with the alumni association used to keep alumni close. For organizations where membership is an integral part of the fundraising, a graduated dues structure is essential. The dues range from basic levels to donor clubs. In a membership program it is important to have a variety of giving opportunities for the prospective member. The basic membership level in most cases ranges from $50 to $100, depending on the type of organization and the benefits offered. To increase the likelihood that people will increase their giving over time, other levels of membership should be established. These levels should be established at intervals that will facilitate a gradual upgrading of a member's giving.

For example, a dues structure of $75, $125, $250, $500 and $1,000 paces the increases at roughly double the amount of the preceding category. This allows for a stepping-stone approach based on the higher levels of membership and also makes possible the increase in a membership category if a member is employed by a company that offers matching gifts.

Category Options

Whether there is a flat or a graduated structure, there are a number of issues to decide. What kinds of membership options should be offered? Should there be individual members? Single Parent Household members? Dual Household members? Family membership? Life members? Student members? Senior memberships? The list could continue. The fundamental philosophy should be to keep it simple. Simple makes it easy for everyone. The potential member (especially those who begin as value members) should not have to mathematically figure out which is the best value, should not have to send "documentation" of student or senior status, and should be able to make a quick decision because of convenience. On the organization side, simple makes data entry much easier. It makes reporting much easier. It makes all financial projections much easier. If the organization is a visitation-based institution, simple makes the admission staff's lives much easier. It is difficult (if not impossible) for a staff member to question the "family" at the turnstile. The fewer the options, the easier it is for member and organization alike. Once again, keep it simple.

Life

The ultimate multi-year membership offer is a lifetime membership. Don't do it. A lifetime membership seldom makes any sense, and especially does not make economic sense unless it is very large and basically endows the membership gift for life. There are, of course, some exceptions. Lifetime membership can be used as a mark of respect or an honor. This may be appropriate for a founder, a lifetime volunteer, or a very major donor. Another possibility is to use it for major endowment gifts, which, in essence, endow the membership gift. These gifts tend to be very large and unusual, falling often into the "honor" category.

If the organization currently has lifetime members and decides not to offer this category any longer, the category can be phased out. First, remove the level from any membership literature. Second, "grandfather" all current lifetime members. Notify life members that they will always be considered a member and list them as such on donor recognition lists. As well, consider soliciting them for upper-level donor clubs. Many are friends of the institution and will become annual givers.

Individual and Dual Members

Individual membership may be a suitable category for single persons or for people whose spouse or significant other does not share their interest or passion for the organization or cause. The great majority of people visit an institution with a friend. Make it easy for the member to bring someone to enjoy the day with. A dual membership is designed for two adult members in a household.

Family or Basic Level

Family has taken on new definitions during the past few decades. What is a family? There is no longer the single pattern of mom, dad, and two children. For this reason, it seems most accepting to the variety that now makes up the population to consider other ways of describing a dual or group membership. For non-visitation-based organizations, consider naming the group "household," since many of the benefits come by way of the mailbox and email; the issue is to mail to one address, be it postal or email. For visitation-based institutions, consider a "basic," "regular," or "household" membership that includes two adults and children up to the age of twelve, sixteen, or eighteen. With this basic membership, the turnstile staff need only look to see if there are two adults and two (or whatever the number of) children.

Some organizations that serve a family audience (children's museums, science centers, zoos) may create categories based on the number of children. For families with more children, a Family Plus category may be created to accommodate the larger family size. These plus-sized family categories will carry a higher price tag. Some organizations may decide to require names and ages of children to make certain that the visiting children are actually part of the family, and not a collection of neighborhood kids all trying to get in with one membership.

Some organizations also offer a "plus one" option to be able to add a nanny, a grandparent, or other guest who may be accompanying the rest of a family on each visit. Typically, another person can be added for an additional price (e.g., $25).

Yet another option is tiered categories with the higher tier receiving more premier benefits. In a tiered category structure, memberships are based on the number of people admitted at one time, rather than on a family cluster. The Museum of Science, Boston offers a basic membership for parties of two ($85), five ($125), or eight ($155). These members receive admission for the number of people specified, plus two Omni, two Planetarium, and two Guest Passes per year. Premier tier members can also receive admission for two ($120), five ($160), or eight ($190) individuals and receive four Omni, four Planetarium, and four Guest Passes per year plus two hours' free parking every visit and priority treatment for select member events. The much-coveted free parking option is not available at the basic-level memberships. Parking can be a very motivating benefit for many institutions in larger cities.

In the case of the Museum of Science, Boston, the institution specifically reworked its membership levels to avoid limiting descriptions such as dual and family. In part, this decision was made because the museum did not want to define eligibility for entry by how people within a group are related to one another. The museum also found the "family" definition to be unenforceable. Attempts to enforce such a requirement upset members who believed staff were making assumptions regarding how members of a household look or do not look like each other. Additionally, findings from a market research study indicated that the museum's members would value the opportunity to have membership categories that allowed them to bring guests. With this in mind, new categories were designed and priced accordingly. As long as one or both of the members named on the membership are present, additional guests—children, cousins, neighbors, or out-of-town guests—need not be named. Many organizations feel as though they have to be the "Membership Police" trying to enforce category restrictions on people in the same household. The new category structure at the Museum of Science, Boston is a relief to admissions and membership staff.

Premier Levels

This level applies mainly to visitation-based institutions. If there are benefits such as IMAX tickets or additional admissions and a need for another level, this is a possibility. The financial side is the consideration here. Remember that for every additional ticket included in the benefit package, there is revenue forgone on the ticket revenue side of the ledger. This is not to say that there should not be a membership program because of revenue forgone, but that the more tickets that are used as benefits, the more revenue that is lost. The original basic membership level needs to be sufficient to attract and keep value members, but not lose money for the institution.

Premier levels can be created to offer more robust benefits for a higher price. These levels can also be fashioned to service the member with more desirable benefits, and service the organization with added financial support. These categories can be a way of identifying members with greater giving capacity and may pinpoint members who are crossing over from a value to a philanthropic member with their increased commitment.

Students

As the definition of family has changed, so has the definition of student. Who is a student? The organization must decide what it is trying to accomplish with this level. Is this an age issue? Or a "go to school" issue? If the real interest is in people in the eighteen- to twenty-three-year age range or younger, then the category definition needs to reflect this. This is different if the goal is attracting students in general or one of access for students.

For a non-visitation-based organization that attracts this age range as the majority of members, use a basic category at an appropriate price level with additional higher-level categories for those who can afford more. For an organization that is interested in students, no matter the age, select a basic level, again, that is at an appropriate price point. Acquisition efforts would focus on those lists or sites made up of the age group or student population. For example, an alumni association might have special lower membership fee for the first few years out of college so that the alum becomes accustomed to belonging to the association.

For a visitation-based institution, there is a direct impact on admissions revenue. Again, the decision must be made whether the issue is age or access. If the issue is age, then the student category definition must reflect this. Usually, students are not a good source for fundraising, so the question becomes why the organization wants student members. The answer is often access. The organization may want to make certain that students have easy access to the institution. There are several ways to work on this issue. The first way is to have a low student admission price so that if a student wanted to come, he or she could come numerous times before it would make sense to become a member. If a defining characteristic is age, then that needs to be clearly spelled out in all materials. If the characteristic is being a full- or part-time student, then student identification is needed and that needs to be clear. Admission staff needs to be trained in what to ask for and how to make the request appropriately. Showing a student I.D. is usually a stated prerequisite for using a membership card in this category.

The second way to approach student membership is from the perspective of access. For example, an art museum might want to make certain that local art and art history students have access. The museum can work with the faculty and sell or donate enough admission passes to make sure that access is available. Most student memberships are a digital membership requiring an email address for contact and benefit delivery. The digital nature of this membership eliminates costly mailings and can justify a lower-cost membership.

For associations, a student membership can be the funnel for future full-dues-paying members. A student membership can be a way to introduce the individual to their future field of endeavor. The membership and annual conference can be a connecting point for potential employment or mentorship. The challenge with student memberships is the ability to stay in touch after graduation and the transition years to employment. Sometimes a membership in an industry association may be a requirement of a graduate program in the field of choice.

Grandparents/Caregiver

This category is aimed at relatives or friends other than parents bringing children to the institution. Grandparents, nannies, aunts, uncles, and other caregivers fall into this category. Children's museums, zoos, and science centers are among the institutions that typically consider a grandparents/caregiver category. Benefits are aimed at caregivers bringing a certain number of children under a certain age. The number can range from two to unlimited; the age range can span from twelve to twenty-one years of age, with most ending by eighteen years of age. Benefits might also include special events. The Saint Louis Zoo offers passes to the Children's Zoo, the Zoo Railroad, parking, and an invitation to a special grandparent/grandchildren event along with a shop discount and the newsletter and calendar. Those purchasing the membership are often asked to provide the specific names and ages of the children involved.

Senior

Offering senior discounts has become a way of life in America. For many visitation-based organizations, seniors may make up the bulk of the membership. Senior, as the above categories, needs a definition. While always age, this category can begin at fifty years old (AARP); however, most organizations and institutions tend to use sixty, sixty-two, or sixth-five years of age. This category is also based on trust; most organizations do not ask to see proof of age. The major reason for this category seems to be "everyone is doing it." The "everyone" includes movie theaters, stores and restaurants, and a variety of other venues.

Demographic information shows that, for the most part, this group can most afford to be members. We also know that the population as a whole is aging, with the senior group increasing. If there is a way to avoid having this category, avoid it. Don't offer it just because other organizations do. If it is something that the organization must do, then make it only a little less expensive than the basic level of membership. The charge for this level should be no more than $5 less than the basic level; at this senior rate all costs must be covered. Some organizations offer $5 or a percentage off any level for senior members. This arrangement allows for the discount-oriented senior population to feel like they are getting their due, while still supporting the organization at higher levels rather than at just one discounted entry price level.

Build Your Own

A newer membership category structure includes a "build-your-own" membership. The proliferation of single-parent households spurred the development of this category. The build-your-own concept allows a household to buy a membership based on the exact number of people who will be utilizing the membership. There is a designated rate for the first adult, and then additional adults and children are add-ons to that initial base membership amount. For instance, the Phoenix Zoo sells the initial membership for $55 for an adult. Additional adults can be added for $40 and children can be added for $30 per child. A similar program at the Woodland Park Zoo in Seattle offers adult passes for $49 each and additional children are $17 each. Yet another variation has been the Georgia Aquarium, which requires separate memberships or annual passes for each individual—$69.95 for adults and $52.95 for children. The only caution is that the more a membership is structured as an annual pass or season pass—like an amusement park—the less likely that the purchaser feels like a member/donor with loyalty to the organization and its mission. It becomes a purchase, not a commitment.

Another form of the "build-your-own" membership is offered at the Whitney Museum of American Art. A "core" membership at the individual level is available for $85. Then a joining member can select the "Curate Your Own Series" that they wish to receive with respect to benefit offerings. The first series selection is free, but additional series are $40 each. The series options include:

- Social: Invitation to a summer and winter champagne hour and two one-time-use guest passes
- Learning: Lectures exploring key issues in modern and contemporary American art with Whitney teaching fellows
- Insider: Special presentations and behind-the-scenes gallery talks featuring perspectives from staff across the museum
- Family: Priority notification and discounts for family programs for kids ages four to twelve and two one-time-use guest passes
- Philanthropy: Enjoy core benefits only and direct more of your membership gift to the museum

This complex array of benefit offerings requires the level of management and operational sophistication of a larger organization.

Discounts

Some organizations offer a discount on membership as an incentive to join. This is another practice to avoid if possible. Offering the membership at a discount cheapens the value of the membership. It also then serves value members to wait until the next discount opportunity to renew. Renewal at the regular or basic level really becomes an upgrade ask and much more difficult. If some form of incentive is desired, consider adding an extra month or two or a premium rather than lowering the price. While it may amount to the same thing, the member will be writing the check for the same amount of money when it is time to renew.

The economic downturn in 2008–2009 precipitated a major move toward discounting in membership. Online discount promotions such as Groupon and Living Social offered deep discounts and provided huge, one-time blips of larger membership numbers for organizations. Few (5 to 15 percent) of these online discount members renewed while the organizations bore the cost of servicing larger numbers of members, raising the question of whether the deeply discounted dues even paid for the servicing and staffing required. Thankfully, this trend of deep discounting appears to have subsided with some organizations, such as the Los Angeles County Museum of Art, now adopting a "no discounting" policy.

Pricing Structure

What should be the price for each of the levels? Each organization needs to decide this for itself. Take a look at the other comparable organizations. Consider the institution's audience. Try different benefit packages and analyze their costs. For those organizations for whom the membership levels move into donor clubs, it's important to know where the fundraising program places the high donor levels. As mentioned earlier, a stepping-stone approach works very well. There are a number of possibilities; several are noted in exhibit 4.1.

The same principles that apply to pricing goods and services in the open market also apply to membership dues. A part of the perception of what a product is worth is dictated by the pricing structure. If a product is bargain priced, that sometimes conjures up the notion that the product is not worth

Typical

Individual	$75
Family	$95
Family Plus	$125
Sponsor	$250
Patron	$500
Director's Circle	$1,000
Trustee's Circle	$2,500
Gold Circle	$5,000
Platinum Circle	$10,000

Sample Tiered Membership Options (Museum of Science Boston)

Basic	Admits:	
	2	$85
	5	$125
	8	$155
Premier	Admits:	
	2	$120
	5	$160
	8	$190
Explorer		$350
Discoverer		$600

Additional levels report to Development

"Build a Membership" Concept (Phoenix Zoo)

Basic	First Adult	$55
	ADD:	
	2nd, 3rd Adult	$40
	Each child, 3 & up	$30
	Example: 2 adults, 2 kids	$150
Caretaker Club		
	Includes 2 adults, up to 4 kids or grandkids	$195
Keeper Club		$250
Curator Club		$500
Guardian Club Membership		
Director's Circle		$1,250 to $2,499
President's Circle		$2,500 to $4,999
Chairman's Circle		$5,000 to $9,999
Maytag Circle		$10,000 or more

EXHIBIT 4.1
Sample Membership Pricing Structures

more than the price. Conversely, if a healthy price tag is attached to a product, there is a perception that it is quality and worthwhile, unless proven otherwise.

Likewise, if a membership program's prices are drastically lower than similar programs, the perception may develop that this product is inferior to the others, not that the others are all overpriced. It may also be the perception that if one institution's membership dues are above the competition in pricing, then its product and institution is superior to the others. However, it is suggested that unless there is a dramatic and perceived difference in quality in an institution and its membership offering, its pricing structure should be in line with others offering similar products and competition within the same market.

Dues Increases

Periodically, it is necessary to raise prices no matter what the product or service. To keep pace with inflation and other institutions, increasing dues on an every-three-year time span is perfectly acceptable. Increasing dues more frequently than that may be necessary, but can present the impression that the organization is greedy. Increasing dues less frequently than that is literally passing up an opportunity to increase the financial support and an institution's revenues from such a program. In this case, the organization is not taking advantage of the ability and willingness of its membership to support the institution. Further, a significant gap in increasing dues can be jarring whereas implementing a regular schedule for increasing dues can help to create a familiar and expected pattern, thereby mitigating sticker shock.

The mechanism and method that an institution uses to increase is dues can help soothe any ill will created by the dues increase. Giving ample forewarning that the increase is going to happen can appease some members. Giving members an opportunity to renew at the old dues structure rate can calm some of those irate or unhappy feelings. Another approach to dues increases is to not make a big deal or a major announcement; rather, enact the increase quietly and without fanfare. Dues increases can be enacted smoothly if they are done in small increments and on a more frequent timeframe. Infrequent dues increases can require a larger increase that will be less well received.

When carrying out a dues increase, expect that some members will write, call, and complain; however, a complaint or two is not an indication that the dues increase should not have taken place. A slight decline in membership renewal may be experienced during the initial year of a dues increase. These are expected responses to an increase and should not be taken as a failure or mistaken decision.

Implementing a membership dues increase can significantly increase the revenues from a membership program in one year. Increases in dues may be a way to allow a membership program to be stable and to acquire more members because of the additional revenues received. If the result of a dues increase is enlarging the membership substantially through aggressive acquisition, then more power to the effort. A new trend is appearing in membership structures at visitation-based institutions: raising the second level membership to a higher amount (e.g., $125 or $150) and the configuration of that level into a Family Plus or Enhanced membership level. At this new level members are offered access to events, tickets to performances, or added guest opportunities. This level is a way to entertain extended family and friends at an institution. For example, at one museum the IMAX Club gives members six free tickets to all IMAX shows. At a botanical garden, the Family and Friends Plus plan allows the member to bring guests.

Record Keeping

If the organization does not have a way to keep accurate and up-to-date records, there is little reason to have a membership program. Record keeping is the basis for all of the work done by and for the membership. Acquisition can be expensive with the financial rewards coming from renewals and other fundraising efforts. Thus, recording the information for a new member is essential. The questions to consider are, first, what information needs to be kept and, second, how to keep it.

The information that needs to be kept depends on the organization and the role of the membership. All organizations need to keep the basics: name, address, amount, and date of gift. Related to this information may be both home and office information for address, telephone, and email. If this is a dual membership, the organization may want both first names. With the proliferation of two members of a couple having different last names, it is important to be able to keep separate names even though there is one membership. The gift level is needed to make certain that fulfillment is correct and so that, if personal renewal and/or thank you letters are sent, the amount can be referenced. The date is essential in order to make the renewal process run smoothly. Other information to keep depends on the organization. Possibilities include donations, names of children or grandchildren, volunteer work, legislative district (for public issue groups), and anything else that is relevant to the institution.

How the information is kept depends on the program's size, complexity (e.g., is it part of fundraising), funding, and computer capabilities. Selection of the right database for an organization's budget and size is always a key, core decision. There are many software options ranging from straightforward database systems such as Access to very complex systems that work with membership, donations, ticketing, event and class registration, and any and everything else an organization might need. The options change continually so it is important to find up-to-date information on any system that is considered. From time to time, resources such as the Chronicle of Philanthropy and the Association of Fundraising Professionals offer information and lists of vendors.

The important issue for an organization is to decide what it wants and needs before doing the research to find an appropriate system. Questions include:

- What is the size of the program (number of records) and what are the plans for growth?
- Is there in-house capability for a server and IT support? Or is cloud computing a better choice?
- What is the budget? Is there money for training and support?
- Does information have to be converted from another system to the new one? If so, what will the cost be for the migration?
- Is there a single user or multiple users?

- Will the membership be the donor base; if so, will donor information be kept as well as membership information? Does it need to interface with an accounting system?
- Is there a user group in the area to help support the system?
- How will the system integrate with other software such as email, ticketing, marketing automation, and the website?
- What type of information and reporting does the organization need to be able to extract from the system?

Answer the above questions and speak to other local and like organizations to find out what they are using and how their programs work. Check vendor websites and ask for information from five or six of the vendors whose programs look promising. After reading and examining the information, ask three of the vendors for a proposal. Make the decision. From beginning to end, this process will take as little as a month or two to a much longer time. Once installed, make certain that the data entry staff have appropriate training and document how records are to be entered and queries that are used for regular reporting.

One of the major tasks is to keep the membership list correct and up to date. This is a constant need. Postal regulations now require that organizations implement a National Change of Address (NCOA) process for each mailing. Once finished, an organization needs to update its database with the changes of address identified by the NCOA. This process matches the organization's mailing list to change of address information that is submitted to the post office by people who are moving. All mail houses provide this service.

THE MEMBERSHIP PROGRAM

The membership program itself is made up of five parts: benefits, service, events, communication, and recognition. When developing the program it is always essential to view it from the member's perspective since the member will make the decision about whether or not to join or renew. This approach is a marketing approach because it is concerned first with the market (the potential members) and then, second, with the organization. The tangible benefits are packaged for acquisition and renewal and have a substantial financial implication for the institution. The intangible benefits, the "feel good" benefits of a sense of belonging, pride, and giving back are achieved through service, events, and communication. These, too, have a financial implication for the institution, but the potential member doesn't necessarily see these benefits as part of the economic package when weighing whether to join.

Benefits

Membership at the basic levels (the first of several levels of dues) most often provides benefits that make it "a good deal." Many will join at these levels because they perceive that it is good value for the money spent. Members who base their gifts on this exchange are "value members." The value member is defined as one who makes the financial calculation of benefits received versus money spent and is willing to become a member on that basis. Many members begin their relationship with the organization in this way. This must be kept in mind when benefits are designed. While an organization does not want to be overly generous with benefits, the benefit package must be compelling enough to attract the prospect interested in value. If the benefits are so good that the person joins based on benefits alone, it will rarely be possible to keep that member. The long-term fundraising goal is to turn value members into support or philanthropic members. If there are other goals for the program, such as community support, the program should reinforce those issues as well. The tangible benefits are that first nudge toward encouraging people to take a look at what the organization is doing.

As discussed previously, there are many reasons why people join an organization. It is essential to understand that, above all, those who join have some interest in the organization and the work that it is doing. Member surveys cite "joining for the purpose of supporting a worthwhile organization and giving back"[1] as one of the top reasons why people join, followed by other benefits. Even if the person is joining for the benefits—free admission to a museum for example—the person still has to want to go to the museum for membership to be considered.

Benefit Package

The benefit package is what the prospect exchanges for dollars. The structure of the package is very important economically and should be designed with benefits relevant to the organization. As well, and perhaps more important, it needs to recognize basic human needs and values. People like to feel special, to have access to things and places that not everyone else can claim, to be given something that is free, to be kept informed, and to feel a sense of belonging. These are some of the issues to keep in mind when constructing the membership benefits and program.

Creating benefits is limited only by imagination. A benefit package takes on the character of the institution. Benefits are limited only by creativity and economic realities. For all organizations, there is the possibility of member-related benefits: the membership card, a window decal, a Facebook cover photo. There can be products with the organization logo such as a mug, a t-shirt, or a baseball cap. All of these items serve to make the person feel that they belong and can make them external advocates for the organization.

There are also program-related benefits (see exhibit 4.2) that can be included in a package. These should always include a newsletter or other publication that is a regular communication vehicle between the member and the organization. Other benefits might be invitations to and/or discounts on program-related special events, lectures, classes, and tours. For example, a history interest group might invite the public to hear a famous lecturer while members are also invited to a reception where they can meet and personally talk to the lecturer. It is also possible to provide members-only information via the organization's website as well as email updates on current events or information of interest. For visitation-based organizations there are the extra added—and usually the primary—benefits relating to visitation. These include free admission, free parking, and discounts at gift shops or for food service.

Constructing the Benefit Package

The chances are good that the potential member also belongs to other like organizations. Thus, in constructing a membership benefit package, one of the first tasks is to look at similar institutions and the types of benefits they offer to their members. Each institution is different; however, it is important to recognize that your program is competing with comparable programs. Often the comparison is geographical. For example, one museum in a city probably needs to be somewhat close in benefits and dues to another museum in the same city. Regional and national groups that attract some of the same audience need to be aware of what the others are offering.

The individual character of the institution will ultimately determine what is appropriate for that institution. But there is no sense in reinventing the wheel. Benefit programs can be modeled after one another and even a copied

EXHIBIT 4.2
Types of Membership Benefits

The benefits listed here are the tangible ones that programs offer to potential members. The combination for any one organization is a combination of the organization's strategy, what is appropriate for that institution, cost of benefits relative to pricing of membership levels, and what members want from the organization. Some of these benefits are also useful as incentives, the offer that encourages the potential member to join. This list is by no means exhaustive, but it is a reference for new programs and for those who are redesigning their benefit programs.

Member-Related Benefits

- Membership card, decal, bumper sticker
- Membership Directory
- Recognition on a wall, in a book, on a list
- Dinners, receptions, previews
- Logo merchandise
- Discounts in shop, catalogue, or online shop or bookstore (10 to 20 percent or a small dollar amount)
- Gift Certificates/coupons (food, merchandise, programs) to use at institution

Program-Related Benefits

- Members-only events, free or with cost
- Lectures, gallery talks, film programs
- Tours and meetings with director, curators, staff
- Tickets to performances, films, special exhibits
- Education Programs
- First opportunity — for programs, events, reservations, travel
- Special benefits for children — own membership card, birthday card, birthday parties
- Travel opportunities
- Library check-out privileges
- Legislative updates
- Ability to register for a conference
- Members-only section on website
- National organizational events in the member's home area
- Discount on events, programs
- Publications — books, magazines, newsletters, catalogues, videos, tapes
- Involvement in programs — volunteer for organization, be part of a testing program (e.g., plants, hunting equipment)
- Reciprocal admission to like organizations in other cities
- Resource directory
- Kit to help member become involved in issue
- Hotline for information

continued...

Visitation-Related Benefits

- Benefits can be related to admission to the institution, or to exhibits or programs within it
- No waiting; members' line to enter
- Free, discounted, or a certain number of passes
- Parking, free for a number of hours, reduced rate
- Access to early/late nonpublic hours
- Guest passes, free or discounted
- Facility rental (access to/discount)
- Restaurant or other food service discount
- Access to special dining rooms, members'/patrons' room
- Concierge service — ability to purchase tickets to sold-out performances
- Audio tours, free or discounted
- Tram/railroad or other transportation at institution

Other Benefits

Discounts for:

- Other memberships in the community
- Relevant retailers (e.g., sporting goods store for outdoors group)
- Community retailers, e.g., restaurants and shops
- Business-related offers
- Magazine subscriptions (not from the organization)
- Hotel/motel/car rental rates

program will take on a character all its own. When beginning to construct the benefits package it may seem that the organization has little or nothing to offer. Creativity then becomes the exercise and what it stimulates can be amazing. Think from a marketing and promotional point of view. Brainstorm ideas with staff, board, and volunteers. Hold a focus group of current or prospective members to ascertain what is important to them. Also collect membership information from other organizations to stimulate your thinking.

Value Member Analysis

The value member takes the tangible benefits package very seriously. The package needs to have a perceived value for this potential member as well as meeting the economic realities of the organization. For the organization, the benefits should not cost more than the dues. It is incumbent on the membership manager to make sure that the benefit package is competitive without offering more than the price of membership. The perceived value analysis is from the member's perspective and underpins the marketing of the program.

For example, the potential member for a visitation-based institution will make some assumptions. He or she will assume visiting three times a year, receiving the newsletter with information about events, maybe attending one or two programs, doing some shopping in the gift shop, and wanting the membership premium of a museum tote bag. If the potential member is a value member, he or she must feel that the organization is worth supporting and that the benefits are worth the expense.

Beyond the financial cost involved in evaluating and structuring a benefit package, there may be other concerns as well. One of the most important is deliverability. In other words, do not offer benefits that cannot be delivered easily by the operating constraints of the organization or institution. Staffing concerns and the capacity to serve the volume of members must be considered. The benefits offered must not create any ill will. For instance, if free parking is offered as a benefit, but it is very limited, the organization needs to make other arrangements for major events so that members do not feel "cheated." In this case, a shuttle service would be a possibility as long as it is able to handle the demand without creating long waiting lines, an impact that would negate the positive benefit of having free parking.

The same is true for the premium that is offered. It must have intrinsic value and be easily available. On the value side, organizations need to select premiums carefully. The perceived value must be in line with what the member might picture in his or her mind. For example, a botanical garden once offered a plant as a premium. The potential members pictured the lush large plants that the garden's gift shop sold. In reality, to keep within budget constraints, the plant premium was a lovely, but very small, houseplant. Members were disappointed. Such disappointment is not a good way to start a relationship.

Support Member Analysis

Support members, those who join at higher levels where the benefits are increasingly intangible, are also often interested in the tangible benefits, but clearly that is not why they are joining above the value level. Many membership staff relate stories about support members who are interested in receiving their tote bags and other benefits. For those who are not interested, the member should have a way of declining benefits so that their gift can be totally tax deductible.

SERVICE

Consumers have been trained to expect good service. Nordstrom has built a department store chain on this concept. Members expect no less from those organizations that they have chosen to join. An institution that can't provide the "service to back up the sale" will experience disappointment when it comes to repeat business—in this case, the renewal of the membership.

On Joining

Membership Payment Processing

Strong membership service is a hallmark of a strong program. The acquisition program has gone perfectly. As a result, individuals are joining. Whether by mail, telephone, or online, people who want to join flood the organization with their responses. This is when membership service begins. Now, what do you do?

Depending on the size of your staff and the number of membership responses, there are three basic ways for you to process membership payments: internally, through a lock box, or online.

Internal Processing

Your organization can receive membership payments either through a post office box or directly to the office. Once received, the staff or volunteers open the envelopes, enter data into the membership computer system, and deposit or process payments. Depending on the volume of responses, internal processing may involve one volunteer with a letter opener or a team of people working in an internal "lockbox" environment involving sophisticated equipment for functions such as envelope opening, check extracting, check encoding, etc. (In the membership context, a lockbox is a service providing all handling of money including deposits.) The principal advantage of internal processing is that it provides the membership manager with the greatest possible internal control over the entire membership process. The downside is that internal processing may not be timely.

Bank Lockbox

If the overall annual response volume is too great for staff to handle or if the responses come at particular times of the year, it might not be beneficial to handle the membership processing internally. For example, a large spike in the number of responses at year end might overwhelm staff and yet not justify creating a year-round internal processing department. Instead, outsourcing the processing may allow for quicker deposits and fulfillment while not necessarily resulting in increased expense. Responses would go directly to the bank where the bank's lockbox department would take care of opening responses, capturing limited data, and depositing payments. The principal advantage to a bank lockbox is that it relieves staff of a tedious function while cost-effectively ensuring that payments are processed on a timely basis. One downside of using a bank lockbox is that banks are often unable to provide the full flexibility that is frequently required for this type of processing, particularly where data capture is concerned. Another downside is that bank lockboxes can become expensive as the volume of responses grows. However, when compared to staff costs and timeliness, they can be an attractive option.

Independent Lockbox

A number of companies specialize in providing lockbox services, sometimes called caging or simply payment processing. Because these companies specialize in lockbox services, they will generally offer better service and, at higher volumes, fees far below those charged by banks. While the minimum volume handled by these companies varies, expect them to be a viable option once the annual volume reaches 100,000 transactions. Responses would be sent directly to the company's post office box or to the organization's post office box where the responses will be reshipped to the processing company. The advantages of independent lockboxes are that they will process payments quickly and cost effectively while also capturing all vital data. The downside to this solution is that these companies will only service organizations with very high transaction volumes.

Joining Online

The "join now" button is a powerful device in the membership toolbox. It's no secret that the web has revolutionized the way we discover, engage with, and buy products and services. The simplicity, instant processing, and immediate gratification of joining online makes it a highly effective channel for acquisition and renewal.

Providing an easy, one-click way to source and enlist new members and donors, an institution's website can process a significant portion of membership transactions. Many organizations are concerned that the older demographic of their donor base will not be comfortable joining or giving online; however, the ubiquity of the web means that there is no longer a deep generational divide in technology adoption. Indeed, there are people of all ages who prefer to order products and purchase services online. It's important to note that the services and features offered via the web should be in addition to current ways of delivering services, attracting members, and processing transactions—not a substitution. An organization's online channels should complement existing face-to-face, phone, and mail activities.

The ability to quickly, easily, and safely transact membership purchases online should be the first priority for all organizations. It is no longer acceptable to require members to process a transaction offline if their preference is to do so online. There are numerous e-commerce solutions that can be used for this purpose, including everything from a plug-and-play PayPal button to sophisticated enterprise-level software.

Whereas single-purpose e-commerce solutions such as PayPal, Amazon Payments, and Google Wallet can get the job done with minimal to no IT resources needed, enterprise-level software typically requires cross-departmental buy-in and implementation support. While the up-front investment in time and dollars is significant for enterprise software, such a solution can provide organizations with a holistic platform for online transactions, including seamless integration with the membership database, comprehensive reporting, and suggestive selling features. Many enterprise software options are "hosted solutions," which include ongoing support and maintenance for a monthly fee.

When it comes to security, Secure Sockets Layer (SSL) is the de facto standard for ensuring that e-commerce transactions are secure. Essentially, SSL encrypts private information such as credit card numbers, personal identifiers like name and address, and passwords that are required to process transactions online. Therefore, SSL is a critical component in protecting consumer privacy online.

The HTTPS at beginning of a URL indicates that the membership transaction form is on a secure site designed for e-commerce. Additionally, many search engines display a padlock icon in the URL field to indicate that a web page is secure. From a design standpoint, there are many ways to increase the perceived security of a web page. Many studies have found that while users have little understanding of the technical aspects of securing e-commerce transactions, they rely on visual cues that indicate trust—such as the look of payment forms, background colors and fonts, and use of "trust seals" or SSL icons (logos used to demonstrate that a web page is secure). With a secure page, prospective members can feel confident transmitting their membership applications and credit card number knowing that the site is protected. People who are accustomed to transacting business online expect this level of security. It is a level of security that membership organizations must provide if they expect to be part of the e-commerce community.

As with many operations in membership, there is often the philosophy or need to do membership work in-house. As programs grow, they often realize that it is not always cost effective to do everything in-house. The staff and financial resources once presumed to be less costly than outsourcing may no longer be economically feasible in-house. This can be true for direct mail campaigns for acquisition, graphics production, telemarketing, website design, and e-commerce capabilities. Each organization must weigh time, money, and staff capabilities to determine what is possible.

One experience demonstrates what can easily happen in an organization. The membership department presented its needs to its two-person IT team. Other departments presented their e-commerce needs at the same time. The requests included membership and donor transaction pages, an online store, class registrations, and a members-only access page that would allow members to ask curators questions. An outsourced proposal was compared to the in-house IT team. The in-house team stated that it could do all of the requested services at no cost, though taking far more time (six weeks versus eighteen months). The organization decided to do the work in-house. Twelve months later the in-house staff had all left the organization for other positions without the wish list being completed. This scenario, in hindsight, could have been prevented if the organization had been more realistic. While outsourcing costs more in the short run, it can save time and provide long-term benefits.

Stewardship

The methods of processing payments and monitoring how they are used are known as internal stewardship. The process of thanking, serving, and reporting to members is known as external stewardship.

Regardless of where membership payments are processed, good internal stewardship requires that processing be timely and accurate. Ideally, payments will be deposited within twenty-four to forty-eight hours of when they are received. To ensure that the member receives the appropriate membership benefits and recognition, the organization must also take special care to ensure that it correctly records membership information. In addition, properly capturing information will help the organization effectively evaluate the performance of its membership marketing efforts as well as the overall membership program.

Once membership payments are processed, the organization should ensure that the funds are used for the purpose outlined to the member. For example, if members are told that a portion of their membership dues will fund educational programs, then the organization should take great care in making sure that those programs indeed receive the funds indicated. Also, the organization must use the membership funds to ensure that the members receive all the promised benefits of membership.

Soon after the organization deposits the membership payment and records it, the organization should send a thank-you letter and membership welcome package. The membership welcome package might include a membership card, guest passes, catalog of membership services, premium, etc. Welcome packages or fulfillment packages can be sent directly from the organization or, if the volume is great enough, a fulfillment house can be contracted to handle this task. A fulfillment house provides the service of generating the membership packet (letter, membership card, decal, or other premium, etc.) and mailing it to the member.

Thank You

As a rule, organizations should thank members a minimum of three times and as many as seven or more times. Members should be thanked when they join as part of the conclusion to the solicitation itself, when they are sent their welcome package, and when they are solicited for renewal. If possible, an immediate phone call thank you, especially to support members, when the gift is received, is always appreciated.

In addition organizations can thank members by publishing a list of them in the annual report, inviting them to special member appreciation events, sending a thank-you letter from the chief executive officer and the membership manager, and listing upper-level support members on a recognition wall. You cannot thank people too much. The only limit is your imagination.

Effective communication with members will help develop the relationship between the member and the organization. "By reporting to donors how their gifts were used, we gain their confidence. With their confidence, the opportunities for future support are greater," according to the Association of Fundraising Professionals Survey Course.[2] The same is true for membership programs. Tell members how their funds and even their numbers benefit the organization. Remind them of the benefits they receive as members and encourage them to use those benefits. If members feel that their membership helps support the organization in some way and if they use the available benefits, they will be much more likely to make charitable gifts to the organization as well as renew their memberships.

Being a member means being part of something; it means joining. The more an organization makes its members feel part of something worthwhile, the more loyal the members will be. Effective internal and external stewardship is about building relationships. Strong relationships are the building blocks of strong membership programs.

A new member should receive his or her thank you and information within ten days to two weeks. If it takes more than two weeks to process the membership, there will be problems. There is immediacy when people join. Often someone joins because he or she wants to visit soon, is interested in the issue and wants information, or wants to become involved in the organization's events. If the member is waiting for three weeks or a month, the initial experience is not good from the member's perspective. There may be, however, spikes in responses at certain times during the year due to campaigns and seasonality. The goal should continue to be to have responses in the mail within ten days to two weeks or sooner. Email can be a great way to acknowledge the new member immediately while the mailed membership package is en route.

For an organization that is having a membership drive, it is important to be able to service the new members. It may be necessary for staff to work overtime, to hire temporary staff, or to enlist other staff to help during this busy time. When planning the calendar for the year, it is imperative to prepare for the required time and staff involved to conduct a membership drive properly. It is important for the new member to have a great first impression; it is this first impression that actually begins the renewal decision.

Membership Cards

A word about membership cards: They come in virtually any form imaginable. One vendor, Membership Cards Only®, advertises that it has "more than 77 different kinds of cards" (1-800-77cards or moreinfo@memcards.com). They can be as simple as a computer designed and generated card to a heavy plastic version much like a credit card. Some visitation-based institutions have begun using cards that electronically monitor tickets to events such as movies. The tickets are subtracted from the membership card as the card is used. The electronic tickets expire with the membership.

Membership card issues include use, cost, ease of fulfillment, and potential abuse. An organization should use material that is suitable for the card's use. If the card is never really used, as might be with a fraternity or sorority or alumni group, then a heavy stock card is appropriate. If the card is used continually for admissions, then a plastic card with a bar code or magnetic strip for swiping might be the right kind. If the card needs to be punched for admissions, then, again, a different material might be used.

Cost can play a major role; the more substantial the card is, usually the higher the cost. Some organizations use an inexpensive card at value levels and then more substantial ones at very high support or donor club levels. Ease of fulfillment has to do with how the card is printed or embossed and whether it is done in-house or by a fulfillment company. Each organization needs to make this decision based on size of membership, revenue generated, and staffing. Membership card abuse has become a topic particularly for those institutions with high admission ticket prices. Some cards have photos to protect against membership usage abuse. Many institutions are now requiring photo identification with the member's name on it for the membership card to be used. This trend is more likely to occur at organizations with higher admission fees. As mobile applications become more integrated to payment, ticketing systems, and member services, members will be able to access their membership card and information directly from their mobile devices.

During the Membership Year

The members view the membership department as their place to have questions answered, get information, and voice complaints. This is a major function for the organization and must be taken seriously. Whoever is in charge of answering the phones needs to smile and be cheerful and positive when talking with a member. Likewise, answering emails or responding to Facebook posts with membership questions needs to be prompt and positive. Membership service personnel are the face and voice of the membership program and should do whatever they can to answer the questions or complaints.

Dealing with complaints can be difficult, but the complaints should be taken seriously. For every complaint that is voiced, there are another ten or more comparable complaints that aren't voiced. There are difficult members. Some will make unreasonable demands. Staff and volunteers need to be trained to cope with these members and situations. For these reasons, it is important to train, support, and authorize membership service workers to do certain things to satisfy members' demands. Depending on the situation, the front-line membership service person needs to be equipped to offer some solutions that will appease members and leave them feeling heard and valued. Likewise, it is important to document complaints and situations in a member's record. Someone who loses his or her membership card with regularity or is a frequent abuser of benefits should have that noted in the record, so that the service personnel can note past experiences and know not to give free months or passes or other special privileges—some members do try to game the system.

At the Institution

Members expect to be treated in a special manner. There should always be a way for members to enter without waiting. If there is some way for the admissions desk to have a list or computer access to the membership list, it is helpful for those members who forget their membership card. This is not an unusual occurrence. Most members are sensitized to the fact that they need to carry their cards, but it sometimes happens that the member is without one. If it is not possible to have an up-to-date list and there is no membership staff member available to check, it is usually best to admit the "member." If the person is really a member, no harm done and the person will be happy. A difficult situation can arise with a real member who is not admitted. If there is a discount in the gift shop, the membership card should be requested for purchases. The admission areas and the shop(s) should have access to the membership database. The institution should have a policy to deal with these situations and staff needs to be trained in how to handle these kinds of situations. Most people are honest.

For an art or other museum with a blockbuster show, it may be difficult to have easy and quick access for the thousands of members who want to see the show. Members, however, should have some way to enter that is less cumbersome and at least somewhat faster than the general public. In these situations, many institutions have separate lines for members—separate ticket windows and staff in visible positions to talk with members. Members also often have access to reservations for timed tickets before the general public.

Some institutions have special a "member room." This can be a dining room, a lounge, or a meeting room. This can be a benefit for an upper-level member if the numbers are such that not everyone can be served. Free coffee, Wi-Fi access, and in some cases, concierge-like service may be provided. At the American Museum of Natural History, upper-level members at the $600 and above position enjoy access to the Member Lounge with concierge services, express ticketing, and free coat check.

Events

Events are a powerful engagement tool for members. There must be events for all members. There are some differences, however, for first-year members and with upper-level or support members. As the program becomes more mature, other segments of the membership can also be selected for special events. For example, there might be programs directed toward life stage scenarios—families, young professionals, seniors, or those members with special interests. Events are important. Participation equals involvement and involvement relates to commitment, higher renewal rates, and more support for the institution.

First-Year Members

The renewal rate for first-year members is always lower than for multi-year members. Some people will "try out" the membership and decide, for whatever reason, that it is not for them. Because of the cost of acquiring new members, doing as much as possible to retain first-year members makes economic sense. Once someone is a member for three or more years, the chances are very good that the person will support the institution for many years to come. For those organizations with multi-year memberships, the first renewal time is really the end of the first-year membership even though the member may have been a member for two or three years. These renewal rates should be closely followed to see if there is a difference between annual and multi-year members. Additionally, there needs to be enough activity and programming so that the multi-year members will want to renew.

Developing a package of information and events for a new member can significantly increase renewal rates and the involvement of the member. New member events can include a phone call or email from a volunteer or staff person welcoming the person to the organization, a special new member reception to meet the director or president of the organization, or an orientation session for the new members to learn about the institution. Depending on the size of the new member group, the events can be held two or more times a year. Again, there is some urgency. When people first join, their interest is at a peak. If the new member activity happens a year after someone joins, the member no longer feels new and the opportunity for engagement is lost.

In an organization that wants and needs its members as volunteers and participants, involving the first-year member is crucial. The member who wants to volunteer and receives no contact to participate will go elsewhere.

Support Member Events

Support members are treated more equally than other members. They need to have special events. For a visitation-based institution, special times (without crowds) to see exhibits are a prime benefit. For all organizations, receptions, dinners, and access to special guests of the institution are well received. As the support members become part of the institution's donor clubs, the donor club events become theirs. It is very important to coordinate these events between membership and development. This is one of the reasons that it is easiest in an institution for membership to be a part of the development office. Remember that the support members are also invited to the general membership events and, depending on the activity, many will attend.

General Events

As our culture has changed, people want more and more. Movies now must have stadium seating, coffee bars, and dining options. Theme parks have to add a new ride every year. Institutions have to "keep up." Having an organization or an institution for someone to join is not enough. The membership program must provide experiences that are of interest to the members. At a visitation-based institution, just visiting is no longer enough. The blockbuster show is a good example of this. Members may not necessarily visit enough times to make economic sense for their membership.

For organizations without visitation, this is even more important. For these organizations, the experiences need to be delivered by print and electronic publications, or by events that are produced from time to time for members to attend (e.g., a lecture, a discussion, or a reception). This is true for both local and national organizations. This means that an institution needs to provide events to encourage members to attend and to demonstrate that the institution is doing a lot even if they, personally, do not participate.

A membership program without the opportunity to be involved via events could lack perceived value.

The membership program, regardless of the kind of organization, should offer some events that are for members only. This may be a large social event, a family oriented event, or an educational program. During the course of the year, the membership program should offer one or more of each type. In terms of cost, the events can be free, at cost, or fundraisers. Again, there should be one or more of each. Free events might include a lecture or an after-hours behind-the-scenes tour of the institution. An event that is at cost might be social with a modest price associated with refreshments or entertainment. Fundraisers can be anything from a special brunch to an auction to a gala benefit. Make certain that the events have a mix so that the members do not feel that the only invitations that they receive are for fundraisers.

Members should also have a special place in events that are scheduled for the public. As with the blockbuster and timed tickets, it is important for members to feel that they are special; in this case, they can make their reservations before the public. For large public events with a charge, members should pay a smaller fee. In some cases with support-level members, the fee should be waived. It is not so much the money involved as a way for the member to feel special.

Communications

A member cannot receive too many communications from the organization. The budget should be developed to include as many mailings or email contacts as possible and necessary. A strong program will mail and/or email at least once a month; a large program may mail or email thirty to forty-eight times per year. The norm for the number of contacts is at least three points of contact per month. Some organizations are in contact with their members and donors several times a week. For most organizations, the piece of mail in the mailbox or the email in the inbox is the major connection with the organization. Sometimes there is the thought that the member will think the organization is wasting time or money by sending all the mailings; this is a rare thought among members. More often the member does not renew because he or she has not heard anything from the organization since the last request for money. For the few members who request not to receive mailings or emails, honor the request.

There should be variety in what the member receives. The effort is to create the perception and reflect the reality that the organization is doing a lot, that the work is important, and that the members are special. A communications plan should be a part of the membership planning. Often the member will receive communications from the organization that do not come from the membership department. If this is the case, the membership department should try to learn what is being sent in order to have a complete view of what the member is seeing.

A good exercise is for the membership manager to put his or her name on the mailing and email list as a "seed." As each communication arrives, it should be dated and saved to provide a complete perspective on what a typical member is receiving. At the midyear mark, review the communications. This will give a look at what the member sees. If there are few communications, the member's perception will be that the organization is not doing much or is not valuing their membership involvement. If the communications are heavy with fundraising appeals, the member's perception will be one of constant fundraising. Conversely, if there are no fundraising appeals it will be clear that it is time to send one. It's also helpful to have a nonmember (e.g., a friend) take a look and give an honest opinion about how the organization appears from its communications.

It is also important to look at the balance between mailed and emailed communications. Some members choose not to give an organization access to their email address. Therefore, it is still necessary to send some communications via postal mail. A bimonthly membership newsletter, renewal notices, and annual appeals are examples of communications that should still be sent via a hardcopy format to maintain contact with the 20 to 30 percent of members without email addresses in the database. Sometimes it is the long-term or support-level members who do not give an organization their email address. These audiences are very important and should receive communications with care and frequency.

Member Communications

Renewal Notice (Three to Six)

Of course, a member should receive a renewal notice. The great majority of members will not renew on their own. The renewal notice should be marked on the outside of the envelope so that it clearly notes what is inside. In the best of all worlds, there will only need to be one renewal notice. Organizations send anywhere from three to nine or more depending on the renewal returns with each renewal touch. Renewals are an example of a communication that must be delivered via postal mail. Email can supplement the mailed notice, but emails are too easily missed, deleted, or blocked in inboxes.

Membership Cards (One or Two)

Once the member renews, he or she should receive a packet with membership cards, a listing of benefits, coupons if they are a part of the membership package, and perhaps a request to volunteer or a tribute envelope to be used during the year. Each organization has its own package of information; it is an important mailing. It is the first communication the member receives at the beginning of his or her membership year. The envelope for this mailing should also be clearly marked so that the member knows to open it.

Invitations to Events (Four to Fifteen)

Separate invitations should be sent for the events. Invitations that appear in the newsletter or a calendar may or may not be seen. Separate invitations are also more special. They convey that sense of belonging to the member. Invitations can be printed or a special stand-alone email. The mailed variety can range from the frugal to the very extravagant. The type of invitation depends on the event and the organization. The design may range from an emailed invitation for a lecture to a postcard for a members-only program to very fancy for a high-ticket-price gala benefit. Email is the most commonly used vehicle for event invitations for most member programming, with mailed invitations now being reserved for higher-level fundraising events. For some value-level-member events, posting notices on social media platforms is possible, but be prepared to check member cards at the door, since nonmembers will also see these postings. However, making member-only events known to the public can serve to make nonmembers aware of the perks of membership and be a way of capturing new members.

For print invitations, with little money to spend, it is best to spend available funds on design, not on fancy paper or complicated printing, and make certain that the size of invitations is a common one and uses as little postage as possible. This may be bulk rate postage or first-class postage depending on the size of the mailing and on the event itself. For a very large event, bulk mail may be appropriate, but for a high-ticket-price gala first-class mail will be important.

Fundraising Appeals (Two to Four or More)

These are fundraising appeals in addition to the membership renewal. The most common ones are for a second annual gift, for gift membership(s), for fundraising events, and for special projects. Members may also be solicited from time to time for capital campaigns. If there is a planned giving program being marketed, members should receive that. The same is true of a tribute fund if there is one. Often a special mailing once a year will encourage tribute gifts.

There will be a difference between what a value member and a support member receives. For some fundraising appeals, support members will be treated individually as major donors; for others, all members will receive the same mailings. This needs to be coordinated with the development effort. Fundraising appeals are sometimes included in newsletters. If it is not possible to send separate appeals, it can be done through the newsletter, though separate mailings can be more effective. The organization needs to test the efficacy of the two approaches. It is also important to remember that the result of fundraising appeals is sending a thank you to those who respond.

The mailed appeal letter is still a requirement. Like renewals, we cannot risk the member not receiving the ask. Complementing the mailed ask with email (especially if there is an engaging video component to drive home the need for support) should also be added. Appeals can also be made via social media to get additional push and to appeal to nonmember followers.

Newsletter/Bulletin (Four to Twelve)

It is essential that the organization have an informational communication regularly sent to members. At a minimum, whether emailed or printed, the newsletter should be sent four times a year. The newsletter should be published and sent as often as possible, up to once a month. A newsletter does not need to be long; better to send a shorter newsletter more often than to wait until a longer one can be published. The organization's newsletter is often a part of the membership and development effort. If it is not, then the membership department should have significant allocated space in the newsletter for information for members.

Newsletters are sometimes written for member and nonmember audiences. It is advised that the newsletter include a member version to make the communication more personalized to the members' special position within the institution.

Other Publications (One to Twelve)

These publications range from an annual report to a book published by the organization to those organizations that offer a magazine as a benefit. For example, the *Smithsonian Magazine* is sent to members once a month while *Air & Space* magazine from the Smithsonian National Air and Space Museum is published seven times a year. Publication formats can vary from a major four-color magazine to self-published books and reports.

Miscellaneous (One to Four)

Other sporadic communications can come from the organization. These can be planned or the result of an unexpected event. Typical might be a membership survey mailing, a special letter about something important at the institution, or legislative updates. The important thing to remember is that when something important happens, the natural audience to hear about it first is the membership.

It is apparent from this list, which is by no means exhaustive, that there is a lot that can be communicated to members. Cost is always an issue. Printing and postage are often among the largest budget items. Email and digital channels have made communicating with members much more accessible and affordable. Developing a communications strategy for members and donors is absolutely necessary. Membership should have control of its ability to communicate with its members. Fear of frequency is sometimes a concern institutionally. However, the greater sin is not to communicate often enough with this high-priority audience. Because the mailbox and email inbox are the major connection between the organization and the member, the rule is the more touch points the better.

Telephone

The telephone is another major way membership programs communicate with members. This includes telemarketing for lapsed members and renewals, for thank-you phon-a-thons, and for encouraging participation in events. Customer service is also delivered via the telephone. Membership surveys can be conducted via telephone. The telephone can be the most personal communication that a member has with the institution. If there is an effective way to use the phone, use it.

The phone is a means of having a live one-to-one connection with a member. The most powerful way to raise money is a face-to-face meeting. This type of personal contact is not possible with hundreds or thousands of members. It is, however, possible to have a personal contact with members via the phone. With the migration to email for many member communications, the phone has been used less and less to connect with members. In the 2014 *Pulse of Membership* survey, only 17 percent of membership programs reported utilizing telemarketing in their membership programs.[3] Despite personal opinions and impressions of telemarketing, it is still a highly effective tool.

Email

Email has become the preferred method of communication for many, and is a timely and inexpensive way to communicate with members. It is particularly useful with time sensitive information—someone is unexpectedly coming to give a lecture, a bill that affects an important issue for the organization is in committee and members need to contact their legislators immediately. Some members now want to receive their newsletter online rather than through the mail. Sending event information a few days before the date may well increase attendance. For those who have given the membership department their email address (typically 70 to 80 percent), it is possible to send them quick updates on important projects on a regular basis, thereby increasing the number of communications at very little cost.

While email is an easy, inexpensive, and effective communications channel, remember that there are strict legal guidelines that govern email marketing. The CAN-SPAM Act of 2003 requires organizations to comply with numerous actions including valid opt-in, a visible and operable unsubscribe function that is present in all emails, and accurate From lines (the displayed sender name) among other requirements.

Gathering and maintaining email address lists is a major undertaking. Essentially the organization is now keeping two mailing lists—one for direct mail and one for email marketing. This takes a concerted effort; keeping a list up to date and "clean" is time consuming and must be tended regularly. Email communications need to have a purpose and be relevant or they will become spam (electronic junk mail). On the membership form, the member can be asked if he or she would like to receive information by email. Other opportunities to collect opt-ins for email include offering something in exchange for the member's email address, email appending, and loyalty programs.

It is also important to remember that email is a two-way communication. When members email a question, complaint, or suggestion, they need a response. Email is a faster medium than postal mail. When a comment arrives, the sender expects a quick response. Forrester Research found that 41 percent of consumers expect an email response within six hours.[4] Someone should have the responsibility for answering the mail in a timely manner. This becomes a service issue in the minds of the members. Organizations should also consider using another solution rather than a "no-reply" mailbox for member communications; this inhibits the opportunity for dialog via email. Remember, every time an institution sends an email to a member, it's an opportunity to receive feedback and strengthen the relationship.

Website

An organization's website, in combination with its other online properties, comprises its digital brand identity. It is an institution's virtual front door. The membership message and an invitation to join needs to be front and center on the homepage. Don't hide it!

Websites don't have to be costly or fancy to be effective. All that is required is an easy way to access information. Today, there is no excuse for an institution not to have some sort of website—whether a simple WordPress blog, a Squarespace template, a fully customized interactive platform, or something in between. The website should include a quick, one-click way to join as well as descriptive content that the user can drill down to on levels, events, and benefits.

Once having joined, a "members only" section can be a great opportunity to give members a feeling of connectedness and exclusivity. A members' only section could contain a variety of information, some of which can be a member benefit. Direct online access to a collection, research papers, the membership directory, and information on upcoming members-only events are a few of the uses for this type of feature.

Ensuring information on membership levels and benefits are up to date and having secure e-commerce capabilities to join or donate online should be the first priority of any membership website. Once this has been accomplished, the organization can focus on providing opportunities for users to opt-in to receive emails, developing a robust content strategy, designing interactive features that encourage online engagement, adding dynamic content, and so on.

While the possibilities for leveraging the website for membership are endless, membership managers should strive for the following capabilities online:

- To acquire and renew members—via a secure transaction page or third-party service;
- To communicate with members—via online newsletters, regularly updated content, and breadth of information including events, upcoming exhibitions, and multimedia;
- To increase participation—including interactive features, email opt-in, social sharing, commenting, and user generated content; and
- To service members—using members-only pages, member portals, contact forms, FAQs, and push notifications.

Recognition

The benefits, the service, the events, and the communications all serve to recognize members and the fact that they are supporters of the organization. The initial recognition is the thank-you email and/or phone call, the mailed packet of information, the membership card, and the other items the member receives on joining. In addition, other things can be done for recognition that make individual members feel particularly special.

The organization's newsletter is the most common way to recognize members. Many organizations, especially small ones, list new members. This is a nice form of recognition as well as alerting current members about who is joining the group. Some list members who upgrade. When a membership program becomes too large to do this, then the organization can move to recognize the support members rather than all members. If not using the newsletter, some groups use their annual report to do this. The newsletter is also the place to recognize members for volunteer work, for length of membership, and for any special events. Often the "member highlight" section about what members are currently doing is the most popular in a newsletter.

Length of membership can be recognized in other ways as well. First, those members who join "in the beginning" should be recognized as charter members, founding members, or a similar title.

If it is at all possible, it is very nice to have the membership card read "member since ___." Recognizing members on special anniversary dates such as five, ten, or twenty-five years of support promotes long-term relationships and shows appreciation for the value of long-time members. A reception honoring twenty-five- or fifty-year members creates nostalgia and enhances that feeling of belonging. Most importantly, it highlights the value of the members to the organization.

Creating and implementing a strong program for members will ensure their continued support. This program can be developed on any level, from very small to very large. The effort and challenge, for any membership program, is to design and include the benefits, service, events, communications, and recognition that the members want and believe are of value.

CORPORATE MEMBERSHIP PROGRAMS

Many organizations extend the membership concept to corporate giving. Some organizations combine all memberships—no matter if the membership comes from an individual or a company. With this system, the person in the company who sends in the membership becomes the member. There are no special corporate-related benefits or events. For many organizations, this is the easiest way to manage corporate members. If the program and its staff are small or new and/or corporate benefits difficult to construct, this is the more effective way to work with companies.

For others, however, a separate set of corporate dues, benefits, and programs is desired. How an organization works on corporate membership depends on the size of the institution, the size of the dues amount, the size of the corporation, and how corporate giving is handled by the company and in the community. Just as with the membership program for individuals, a corporate program needs acquisition, renewals, and dues as well as the same basic five elements: benefits, service, events, communication, and recognition. Although the membership manager is soliciting funds from a corporation, it is important to remember that this is still a decision made by an individual. Just like the individual program has to be viewed from the perspective of the individual member, it is crucial to view the corporate program from the corporate perspective.

There are three very important concepts to keep in mind when constructing a corporate membership program. First, do not develop benefits for the employees of a corporation that are a disincentive for individual membership. Second, the corporate program is much more like a major gifts program than a membership program and needs to be designed as such. Third, corporate members do need that personal solicitation and an individual ask. It is rare that corporate members are acquired through the typical means used by programs designed for individuals.

Acquisition, Renewals, and Dues

Acquisition is most often accomplished through personal solicitation by volunteers or staff rather than by direct mail or telemarketing. In general, the larger the company and the larger the dues amount, the more personal is the appeal. Dues for corporate members typically start at a much higher level than those for individual members and there tend to be fewer levels. They range from hundreds of dollars for small organizations to many thousands of dollars at large, major institutions. Corporate programs should be designed to produce significant income.

Benefits

Corporate benefits can be linked to employees, use of a facility (for a visitation-based institution), and advertising or product promotion. Benefits linked to employees include an employee day or event at the institution, or the organization coming into the workplace and presenting information or entertainment for the employees. Facility use for corporate functions is sometimes limited to corporate members, sometimes free of charge and sometimes tied to a discount for their use. Advertising and/or product promotion might include the ability of the corporate member to sponsor an exhibit or program.

Service

Corporate members want the same type of service as individual members. Payments need to be processed efficiently, thank yous sent, calls and questions answered promptly, and use of benefits (e.g., facility use) handled in a professional manner. With a corporate membership, a number of people on the corporate side may need service. The accounting department may deal with the payment, a community relations person with setting up an event, and the human resources staff with membership cards for employees. For this reason, the data that are kept for a corporate membership may be much more extensive than that kept for an individual member. On the institution side, more people may also be involved—membership, facility rental, public relations, education, events. When constructing the benefits package it is important to include other departments that may be called upon to service the corporate membership.

Events

The events for corporate memberships will depend on what the corporation wants to receive and on what the institution can provide. A visitation-based institution may offer an employees' day for the company's staff. For an organization that doesn't have a place to visit, there might be a lecture or a short course for interested employees. A service club that works with children might offer a parenting course; a library might offer volunteer opportunities in the library's literacy program.

Communications

Because a corporate membership is often the size of a major gift, it needs to be treated accordingly. It is important to communicate with all the people in the corporation who are involved with the membership. As is the case with servicing the membership, this may include the CEO's office, community relations, human relations, marketing, and others. In large companies, there may also be the possibility of communicating with all of the employees. If the company has an internal newsletter or intranet, this is a great audience to hear about what is happening at the institution, upcoming events, and volunteer opportunities.

Recognition

Corporate members should receive any recognition given to individual members. In addition, the organization might include their logos in print and electronic media (this may be positioned as recognition rather than an explicit benefit). Corporate logos cannot be used for pieces mailed with nonprofit mail classification; check postal regulations for exact limitations. If there is an event such as an employees' day at the institution, recognizing the corporation that day should be done in every way possible.

SUMMARY

The Membership Program is a complex set of components that defines the overall program—categories, dues, and benefits—all defining the product that is membership. The membership infrastructure is developed around the type of organization and people being served. Regardless of the type or structure of the program, there are essential elements that are required for all membership programs—the commitment to quality service in the delivery of the membership product and the need for frequent contact through live events and programming and for ongoing relevant communications. Finally, recognizing and celebrating members' commitment and involvement is a way of thanking them for their valuable support. A well-rounded membership program excels in all of these areas.

NOTES

1. Membership Consultants, Inc., "What Members Say," accessed June 10, 2015, http://knowledge.membership-consultants.com/what-members-say.

2. *Survey Course in Fundraising, Faculty Manual* (Alexandria, VA: Association of Fundraising Professionals, 2001), E-16.

3. Membership Consultants, Inc., "[Webinar Recording] Pulse of Membership Survey Results Year-End 2014," accessed April 21, 2015, http://knowledge.membership-consultants.com/pulse-of-membership-year-end-2014-webinar-recording.

4. "Multichannel Customer Experience Study," *Eptica*, accessed March 20, 2015, http://www.eptica.com/mces2015.

5

Leadership, Management, and Staff

There are three kinds of people: those who make things happen, those who watch what happened, and those who wonder what happened.

—*Unknown*

LEADERSHIP AND MANAGEMENT

Membership programs with strong leadership and management make things happen. They are proactive rather than reactive; they try new and different activities while keeping the successful ones fresh. Effective leadership and management are the hallmarks of successful membership programs. Who provides that leadership and management in a membership program? As with almost everything involved in a membership program, there are a variety of answers. The answers are interwoven with the type of membership program, the founders, the strength of volunteer involvement, the addition and quality of staff, and the role that the membership and program play within the total organization.

In a large institution with a strong membership program, leadership may come from a committee of the board, or a members' board and management from staff. In a large staff-driven organization, staff may provide both. In a small participatory or volunteer organization, leadership and management will both come from the members.

Leadership shows itself during the planning process for the membership program, where those who have a vision for the organization make it known. It shows itself in the willingness of staff or volunteers to take on projects, persuade others to participate, and implement them successfully. Effective management makes certain that goals are set and met, that day-to-day operations of the program run smoothly, and that the members are well served.

STAGES IN THE GROWTH OF MEMBERSHIP PROGRAMS

Typically a membership program will start small and many will stay small. The support group for a library in a small town will never be very large. On the other hand, Mothers Against Drunk Driving (MADD) is a good example of a small group that grew very large. Started by several women in California when they were angered about a drunk driver who had killed a child, it has now grown to many thousands of members and multiple chapters across the country.

There are four stages that a growing program will go through, although a program might always remain at any one stage, or, if there are problems, return to a prior stage. We are calling the stages founder, growth, expansion, and comprehensive. The descriptions below are meant as a general guide describing what happens in programs. Most organizations will reflect parts of several of the stages. Every organization will evolve differently, and at its own speed. The only constant is that all programs will change over time.

Founder Stage

Someone has to initiate the program. That person is the founder, and most often a volunteer. Sometimes there is a group of founders, the "founding members," though usually only one or a few consider themselves the founders. Founders have a special pride in what they have accomplished, as they should. They had the vision to begin the program, implement its first activities, and watch it begin to prosper. Many founders work tirelessly, giving of themselves with time as well as finances. They bring together their friends, family, and colleagues to support the cause. For some, it is their life's work.

The initiation stage revolves around the founders. These people lead the group. At some point, this isn't enough. Typically, the program will begin to grow. Membership acquisition increases, programs are developed, and a newsletter may be created. The group is now up and running and there is an active, vital program.

Difficulties begin when there is more work than the group can manage on its own. This time comes when the organization has between 500 and 1,000 members. By the 1,000-member level, some staff becomes essential unless there is the luxury of consistent ongoing volunteer staffing.

Growth Stage

The program has begun to be institutionalized and the active members share the work and power. At this point the founders know that they can't do it all by themselves and there is considerable delegation of tasks.

The greatest rite of passage is that the organization has to hire paid staff. The management of the membership program has become too large a task for volunteers. It is important to keep donor records, do the financial bookkeeping, issue membership cards, issue tax-related information if necessary, send out renewals on a timely basis, conduct acquisition programs, and produce events.

Hiring staff is a large commitment, of both time and money. While the membership manager will be learning and able to help from the day of hire, it will take a full calendar year for him or her to be conversant with all the operations of the membership program. This position is a "jack-of-all-trades," doing data processing as well as working on events. If part of an institution, the membership program becomes more integrated into the organization when the staff arrives since there is someone available at all times. Often, early staff serves a variety of needs, including public relations, marketing, or administrative duties for the greater organization along with the membership portion of their job.

At this point in the evolution, it is important for the volunteers to stay involved at a high level, though many of the tasks can be delegated to the staff member. For more information and resources regarding volunteers, visit www.themembershipbook.com.

Expansion Stage

With everything running smoothly, the volunteers and staff may decide that it is time to drive growth, add more programs, and, generally, expand what the program offers. This may take more paid staff to implement the activities. An assistant for the membership manager may be the next person hired to help with inquiries, processing duties, and other tasks. With membership growth, by the time the numbers reach 4,000, it is time to add a full-time data processing staff member. The membership manager has now become the full-time manager of the program and may also be providing some of the leadership.

At this stage, acquisition and renewal efforts become very aggressive and may increase with a phon-a-thon and on-site sales. The membership software may become more sophisticated with the ability to track all acquisition and renewal efforts. A membership survey may be instituted. New people are included in leadership positions. In all, the program is becoming institutionalized with systems in place, with day-to-day operations moving at a healthy pace.

Comprehensive Stage

This is a fully mature program, staffed with a number of paid people, all dedicated to serving the membership and its volunteer activities. With growth, one data processing person is needed for approximately every 7,500 members. By the time the total reaches 15,000, there will probably also be a need for part- or full-time supervision of the database management operation, including reporting and supervising the data entry staff. The membership manager manages and works in partnership with the volunteers to provide leadership for the membership program. More staff may be added to handle additional projects including a large fundraiser, a membership month of activities, or a membership desk in a visitation-based institution.

Other membership programs may be added such as online membership or special interest groups. More complicated benefits may be negotiated such as travel, insurance, or concierge service. An upper-level membership solicitation program is added. The volunteers have become an integral part of the institution and their contributions of time, energy, and money are greatly appreciated. The program is fully institutionalized, not dependent on any one person or group, and there is a guarantee that it will continue into the future.

There can be other stages or circumstances with respect to the stages of development of a membership program. All membership programs do not grow and prosper. Some programs hit roadblocks, staff turnover can stall management, institutional malaise or even scandal can occur, and membership will suffer as a result. Sometimes membership is neglected by management. Membership may not be properly funded, or other issues are higher on the priority list institutionally. In these cases, membership can plateau, staying flat without growth, or even experience a decline. When these issues affect membership negatively, it will take effort to correct the situation. New leadership or a turn of events may need to occur for membership to grow and prosper. A full audit of the membership program is required to analyze all aspects of the program and to commit to a comprehensive strategic plan for membership to regain its place within the institution.

RELATIONSHIP BETWEEN STAFF AND VOLUNTEERS

There may be tension between paid staff and volunteers in any organization. In the membership program, where often the volunteers have created the program and there is a sense that it is "their program," this feeling may be very strong. The issue is the volunteer time available. By the time a group reaches a critical mass of 1,000 or more members, staff becomes essential. The relationship between staff and volunteers is one that both the staff members and volunteers must manage carefully and carry out thoughtfully.

This is the point at which issues arise; the program becomes managed much more by staff than by volunteers. As well, activities that may be valued by volunteers can no longer be handled in the same way due to the size of the program. For example, the personal touch of hand-addressing invitations to a members-only event or providing homemade refreshments may no longer be possible with thousands of invitations to send and hundreds of people to feed. There is a loss of the personal touch and there is the feeling among the volunteers that their work is not valued. Many will also feel that they have lost control of a program that they may have created. This feeling of loss needs to be overcome with a bright vision for the future, interesting volunteer activities that work to increase the personal touch (e.g., having greeters and hosts at events, calling new members), and a staff that meshes well with the volunteer workers.

If this is an institution deciding to add staff to the program and a founder involved is still present, it is important to enlist his or her help and understanding. It is important for the founder to understand that the management of the program needs to grow with the program. When programming develops and the management side does not, there can be problems of service for the members, difficulty in keeping the processing running smoothly, and overwhelmed volunteers. When this occurs, the program is suffering from what has been called "founder flounder." Much like a business entrepreneur providing the vision and the passion to begin a company and then needing managers to take it to the next level, the developing membership program has the same growing pains.

When staff is added, there are several possible outcomes. No matter how well the situation is handled by the staff, there may well be some volunteers who feel that they are no longer needed and will decide to volunteer elsewhere. While this isn't what an organization wants, the priority becomes managing the program well and that will include a staff component. If not handled well, the program may lose some or all of its volunteers, which is not a desirable outcome. It is vital for the leadership of the organization to work with the volunteers to make certain that there is a smooth transition. It is also essential for the staff to have excellent interpersonal skills. The mandate for the staff is to involve and include the volunteers as possible and in as many activities as possible.

From the staff viewpoint, involving volunteers increases the amount of time that an activity takes. For example, it may well take the membership manager longer to coordinate a volunteer group to hand-address invitations than to print and affix computer labels; however, there will be instances when working with the volunteers on this project is time well spent. The volunteers who are involved in the hand addressing will make certain to ask their friends and colleagues to attend. They now have a stake in it. The same is true with events. The membership manager can organize an event fairly quickly; however, volunteer involvement is often essential to guarantee an audience.

On the volunteer side, those volunteers who are not happy about the addition of staff have two choices: they may find a different organization with which to work, or they may partner with the membership manager and work together. The point is for the volunteer to make the decision; it is not helpful to anyone to have an irritated volunteer involved who participates with grumbling. When this happens, the volunteer leadership needs to speak with the unhappy volunteer and resolve the situation in as pleasant a way as possible.

For staff and volunteers to work together in harmony takes work on both sides. There needs to be mutual respect, a delineation of roles, and the commitment of all to work for the organization together. When this partnership works well, the membership program and the organization will flourish. If it is not working well, the staff and volunteer leadership need to sit down and talk through the situation to resolve it. The effort is for staff and volunteers to become a team to carry out the work of the membership program. See www.themembershipbook.com for helpful volunteer resources.

STAFFING THE MEMBERSHIP PROGRAM

Tasks

There are numerous tasks in the membership program that need attention. It is irrelevant whether the membership manager or the volunteers accomplish the tasks; they just need to be done. The tasks run the gamut from keeping records to developing and implementing events to creating the strategic or long-range plans for the membership program. Each of these tasks can be done at a minimal, basic, or very high and sophisticated level.

The following suggested time allocations are a percent of the effort spent on the program assuming the entire program takes 100 percent. It is not necessarily related to the importance of the task, because some tasks just take longer than others, even though they might be less important. For example, acquisition is the most important task for any program since it is imperative to bring in new members; however, a program may well spend more time on events because they are incredibly time consuming and the acquisition is outsourced to a direct mail professional. As well, the time spent will vary depending on the day, week, or month. Juggling and setting priorities become important skills. Of course, there is overlap between and among the activities. Look at the time suggested here with these caveats, and consider them as guidelines based on experience.

Acquisition: No matter the type of acquisition program, it must be planned and implemented. This also includes planning the benefits for the program. Time: 15 percent.

Renewals: There must be a schedule for renewals. They must be sent promptly with as much follow-up (letter, email, and phone) as possible. Time: 10 percent.

Processing and Record Keeping: Someone must process the membership application and keep the records of who joined when, membership level, and information such as addresses, email, and phone numbers. Processing may include sending a welcome letter, a membership card, and any benefits. If memberships cannot be processed promptly and the records kept with accuracy, there is a real question about whether there should be a program. This also includes providing monthly reports on new members, renewals, and upgrades. Time: 15 percent.

Member Services: Members need someone to call. If a membership card is lost, information wanted about an event, or an RSVP required, someone must answer the questions and provide the information and service. Time: 10 percent.

Communications: Where the membership program is a part of the larger organization, another department may handle this. In this case, the membership program needs to coordinate so that the appropriate communications vehicles have membership information. When the membership program is the organization or the membership department has the responsibility for communicating directly with members, one of the largest tasks is communication. Time: 10 percent.

Events and Programs: At a minimum, there should be three to four events and/or programs a year planned for members only. They can be as easy as a lecture or as complicated as a major fair. There may also be events that the volunteers want to plan for the public. Additionally, there may be interest in having volunteers work on fundraisers for the organization. Time: 20 percent.

Coordinating Volunteer Activities: For a program with an active volunteer component, the membership manager is often called on to coordinate the volunteer work. This can be time consuming, but it is very important to have the volunteer corps involved; they give enormous amounts of time and energy. Time: 10 percent.

Planning: Every year an operational plan based on the program's strategic plan must be developed. This includes planning all of the work for the year, the budget, and the calendar. At least every three years, the organization should take a strategic look at the program and determine whether to make any major changes. With a plan, small changes can be made at any time. The major changes are those that are strategic, such as beginning direct mail acquisition when there has been none, increasing the number and type of communications, or deciding to appeal to a new market segment with a new acquisition program, events, and services. Time: 5 percent.

Other: There are myriad other tasks that can be a part of the program. These include tasks such as market research, travel programs, interest groups, and so on. Time: 5 percent.

Possible Staff Configurations

Programs that add staff usually do it slowly but surely. The following configurations will give some idea of what can be accomplished by adding staff. Size of the membership and the amount of volunteer help available are the two variables that make the greatest difference in what can be accomplished by staffing. The configurations provided here are meant as a guideline; each program needs to decide for itself how to succeed at the work at hand.

A Few Hours Each Week: When a small program reaches the point that it needs help with record keeping, renewals, and mailings, a part-time staff person is a great help. With this type of staffing, the volunteer responsible for membership would have the tasks planned so that the staff person could accomplish them in the limited time available.

One Half-Time Equivalent Staff Member: This might be some of the time of the development director or the public relations staff person or it might be a half-time membership manager. Volunteer coordination, record keeping, some of the acquisition and renewal work, and some member services would be the first tasks for a new staff person.

One Full-Time Equivalent: All the tasks could be tackled at the levels suggested above.

Two Full-Time Staff Members: One staff person would be assigned the acquisition, renewal, record keeping, and member service. The other would be responsible for the communications, volunteer coordination, events, and planning.

Three Full-Time Staff Members: By this time, the program would be large and require a full-time person working on record keeping, renewals, and member services. The other duties would be divided between the other two staff members. The director of membership would have supervisory responsibilities by this time.

Four Full-Time Staff Members: At this stage, the director now has a growing staff and supervision will take more time along with the basic membership responsibilities. One staff person might be totally committed to working with the volunteers and events. Two might be assigned to the record keeping, renewals, and services.

More Staff: As time goes by and the program becomes larger, more time must be spent on data processing, reports, and analysis. More members require more events and communications to reach the different segments of the membership. Additional programs, such as interest groups, can be added. The sky's the limit.

Two sample organizational charts involving membership are shown in figures 5.1 and 5.2. In both of these charts, the membership department is a part of the development effort. The major difference is the size of the department.

In both charts the events coordinator is responsible for member and donor events and the membership service staff is responsible for phone calls and dealing with member issues. The on-site sales assistant may be full- or part-time. There are, of course, many ways to design the organizational chart for membership. Another possible structure exists when membership is part of the marketing department (see figure 5.3).

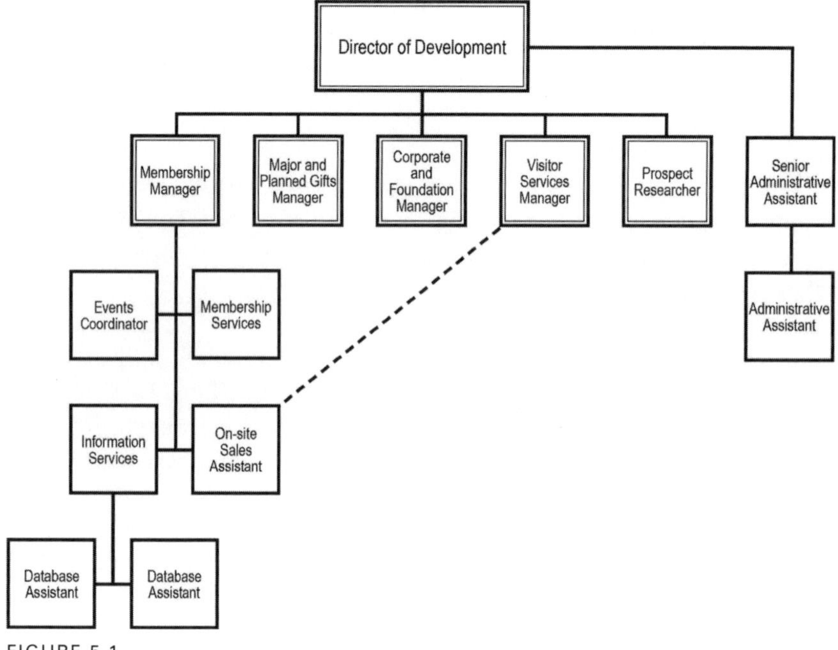

FIGURE 5.1
Large Membership Staff—Organizational Chart

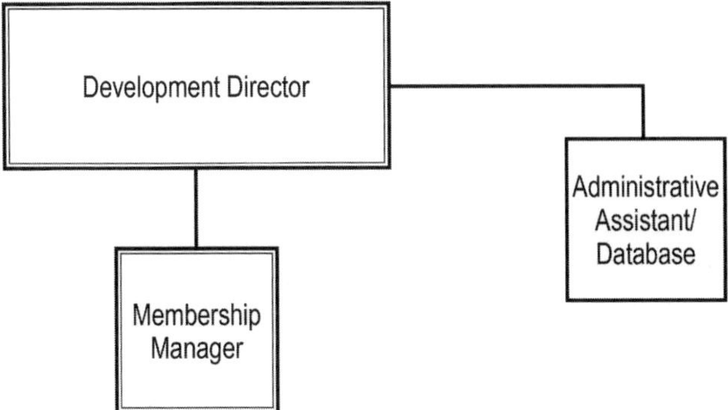

FIGURE 5.2
Small Membership Staff—Organizational Chart

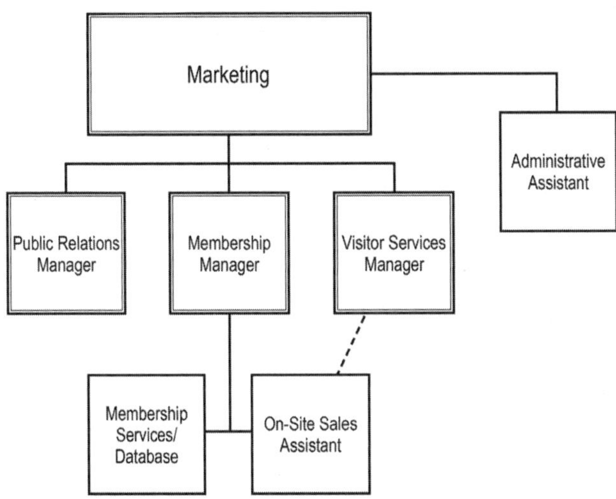

FIGURE 5.3
Membership in Marketing—Organizational Chart

Hiring Staff

The first effort in hiring staff is to develop a position description that outlines the responsibilities of the staff person. In *Starting & Building a Nonprofit: A Practical Guide*, author Peri Pakroo notes that creating a job description will "help in the hiring process but will also be valuable when it's time to review the worker's performance."[1]

The volunteer group can do this in conjunction with the current staff person responsible. If this is the time when the volunteer-founded membership program is first hiring staff, the volunteers should be directly involved. Since some of their work will go to the staff person, they should determine which tasks to move to staff. The position description should include specific tasks for which the new person will be responsible, to whom he or she reports, and any results that are expected. If the membership program has a plan, the goals and objectives in the plan should be discussed with the potential new staff person so that she or he has an idea of what is expected.

Those involved in the hiring must determine what skills are needed. The skills may range from data entry to social media to event planning. As important as the skills are, the personality traits of the person to be hired are perhaps more important. He or she must have excellent interpersonal abilities. These traits enable a person to work well with others. Membership involves working with other staff, volunteers, and the members. The appropriate person will enjoy working with people and know how to do it skillfully. It's always good to have someone who is cheerful and enthusiastic about the organization and its mission.

Finding the person who is the right fit for the organization can take some time. Look in all the usual places, including the volunteer and member ranks of the organization. Someone who is already a volunteer or member knows about the organization and has voluntarily already made a commitment to it. It is sometimes difficult to make the transition from volunteer to staff, but it is often done successfully. If the person is the right fit, consider this option. Other usual places will include advertising on the institution's website, networking with groups in the community to find out who might be available, and leveraging social media (e.g., posting the position to Facebook and LinkedIn). It may take two to three months or more from beginning the search to having someone in place. Sample membership job descriptions are available at www.themembershipbook.com.

Staff Orientation

Once the person is in place, it will take time to train him or her. If it is necessary to train the person on the database, take the time and money to do it. It will pay rewards in the future. If the person has never worked in membership before, consider sending him or her to a seminar on membership programs; two days at a seminar will shorten the learning curve considerably. It takes one calendar year for anyone to be completely familiar with a job. This is because so many activities are calendar dependent. It is necessary for the person to experience the year and the ebb and flow of membership to understand the position.

Staff Evaluation

The new staff person should be evaluated at the end of a probationary period, often three months. This is the time at which the person can be terminated if it is determined that he or she is not the right fit for the organization. If all is well, the next evaluation will be at the end of the first year. Every organization should have some form of performance appraisal where the employee is evaluated against the position description.

Once the membership manager is a part of the membership team, it is important for him or her to have personal objectives to meet from the membership plan. The membership manager and his or her supervisor should agree on what the membership manager needs to accomplish. This becomes an ongoing process.

When to Increase Staff

As the program grows in numbers and activities, the time comes to add more staff. In the data processing area, a new staff person is needed with each addition of 7,500 members. In events, it will depend on the amount of volunteer help and the extent of the programs. Large public events and fundraisers may signal the need for additional help.

The need for more staff is often a signal that it is time to review the plan for the membership program. The plan will detail the work for the year; having a plan gives the current staff and volunteers a way to decide what is needed. This is very much an individual situation with each organization needing to find the level of staffing for what it wants to accomplish as shown in the membership plan.

MANAGEMENT'S LEGAL AND ETHICAL ISSUES

The membership manager (whether volunteer or staff) must make many decisions for the program. Some of the issues involve ethical decision making and some deal with the legal requirements for any program that receives money.

The public has a right to hold nonprofit organizations to a high standard. Society grants nonprofit organizations special status and benefits including exemption from certain taxes. In exchange, the public expects nonprofit organizations to make society better, to fulfill their missions, and to act ethically. Nonprofits also must follow the law. Legal and ethical concerns are not necessarily the same. Generally, society first reaches a consensus of what is unethical and then it is codified into law. Therefore, many things can be considered unethical even though laws and regulations have yet to be written on the subject. Society's views change and then laws and regulations are rewritten or even repealed.

It is a best practice and essential to obey the law. The Association of Fundraising Professionals (AFP) Statement of Ethical Principles states:

> Members shall:
>
> . . . ensure that all solicitation and communication materials are accurate and correctly reflect their organization's mission and use of solicited funds.
>
> . . . ensure that donors receive informed, accurate and ethical advice about the value and tax implications of contributors.[2]

The AFP Code of Ethical Standards (exhibit 5.1), as well as the Donor Bill of Rights, can be found at www.afpnet.org. Other professional organizations and individual nonprofits have also developed codes. While many of the points addressed in these codes address fundraising and/or prospect research activities, many of the principles are equally valid for membership professionals.

Unfortunately, codes suffer from the same limitation as the law. They cannot be all inclusive. Like conscience, the law and codes are only of value when confronting the specific situations they address.

Key Issues

Membership professionals must be prepared to deal with any number of ethical issues on any given day. However, three broad areas in particular affect membership professionals most often: privacy, list ownership, and stewardship.

EXHIBIT 5.1
Code of Ethical Standards

Adopted 1964; amended Oct. 2014

The Association of Fundraising Professionals believes that ethical behavior fosters the development and growth of fundraising professionals and the fundraising profession and enhances philanthropy and volunteerism. AFP Members recognize their responsibility to ethically generate or support ethical generation of philanthropic support. Violation of the standards may subject the member to disciplinary sanctions as provided in the AFP Ethics Enforcement Procedures. AFP members, both individual and business, agree to abide (and ensure, to the best of their ability, that all members of their staff abide) by the AFP standards.

PUBLIC TRUST, TRANSPARENCY & CONFLICTS OF INTEREST

Members shall:

1. not engage in activities that harm the members' organizations, clients or profession or knowingly bring the profession into disrepute.
2. not engage in activities that conflict with their fiduciary, ethical and legal obligations to their organizations, clients or profession.
3. effectively disclose all potential and actual conflicts of interest; such disclosure does not preclude or imply ethical impropriety.
4. not exploit any relationship with a donor, prospect, volunteer, client or employee for the benefit of the members or the members' organizations.
5. comply with all applicable local, state, provincial and federal civil and criminal laws.
6. recognize their individual boundaries of professional competence.
7. present and supply products and/or services honestly and without misrepresentation.
8. establish the nature and purpose of any contractual relationship at the outset and be responsive and available to parties before, during and after any sale of materials and/or services.
9. never knowingly infringe the intellectual property rights of other parties.
10. protect the confidentiality of all privileged information relating to the provider/client relationships.
11. never disparage competitors untruthfully.

SOLICITATION & STEWARDSHIP OF PHILANTHROPIC FUNDS

Members shall:

12. ensure that all solicitation and communication materials are accurate and correctly reflect their organization's mission and use of solicited funds.
13. ensure that donors receive informed, accurate and ethical advice about the value and tax implications of contributions.
14. ensure that contributions are used in accordance with donors' intentions.
15. ensure proper stewardship of all revenue sources, including timely reports on the use and management of such funds.
16. obtain explicit consent by donors before altering the conditions of financial transactions.

continued...

TREATMENT OF CONFIDENTIAL & PROPRIETARY INFORMATION

Members shall:

17. not disclose privileged or confidential information to unauthorized parties.
18. adhere to the principle that all donor and prospect information created by, or on behalf of, an organization or a client is the property of that organization or client.
19. give donors and clients the opportunity to have their names removed from lists that are sold to, rented to or exchanged with other organizations.
20. when stating fundraising results, use accurate and consistent accounting methods that conform to the relevant guidelines adopted by the appropriate authority.

COMPENSATION, BONUSES & FINDER'S FEES

Members shall:

21. not accept compensation or enter into a contract that is based on a percentage of contributions; nor shall members accept finder's fees or contingent fees.
22. be permitted to accept performance-based compensation, such as bonuses, only if such bonuses are in accord with prevailing practices within the members' own organizations and are not based on a percentage of contributions.
23. neither offer nor accept payments or special considerations for the purpose of influencing the selection of products or services.
24. not pay finder's fees, commissions or percentage compensation based on contributions.
25. meet the legal requirements for the disbursement of funds if they receive funds on behalf of a donor or client.

Privacy

Public concerns over privacy rights generally continue to increase. "Public opinion polls consistently find strong support among Americans for privacy rights in law to protect their personal information from government and commercial entities."[3]

Privacy issues of one type or another are regular news. A simple web search in 2015 using Google found more than 5,580,000,000 websites with the word "privacy." With media attention and public pressure, the government will continue to look at developing new consumer protection laws and regulations. For the membership professional, adhering to these new rules is critical. Beyond that, being sensitive to the public mood is likewise important.

Membership files should only contain the information relevant to the membership effort. As a rule, the membership professional should never feel uncomfortable about showing a member his or her file if asked. If the professional would be uncomfortable doing so, it is a possible sign that the file contains information that should not be included.

Membership files should be kept secure with authorized access granted only to those who need access to perform their jobs. Security has become an enormous issue with the arrival of hackers breaking into private data of well-known companies. Security for the database is essential.

Privacy and security also extend to the website. A privacy policy should be displayed on the website and should describe how a site visitor's information will be collected and used. Additionally, organizations must ensure payment processing is compliant with the Payment Card Industry Data Security Standard (PCI DSS).

Members should have the opportunity to have their names removed from lists that are sold to, rented to, or exchanged with other organizations. A small-print note including contact information should be included in every newsletter or other regular communication reminding members that they may choose to have their names deleted from any list sale or exchange. The item should be clear about how members go about removing their names.

AFP states that members shall:

> not disclose privileged or confidential information to unauthorized parties . . . give donors and clients the opportunity to have their names removed from lists that are sold to, rented to or exchanged with other organizations.[4]

List Ownership

AFP members agree to "adhere to the principle that all donor and prospect information created by, or on behalf of, an organization or a client is the property of that organization or client."[5] When the professional moves on, the data remain behind.

When working with direct response agencies, organizations should negotiate contracts that provide the nonprofit organization rather than the agency with list ownership rights. Members are establishing a relationship with the organization. Members expect that the organization will protect their personal information and not share it with a third party for other purposes. However, some direct response agencies may maintain an interest in the list without asserting rights of ownership. For example, an agency might receive a fee if the nonprofit organization rents its membership list to another party.

But this is only if the organization intends for the list to be rented and it gives its consent. However, a nonprofit organization should always retain control of the list. An organization can decide to put its list on the rental market, legally and legitimately, and it becomes a source of income. Even if the list is "on the market," the organization controls who may rent it. Some national groups make significant income from the rental of their lists.

Stewardship

Through sound stewardship, membership professionals will develop loyalty among their members. Loyalty will lead to long-term relationships and the possibility of additional support through charitable giving along with membership dues.

Stewardship means many things. Professionals should make certain that members receive the acknowledgment and the benefits promised on a timely basis. Members should receive updates of how their money is used if there is a charitable gift component to the membership dues. Membership professionals should be sure to fulfill members' opt-out requests. Membership professionals should report to each member how much of his or her membership dues is tax deductible.

LEGAL ISSUES

Ethical situations and issues can provoke discussion and are sometimes gray rather than black or white. Legal issues involving nonprofit organizations are more straightforward. For those membership programs that are the organization, it is important to meet all legal requirements. For a membership program that is part of a larger organization, most of the legal concerns are addressed by the organization itself. The membership program, though, along with development, is usually responsible for the legal issues related to fundraising matters.

Nonprofit Status

Many membership groups never become formal organizations. The neighborhood book club, the group devoted to bringing volunteers together to clean a stream, and the social dinner club that convenes over food are very informal, providing something for their members, but little or no real need for organizational structure or to ask the public for funds.

If a group decides to formalize its status, the first issue is to become a non-profit organization. The Internal Revenue Service confers this designation. A group that meets the requirements of becoming a 501(c)(3) organization will be able to offer tax deductibility for gifts. To become a 501(c)(3), IRS form 1023 must be completed.[6] Some organizations are able to do this on their own; others consult with or hire a lawyer to help. It is a major project.

Form 990

The "cost" of tax deductibility is submitting Form 990 to the IRS each year. This form details an organization's financial status. It is due by the fifteenth day of the fifth month after the end of the organization's fiscal year. It is federal law that Form 990 must be given to anyone who asks for it. Some organizations post Form 990 on their own website or on a database site on the Internet. GuideStar® (at GuideStar.org) calls itself "The National database of Nonprofit Organizations." Indeed, it now lists information for many of the country's nonprofits.

While often the membership manager is not responsible for filling out Form 990, there is an opportunity to have input. From 990 asks for basic information, which, if viewed from a marketing perspective, is an opportunity to talk about the work of the organization and mention how, if appropriate, members play a role. Considering that many will be looking at 990s on the Internet in the future, don't overlook this occasion to market the organization and membership.

Tax Deductibility

The most common question about membership dues is "how much is tax deductible?" The following is adapted from IRS Publication 526, Charitable Contributions; Contributions You Can Deduct.[7] This information is also shown in exhibit 5.2, Charitable Gift Receipt and Disclosure Rules, reprinted courtesy of the law firm Faegre Baker Daniels, LLP, of Minneapolis, Minnesota.[8]

If an organization has 501(c)(3) status, a member may be able to deduct membership fees or dues paid. However, the member can deduct only the amount that is more than the value of the benefits received.

Certain membership benefits can be disregarded. The member and the organization can disregard certain membership benefits given in return for an annual payment of $75 or less to the qualified organization. The member can

EXHIBIT 5.2

Charitable Gift Receipt and Disclosure Rules

Written Statements

All gifts in cash or by check	Donor must have bank record or written receipt from charity stating charity's name and the date and amount of the gift	
Gifts of $250 or more	Multiple gifts of <$250 from one donor in same year are not aggregated for purposes of this rule	*Gift* portion, not the entire payment, must be $250 or more
Content	• Amount of cash, description of non-cash items donated • Statement of whether charity provided any goods or services ("benefits") in exchange (other than those that can be disregarded) • If benefits are provided — a description and good faith estimate of their value • Special rules apply to gifts of motor vehicles, inventory, personal property, and certain other property	Need not provide value of goods and services provided to employees or partners of donor Need not mention benefits that can be disregarded
Timing	Donor must have statement by earlier of due date for return or actual filing date; single statement may cover multiple contributions by same donor	
Penalty	Contribution not deductible	
Volunteer expenses	Statement must include description of services provided by volunteer instead of description of donated cash or other property	Need not specify date of services
Payroll deduction	Charity provides pledge card or other document stating that no benefits are provided in exchange for gift	Amount withheld from each paycheck is separate gift
CRTs & CLTs	No substantiation required for gifts to charitable remainder trusts or charitable lead trusts	
Gift annuities	Substantiation required; annuity interest not treated as benefit received in exchange for gift	
Matching gifts	Benefits are listed on the substantiation provided to the party receiving them, even if attributable to matching gift made by another party	
Donor-advised funds	Receipt for a gift to a donor-advised fund must state that the donee organization has legal control of the contributed assets	
Quid pro quo gifts over $75		Entire payment, not gift portion, exceeds $75
Content	• Statement that the amount deductible for federal tax purposes is limited to the excess of the value of the property contributed over the value of any goods or services provided by the organization • Good faith estimate of value of benefits provided	
Timing	In connection with solicitation or receipt of the gift	
Penalty	$10 per gift, up to $5,000 per campaign or event, payable by charity	

Benefits to be Disregarded

Insubstantial value	Items of insubstantial value, if value of all benefits is ≤2% of payment and ≤$105*	
Token items	Token items bearing charity's name or logo, if: • Donor's payment is ≥$52.50*, and • Benefits received are bookmarks, calendars, key chains, mugs, posters, T-shirts, etc. bearing the organization's name or logo, and • Aggregate cost of all such items for this donor for year is ≤$10.50*	
Newsletters	Members-only newsletters and program guides not of commercial quality (with primary purpose of informing members about activities)	
Frequently exercisable benefits	Annual membership benefits (other than access to college athletic tickets) that can be exercised frequently. Same benefit must be offered at a membership level of $75 or less	Ex.: Free or discounted admission, gift shop discounts
Member events	Admission to members-only events with projected cost per person of ≤$10.50*. Same benefit must be offered at a membership level of $75 or less	Ex.: "Meet-the-celebrity" event for members
Employees	Benefits provided to employees of a corporate donor or partners of a partnership donor may be disregarded according to the same rules	Ex.: Open house for employees of corporate donor

**For 2015 gifts. Adjusted annually for inflation.*

Good Faith Estimate of Value

Market value	Fair market value: price at which the property would change hands between a willing buyer and a willing seller, neither being under any compulsion to buy or sell and both having reasonable knowledge of relevant facts	
Method	May use any reasonable method for valuation	
Unique items	Unique items can be valued based on similar or comparable items, without regard to the unique feature	Ex.: Value of dinner in art museum has same value as comparable dinner in restaurant
Celebrities	Celebrity presence has no additional value	Ex.: Dinner at Oprah Winfrey's house has same value as dinner at any private home
Ticket access	Right to purchase college athletic tickets has value equal to 20% of the payment	Ex.: Where $200 donors have right to purchase tickets (at full price), value of the access to the tickets is 20% of $200
Auctions	Tip: For auction items, list estimate of value (in addition to "minimum bid") in auction book	

Source: Faegre Baker Daniels LLP.

pay more than $75 to the organization if the organization does not require a larger payment to get the benefits. The benefits that can be disregarded under this rule are as follows:

Membership Fees or Dues

1. Any rights or privileges that can be used frequently while a member such as
   a. Free or discounted admission to the organization's facilities or events,
   b. Free or discounted parking,
   c. Preferred access to goods or services, and
   d. Discounts on the purchase of goods and services.
2. Admission, while a member, to events that are open only to members of the organization if the organization reasonably projects that the cost per person (excluding any allocated overhead) is not more than a specified amount, which may be adjusted annually for inflation. This is the amount for low-cost articles given in the annual revenue procedure with inflation-adjusted amounts for the current year. This figure is available from the IRS.

Token Items

You can deduct the entire payment to a qualified organization as a charitable contribution if both of the following are true.

1. There is a small item or other benefit of token value.
2. The qualified organization correctly determines that the value of the item or benefit received is not substantial and informs the members that they can deduct their payment in full.

The organization determines whether the value of an item or benefit is substantial by using Revenue Procedure 90-12 and 92-49 and the revenue procedure with the inflation-adjusted amounts for the current year.

Written Statement

A qualified organization must give the member a written statement if he or she makes a payment to it that is more than $75 and is partly a contribution and partly for goods or services. The statement must tell the member that he or she can deduct only the amount of the payment that is more than the value of the goods or services received. It must also give a good-faith estimate of the value of those goods or services. The organization can give the statement either when it solicits or when it receives the payment.

Exception

An organization will not have to give the member this statement if one of the following is true.[9]

1. The member receives only items whose value is not substantial as described under token items, earlier.
2. The member receives only membership benefits that can be disregarded, as described earlier.

Reporting to Members

Members today are cognizant of the tax-deductibility issue. Many will want receipts that state that their gift is fully tax deductible even if they do not need one. The membership manager needs to be ready to send the appropriate information when requested. Letting donors know how much of their gift is tax deductible can be done on the membership form itself or included in the information that the donor receives with his or her membership card and packet. Examples of wording that are most helpful to members include, for lower level members, "Membership is 100 percent tax deductible," or for the higher levels, "$950 tax deductible" (of a $1,000 membership). Another way of say this is "All but $50 of your membership is considered to be tax deductible."

At the higher levels, every organization will have a different amount of tax deductibility for each of its levels, depending on the benefits offered. For one organization it may be $950 of $1,000, for another it may be $890 of $1,000, and for yet another it may be $825 of $1,000. It is the responsibility of the organization to figure out what the tax-deductible amount is for the purposes of informing the members. Giving the amount or percentage of tax deductibility is far preferable to saying, "Your membership is tax deductible to the full extent of the law."

The membership manager may have to send another letter close to tax season when the donor cannot find the original letter. Keeping copies of these letters or being able to generate them quickly is helpful for this reason. Some organizations choose to send a blanket acknowledgement to all donors at the end of the year along with another thank you.

Closer to home, many states have their own nonprofit statutes. It's important to be up to date on what they are. If the state has laws governing fundraising, membership professionals should be aware of any that might have an impact on membership solicitations. Many states have registration and annual financial reporting requirements. Many states require specific wording on direct mail solicitations. Additionally, some states have rules governing telephone solicitation, which must be followed. These rules must be followed for the nonprofit's home state, and also for any state in which the nonprofit solicits.

Further, as online fundraising has become mainstream, nonprofits must ensure that the organization is meeting requirements for solicitation via the website, mobile, and social media. The National Association of State Charities Officials (NASCO) has provided recommendations and tips to help nonprofits navigate the vast opportunity of online fundraising. Ultimately, nonprofit organizations should consult with a legal advisor and state charity officials regarding online fundraising.

Nonprofits need to be cognizant of what is happening locally and nationally. Membership programs that are nonprofits need to be mindful of those laws that all nonprofits must heed. All membership programs need to be aware of the tax-deductibility issues. Keeping up with these topics is not difficult; there is a lot of information available. AFP nationally provides legislative updates for members. Reading periodicals that follow the nonprofit sector (for example, the *Chronicle of Philanthropy*) is another way to stay abreast of changes. As noted above, information is also available online on websites such as GuideStar®. In the case of legal and reporting issues that can have an impact on a membership program, ignorance is not bliss.

Conflict of Interest

Another legal issue that a membership manager can face is that of conflict of interest. It is always an ethical question and can become a legal one depending on the state statutes regulating nonprofits. Conflicts of interest occur sometimes because someone is trying to help and sometimes because people are interested in personal gain. Because a large membership program can spend a significant amount of money for vendors selling items such as printing, direct mail, telemarketing, catering, premiums (the token gifts), and market research, it is helpful to have policies in place to avoid these situations. IRS Form 990 now asks if the organization has a conflict of interest policy.

The conflict occurs when someone active in the program, perhaps a board member or his or her relative, receives personal gain from a transaction. Having a policy that requires three bids on items over a specified amount of money makes certain that transactions are fair to both the vendors and the nonprofit. This does not mean that those who are involved cannot do business with the nonprofit. The issue here is the appearance and the reality of fairness. It does a program no good in the community if it appears that all business is going in one direction without others having an opportunity to bid on it.

Obeying the law, learning from various codes of ethics, using a sound ethical decision-making model, protecting member privacy, maintaining proper list ownership, and providing effective stewardship will all build trust between the organization and its members. This in turn will help secure the future for the organization and help ensure a successful career for the membership professional.

SUMMARY

As author John Bryson notes in *Strategic Planning for Public and Nonprofit Organizations*, effective leadership in nonprofit organizations is "a collective enterprise involving many people playing different leader and follower roles at different times."[10] Legal considerations, hiring decisions, management of volunteers, establishing departmental roles, and ethical decision making are all aspects of leadership within membership. Leaders must be proactive in addressing issues within membership that threaten the program, staff, volunteers, or mission. Obeying the law, using a sound ethical decision-making model, protecting member privacy, maintaining proper list ownership, and providing effective stewardship will all build trust between the organization and its members.

NOTES

1. Peri Pakroo, *Starting and Building a Nonprofit: A Practical Guide*, 6th ed. (Berkeley, CA: Nolo, 2015), 94.

2. "Code of Ethical Standards" (Association of Fundraising Professionals, 2014), adopted 1964; amended October 2014; accessed June 4, 2015, http://www.afpnet.org/files/ContentDocuments/CodeofEthics.pdf.

3. "Public Opinion on Privacy" (Electronic Privacy Information Center, 2015), accessed March 3, 2015, https://www.epic.org/privacy/survey.

4. AFP, "Code of Ethical Standards."

5. Ibid.

6. IRS, "Form 1023, Application for Recognition of Exemption Under Section 501(c)(3) of the Internal Revenue Code," last updated June 10, 2015, accessed June 13, 2015, http://www.irs.gov/uac/Form-1023,-Application-for-Recognition-of-Exemption-Under-Section-501(c)(3)-of-the-Internal-Revenue-Code.

7. IRS, "Publication 526, Charitable Contributions," 2014, 4, accessed June 4, 2015, http://www.irs.gov/pub/irs-pdf/p526.pdf.

8. Faegre Baker Daniels, LLP, "Charitable Gift Receipt and Disclosure Rules," 2015.

9. IRS, Publication 526.

10. John M. Bryson, *Strategic Planning for Public and Nonprofit Organizations*, 4th ed. (San Francisco: Wiley, 2011), 356.

6

Membership Acquisition

The beginning is the most important part of the work.

—Plato, Philosopher and Mathematician

THE CRITICAL TASK

Acquisition is the beginning and the most important part of membership. Without members, there is no program. Acquiring new members is the most critical function of membership marketing. It is the membership manager's primary responsibility; it is a great challenge and, at times, the most frustrating aspect of the position. At the same time, it is often the most costly component of the membership budget, while also being the most time consuming and the least predictable. There are a number of methods of membership acquisition that differ depending on the size and type of an institution, the budget, and the amount of volunteer and/or staff time available to carry out the functions described in this chapter.

Before embarking on a membership acquisition effort, it is important to assess the organization's commitment to its membership operation. Verbalizing a commitment to membership acquisition is not enough. Sufficient funds need to be dedicated to this effort to give any statement of commitment real strength. Also, it must be understood that membership acquisition is a long-term commitment. An institution must dedicate sufficient funding for acquisition on an ongoing basis, not just for one year or sporadically.

Important questions that need to be answered are: Does the leadership of the organization understand that acquisition efforts are usually a break-even proposition at best? That it may take two years to recoup the cost to acquire a member? That the benefits of membership acquisition are usually only seen in succeeding years when membership renewal income is realized? In membership acquisition, more than in any other area, it is critical to have realistic expectations. Expectations and projections must be attainable or it is likely that the decision makers involved will discontinue funding membership acquisition efforts, especially in smaller organizations or when budgets are less stable.

An on-again, off-again commitment to membership acquisition is possibly more destructive than having no commitment to acquisition at all. Without a constant, ongoing effort to acquire new members, membership totals and revenue are merely maintained or even decline over time. Spikes in membership totals will be followed by dips when funding or commitment to membership does not remain constant. If there is no commitment, money is neither spent nor generated, so garnering that initial commitment for membership acquisition for a period of several years is a most crucial point to be made and understood.

MEMBERSHIP PROSPECTS

The first step in membership acquisition is to decide to whom the membership promotion efforts should appeal. The best way to identify prospects is by looking at people who have already become members—current members. The easiest and most cost effective new members to be acquired will look, act, think, and behave like current members. Trying to convince people who are too different from existing members can be very expensive and have minimal results.

Developing an accurate member profile is achieved through a membership survey. Using an online membership survey, ages, incomes, household composition, and other important demographic information as well as lifestyle characteristics such as hobbies and leisure time activities of current members are pinpointed. Marketing efforts are most successful when directed at a group that very closely approximates the group of current members. A survey may also identify other, less obvious segments of members.

For example, one organization had already identified the wealthier population in its community as a primary segment of its membership. After surveying its membership, however, it came to realize that it had two other significant segments, retirees with significant free time to visit the institution, and families with children who belonged to the institution in order to use the free admission benefits for frequent family outings. This organization now had three distinct target populations to whom to target their membership promotional efforts.

To find an organization's membership prospects it is also important to determine the best "season" for the heaviest membership promotion. For outdoor venues in the north, that season may be spring or summer. For indoor venues, the season may be the academic year schedule—fall and winter. For alumni associations, the season may be graduation times and homecoming. Knowing when most people would naturally turn to the organization for advice, help, or the services it provides is the key.

MOTIVATIONS FOR BECOMING A MEMBER

Before deciding whom to target as a prospective member, it is important to be aware of people's motivation for becoming a member. The need for belonging and being part of groups is one motivation. But other conditions include the prospect's interest, experience, and ability to join. These are necessary ingredients for a person to even consider the invitation to become a member. The presence or absence of each of these factors should be considered when making membership acquisition targeting decisions.

Interest

Does a person have an interest in the organization that is promoting membership? Membership is unlikely if there is not some interest on some level. A person will not join a zoo if they have no interest in animals, or conservation efforts, or don't care to visit and stroll the grounds. However, if someone has even one of these interests, then he or she is a likely candidate.

Experience

People who have never been to a zoo are not likely to join. Once they have had this experience, they become likely candidates. On-site sales are a productive source of new members for some organizations, largely because if a person is visiting he or she has at least one of the necessary ingredients for membership—experience.

Ability

A person must have the financial wherewithal to be a likely candidate for membership. Usually, membership does not require a major financial commitment; however, for some, a $75 expenditure for a membership is not possible.

Therefore, it is necessary to target groups of likely members from pools of people with discretionary income.

VARIETY IN METHODS

How does an organization reach the group of prospects most likely to respond? A variety of methods is frequently used to reach various populations, including:

- Direct mail
- On-site sales
- Email campaigns
- Social media
- Mobile marketing
- Personal solicitation
- Member-get-a-member promotions
- Employee campaigns
- Brochure distribution
- Gift membership promotions
- Online membership sales
- Membership month
- Charter membership drives
- Advertising

Generally, the smaller the organization or institution, the more personalized the solicitation process can or may be, and such personalization often relies more heavily on volunteers than a larger program with a significant budget.

Also, generally speaking, the larger an institution or organization, the larger the budget and the greater the reliance on mass campaigns (e.g., direct mail) that are costly. These larger campaigns generate large numbers of members, whereas the personalized, one-on-one efforts undertaken by smaller institutions are less costly but garner fewer members. One set of circumstances is not better than the other, but there needs to be the realization that institution size, budget, availability and willingness of volunteers, and other resources make a great difference in the program design.

Regardless of acquisition methods or the size of the institution, diversity is the key. A membership program should not rely totally on one method of acquisition. Just as one would not commit his or her life savings to one form of investment, neither can an institution rely on a single source for new members. The more diverse the sources of acquisition, the more stability there will be in the number of new members.

As an example, one institution might employ the following methods of membership acquisition. (Each method is listed with the percentage of members attributed to that method.)

Direct mail	30 percent
On-site	45 percent
Gift memberships	5 percent
Email campaign	10 percent
Online	5 percent
Miscellaneous	5 percent

The importance of diversification of membership sources is that if one method is less successful than anticipated, other methods are in place and will, hopefully, make up for those that did not perform as well.

What becomes clear is the necessity to track the productivity of each membership source. In a direct mail campaign it is necessary to code responses by each list used so that the source of the new member is readily known and trackable. The same is true with the on-site methods, gift memberships, online advertising, email marketing, and other methods. If tracking or coding is not done, it is impossible to separate successful membership promotions from unsuccessful ones. With accurate tracking of each effort, it will then be possible to evaluate the financial viability of each separate source of membership, and thus make decisions based on what is most cost effective and what is not producing at an acceptable level.

BASIC METHODS

Examples of how some membership acquisition efforts work or have worked at other organizations is always helpful. It is important to realize that every organization is different, and the circumstances around an organization may be different. The membership manager may never know what will work for his or her program unless it is tested.

For large-scale acquisition efforts, there are three basic methods: direct mail, email, and on-site sales. All three can be used by any type of group, whether all volunteer or with paid staff. Direct mail in a small organization will be personal letters from board members to prospective members, email will involve including an offer to join in the e-newsletter and occasionally sending stand-alone membership promotions, and on-site sales will involve volunteers at an event encouraging the participants to become members. At a large organization, direct mail will include many thousands of letters, email will be highly sophisticated leveraging segmentation, marketing automation, and expanded email marketing, and paid professionals will staff the on-site sales effort.

Direct Mail

Direct mail is the most popular method of membership acquisition for most organizations. It is, or can be, an expensive method of acquisition that requires a minimum of $5,000 to $10,000 to initiate. In some cases, a budget of $100,000 or more is needed, depending on the size, sophistication, and frequency of the mailing.

Direct mail approaches a targeted group with a specific offer and a response device that allows the prospect to act upon the request to become a member. This offer can be targeted via list purchases that most closely replicate the type of person the institution seeks. Cost can range from approximately $0.40 per piece (not including postage) for a large mailing (50,000 or more), to $1.25 per piece for a small mailing (5,000 to 10,000). Typically response rates of 0.7 to 1.0 percent are considered acceptable. Response rates greater than that are always welcome, but are not to be expected unless it is a popular institution, an organization making an appeal for the first time, or the appeal is related to a very significant event—a major anniversary of an organization or a blockbuster exhibition. Acquisition mailing response rates less than 0.7 percent can occur if the institution is a non-visiting institution or has few tangible benefits.

Email

Email marketing is cost effective and can reap results quickly. In 2012, a survey of online consumers by ExactTarget found that 66 percent of people made a purchase as a result of an email marketing message.[1] Email works best in a supporting role, complementing direct mail, advertising, and on-site sales strategies.

At a minimum, organizations should be leveraging in-house ticket buyer lists, lapsed member lists, and other internal email list assets such as corporate partners, teachers, and events for membership acquisition. Membership offers should be regularly featured in institutional e-newsletters and other communications to visitors and ticket buyers, and it is recommended to send a quarterly stand-alone membership acquisition email to the entire in-house email list. Because of its importance as an acquisition channel, every effort should be made to capture email addresses for visitors, ticket buyers, and social media followers. Other acquisition opportunities include sponsored email marketing to non-owned lists such as subscriber lists for a local mommy blog or a nature magazine.

In addition, there is an opportunity to supplement in-house lists with expanded email lists that mirror the demographics and lifestyle of the current member base. Such expanded lists are composed of people who have opted in via a third party to receive special offers and promotions that would be of interest to them. These expanded email lists are similar to rented mail lists in that the organization does not physically possess or send to the list directly from its in-house email system. Rather, the email campaign is executed entirely by a third party.

It is critical that organizations comply with the requirements of the 2003 CAN-SPAM Act, including a working unsubscribe mechanism and a valid opt-in process. The process of keeping an email list up to date and "clean" is time consuming and must be tended to on a regular basis. This includes scrubbing lists for hard bounces, updating records with new email addresses, and continually collecting new emails to account for list churn. Due to inactive email accounts, unsubscribes, hard bounces, and spam complaints, annual list churn can average between 10 to 50 percent per year,[2] which means an organization's email subscriber list can quickly become obsolete if there is not an effort to keep the list up to date. List churn can have a major impact on the deliverability of an organization's email marketing. The Internet Service Providers (ISPs) that monitor the number of undeliverable emails sent by an organization will redirect all emails into every recipient's spam folder if there is a high number of bad email addresses. In the worst-case scenario, an organization can be blacklisted from sending any emails.

Another consideration for email marketing is that mobile readership accounts for 66 percent and is continuing to increase.[3] Thus, organizations must ensure their emails are mobile-friendly and that all links are redirected to mobile optimized web pages.

On-Site Sales

For organizations with a place to visit, on-site membership acquisition is an opportunity to reach prospective members with few out-of-pocket costs.

If paid staff are used there is the cost of staff time, and, in all cases, there will be some cost for materials. This form of acquisition is even less expensive if volunteers staff a membership desk. This type of membership solicitation captures visitors who have already experienced some of the benefits the organization may be offering through membership. For an organization with a visitation-based membership, this form of membership acquisition is essential. This form of membership solicitation is enviable in that it is the most personal and the least expensive.

On-site sales can be conducted in many ways, ranging from a low-cost, volunteer-run program to one implemented with a professionally staffed sales force, whether with an in-house or outsourced sales team.

Volunteer Driven

This type of on-site sales program is virtually 100 percent pure profit. It requires, however, adequate staff time to organize and manage. A core group of dedicated volunteers is necessary on an ongoing, long-term basis. Essentially, this group of volunteers commits to selling memberships year-round, at high traffic times and at events selected by membership staff. For instance, staffing will probably be required every weekend, and at other busy times when key periods during the day must be covered. The volunteers should work at a desk or in the lobby or entry area, at a position where they can influence visitors before their approach to the admissions desk or ticket counter. The volunteers must be well trained, personable, and willing to sell.

The benefits of such an arrangement with a volunteer sales staff are many. First, the cost is extremely low—virtually nothing more than the cost of the brochures they distribute. A volunteer force is usually one of the organization's best ambassadors, or they would not be so enthusiastic about volunteering. This type of volunteer assignment is usually very rewarding—there is contact with the public, an opportunity to sell an organization that they care a lot about, and quantifiable results. At the end of the day, week, or year, the organization will know exactly how many memberships and dollars the group generated.

The downside of a volunteer operation is that staffing may be an arduous and difficult. This endeavor will require volunteers to give up some of the best hours in their schedules—weekends. Few people will want to dedicate a whole day to this task, so it may be necessary to fill several shifts per day. The management of a volunteer pool of the size necessary to cover all the hours needed on an annual basis may be a significant portion of a manager's job.

Associations are prime examples of membership organizations that rely on volunteers to run chapters across the country. Chapters are usually volunteer driven, yet supported by the national organization's staff. Chapter volunteers have a dual role of finding new members while also providing the connections and the content at monthly meetings that keep people engaged and excited about the organization. With the increasing demands on people's personal time, in some cases it has become increasingly difficult to find local leadership that can do all that is expected; more may need to be done from a national office to attract new members in less intensive, personal one-to-one ways. For more information and resources regarding volunteers, visit www.themembershipbook.com.

Staff Driven

In many organizations, such a committed group of volunteers as described above is not a possibility. Therefore, it is necessary to use either existing staff or special membership sales staff to transact membership sales on-site.

Paid staff that has other duties can conduct membership sales. Admissions desk or gift shop staff may also be asked to sell memberships. These staff members are already in contact with the visiting public, so it makes sense that they may also be able to suggest the purchase of a membership. Many times, the mere suggestion of membership is all that is needed. The word membership should roll off the lips of any front-line person. Compare this with shopping at an upscale department store. If you are about to make a significant purchase and not using the house credit card, you will be asked to apply for a credit card and receive 10 percent off your purchase immediately. Organizations can be just as opportunistic. Everywhere we go, people we meet are upselling us on whatever we are buying or doing, and membership can be sold and upsold, too.

Professional Staffing

If neither of the aforementioned two options is a possibility or a huge event is approaching and an organization knows it cannot handle the volume of visitors (prospective members), then professional membership on-site salespeople should be considered. These are people who have been professionally trained to sell memberships and who are then trained to be knowledgeable about the institution they will be promoting. They are usually contracted to sell on behalf of the organization for a specific event (grand opening or signature event) or for an entire run of a special exhibition or expected high traffic period. This type of sales staff can complement an organization's standard on-site sales staff and activities throughout the year.

At a major aquarium, the membership program is robust and successful with approximately 70,000 members. The aquarium has highly trained visitor experience staff to work the admissions desk. The responsive staff and streamlined layout of the box office allows for a high volume of visitor traffic to flow efficiently into the aquarium. That flow, however, was not conducive for membership sales. The entry process was so streamlined that there was not time to have a conversation about the possibility of a membership purchase. The aquarium had on-site sales specialists analyze their entry process with secret shoppers and a site evaluation. The result of the analysis was to add salespeople on the entry plaza as visitors approached, and before they went through the regular visitor lines. Outsourced professional on-site salespeople managed this intercept process. The professional sales team demonstrated how the sales process could work and modeled the selling techniques. For several years the team has returned during the highest traffic times to maximize membership sales for the aquarium. The results included more than five membership sales per person per hour, almost 10,000 memberships sold over a 107-day period with and average sale of $184 (see table 6.1).

Another on-site success story is the St. Louis County Library Foundation. The library foundation hosts one of the most popular library author programs in the country. Popular authors participate in lectures and discussions of their books at events at the library headquarters. These events are attended by 200 to 500 people. Foundation staff realized that these involved library patrons were wonderful prospects for the library's friends support group. People line up for an hour or more before the event to get a seat at the author chat. The foundation staff wrapped some special benefits and privileges—preferred seating, a line ticket for an autograph, and even a book—as a benefit of joining the friends at the event. Professional outsourced sales staff work the lines before the doors open, selling ten to fifty-plus memberships before each event, depending on the size of the crowd and the draw of the author.

Table 6.1 Aquarium On-Site Sales History

2012	Memberships Sold	Revenue Raised	Number of Days	Average Sales per Hour	Average Gift Amount	Conversion Rate	Cost per Dollar Raised	Return on Investment
JUL 2012	353	$67,360	5	3.82	$190.82	1.09%	$0.41	$2.42
NOV 2012	179	$34,635	4	2.49	$193.49	1.59%	$1.01	$0.99
2012 Totals	**532**	**$101,995**	**9**	**3.23**	**$191.72**	**1.22%**	**$0.62**	**$1.62**

2013	Memberships Sold	Revenue Raised	Number of Days	Average Sales per Hour	Average Gift Amount	Conversion Rate	Cost per Dollar Raised	Return on Investment
FEB 2013	384	$66,215	4	5.51	$172.43	1.90%	$0.61	$1.65
MAR 2013	702	$130,605	10	3.94	$186.05	1.37%	$0.31	$3.25
MAY 2013	608	$111,515	10	3.38	$183.41	1.58%	$0.36	$2.78
JUL 2013	858	$162,540	10	4.52	$189.44	1.40%	$0.25	$4.05
AUG 2013	893	$169,290	10	5.15	$189.57	1.29%	$0.24	$4.21
SEPT 2013	441	$76,145	4	6.26	$172.66	1.78%	$0.53	$1.90
NOV 2013	223	$41,030	3	4.07	$183.99	1.86%	$0.98	$1.02
2013 Totals	**4,109**	**$757,340**	**51**	**4.49**	**$184.31**	**1.48%**	**$0.37**	**$2.69**

2014	Memberships Sold	Revenue Raised	Number of Days	Average Sales per Hour	Average Gift Amount	Conversion Rate	Cost per Dollar Raised	Return on Investment
FEB 2014	560	$100,110	4	9.66	$178.77	2.97%	$0.39	$2.57
MAR 2014	774	$133,205	9	5.35	$172.10	2.44%	$0.29	$3.43
APR 2014	1,024	$188,250	9	6.23	$183.84	2.25%	$0.21	$4.84
MAY 2014	482	$86,565	4	6.54	$179.60	2.48%	$0.45	$2.23
JUL 2014	556	$105,540	5	5.99	$189.82	1.89%	$0.37	$2.71
AUG 2014	532	$100,655	5	5.57	$189.20	1.83%	$0.39	$2.59
OCT 2014	219	$39,090	3	3.81	$178.49	1.83%	$0.99	$1.01
2014 Totals	**4,147**	**$753,415**	**39**	**6.04**	**$181.68**	**2.23%**	**$0.36**	**$2.77**

2015	Memberships Sold	Revenue Raised	Number of Days	Average Sales per Hour	Average Gift Amount	Conversion Rate	Cost per Dollar Raised	Return on Investment
MAR 2015	972	$185,720	8	6.75	$191.07	2.31%	$0.18	$5.61

	Memberships Sold	Revenue Raised	Number of Days	Average Sales per Hour	Average Gift Amount	Conversion Rate	Cost per Dollar Raised	Return on Investment
Total Cumulative	**9,760**	**$1,798,470**	**107**	**5.11**	**$184.27**	**1.78%**	**$0.36**	**$2.77**

In this way, the outsourced sales staff and in-house membership staff complement each other by relying on each other's strengths. Once the salesperson closes the sale, the person joining is escorted to the membership desk for staff processing. While the staff is making sure the form is filled out correctly, processing payment, and issuing the premium and/or free admission ticket, the salesperson is approaching more visitors. The goal of the salespeople is to talk to as many people as possible and staff helps them do this by handling the financial transaction and fulfillment.

At times, with long lines of people waiting to enter the venue or to make purchases, a membership sale by admission staff may not be possible. At these times, it is necessary to have a membership desk or table at which to handle membership sales. This desk or table needs to be staffed with people who solely sell and fulfill membership purchases. If volunteers are not available, then a paid staff person should be at this station. It may be possible to hire part-time workers to fill these types of positions. The revenues generated by membership sales should more than cover the cost to staff this position. If that is not the case, then the person may not have the sales skills necessary or the station is not being staffed at the best times to take advantage of high visitation.

Compensation may affect the productivity of the sales staff. Cash is the biggest motivator. A sales incentive program where salespeople are paid for each membership sold can produce the best results. If an organization does not allow such compensation, the reason for not doing so needs to be questioned. In some cases, public institutions do not allow for any type of incentive plan. Regardless, some form of incentive needs to be provided to motivate sales. Use gift dollars in the gift shop, coupons for movies or restaurants, or pizza parties to reward the admissions desk sales staff if they have a particularly productive month or weekend—whatever works.

Positioning the membership salespeople is key. Membership salespeople must be the first people the visitors encounter when entering. The professional salespeople have clipboards containing applications, newsletters, and brochures in hand and approach the visitors, asking them to consider joining. They are on their feet, not sitting behind a desk. The membership sales pitch, highlighting all of the benefits of membership, and perhaps an incentive for joining that day, is direct. The results are significant: A well-trained salesperson who is eager to sell will be able to achieve a 2 to 4 percent conversion rate of visitors to members.

Regardless of who is selling memberships, the necessary tools are the same. First, there is signage. It is important for the group's sales efforts to be supported by strategically placed signage. "Join here" or "Become a member and enter free" point the visitor in the right direction and indicate to them what is going on that day. Signage at the admissions desk might read "Join now, save $$$ in admission." At the point of sale in a gift shop the sign might read, "Join now. Members receive 20 percent discount!" Salespeople or circulation desk personnel might also wear buttons or t-shirts that say "Ask me about membership." Whatever the message, it should help make the sale by drawing attention to the possibilities of membership.

Sales tracking should include the person selling, the time, and the day. Knowing that one salesperson has a better track record then another, or that the 10:00 a.m. to noon period is the most productive, will enhance future sales at similar events. Sales can also be tracked by new, renewal, or gift membership. On-site sales, just like direct mail, can become a science if the proper tracking and analysis takes place. A sample on-site sales report is shown in exhibit 6.1.

OTHER MEMBERSHIP PROMOTIONS

Other membership promotions such as charter memberships, member-get-a-member drives, and referrals from current members are a sampling of creative ways to encourage membership. Programs such as these can be designed with an organization's capacity in mind. Creative campaigns have included rewarding the person bringing in the largest number of memberships or offering a special benefit to any person bringing in multiple memberships. These promotions can be designed cost effectively.

Social Media and Mobile Marketing

Social media, Short Message Service (SMS) texting, and mobile apps with push notifications are becoming preferred communications channels for many consumers, especially among younger generations. Social media and mobile marketing campaigns can be used to create a path to membership by collecting one-to-one contact information, including email and mailing address. Opportunities to leverage social media and mobile for membership acquisition include mission-aligned contests, text-to-win promotions, and crowdfunding campaigns. Often, these kinds of fun, engaging, and mission-oriented campaigns

Friday	FamilyPlus	Family	Individual	Senior	Student	Total Sales	Total Sales Hours	Sales per Hour	Revenues	Average Gift
	$150	**$115**	**$75**	**$75**	**$75**					
Laura	5	20	20	0	3	48	5.5	8.73	$4,775.00	$99.48
Dave	7	20	5	2	1	35	5	7.00	$3,950.00	$112.86
Fran	7	26	19	0	0	52	5	10.40	$5,465.00	$105.10
					Total	**135**	**15.5**	**8.71**	**$14,190.00**	**$105.81**

Saturday	FamilyPlus	Family	Individual	Senior	Student	Total Sales	Total Sales Hours	Sales per Hour	Revenues	Average Gift
	$150	**$115**	**$75**	**$75**	**$75**					
Laura	5	16	9	0	8	38	5.5	6.91	$3,865.00	$101.71
Dave	11	11	7	4	0	33	5	6.60	$3,740.00	$113.33
Fran	0	29	22	0	2	53	5	10.60	$5,135.00	$96.89
					Total	**124**	**15.5**	**8.00**	**$12,740.00**	**$103.98**

Sunday	FamilyPlus	Family	Individual	Senior	Student	Total Sales	Total Sales Hours	Sales per Hour	Revenues	Average Gift
	$150	**$115**	**$75**	**$75**	**$75**					
Laura	3	8	10	1	4	26	5.5	4.73	$2,495.00	$95.96
Dave	5	10	6	1	3	25	5	5.00	$2,650.00	$106.00
Fran	8	13	7	1	1	30	5	6.00	$3,370.00	$112.33
					Total	**81**	**15.5**	**5.23**	**$8,515.00**	**$104.76**

TOTALS	*FamilyPlus*	*Family*	*Individual*	*Senior*	*Student*	*Total Sales*	*Total Sales Hours*	*Sales per Hour*	*Revenues*	*Average Gift*
Laura	13	44	39	1	15	112	16.5	6.8	$11,135.00	$99.05
Dave	23	41	18	7	4	93	15	6.2	$10,340.00	$110.73
Fran	15	68	48	1	3	135	15	9.0	$13,970.00	$104.77
Grand Total	***51***	***153***	***105***	***9***	***22***	***340***	***46.5***	***7.3***	***$35,445.00***	***$104.85***

EXHIBIT 6.1
Sample On-Site Sales Report

can serve as a way to raise visibility quickly and reach a new pool of qualified prospects. Organizations with an institutional mobile app should be sure to include acquisition messaging, special members-only features, and, if possible, an easy way for users to join directly via the app.

Personal Solicitation

Particularly in new or small organizations, personal solicitation of memberships is a good way to acquire members. Some members will ask friends and colleagues to join a group in which the member believes the friend might be interested. This may be as simple a process as an email, a phone call, or a letter. Or it may be more elaborate with a member willing to hold an event such as a luncheon and invite potential members. The organization has the opportunity to tell its story and enroll the interested guests. This format can also be used at civic group meetings where one of the institution's members is willing to invite someone from the organization to speak. This is very much a one-on-one solicitation.

It is up to the membership manager to make certain that the solicitations are happening. Because this is time consuming, though inexpensive, this type of acquisition is often used for acquiring support members rather than value members.

Member-Get-A-Member Campaign

Member-get-a-member campaigns have been run with varying degrees of success by many organizations. The key question is, how much effort will current members extend to recruit a new member? In some cases, a member may go to great lengths to help enlist a new member (e.g., an alumnus taking a fellow alumnus friend to dinner to solicit him for membership). In other cases, a member may only be mildly committed to helping an organization expand its membership program.

One organization devised an elaborate membership sales competition with a sizable reward for the winner. The organization was known for its foreign travel programs. The incentive for the winner of the member-get-a-member campaign was a free European trip. Luckily, at least one member took this challenge very seriously and sold more than 100 memberships to win the prize. The next highest member, however, sold only five memberships. If the winner had not worked so diligently to sell memberships, this campaign would not have been a success.

Another model for a member-get-a member campaign involves direct mail to existing members. The campaign was designed to reward each member who found at least one member to join. The mailing was designed around an oversized post card with a rallying message on one side, "Your friends belong at the Zoo"; the postcard had a mail panel and explanation of the offer and a response mechanism on the reverse. Both the existing member and the new member are offered a premium if the new person joins. It is easily trackable—the existing member's name and member number are in the address section, and the new member fills out the form on the same side of the post card.

A similar type of campaign could be conducted online leveraging a combination of email marketing and a customized online join page. In this case, existing members would receive an email invitation to share with friends and family that includes a unique identifying code tied to each member. The member can then send the invitation out to friends via email, a post on Facebook, or even a text message. The online form should include a field for the new member to enter the code to attribute sales back to the member.

Yet another form of a member-get-a-member campaign was conducted for years in a southern art museum. The promotion began when the museum itself was in its infancy. This volunteer effort involved training volunteers in the details of membership, motivating them, and sending them out to sell memberships to their friends, neighbors, and business associates. Originally, the campaign was designed to sell new memberships, and it was quite successful, selling hundreds of memberships. Over time, however, with not much change in the membership of the volunteer group, it became a renewal effort, since a person's sphere of contacts does not change much from year to year.

A similar effort has been the mainstay of the membership program at the Henry Doorly Zoo and Aquarium in Omaha for many years. The campaign presents itself similarly to campaigns initiated by the United Way. Volunteers from all major employers in the area are recruited, trained, and entertained, and then they sell in their workplaces. It is a very labor-intensive effort, but it is so successful that little direct mail is required for renewals, and none is required for acquisition. The zoo has more than 90,000 members.

Employee Campaign

Another type of membership promotion that is similar to member-get-a-member promotions is an employee membership sales contest. It should be time limited, conducted in conjunction with Membership Month, structured with prizes for the most sales overall by department, and presented as an enjoyable way for all staff to help promote the institution for which they work.

At the Saint Louis Zoo a very successful staff membership sales incentive program was designed and implemented. Donated prizes were collected. A television was the grand prize. Gift certificates to stores and restaurants were departmental prizes. The program was designed so that everyone working at the zoo, including volunteers, could participate. One of the unexpected by-products of the program was a better understanding of the importance of the membership program by all staff.

To launch the program, the membership manager attended all department staff meetings, explaining the membership program and the reason for the contest. As a result, staff gained a greater appreciation for the membership program and the role it plays in supporting the Zoo. The primary concern as the program was being launched was that the front-line staff would have an unfair advantage of selling to the public. In the end, the person who won the contest was a person who worked in Receiving in the warehouse. She asked vendors who made deliveries to the warehouse if their companies were members. They were, after all, selling their wares to the zoo.

BROCHURE DISTRIBUTION

Distributing membership brochures via welcome wagons, point-of-purchase displays, on-site, and as billing statement stuffers or enclosures in utility bills are yet other ways to spread the word about membership opportunities and give people a way to join a membership program. The success of these programs can be calculated by the number of responses received from these promotions via coded response forms. The cost of printing is often the only cost involved in these methods, since the organization is not responsible for distributing the brochures or flyers. An important note: the per-piece cost of the membership brochure should be inexpensive enough to distribute widely.

One organization used statement stuffers to announce and promote its newly constructed attraction. The Aquarium of the Pacific in Long Beach attracted nearly 60,000 members without incurring the expense of a direct mail campaign. The city-owned utility company allowed the aquarium to include a membership application in its regularly scheduled electricity bill mailing to residents on several occasions—and the memberships flowed in. The same phenomenon occurred at Colorado's Ocean Journey in Denver. Statement stuffers and free publicity about the aquarium's opening on radio stations allowed the aquarium to open with more than 40,000 members and with virtually no cash outlay to acquire those members. New attractions have an amazing capacity to leverage the pent-up interest in a new venue to benefit of membership.

GIFT MEMBERSHIP PROMOTIONS

Gift membership solicitation relies on a third party to purchase a membership as a gift for someone else. Membership promotions revolving around gift-giving opportunities can be designed around a variety of occasions. Appropriate times might include the winter holiday season, birthdays, Valentine's Day, Mother's or Father's Day, as well as others.

Gift memberships can be promoted via direct mail and email to the current membership file, marketed online via the institution's website or Facebook page, or by advertising in print ads in publications, out-of-home ads (e.g., mall advertising), or TV ads. These promotions are considered successful if they are operated on a break-even basis when including postage, printing, artwork, cost of media, etc. In general, the people most likely to give membership as a gift are those who have already joined the organization. They are aware of the benefits of membership and the enjoyment that results from using it. Thus, most of the promotion for gift memberships needs to be directed at this already committed audience.

Gift memberships to cultural organizations can be promoted as a great family gift—something for everyone in the family regardless of age, size, or makeup. Memberships to professional organizations might be a nice gift to a professional starting out in her field, given by a person in a mentoring position. A gift of a membership to an alumni organization might be a great graduation gift.

The Museum of Science, Boston implemented a multichannel gift membership campaign during the holiday season. The campaign included a mix of online and offline marketing components, including email, Facebook advertising, a postcard, on-site signage, online display and pay-per-click advertising, website promotion and retargeting, and a blogger giveaway.

The campaign used a series of offer-specific landing pages hosted on the subdomain of the primary website (membership.mos.org) to optimize click-through conversions and improve measurement. Importantly, a key goal of the campaign was to test a set of messaging and offers to determine which would be most compelling, such as experiential messaging versus convenience messaging and 20 percent off versus $25 off. A complete case study of the Museum of Science, Boston holiday gift campaign concludes this chapter.

It is advantageous to consider a tangible gift in addition to the membership itself, so that an actual gift that represents the membership can be physically presented to the recipient. A coffee mug, a tote bag, or something that relates to the institution or the occasion being celebrated can be used. For Father's Day, car wash coupons can accompany the gift membership. On Valentine's Day a single red rose would be appropriately delivered with a heart-shaped membership packet. For a holiday gift membership, an ornament or a packet of writing cards with a scene from the organization might be given. For Mother's Day, a wind chime might be the tangible gift.

The first and second renewal notices for membership gifts are usually sent to the gift giver. Subsequent notices are then sent to the members themselves. Typically, the renewal rate for gift memberships is about 50 percent.

ONLINE MEMBERSHIP SALES

Today, the web plays an integral role in the acquisition of new members. For many organizations, the volume of membership sales attributed to online sales will be dependent on how computer and Internet savvy its target population is. The key, however, is to have a strong online presence, including a user-friendly website capable of processing secure online transactions and a social media strategy that incorporates membership messaging. Membership should be prominently promoted on the homepage and throughout the website and the site should be included in printed membership materials to encourage joining online.

In the coming years, the number and percentage of members joining online will continue to increase, and organizations should be actively promoting the ability for new members to join online. Indeed, many prospects will be prompted to join via direct mail, but will elect to purchase their membership online. The National Baseball Hall of Fame and Museum acquires about 20 percent of its new members online. For others the percentages are small, yet growing every month or year.

The Metropolitan Museum of Art has one of the leading membership websites among cultural organizations. Not only can a member join or renew online, but there is a special Net Met Membership where benefits are delivered online—a digital newsletter, a screen saver membership premium, a virtual tour of the collection, and special access to member-only areas of the website.

One of the greatest membership potentials of the web is that it exposes an organization to an immense universe of prospective members worldwide. An organization that does not have the budget to market its program via traditional offline channels can attract national or international members by offering something of value online. Online benefits could include exclusive access to digitally housed information, an "Ask the Expert" feature via an online forum, discounted shopping at the online store, or behind-the-scenes updates delivered via email on the latest discovery, acquisition, or breakthrough research. Members can also be cultivated and engaged by participating in social media, online surveys, and interactive features on the website. This medium may also make traditional institutions available in a totally new light to a younger, more connected population than organizations have appealed to in the past.

Importantly, organizations need to be prepared to meet the expectations of younger generations and tech-savvy consumers including ensuring that the website and e-commerce pages are user friendly and optimized for mobile devices. If an organization is not able to support an easy-to-use, mobile-optimized transaction process as part of the primary website, then a third-party solution should be considered. Additionally, organizations should evaluate opportunities for suggestive selling and abandoned cart strategies, such as automatically triggered emails, during the online sales process. Without these e-commerce functions, there is a risk of lost sales.

MEMBERSHIP MONTH

Membership never seems to get the attention it deserves—internally or externally. One way to change that situation, at least for one month out of the year, is by hosting Membership Month. Pick a high traffic time during the year and designate it "Membership Month." To add excitement to the month, schedule special entertainment on weekends, create big "Membership Month" banners, invite radio stations to do live remote broadcasts where they have on-air contests and give away free memberships as prizes, and invite people to come to the venue and become a member. Other events such as a membership appreciation night can take place during this month. Perhaps an already scheduled direct mail campaign can be moved to this month. An employee sales incentive contest can take place during Membership Month. Suddenly, there is an event that can be pitched to local news outlets for earned media. Maybe a local newspaper's business section would be interested in writing an article on the business of membership in the area—with your program as the lead, of course.

CHARTER MEMBERSHIP OPPORTUNITIES

For new organizations, or organizations with new beginnings, a charter membership program may be in order. A charter membership program is one in which the original group of members will receive special designation and forever be remembered as the founding mothers and fathers of an organization. The key is to impress upon people that to remain a charter member, they must keep their membership intact year after year, without lapse. Charter members may sign on at an increased monetary level, should get memorabilia that connotes their status, and should be reminded of their status at all future fundraising times. This group has the potential of being a loyal group of supporters for many years to come if properly treated.

ADVERTISING

Generally, it is not recommended to use awareness building advertising as a stand-alone strategy to market membership. There are two reasons: First, advertising is very expensive and second, it is not targeted enough. If the marketing department has a budget for advertising to drive attendance, collaborate on a theme and have the advertising support the direct mail acquisition campaigns. This is usually done quite well when museums are sponsoring a major exhibition and the entire organization works together to plan the opening, including media buys, free publicity, and membership direct mail and email campaigns. Also, many zoos and gardens coordinate their spring attendance push and membership drives with each form of media—direct mail, online advertising, email, and print ads—supporting one another.

In recent years, the old "no advertising" rule for membership has been turned upside down by the ability for highly targeted advertising opportunities now possible via social and digital media. For example, Facebook's ad platform allows for in-depth targeting based on demographics, lifestyle, interests, and offline buying behavior as well as targeting based on an organization's in-house email and lapsed member lists. Other opportunities include leveraging a cookie-based technology that allows an organization to serve tailored advertising to website visitors based on the content they view and behavioral advertising that uses an individual's browsing history to deliver targeted ads. This targeting capability adds a new level of sophistication to reaching prospective members with online marketing.

What usually does not work for membership is broad-based image or "awareness" advertising (billboards, for example). This type of advertising is not targeted, nor is the impact measurable. For most organizations, the exception to this rule would be advertising specific gift membership in targeted publications. This would include an ad in a business journal around the holidays when businesses are buying gifts for clients or employees, or placing an ad in a local newspaper for a Valentine's Day gift membership promotion. Another possibility might be to advertise through a service such as Welcome Wagon or other groups that welcome new residents in town.

Many organizations do not have large enough budgets to support a sustained advertising campaign. However, even organizations with very limited budgets could benefit from a discrete, targeted investment in advertising. For example, a small library might collaborate with a local parents' magazine to negotiate an advertising agreement that includes a set of online banner ads, promoted email blasts to readers, and a targeted social media ad. For large national and international organizations such as AARP and the World Wildlife Fund, advertising may be the best way to reach many more people than by any other means. Regardless of the budget, to be effective, advertising needs to be professionally designed and well placed. It needs to be in print, radio, TV, and digital media where qualified prospective members may see or hear it. Market research is the primary way to discover what current members read and the how they spend their time online. Advertising placed without the research beforehand puts significant funds at risk.

When advertising is used for membership acquisition, it is important to include tracking codes or "pixels" as well as unique landing page URLs and customized promotional codes in order to measure the impact of the campaign by channel.

MEASURING ACQUISITION SUCCESS

The success and productivity of each type of membership acquisition can be measured in both immediate and long-range terms. As mentioned earlier, membership acquisition on a break-even basis the first year is successful. In his book *Fund Raising*, James Greenfield notes that when acquiring new members or donors, it may be necessary to spend $1.25 to $1.50 for every dollar raised.[4] The profitability in membership acquisition comes in succeeding years with membership renewal monies. In calculating succeeding year incomes, memberships from any method should be income producers by the second or third renewal year and should produce a surplus in revenues when considered over a five-year basis. To determine this kind of multi-year success evaluation, it is necessary to determine renewal rates by sources each year. Careful coding and attention to detail is a necessity and it is important to know how each source produces over time to evaluate fully its success or failure as an acquisition method.

To calculate membership income over time, follow the mathematical process as shown in exhibit 6.2.

This equation can be extended as many years into the future as necessary. Also, if only the overall renewal rate is known, that rate can be used. In the example illustrated above, a per membership acquisition cost of $75 could be justified, but an acquisition cost of $150 or more could not, since it would take four years to recoup the cost to acquire the member. In general, the cost to acquire a member should be recouped in year two.

Membership acquisition will probably be the largest single line item in a membership budget. It will most likely outpace the salary line item. And the membership manager's job may be in jeopardy if the acquisition line item doesn't produce expected results. That is why understanding that the true cost of acquisition is vitally important and that it will most likely cost more to acquire a member than that member produces in the first year. It is the membership

Membership dues rate year one		$75.00
+ (Dues *x* 1st year renewal rate – 40% in this case)	+ ($75 *x* 0.4)	$30.00
+ (Dues *x* 1st year renewal rate *x* 2nd year renewal rate)	+ ($75 *x* 0.4 *x* 0.60)	$18.00
+ (Dues *x* 1st year renewal rate *x* 2nd year renewal rate *x* 3rd year renewal rate)	+ ($75 *x* 0.4 *x* 0.60 *x* 0.70)	$12.60
+ (Dues *x* 1st year renewal rate *x* 2nd year renewal rate *x* 3rd year renewal rate *x* 4th year renewal rate)	+ ($75 *x* 0.4 *x* 0.60 *x* 0.70 *x* 0.85)	$10.71
	Total	**$146.31**

EXHIBIT 6.2
Five-Year Income from a Member

manager's job to get everyone else at the organization to understand this as well. Overall membership will decline if too few new members are attracted on an annual basis. As mentioned previously, the acquisition of new members is perhaps the most important function of a membership manager.

The keys to acquisition are to be creative, cost effective, and yet confident enough so that membership growth can occur. The following are key metrics in membership acquisition:

- Response Rate: Number mailed divided by the number of responses (e.g., mailed 5,000 divided by 50 responses = 1.0 percent response rate).
- Average Gift: The average of all gifts received (e.g., $5,000 in donations divided by a total of 50 gifts = $100 average gift).
- Cost Per Dollar Raised (CPDR): The cost to raise $1 in donations. Divide the total cost of the campaign by the total amount raised (e.g., cost of $4,000 divided by $5,000 = $0.80 cost per dollar raised).
- Cost Per Response (CPR): The cost of generating each response. Divide the cost of the campaign by the number of responses (e.g., $4,000 cost of campaign divide by 50 responses = $80 cost per response).
- Return on Investment (ROI): The return on the money invested in a campaign or the amount that will be returned to the organization for every dollar spent. Divide the total amount raised by the total amount spent (e.g., divide the $5,000 raised by the $4,000 spent = $1.25 ROI).
- Five-Year Income: What a campaign produces financially if the five-year life of a donor or member is taken into consideration. First, second, third, and fourth year renewal rates must be known and taken into consideration.

Which of these is most important? This depends on the organization and its strategy. If the organization is small and beginning a membership program, the most important issue is to develop a critical mass of members. For this group, the response rate will be most important since gaining members is the strategy. If the institution has a long history and many members, the five-year income projections may be most important. If the organization has mainly corporate board members who work with return on investment on a daily basis, this may be the most important number so that the board members understand the program. When budget is an issue, average gift becomes important and the basis for knowing whether an upgrade program is working or not.

Table 6.2 St. Louis County Library On-Site Membership Sales History—Membership Consultants Results for Memberships Sold

Year	Total Number Sold	Sales Revenue	Number of Hours	Cost Per Dollar Raised	Average Gift
2009	120	$8,100.00	22.75	$0.61	$67.50
2010	163	$8,592.00	43.00	$0.59	$52.71
2011	77	$5,230.00	24.00	$0.75	$67.92
2012	103	$7,450.00	27.00	$0.66	$72.33
2013	86	$6,425.00	22.00	$0.62	$74.71
2014	31	$2,320.00	12.00	$1.18	$74.84
Totals	**580**	**$38,117.00**	**150.75**	**$0.67**	**$65.72**

On-Site Sales History. St. Louis County Library Foundation.

Because of the many ways that the numbers can be figured and counted, it is important to decide ahead of time what is significant for the organization. When planning the program, determine the strategy, implement it, measure it, and then there can be an honest evaluation. Table 6.2 shows the on-site membership acquisition sales history of the St. Louis County Library.[5]

SUMMARY

There are boundless opportunities for acquiring new members, and diversification of membership sources is important to ensure sustainability of the program. The keys to successful acquisition are to use a blend of new and tried-and-true methods that can reach the target audience. The effectiveness of each method of acquisition should be measured for both immediate and long-term results. Understanding the true cost and expected return of acquisition is important as the profitability of such efforts comes in succeeding years from renewals.

CASE STUDY: MUSEUM OF SCIENCE, BOSTON

Seeking a new way to drive membership, the Museum of Science, Boston implemented a multichannel holiday gift membership campaign to generate exposure to new audiences online. With an already thriving gift membership program, the museum introduced several new acquisition channels, including email, Facebook, display advertising, website retargeting, and paid search as well as a blogger giveaway to boost visibility.[6] Exhibit 6.3 shows the gift membership campaign creative.

EXHIBIT 6.3

Museum of Science, Boston Holiday Gift Membership Campaign Creative
Source: Museum of Science, Boston

The campaign goals included:

- Acquiring new givers from untapped sources, specifically social media and online advertising;
- Evaluating the current gift membership program and identifying opportunities to increase revenues via acquisition, retention, upgrades, and multi-buy from current/past givers;
- Testing a set of messaging and offers; and
- Establishing a baseline for leveraging digital marketing channels for membership.

Holiday Gift Membership Campaign Results

The campaign was very successful, generating membership sales in previously slow periods and establishing a baseline for future campaigns (see exhibit 6.4). The campaign demonstrated a capacity for growth and a clear

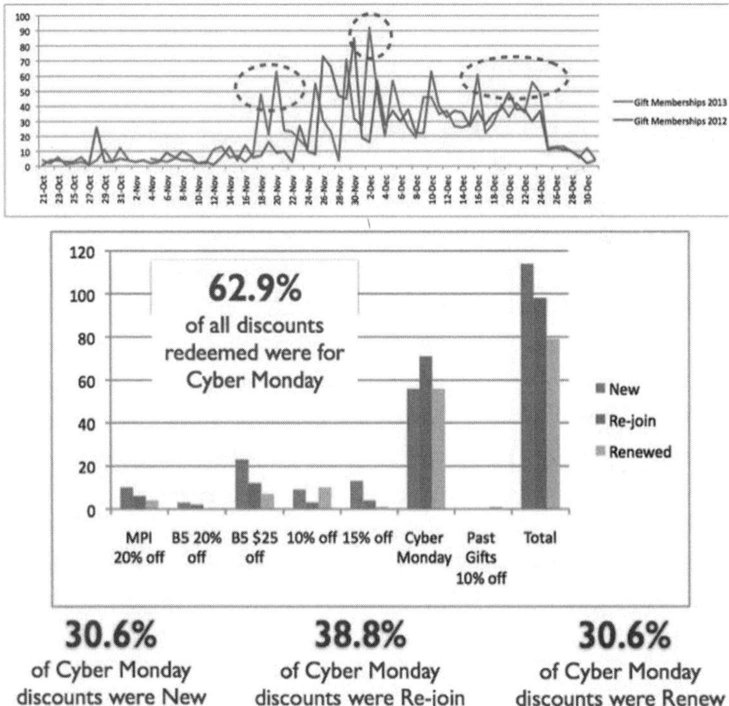

EXHIBIT 6.4

Museum of Science, Boston Holiday Gift Membership Campaign Results
Source: Museum of Science, Boston

opportunity to reach new audiences via digital channels. Additionally, the museum learned that experiential messaging is more compelling than convenience messaging for gift givers, and that a dollar off is more motivating than a percentage discount.

Leveraging Cyber Monday for the first time, the museum was able to reach new gift givers and increase gift membership sales by 9 percent overall. The museum saw a positive return on its investment resulting in a 17 percent increase in new gift memberships sold and a 25 percent increase in gift memberships sold online over the prior year.

EXHIBIT 6.5
Museum of Science, Boston Mother's Day and Father's Day Gift Membership Campaign Creative
Source: Museum of Science, Boston

Mother's Day and Father's Day

Building on the success of the holiday gift membership campaign, the museum decided to implement a second multichannel strategy to grow gift memberships during Mother's Day and Father's Day. This would be the first time that the museum had proactively marketed gift membership for these holidays.

The museum hosted a series of offer-specific landing pages on the subdomain membership.mos.org to increase click-through and maximize online conversions. Channels included email, Facebook, display advertising, website retargeting, and paid search. Applying the learnings of the holiday gift membership campaign, the museum emphasized experiential messaging and introduced new techniques to boost online gift membership sales. Exhibit 6.5 shows the creative for the Mother's Day and Father's Day gift campaigns.

Mother's Day and Father's Day Gift Membership Campaign Results

The campaign helped to raise awareness of the museum's brand and mission, keeping the museum top of mind as a unique and thoughtful gift idea. The campaign successfully created a path to membership, increasing online gift membership revenues by 63 percent over the prior year and driving a 53 percent increase in the number of gift membership sold (see exhibit 6.6).[7]

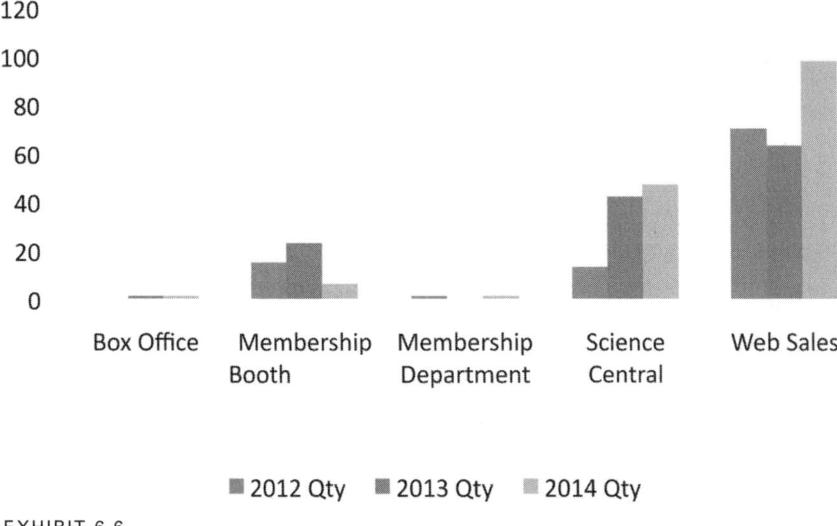

EXHIBIT 6.6
Museum of Science, Boston Mother's Day and Father's Day Gift Membership Campaign Results
Source: Museum of Science, Boston

NOTES

1. Jeffrey K. Rohrs, "Channel Preferences Survey," *ExactTarget*, February 2012, 17, accessed October 12, 2014, http://image.exct.net/lib/fe641570776d02757515/m/1/SFF14-The2012ChannelPreferenceSurvey.pdf.

2. Loren McDonald, "Revisiting Email Address Churn," *Email Insider*, April 3, 2014, accessed December 2, 2014, http://www.mediapost.com/publications/article/222904/revisiting-email-address-churn.html.

3. Greg Sterling, "Mobile Devices Drive 66 Percent of Email Opens—Report," *Marketing Land*, May 9, 2014, accessed December 2, 2014, http://marketingland.com/34-percent-email-opens-now-happen-pc-83277.

4. James M. Greenfield, *Fund Raising*, 2nd ed. (New York: Wiley, 1999), 119.

5. Membership Consultants, Inc., "St. Louis County Library Foundation On-Site Membership Sales History," 2014.

6. Membership Consultants, Inc. and FIVESEED, LLC, "Case Study: Museum of Science, Boston," 2014.

7. Ibid.

7

Membership Retention and Renewals

It's like déjà vu all over again.

—*Yogi Berra, Hall of Fame catcher for the New York Yankees*

RENEWALS: THE BACKBONE

Membership renewals are very much like "déjà vu all over again." Once the organization has found the right renewal combination, the renewal process is repeated over and over and over again. The key is finding what works best for the members, the organization, and the staff structure.

Renewals are the backbone of the membership program. It is much less costly to retain a member than to acquire a new member. It costs pennies on the dollar to renew a member, but it may cost the entire amount of the membership dues, or more, to acquire a new member. According to customer satisfaction researchers, it will cost five to fifteen times more to acquire a new member than to keep a current one.[1] If membership growth is a priority, then membership renewals at a fairly high and consistent rate are essential. For every member who does not renew, a new member must be acquired to replace him or her, just to stay even, and two members have to be acquired to grow.

The successful membership renewal process is a combination of motivation and mechanics—motivating people to renew their memberships and employing the mechanics needed for the membership to be renewed.

RETENTION

The ability to retain the greatest number of members is the key to growth in membership. The process of retention is one that is ongoing, inherent in the management of the membership program, and is a direct result of the philosophy of the organization. Retention is the process of keeping members engaged, involved, and in a positive mindset with respect to the organization or the cause that they support. Such engagement is a result of the organization's treatment of the member, the organization's ability to deliver benefits successfully, and services at a level acceptable to the member. Retention is also dependent upon a member's judgment that an institution is remaining true to the mission to which the organization and the individual are committed.

The act of retaining members is a matter of keeping members satisfied, content, and pleased with their membership experience so that the member chooses to continue the membership relationship. Membership retention results when the cultivation of existing members has been a success. The ingredients of membership retention include quality customer service, successful stewardship, and a "member first" orientation on the part of membership staff. Membership retention is a yearlong process. It is the day-by-day process of responding to members' needs, anticipating those needs, dealing with members in a friendly, professional manner, and delivering a quality product that will translate into membership retention.

The member's decision whether to renew is dependent on myriad factors. A member subconsciously asks, "What was my membership experience like? Did I use my membership? Was I happy with my membership experience?" The issues of benefits, value, involvement, communication, and membership service provide answers to those questions that the members are asking themselves when deciding whether to renew.

BENEFITS AND VALUE

Efforts to renew a member begin the moment a person joins. Every experience that a member has during the membership year will help determine that member's likelihood of renewing his or her membership. The factors that influence a person's decision to renew include the benefits offered, their frequency of use, the number of visits to the institution, the treatment received during the membership year, and the quality and frequency of communications received during the membership year.

Use and Involvement

The quality of the membership experience can be affected by the benefits offered. For acquisition it is important to create an appealing benefits package; however, it is as important to plan as many benefits as possible that encourage member involvement during the year. Events and activities such as lectures, educational opportunities, and most importantly, those occasions that truly entertain the member, can also affect membership renewal. Museum and library professionals and membership personnel now realize that it is permissible and necessary for programming to be "fun" while also educational and at least tangentially mission focused.

The success of many alumni organizations, located far from their alma mater, is involvement of alumni in activities in their current city. This allows involvement with other alumni who have a commonality—their college or university. Scheduling and planning programming that is entertaining, while sometimes also educational, involves both visitors and members in a way that provides memorable and satisfying experiences that will draw those people back to the institution repeatedly, creating that repeat usage or visitation that will have a strong link to the renewal decision.

Even though few members will take advantage of every activity or benefit, the mere offering of such opportunities can affect membership renewal. For instance, if an institution has a wide range of activities and publicizes those happenings with frequent announcements and invitations, members can feel as though the programming was there for them to take advantage of if they so choose. It is the perception of the availability of event offerings, especially for members, that is important.

Communicating with Members

The frequency with which an organization communicates with its members greatly affects the decision whether to renew a membership. Frequent communication in a variety of forms brings an institution close to its members. Frequent communication, just as in friendship, is a way to keep a relationship strong. These communications should be timely and attractive, but need not be expensive. Communications can take the form of newsletters, emails, reminders of events, course brochures, as well as other fundraising communications relating to annual funds, tribute gifts, or special projects.

A recommendation for the frequency of communications ranges from one to three contacts per month, or more. As long as there is a reason to send, there is no reason to be concerned about too many mailings. It only solidifies the relationship. It is almost impossible to communicate too often. Most organizations err on the side of not communicating often enough.

Email communications have become the norm for most member communications, at least for informational communications. When asking for money, mail is still the norm, but can be supplemented by email. As long as the member has given permission for this kind of communication, and the frequency and content are at an acceptable level, then this is an easy and cost-effective way to stay connected to members.

In the 2014 *Pulse of Membership* survey, 44 percent of respondents reported emailing members a few times a month while equal percentages report emailing once a month (18 percent) and every day (18 percent).[2]

In the current digital environment, there is frequently concern with "over emailing" members. There is also an often unwarranted fear of unsubscribes. These are two separate, yet related issues.

First, members expect to receive regular communication from the organization. While there is not a golden rule on the number of emails an organization should send to a member, the best practice to follow is "when in doubt, always over-communicate." Because communication is closely tied to satisfaction and use of benefits, emailing members should always be considered as providing value and service to the member.

Second, while organizations need to be cognizant of the unsubscribe rate for its email lists, this metric alone does not tell the full story. Too often, organizations prioritize protection of the email list from unsubscribes over customer service and good communication. Unsubscribes alone are not indicative of an overuse of email. Many factors could be contributing to the unsubscribe rate, including lack of relevance, inbox overload, interest and life changes, and inability to update email preferences. It is important for the organization to determine what is an acceptable unsubscribe rate, to increase the number of email communications, and then monitor the number of unsubscribes. If the organization is anxious about increasing email communications for fear of a spike in unsubscribes, then a sample of the full list may be used to test the impact of a more frequent email schedule.

Membership Service

Another key factor in a member's decision to renew is the quality of service received during the membership year. Were the membership materials received promptly? Were phone calls and emails answered promptly? Were the responses they received when calling or visiting the institution courteous and helpful? A new area of concern for membership service is the adoption of social media as a customer service channel. Research indicates that one in three social media users prefer to use social media over the phone for customer service issues,[3] and eighteen- to twenty-nine-year-olds are more likely to use a brand's social media site for customer service interactions.[4] While social media is an evolving customer service channel, members still expect the same level of prompt and courteous service provided via other channels.

All of these aspects affect the membership experience and the decision whether to renew. Service in membership, as in any other consumer experience, has a negative or positive effect on a person's decision to continue doing business with the organization.

There are also conditions that are beyond control that affect a person's willingness to renew. These include personal financial state, health, and change of address. To achieve the greatest success in membership retention, the organization should focus on those factors that are within control.

RENEWALS

Anniversary Membership or Calendar Year Membership

Memberships are best managed when they are based on an anniversary year membership rather than a calendar year basis. In other words, a person should receive twelve months of membership in exchange for his or her donation, not a prorated portion of a calendar year membership dependent on when in the year he or she joins. Spreading the memberships and thus their renewal dates throughout the year balances the workload for membership processing staff. There is seasonality to memberships. Some members will tend to join and renew their memberships at certain times of the year. Members should not have to make decisions at a specific time of the year for the organization's convenience. In a large organization, if all members were due to renew at the same time of the year, the workload would be unbearable and impossible. The exceptions to the anniversary dues rule are very small organizations with little change in membership. For example, with a group of fifty, it will be much less work to ask the fifty members for their dues at the same time.

Renewal Rates

No matter what the membership effort, 10 to 25 percent of members will not renew. This portion of the membership is lost due to moving, death, or some other personal situation that prohibits them from continuing as members. These conditions are beyond the control of the membership program.

Depending on the type of organization, it is possible to renew 50 to 80 percent of current members. This is obviously a wide range to be considered acceptable. However, a great deal depends on the type of organization. With an organization that is not visitation-based, it can be much more difficult to renew members since the entire relationship revolves around exchange of information online or by mail. This lack of personal contact or experience at a physical place may significantly affect the renewal behavior. National or professional organizations can make membership a prerequisite for attendance at conferences or professional certification. This situation can be strong "encouragement" for renewing and is effective as long as the certification, conference, or meeting is a sought-after product.

For membership organizations that are not visitation-based, the need is to communicate in stronger, more consistent ways. It may be incumbent upon the organizations to communicate occasionally by phone, for fundraising purposes, membership service, and market research. Some national organizations host annual conferences or local or regional events. Alumni organizations encourage and invite members to homecoming events, and to local booster clubs that encourage lifelong affinity. A major national conservation organization connects with its mid-level members by hosting receptions at various sites across the country that are held at the homes of donors or at local zoos that share the mission of preserving endangered species.

Even for organizations with a site and a visitation-based membership, the renewal rates can vary greatly. If an institution depends heavily on major exhibitions to recruit or retain its members, renewal rates can be closer to the 60 percent range. The same is true of an institution that has exhibitions or offerings that are generally static in nature, such as an aquarium. Organizations that appeal to young children such as children's museums and science centers face a special challenge; when the children are too old for what the institution has to offer, it is difficult to keep the family engaged in membership.

Institutions that are constantly changing and offering new opportunities and exhibitions are blessed with the ability to attract their members to the institution repeatedly during any given year. In this situation it is possible to achieve renewal rates in the 75 to 80 percent range.

It is also important to note that the length of membership and the level of membership also affect the likelihood of renewal. A member who is new to the institution is less likely to renew than someone who has been a member for several years. A member who has committed to a higher membership category is also more invested and therefore more likely to renew than someone in a lower membership category. Both length of membership and amount of financial commitment correlate to the member's overall commitment to the institution. The more commitment expressed, the greater the likelihood that the member will continue to support the institution through its membership program. For first-year members a renewal rate of 40 to 50 percent is as good as can be expected. Renewal rates can exceed the 90 percent mark with members who have surpassed the three- or four-year mark as members. If an organization has a renewal rate that is 85 percent or above, that can be a warning sign that the organization may not be doing enough to attract new members since new members renew at lower rates and decrease the overall membership renewal rate. In the absence of a significant number of new members, renewal rates can be very high.

Another issue to take seriously is the consistency of the renewal effort. One midwestern zoo had a renewal rate of about 68 percent compared to other venues in the same market with mid-70 percent renewal rates. The zoo had fifteen thousand members, but only one staff member to send and process all the memberships. The person was overburdened and always behind. The staff person would send renewal notices whenever the pile of data entry became manageable. Thus, June 1 renewals were being sent in July or August rather than in May. Additional staff was added along with more efficient procedures and renewals were put on a very specific and rigid schedule. The renewal rate improved by six percentage points. Renewal schedules are crucial in membership!

Figure 7.1 provides an overview of how varying scenarios may affect renewal rates.

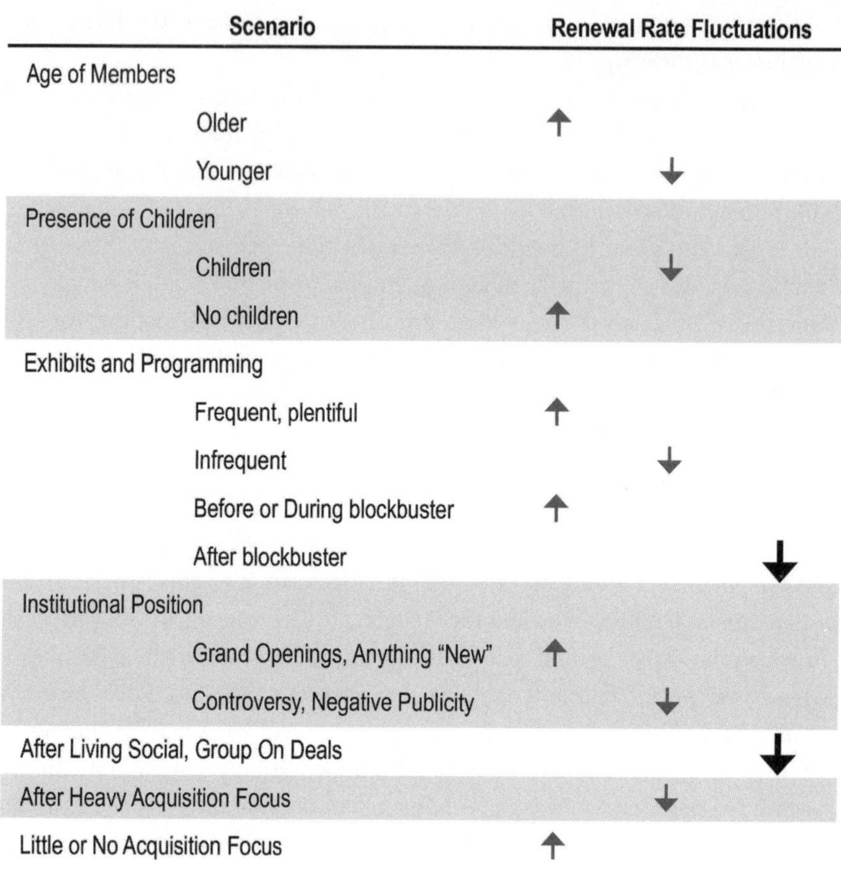

Scenario		Renewal Rate Fluctuations		
Age of Members				
	Older	↑		
	Younger		↓	
Presence of Children				
	Children		↓	
	No children	↑		
Exhibits and Programming				
	Frequent, plentiful	↑		
	Infrequent		↓	
	Before or During blockbuster	↑		
	After blockbuster			⬇
Institutional Position				
	Grand Openings, Anything "New"	↑		
	Controversy, Negative Publicity		↓	
After Living Social, Group On Deals				⬇
After Heavy Acquisition Focus			↓	
Little or No Acquisition Focus		↑		

FIGURE 7.1
Renewal Rate Scenarios

SPECIAL SITUATIONS

First-Year Membership

First-year members are special. They need special treatment. First-year renewal rates are always less than multi-year renewal rates. The long-time member knows the organization and has made a commitment of time and money. The first-year member may be "trying out" the organization to determine if it is a group he or she wants to be associated with for years to come. The organization wants to be careful in its membership acquisition not to "over-promise," a cardinal sin of marketing. If the acquisition promises the new member all kinds of programs, events, and volunteer opportunities and then is not able to fulfill the expectations, the member will certainly not renew. For organizations with multi-year memberships, a first-year member is really any member who has not renewed. This means that the first-year programming needs to continue until at least one renewal cycle has passed.

For first-year members, special events and activities, communications, service, and recognition are helpful in bringing the new member closer to the institution and increasing the chances of the member becoming involved. While a strong membership program is essential for keeping all members, if the organization can do even more for the first-year members their retention rate will be higher than expected. These special activities can be as modest as a phone call thanking the member for joining or calling midway through the year to find out if the member has been attending events or enjoying the publications. More elaborate activities might include a new member behind-the-scenes tour for a visitation facility or a new member reception to meet the director.

The first-year renewal rate of an organization will depend on the type of organization, just as the overall renewal rate will depend on the type of organization and the demographic it serves. The older the demographic, the higher the first-year renewal rate and the overall renewal rate will be. Conversely, younger demographics and organizations whose membership attracts families with children will have lower first-year and overall renewal rates.

The best first-year renewal rate will likely be about 40 percent. Some first-year renewal rates will be as low as 20 percent or less, especially the year after a major event or a blockbuster exhibition or a deeply discounted acquisition offer. Generally, an organization's first-year renewal rate will be half of its overall renewal rate.

Members have become ever more fickle and less consistent with renewals since the economic downturn of 2008. They have been trained to get discounts, they are more focused on the value proposition than ever before, they renew later in the cycle, or in some cases wait to renew when they know they will be using their benefits right away (e.g., waiting to renew until they visit again).

Recapturing Lapsed Members

Lapsed members are the richest pool of prospects for membership—"they have been there, done that" and they understand the concept of membership and what it entails. Recapturing them should be an ongoing, relentless focus. They will rejoin in record numbers, often with the highest response rate of all prospects. Lapsed members are the "low-hanging fruit" of a membership program. It is acceptable to solicit them eight to ten times a year. These solicitations occur in a once or twice a year freestanding renewal mailing or emailing, separate lapsed mailings, and in all acquisition efforts. Additionally, contacting them by phone at least once a year is also advised.

Upgrades/Downgrades

Renewal time is the time to suggest upgrades in those organizations with graduated dues levels. If renewals can be personalized, suggest an upgrade to a member who has been a member for two or, preferably, three years. Once people have been members for three years, they have made a commitment. First-year members should not be asked to upgrade; the issue with first-year members is to encourage them to renew.

If upgrading within the value levels (those most dependent on benefits) discuss the additional benefits that an upgraded level will bring. Because this becomes more of a charitable gift, also talk about the important work of the organization. Other ways to promote the upgrade include mentioning it in the P.S. of the letter and in offering a premium to upgrade. If it is not possible to personalize renewal requests and all members receive the same request, a premium will be helpful in encouraging upgrades.

Downgrades will also occur. Downgrades happen most frequently when the membership rates increase, especially if they increase by a large amount. This will be an issue with value members much more than support members.

As with renewals in general, it is very important to track upgrades and, of course, downgrades. By tracking, the membership manager can see on a month-to-month basis whether an offer is working. If the upgrade effort is working, keep it going. If not, make changes to see if they will work. If downgrades become too prevalent (there will always be some), then it is time to make a change to stop the trend.

A proactive program that wishes to grow membership revenues will take a more aggressive approach to membership upgrades. Upgrade mailings have proven to be a source of added revenue and a way to put a focus on mid-level membership categories—usually in the $200 to $1,000 range. The upgrade push is usually best engineered with a separate, single-focus mailing sent to a group of members who are in the middle of their membership year, and not around their renewal time. The letter clearly states that this is not a renewal, but a special request for the member to upgrade their experience and their commitment to an organization. The letter will suggest a level or two above the member's current level while also communicating the benefits at each of those levels. The letter also serves as a thank you for past continued support, and a reminder that their increased gift will support the organization's mission. A premium offer is a good way to entice the member, and an even nicer premium or event might be promised if they upgrade to a significant level, such as $500 or $1,000.

These upgrade efforts will help membership and the fundraising department identify these generous members as potential future major donors, and provide the member with a way to be ever more connected to an organization that they are passionate about. In membership, part of the purpose of the program's existence is to move people along a pathway as shown in figure 7.2.

These appeals allow organizations to move people along the member/donor pathway. Typical response rates will be 3 to 8 percent or more. Some people will not read the entire letter and will assume it is a renewal ask and will simply renew at the same level. That is acceptable, too, and the revenue from early renewal is always a good thing. Expiration dates should be moved forward by one year, giving the upgraded members the additional time to enjoy the extended benefits (e.g., if someone is due to renew in June, and they upgrade in January, the expiration date should be moved to the following June). The upgrade effort should be repeated six months later, but to the other half of the membership audience who did not receive it the first time because they were in the renewal cycle. Upgrade letter appeals can be supplemented by an email. Some organizations choose to use telemarketing to make a personal ask for a membership upgrade.

Renewal Efforts

Just as in membership acquisition, there are several avenues available for renewing the existing member. As in acquisition, the primary method of renewal is by mail. In addition, there are the possibilities of a member renewing

FIGURE 7.2
Membership Path

in person at a visitation-based institution and renewal telemarketing. Increasingly, online renewal strategies are becoming standard practice. The methods suggested can be used in any size organization.

Direct Mail

The greatest effort to renew a member should be direct mail notices to members. The content and timing of the mailings are the most crucial factors in this effort. There should be a minimum of three renewal mailings, with four to five renewal efforts being the norm. The timing of the mailings should be tested and customized to the particular audience that an institution serves. For instance, an institution that serves an older population may find it advantageous to mail its first renewal notice several months before the expiration date.

Generally, older people may be more likely to renew ahead of time so that their membership does not lapse because of delayed renewals. Younger people may be more spontaneous and delay payments until the last possible moment. Therefore, it is necessary for each institution to decide what timing will work best. Figure 7.3 shows a typical renewal schedule.

Regardless of the renewal schedule, it is necessary to allow enough time to lapse between mailings so that the member has a chance to

- Receive the mail;
- Respond; and
- Have the renewal processed before a second renewal notice is sent.

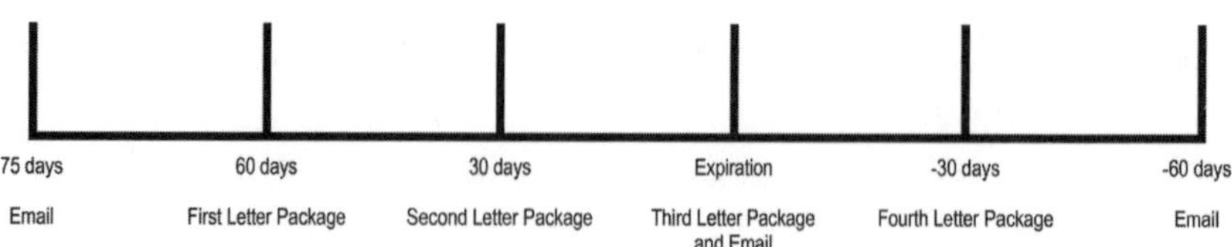
75 days
Email
60 days
First Letter Package
30 days
Second Letter Package
Expiration
Third Letter Package and Email
-30 days
Fourth Letter Package
-60 days
Email
• Test Schedules; the younger the members' audiences the more aggressive the renewal efforts have to be
• Find a renewal schedule that works for your organization
• Stick to the schedule; don't alter or miss any renewal notices; it will affect cash flow
• Speed of processing can affect schedule; must be up-to-date on processing or reminders and payments will 'cross in the mail' and may cause members confusion/dissatisfaction

FIGURE 7.3
Sample Renewal Schedule

If a membership office can provide quick turnaround in processing memberships, it is possible to mail renewal notices within six weeks of one another. This timing will also depend on whether first-class or third-class mail is used and the workload of the data processing personnel. One word of caution: members who renew early should have the same renewal date as the year before. For example, if a June renewal sends in the renewal in May, that member's renewal date should remain the end of June. If the renewal comes in July, the new renewal date should be the end of July.

Generally, the membership renewal package should include a renewal letter signed by the director of the institution or by the leader of the membership or friend's group, a renewal application, and a return mail envelope. The letter personalizes the renewal effort, and the response form and envelope make it easy for the member to respond. Other materials can be included in this mailing as well, including notices of upcoming events that will entice the members into renewing so that they may attend. A window sticker or other small inexpensive premium item that will encourage them to reenlist as a member, or other reminders regarding premiums for renewing or for upgrading memberships are always beneficial.

Just as in the acquisition mailing, the copy is promotional in nature. It should be upbeat and highlight the benefits of membership. Special "pleas" can be successful, especially if the member was a charter member or a long-term member, or if a special institutional anniversary is coming up. The letter should contain several suggestions that the member renew along with a suggestion that the member do so immediately by charging their membership by phone or online. A "P.S." should feature a special or crucial message. The renewal form, if possible, should include the current level of membership, how long he or she has been a member, and an encouragement to upgrade the membership level in exchange for increased membership benefits. The member's name, address, and ID number should be preprinted on the reply device.

The reply envelope can be a postage-paid business reply envelope (BRE) or a courtesy reply envelope (CRE); testing has shown that neither gives an advantage. The postage-paid envelope can make responding easier, but the crucial factor is simply supplying an envelope. The envelope makes a mailed response possible if that is the member's choice for response. The envelope differentiates the letter package versus a mailed postcard or self-mailers, two options that some programs use. The older the audience, the more important it is to provide an envelope. Expecting to change behaviors of people who have been responding in a certain way is a dangerous thing to try when money is involved. Younger audiences and programs that have attracted a larger percentage of members in more recent times may be able to get a higher percentage of its renewing members to transact renewals online.

The second, third, and subsequent renewal letters should be increasingly more urgent than the first, highlighting even more of what the member will miss if the membership is not renewed. Also request a note to let you know why he or she is deciding not to renew if that is the case.

It is possible to continue subsequent renewal mailings as long as the dollars generated from a particular mailing exceed the cost of the mailing. Some institutions employ three, four, five, six, or more membership notices, depending on their profitability.

Email

Email reminders to complement mailed renewal notices are becoming the norm. What will not work is replacing mailed renewal notices with emails. A typical renewal schedule will include mailed notices supported by a simultaneous email. If the member gets both the email reminder and mailed reminder at roughly the same time, he or she can respond in either way. Offering members the "green" alternative of renewing in a paperless environment can be achieved by sending a first renewal reminder via email noting that a quick response to this first notice will prevent a series of mailed efforts to get that member to renew.

To comply with CAN-SPAM, emails for renewals should be deployed via a commercial email platform, not via the membership manager's personal email client such as Outlook or Gmail. Additionally, testing should be conducted to understand which email in the sequence, which subject lines, time of day, or day of the week produces the greatest results for open rates, click-through rates, and renewals. Emails for members should be regularly updated and an email append may be used if there is a significant gap in the number of member email addresses in the file.

Telemarketing

Telemarketing is another means to renew members. This more personalized contact with members is sometimes more successful than mail. In some cases a phone call merely serves as a reminder that will trigger the member into making a personal commitment to renew the membership. In other cases, for a member who has decided against renewing, it is a way to gauge any dissatisfaction with the membership program or other reasons for not renewing. Frequently volunteers or staff with training, a script, and proper supervision can conduct a renewal telemarketing effort. However, the best results are seen when a professional telemarketing firm is hired to reach the lapsed members. Substantial volume is one reason to use a professional firm rather than volunteers. The quality of the call and the ability to make the sales ask are other issues to consider. Many volunteers feel uncomfortable making a financial ask.

Unlike other forms of telemarketing, renewal telemarketing is not a "cold call." There is past experience between the member and the institution. This relationship provides more positive results than if there had been no relationship at all. Again, the profitability of using telemarketing is determined by comparing the dollars raised to the cost of employing professional telemarketers.

On-Site

On-site renewals are possible with a visitation-based institution. Again, the one-to-one personal experience of asking a member to renew can be advantageous. This experience is especially successful when someone with an expired membership visits the institution and is denied free admission unless the membership is renewed. This is an excellent time to "catch" that member and gain another year's support. It is also possible to alert staff to be cognizant of members who have expiration dates coming up in the next thirty to sixty days and have them suggest renewing on the spot while visiting. This can be considered a service to the member to facilitate the renewal while they are at the desk.

Online

Online renewals can be proactive, sending a renewal request via email prior to the mailing of the first renewal notice. The member can be encouraged to "renew now, save time and eliminate the need for future mailings." The ability to renew online can also be promoted in renewal letters and emails. "Save the cost of postage, renew online, get immediate confirmation, and visit tomorrow hassle free!" On member web pages and within the FAQ section of the website, a quick link to "Renew my membership" can help get members to the right place to quickly process their renewal online. To limit the potential for downgrades, it is helpful to drive the member to a pre-populated e-commerce page with their current membership level already added to the shopping cart. Options for upgrading can be presented to the member during the online renewal process, and a full list of membership levels should be available should the member wish to change his or her level at the time of renewal. All e-commerce pages should be secure, mobile optimized, and user friendly to mitigate cart abandonment.

A budding opportunity for membership renewals is using member lists to find members online and send them targeted renewal messages. This advertising technique, often referred to as "CRM retargeting," uses offline lists to find members online. For example, Facebook offers a feature that allows an organization to upload its segmented member lists and match between 50 and 60 percent of email addresses or phone numbers to serve tailored renewal or upgrade ads to users. Similarly, member lists can be uploaded and matched to online user pools to find individuals and serve them with tailored display ads. Because new channels such as social media and CRM retargeting can be expensive and require significant time and expertise to be effective, it is recommended to add these channels only to already highly performing methods.

Timing and Frequency

The timing and frequency of renewal reminders is important in the renewal process. Three mailed renewal letters is the minimum activity to get members to renew at desirable rates. The younger and less entrenched the members, and the larger the membership pool, the more difficult it will be to arrive at a desired renewal rate and the more attempts will be required. Zoos and science centers attract younger, family oriented members, and may require more efforts to get them to renew. Four to six renewal touches may be required to achieve a 60 to 65 percent renewal rate. Conversely, three notices may be all that are required to get a history museum, library friends group, or botanical garden audience (with older members than zoos and science centers) to renew at a 75 to 80 percent renewal rate.

Whatever schedule is adopted, it is important to remain true to that schedule. Strict adherence to a schedule will offer predictability, consistency, and cash flow to the organization.

Renewal Response Flow

Before the economic downturn in 2008 the best response to renewal reminders was expected from the initial renewal reminder. Now it is more common to see the largest response from the second renewal reminder, or one that is closest to the actual renewal or expiration date of the membership. Quite simply, during the recession, people were holding onto their money longer. In some cases people were not renewing until they knew they were going to need the benefits—as in visiting and using their free admission benefit. As a society, we seem to plan less, be more immediacy driven, and sometimes not take an action until it is absolutely necessary. But again, every organization if different, so it is highly recommended that membership managers carefully track the effects of each renewal reminder with a simple renewal spreadsheet that shows the effectiveness of each renewal touch. Carefully tracking renewal flow allows membership managers to have a finger on the pulse of their membership program in a quantifiable way.

Calculating and Reporting Renewal Rates

Pinpointing a membership program's renewal rate can be a more daunting task than one would imagine. The important thing is to be consistent in how to calculate and report the renewal rate for your program.

To figure the renewal rate, it is best to calculate the rate by how many people have not renewed:

> Retain the number of people originally due to renew in a given month (e.g., for May, there were 1,000 people with May renewal dates).
>
> Query the number of people who have not renewed who still have a May renewal date (e.g., in July, that number of May nonrenewals could be 400; renewal rate would be 60 percent at this point).
>
> Decide when (or if) a month's renewal rate is capped off and how to report renewal rates. Some organizations report renewal rates at the date of expiration. This would make an organization's renewal rate artificially low, since the renewal process is still in progress. If an organization is going to have a "cut-off date" for reporting a renewal rate, it should at least be thirty days past the last renewal notice being sent. Another way to report renewal rates for a given year is to look at the overall renewal rate at the end of the year—January and the early months of the year would have very mature renewal rates, having a substantial part of the year to gain as many renewing members, while October, November, and December would have lower, less matured renewal rates. However, the overall effect would be a renewal rate averaged over an entire year.

Renewal Offers

Renewal offers have become as important as new membership acquisition offers. The same questions arise: To discount or not discount? What is the most compelling offer? Do you reward "bad" behavior by giving more to those who do not renew on time? Just as in acquisition offers, discounts have become an expectation of some members, and managers sometimes acquiesce. If a discount is used, it is best used when it is positioned in the first renewal notice for anyone renewing by the expiration date. Other offers include a premium or free months of membership. Premiums, if well selected, can be a very motivating offer, especially if used for on-site renewals, but can also be used in mail or emailed notices. If using a premium, it is best to require that the member make a visit to collect the free renewal premium, rather than incurring the cost to mail it. Additional months of membership can be an attractive offer, especially to cost-conscious families who want to get the most for their membership dollar.

Renewal Fulfillment

The end of the renewal process, but the beginning of the next cycle for retention is the renewal fulfillment. A new member receives a packet of information, and so should a renewing member. The packet should include a thank you acknowledging the member's continued support and, if possible, referencing the length of the membership. The membership card should also have this reference if feasible. In the packet include information about membership benefits, upcoming events, and anything else that might be of interest to the member. If there are special interest groups within the organization, offer membership in them in the fulfillment packet. This is also a good opportunity to send the member a tribute envelope for future gifts, if the organization has this type of fundraising program. Last, but not least, it is also a great time to solicit volunteer help, detailing the volunteer opportunities that are available at the institution.

The fulfillment packet should be considered the first step in the continuing retention of the member. The packet should make a good impression, reinforcing the members' feeling that they have made a wise choice in renewing and in supporting the organization.

Auto-Renewals

Auto-renewals may be the latest, greatest trend for membership renewals. Auto-renewals can take at least two possible forms—the public radio and TV model where membership dues are paid in monthly installments or an automatic credit card charge of the membership dues on the renewal date.

Monthly or sustainer giving is becoming a more commonly accepted phenomenon in the United States. It has been a mainstay of charitable giving in Europe and Canada for some time, but has been just gaining acceptance in the United States in recent years.

A second model is one employed by the Museum of Science, Boston, where members can elect an auto-renew option where their credit card will be charged the full amount at one time (less a 10 percent auto-renew discount) on their expiration date. The museum has an amazing 50 percent of its membership signed up for this option!

The challenge with auto-renew options is to have a PCI-compliant resource for storing member credit card numbers and being able to address credit card expiration dates. PCI compliance refers to the Payment Card Industry Data Security Standard, a set of requirements designed to ensure that organizations that process credit card information maintain a secure transaction environment.

SUMMARY

Renewals are the backbone of any membership program, and a strong retention rate is essential for growth. Membership retention is a day-to-day, yearlong process that involves responding to, and anticipating, members' needs. Customer service and communication have a significant effect on a member's decision to renew. A structured and consistent renewal schedule that includes a multichannel approach will ensure the best possible renewal rates.

CASE STUDY: SANTA BARBARA ZOO

The Santa Barbara Zoo has almost 15,000 members and outsources its membership renewal mailings and email reminders. The zoo mails four renewal letters with reply devices and a return envelope in an outer envelope that bears the offer for the specific renewal mailing. A $5-off offer is included in the first and second renewal notices, and two free months of membership are offered in renewal notices three and four (see table 7.1).

Table 7.1 Membership Report—Mail Renewals

Month	First Renewals Sent	Second Renewals Sent		Third Renewals Sent		Fourth Renewals Sent		Still not Renewed	Renewal Rate to Date
January	1,215	901	26%	650	47%	442	64%	335	72%
February	897	705	21%	556	38%	367	59%	267	70%
March	567	439	23%	315	44%	192	66%	132	77%
April	413	302	27%	234	43%	196	53%	154	63%
May	998	768	23%	564	43%	442	56%	328	67%
June	1,254	965	23%	658	48%				
July	986	754	24%						
August	439								
September									
October									
November									
December									
Total	**6,769**	**4,834**	**24%**	**2,977**	**44%**	**1,639**	**60%**	**1,216**	**70.27%**

Four years ago, the zoo also started sending an email reminder in addition to mailed reminders. Emailed reminders precede the mailed notices by one week, giving members a chance to renew ahead of the mailing to save paper and dollars (see table 7.2). Initially, the zoo had emails for about 65 percent of members; now that rate is closer to an 85 percent email saturation rate. Since instituting the emailed reminders, the zoo has grown the percentage of members renewing online from about 5 to almost 40 percent of members renewing online.

NOTES

1. Arlene Farber Sirkin and M. P. McDermott, *Keeping Members* (Washington, DC: Foundation of the American Society of Association Executives, 1995), 7.

2. Membership Consultants, Inc., "[Webinar Recording] Pulse of Membership Survey Results Year-End 2014," accessed April 21, 2015, http://knowledge.membership-consultants.com/pulse-of-membership-year-end-2014-webinar-recording.

Table 7.2 Membership Report—Email Renewals

Month	First Renewals Sent	Second Renewals Sent		Third Renewals Sent		Fourth Renewals Sent		Still not Renewed	Renewal Rate to Date
January	1,012	950	6%	657	35%	392	61%	324	68%
February	897	845	6%	549	39%	331	63%	244	73%
March	567	542	4%	379	33%	196	65%	130	77%
April	413	381	8%	269	35%	182	56%	148	64%
May	998	932	7%	623	38%	420	58%	304	70%
June	1,254	1,189	5%	728	42%				
July	986	945	4%						
August	439								
September									
October									
November									
December									
Total	6,566	5,784	6%	3,205	38%	1,521	61%	1,150	70.41%

3. Deirdre Bannon, "State of the Media: The Social Media Report." Nielsen, December 4, 2012, 16, accessed November 1, 2014, http://www.nielsen.com/content/dam/corporate/us/en/reports-downloads/2012-Reports/The-Social-Media-Report-2012.pdf.

4. Jacqueline Anderson, "Social Media Benchmark Study[SM]," J. D. Power and Associates, February 14, 2013, accessed October 22, 2014, http://www.jdpower.com/press-releases/2013-social-media-benchmark-study.

8

Direct Mail

The reports of my death have been greatly exaggerated.

—Mark Twain, American Author and Humorist

The death of direct mail has certainly been exaggerated since email has become such a primary way of communicating. Early email marketing consultants in the beginning of the 2000s eagerly predicted the demise of direct mail as a method of fundraising. In fact, Vinay Baghat, the founder of Convio, one of the leaders in email CRM programs, confessed at the time of the sale of his firm in 2012 that the only thing he had been wrong about was the death of direct mail. Direct mail was as alive and well then as it was when he founded Convio in 1999. Not to say that email has not had an impact on fundraising; it certainly has. But getting to large numbers of new member and donor prospects has still been much better received via the mail than from unsolicited emails from strangers. In 2014, Tom Belford, a contributor to the online fundraising blog *The Agitator*, noted the ongoing increase in online fundraising, but calculated that it would take another seventeen years (2031) until online fundraising would get to a point where it equaled the impact of direct mail.[1] Direct mail is still very much alive and well!

PROACTIVE ACQUISITION

Direct mail is the most proactive, controllable source of new memberships that an organization can have. It is proactive because it initiates the action with the prospect. It is controllable in that the manager controls the timing and the number of new members generated. If 1,000 new members are needed during March, the manager plans a campaign of 100,000 to 120,000 mailing pieces in February. Other acquisition methods may be dependent on factors out of control of the membership manager, such as weather, attendance, or the independent decision of a person to join on his or her own without invitation or suggestion.

Direct mail is a form of direct marketing that is just that—direct. It's a direct ask to join. Direct marketing attempts to create behavior in the present. Its goal is to persuade the prospect to overcome inertia, to encourage him or her to indicate, "I'm interested." This call to action means that direct marketing messages tend to be highly conversational and explicit. This is necessary because direct marketers must supply ample justification for the prospect to take immediate action.

It also means that direct marketing involves database work. Because response involves returning a response card, joining online, or using a toll free (e.g., 800) telephone number, human behavior can be tracked, recorded, and analyzed. Program results are objective. This means it is determined which lists, package, ad, or premium worked and which did not. A larger test of the programs that proves to be successful can be conducted with confidence while eliminating the unsuccessful ones. These elements of testing, trackability, and measurability are the great appeal of direct mail.

DIRECT MAIL COMPONENTS

There are three basic components in any direct marketing program:

- The list
- The offer
- The creative execution

Experts argue continually over which of the three is the most important element. There are certain facts that are true, however. The list is important because without it there would be no one to whom to send mail. The offer is important because it focuses behavior that triggers a response. The creative execution or form the offer takes can help or hinder the involvement of the customer or prospect.

Direct mail experts attach 60 percent of the success or failure of the productivity of a campaign to the lists and 30 percent to the offer. That leaves 10 percent of a campaign's success dependent on the creative execution. Ironically, most managers spend the bulk of their time laboring over the creative part of the campaign—the design and copy.

Lists

Most people are on hundreds of lists including compiled business and professional lists, magazine subscription lists, hobby or club lists, enthusiasts' lists, financial lists, credit approval lists, catalog lists, and resident lists. The challenge in building a mailing list is to develop an accurate profile of the current member, donor, or customer and then to target future mailings to prospect lists with like profiles. This approach leverages marketing to strengths rather than spending time and money trying to convert the unconvertible.

One good way to profile is to survey current members. Ask them who they are, what their interests are, what publications they subscribe to, and what organizations they belong to. It will be surprising to find the number of people who will complete the survey and provide vital information. When surveying a loyal membership base, it is possible to obtain a 15 to 20 percent response rate. This is a phenomenal response. Market researchers in the for-profit world are usually pleased with a 2 to 5 percent rate of response. The information gleaned from a survey is especially important in our fast-paced world where lifestyles change rapidly and where last year's target market is this year's marginal market.

Another way to profile members is to have the current membership list demographically or psychographically enhanced. A list can be broken down by numerous characteristics such as median income, home ownership, education level, retail spending index, number of family members, age, and even number or types of automobiles. This demographic profiling (usually done for large lists) will identify the most prevalent subgroups within a larger database, and by their descriptions such as "shotguns and pickups" or "blue-blood estates" and definitions, describe the target audience.

To acquire lists for mailing, the first step is to look at establishing reciprocal list trades with similar institutions or organizations. Surveying the organization's members, asking them which other organizations they support, identifies the similar institutions. The more frequent responses will be the organizations to use. Frequently, list exchanges can be made on a name-per-name basis at no cost to either institution, thereby circumventing expensive list rental costs, which may exceed $100 per thousand names.

By exchanging lists, the appeal reaches people who are already predisposed to belonging or donating to similar organizations. List trading can cost very little and require only the spirit of cooperation when it comes to timing of mail drops among the participating institutions. One caution, however, when trading: A name duplication factor of as much as 50 percent is possible since the lists being collected are like-minded in nature. Thus, the lists must go through a deduping process, which means merging lists to eliminate this duplication. It should be noted that the higher the duplication rate, the more certain it is that a good list has been identified, since that list has almost the same profile and many of the same people.

Some organizations have a policy against list trades. This type of policy is a major impediment to a direct mail program. Traded lists from like-minded organizations will perform at twice the response rate or more, than any other lists that are rented. So, right away, without cooperative list trades, the response rate may have just fallen by half, without even having mailed.

To circumvent such a policy and to make all involved more comfortable with the concept of list trades, a mailing list exchange letter of agreement (see Appendix F) should be used. An agreement specifies the number of times the list can be mailed (usually once), that the list is for mail purposes only (not phoning or emailing), that it may not be reserved or incorporated into the user's database, that no coding be used that identifies the source, and the timing of the mailing. A review of the mailing package may also be required.

It should also be noted that when an organization agrees to be involved in list trading, it still reserves the right to trade with whomever it chooses, such as not trading with commercial entities. It may trade with some organizations and deny others. Nonprofit organizations should not exchange lists with political organizations lest they risk the loss of their tax-exempt status.

Demographic information is accessible on all lists available for rental and it is necessary to match those lists as closely as possible to the current membership list. This information on the profile of the rental list is provided on a data card. This card lists the percentage of male and female respondents, the income or educational level, and perhaps most importantly, names of other organizations who have rented the file. One can determine by viewing the list of other users whether these may be like-minded organizations and whether the list is desirable. In some cases, the list manager may even have data on how the list performed for some organizations that used the list previously.

Another type of list that is readily available is the compiled list. Compiled lists are lists of people who have probably filled out information from a warranty card and listed their demographic information as well as interests, hobbies, and likely future purchases. Many compiled lists are just that, compiled from some source, but not necessarily from a source of purchasers such as subscribers or catalog buyers. Usually compiled lists are not advisable to use unless all other list options have been exhausted. The reason for this is that in direct mail, the important factor is that a person is direct mail responsive and he or she has taken action by mail to purchase something. That action needs to be repeated. With a compiled list that past action is not guaranteed. A marketer, however, may recommend a compiled list to a membership manager because it is the easiest list to acquire and the marketer makes a commission on the list rental. However, in reality, a list trade may work much better, but be more labor intensive to acquire, and provide no revenue for the marketer.

One of the best lists an organization can use is a list that the organization itself has compiled, known as the house list. If the organization hosts events, names should be collected and added to a database for future use. Each such event or group of names should be coded so the list can be used in the next membership acquisition mailing and tested for productivity.

The absolute best-producing list for any acquisition mailing will be the list of lapsed members whose membership has expired. These former members understand the organization and what it represents better than any other prospect. Since they have been a member in the past, they know what to expect, and they understand the mission and other reasons for joining. Many times a lapsed member still has an interest in the organization and a passion for what it offers; they just happened not to renew when asked. As is frequently the case, they might have been busy, financially stretched, or just not paying attention when their membership expired. So these former members should be included in all acquisition efforts as well as dedicated lapsed member appeals of all kinds—mail, email, and phone.

When evaluating the lists an organization should use when prospecting for new members, those with the highest to lowest response rates might look something like this:

Lapsed member file: 2 to 3 percent

Trade lists from like-minded organizations: 1 to 1.5 percent

In-house compiled lists: 0.75 to 1.25 percent

Consumer rental lists: 0.5 to 1 percent

Compiled lists: 0.1 to 0.5 percent

Merge/Purge Processes

Duplication of names is an issue when more than one mailing list is used in a prospect mailing. It is a waste of money for the organization and an annoyance for the recipient, if he or she receives more than one piece of mail from a single mailing. It is even worse if a current member in good standing receives an invitation to join the organization. Merge/purge processing removes duplicates between, among, and within lists. List merge purging is quite sophisticated now; however, some duplicates will always slip through. These are people who are on every conceivable list, spouses with different last names, or people who are on one list at home and another list at the office. One very important list that every organization that uses direct mail should compile is a "do not solicit" list. In every direct mail campaign, the organization will receive "hate mail"—mail from people who make it known that they do not want to receive any future solicitations from the organization. This is typical. To save money and future annoyances, it is best to list all of these people in a "do not mail" file to use as a kill file in the next deduplication process.

Compiling your own "do not mail" file is just the first step in complying with the "Privacy Promise" sponsored by the Direct Marketing Association. (See http://testimis.the-dma.org/privacy/privacy_promise.pdf for greater detail.) This program is a nationwide effort to remove people from mailing lists who really do not want to receive solicitations by mail or other means. It is also an act of self-policing by conscientious direct marketers. The components of the program are:

A person who does not wish to receive mail notifies the Direct Marketing Association in New York. The name is added to a national "do not mail" list.

Responsible marketers have free access to this national "do not mail" list, and with every prospective mailing use the national list as a kill file.

Organizations compile their own "do not mail" file and remove those people from any mailing the organization sends.

Organizations that trade or sell names make people on their own database aware of this fact, giving them a chance to place themselves on a "do not mail" list.

This type of self-policing is good for everyone, for the people who do not want to receive mail, for the organization that will not waste money on mailing to nonresponsive households, and for the industry as a whole. Organizations should ask their marketing firms and mail houses whether they adhere to the Privacy Promise.

Mail Quantities

Determining the appropriate number of pieces to mail is sometimes a difficult task. Every organization probably has a quantity range within which it will be most successful. This is arrived at by trial and error, or by using the expertise of a direct mail professional. It is best to start small. The larger the mailing, the further from the target audience some of the prospects may be, thereby decreasing the response rate. Thus, it is best to start small and increase the quantity from one campaign to the next.

Different situations may call for different mail quantities. Whether an organization has a major event, activity, or anniversary or has nothing in particular happening will dictate campaign size. For instance, an art museum that has a major exhibition on the horizon is justified in doubling its usual mail quantities. In an organization's slow or off-season, a decision may be made to mail a smaller quantity. With every organization there is a target audience that is within its service area. Finding that audience, and then mailing to those prospects time after time with new offers and new information is what is recommended to find the optimal size of a mailing in a targeted geographic area. The Missouri Botanical Garden in St. Louis found that one mailing of 240,000 pieces in the St. Louis region (population 2.5 million) was too large, but a mailing of 140,000 was optimal, and that mailing 240,000 pieces over three spring campaigns every spring worked very well, which entailed mailing to some of the same lists two or three times.

Sometimes it is difficult to find sufficient numbers of names to use in rollout (the larger mailing after testing smaller quantities). List brokers often require purchasing a minimum number of names, usually 5,000 to 10,000. What may seem like a perfect list may not have 5,000 mailable names in the target area. Sometimes the minimum name requirement can be made flexible by working with the right list broker. If a list performs well, it should be used time after time. This is in keeping with the direct marketing principle that states, "You can mail the exact same package to the same list three to five times without the risk of lessening the effectiveness of the offer or creative."

Where some organizations fall short, literally, is in gauging the number of mailable names available after the merge/purge process. In planning a campaign, an estimated mail quantity is established at the beginning of the effort. When mailing lists and mail quantities are amassed in preparation for the campaign, the total number of mailable names collected must exceed the intended mail quantity. Since some prospects will appear on multiple lists, excess names must be included in the deduplication, or merge/purge process. In other words, it may be necessary to collect 70,000 names to reach a target mail quantity of 50,000 names.

The duplication rate may not be known in advance when an organization is planning its first-ever direct mail campaign. In this case, an educated guess or the experience of a seasoned direct mail consultant may be necessary. The duplication rate will vary by the size of the mailing and the size of the target area. For organizations that serve a limited geographic area, and are aggressive in their direct mails strategies, a duplication rate of 50 percent may not be uncommon. For an organization mailing nationally, however, the duplication rate may be minimal, closer to 5 percent. Knowing this number is critical. In some campaign scheduling, the printing and the list deduplication may occur at the same time. An undesirable outcome would be to print 50,000 mail pieces and have only 30,000 names to which to mail. Hence, planning and knowledge of the mailing universe is critical.

Some large national mailers, mailing solicitations by the hundreds of thousands or even millions, do not merge/purge or dedupe lists. The thinking may be that the chance for duplication is minimal and that when prospecting for value-level members, they will take the risk of alienating people who receive multiple pieces rather than go to the expense or the time delay of merge/purge processing. This practice is not recommended. Alienation of potential members is one consideration, as is alienation of some trade list sources. In fact, the best prospects may be on many like-minded lists if it is a cause to which they are very committed. For instance, a single prospect may contribute to the World Wildlife Fund, the National Wildlife Federation, and the African Wildlife Federation. If a like-minded organization used these three files in its prospect mailing and mailed three pieces to this generous prospect, this may well alienate the prospect and lose the donation.

List Hints

Some important points to remember when implementing a direct mail campaign:

Duplication: This means, of course, that there must be an overage in purchase of names to have enough names to meet the projected mailing quantity. It also means that particular attention must be paid to computer work so that as many duplicates as possible are removed from the mailing. The current membership file is used as the primary source file, against which all lists are run. There may also be a special file of people who do not want to receive mailings. This becomes the purge file. A good merge/purge program should not only be run among the lists, but also *within* the lists as well.

A multi-hit list matrix shows the duplicate names appearing on each list. It can be a valuable way of judging the quality of the lists. If there is a lot of duplication among the lists, it demonstrates that the selected lists are similar, thereby ensuring success. If few duplicates are found, it is an indication that either the list is not a good one to use, as it does not mirror the type of prospect being sought, or it is an indication that the merge/purge process is faulty.

Coding: Ensure that all lists are coded so that response rates by list can be determined. This will determine which lists should be used again.

Variety: In a test mailing, use the minimum of 5,000 names from a variety of lists. Depending on each list's success, then use larger quantities of those successful lists in a rollout. Using all the available names on a large list without some idea of how that list is going to perform is a gamble. Never pin the hopes of a campaign on just one list. Spread the risk around; use five lists of 5,000 names each rather than one list with 25,000 names. If one list does not perform, perhaps the others will do well enough to make the mailing a success.

Repetition: Continue using the most successful and productive lists. It takes many mailings to "wear out" a list, if in fact that happens at all. Some organizations have used some of the same prospect files for fifteen to twenty years, as long as those lists keep producing good response rates.

Multi-hits or "Multis": Multis are the names of people that show up on several lists. They receive only one mailing, but the names have come from several organizations. Thus, this group can be mailed to again as a follow up to the first campaign. This group may be the most productive since they were on several lists.

The Offer

The offer is the "deal" that is presented to an individual in the direct mail package:

> Join now and receive a free tote bag!
>
> Money back guarantee!
>
> Respond now and get two months free!

The offer is the "hook" that hopefully entices the prospect to respond. Numerous offers can be made to enhance a program and overcome human inertia. There are examples of various types of offers available in magazines, on the web, and on television. Some examples are free trials, free samples, free gifts, sweepstakes, money-back guarantees, easy terms, yes-no involvement devices (affix a stamp indicating "yes" or "no" to acceptance of the offer), expiration dates, two-for-one offers, discounts, charter memberships, and exclusive terms. These are but a few of the many offers promoted in today's world.

One way to determine which offer is more productive than another is to test two offers simultaneously, mailing from the same list and having only one item in the package that differs: the offer. Results can be compared and the winner determined by response rate and dollars generated.

Premium items (also known as incentives) are a great way to enhance an offer of a membership. Tangible premiums offer a great way for a person to show his or her affiliation with an organization, to say, "I belong." These premiums are also a good way for the organization to obtain a bit of free publicity while also offering something of value that is appealing to the prospective member.

The following are a few examples of premiums that have proven successful for many membership organizations:

- Tote bags
- Umbrellas
- Mugs
- CDs, tapes, videos
- Note cards
- Posters
- Bookmarks
- Books
- Backpacks
- T-shirts
- Baseball caps embroidered with a logo

The key is to find a premium that is related to the type of organization. A history museum might give books on historical topics; a botanical garden might give seeds, gardening tools, or an umbrella; a library might give a bookmark. It is also important to find premiums that are attractive to the widest possible audience, young and old, male and female.

Premiums do work. No matter what people may say, when a package without a premium is tested against a package that offers a premium, the package with the premium will most often win. Premiums can also be used to boost average gift sizes by offering them for upgrades or for joining at a certain level. For example, a premium can be offered to anyone who agrees to move to a higher level of membership. Such an offer will produce better results than a package that asks without the premium.

A distinction should be made between front-end premiums and back-end premiums. Front-end premiums are the address stickers, note pads, or greeting cards included in a direct mail membership or donor appeal that some organizations use. Back-end premiums are usually higher-value items that are offered to prospects *after* they join or respond.

Creative Execution

The third component of the direct mail campaign is the creative execution. Once the list decisions and the offer have been determined, it is time to package it all in the physical form that actually carries the offer to the intended parties. But before the creation of the graphics and copy for a direct mail campaign can begin, some fundamental decisions about the number and size of pieces to be included in the package must be made.

Format of the Package

It's important to understand some direct mail formats and remember that there are some environmental differences between direct mail and other media. People read the newspaper, watch television, surf the web, or listen to the radio while sitting down. Be it good or bad, most people tend to scan direct mail while standing in the kitchen near a wastebasket. The first order of business, then, for a successful direct mail piece is to sustain enough interest to be included in the pile to be opened.

Unlike other media, direct mail is not restricted to time or space. Large or small formats can be used for brochures with multiple folds and numerous inserts. The only limitation is budget and maintaining a look that is in keeping with an organization's image. Many other media, like billboards, banner ads, or commercials, make an impression and build an image, but are not good for eliciting a decision.

The classic direct mail format is a letter package. The letter package consists of an outer envelope, letter, reply device, a return envelope, a brochure, and perhaps other inserts. Some organizations use other formats to save money, such as self-mailers or postcards. These formats do not offer a return envelope into which the respondent can include a check or their credit card number for return to the organization. By using these mail formats, the organization forces the recipient to join online, to phone, to wait and join when visiting, or to find an envelope to send a mailed response. These formats create a roadblock to the person who wants to respond via return mail. Until an organization has trained its audiences to interact with it almost exclusively online, not offering a return envelope can be a gamble. Each organization will have its own mix of ways that its prospects respond—via mail, phone, online, or in person. The percentages of how people respond should be tracked and monitored from year to year. To find the best package format for each organization, testing is recommended.

Outer Envelope

Its purpose is twofold: to prepare the prospect for what is inside and to generate enough interest for the prospect to open the envelope. In direct mail, a highly illustrated envelope tied to an offer inside or a plain white envelope (with nothing on it but the name, address, and a stamp) will most likely ensure that the package is opened and, thus, increase responses. The aim is to involve the recipient in the process of exploring a direct mail piece. There are a variety of sizes and types of envelopes, both standard and custom. There are no hard facts about which size to use. What must be considered is the overall objective, the look of the mailing package, where it will be opened (home or business), and the competitive environment. This last point deserves elaboration. In many cases an organization is in competition with others. Colorful graphics, catchy teaser copy, a plain white envelope, or an interesting return address might catch a person's attention and increase the likelihood of the piece being opened before or instead of another item.

Four-color graphic envelope versus plain white envelope package: That is the question. The answer is in the testing. What works for one organization may not work for another, but this is certainly a hotly debated issue in the membership acquisition world. The consensus may lie in going to one extreme or the other to have the package opened. A plain white envelope is used to raise the level of curiosity: "Who is writing to me and why?" is a question the reader may ask when looking at a package that looks personalized or does not give the reader a hint of who/why/what on the outer envelope. On the other hand, a very bright, lively, and visually appealing package may jump out at a reader and scream "Open me first!" This can be tested using a plain versus a four-color envelope. Envelopes that have worked well are shown in exhibit 8.1, exhibit 8.2, and exhibit 8.3.

The Letter

The letter is the personal appeal to the prospect. In keeping with what has been proven to work in direct mail, always include a letter, even if it is not personalized. Personalization includes addressing the letter to a specific person. In direct mail acquisition, personalization is not necessary. What is necessary is to keep the costs as low as possible, and personalization costs money. Begin to use personalization after someone has joined as a member and the solicitation is for another gift from the member. At the prospecting

EXHIBIT 8.1
Desert Botanical Garden—Envelope
Source: Desert Botanical Garden. Copyright 2015. All Rights Reserved.

stage, after all, there are no relationships with the prospects; they are anonymous. A "Dear Friend" salutation is appropriate.

An age-old debate in direct mail circles is "What should the length of a letter be?" The answer to that question may be answered by what type of organization this letter represents, and how familiar people are with the organization.

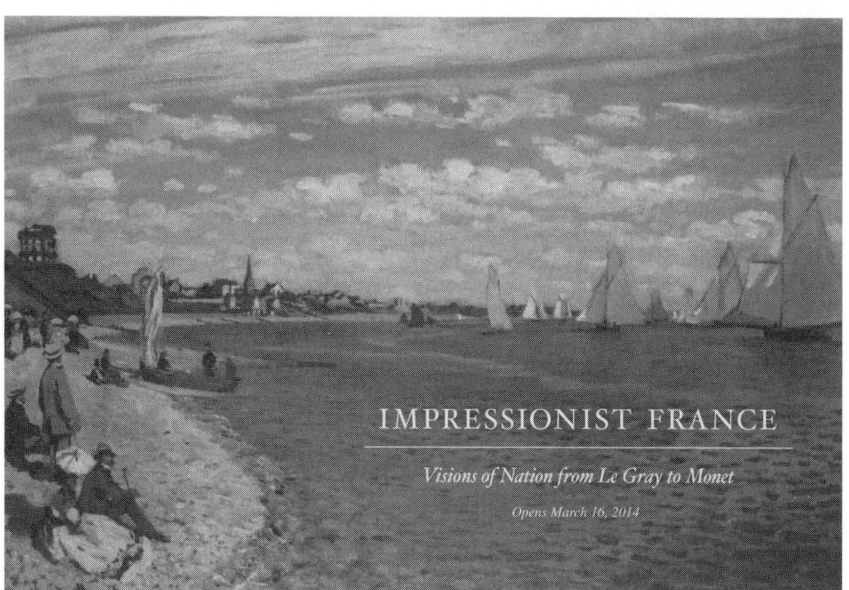

EXHIBIT 8.2
Saint Louis Art Museum—Envelope
Source: Saint Louis Art Museum. Copyright 2015. All Rights Reserved.

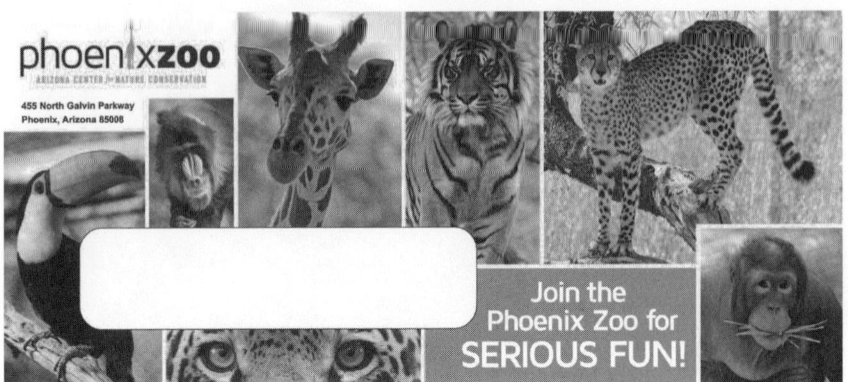

EXHIBIT 8.3
Phoenix Zoo—Envelope
Source: Phoenix Zoo. Copyright 2015. All Rights Reserved.

For some organizations, a one-page graphically enhanced mailing might be sufficient. For very small organizations that are really using personal solicitation from a known friend as direct mail, one page with the friend's signature and a personal note should work well.

For organizations that already have a connection to their prospects, such as alumni associations, a two-page letter may be appropriate. The alumni are already familiar with the alumni association and the concept of the organization. For an organization that has a physical presence in a geographic area and a fair amount of awareness surrounding that organization, such as a well-known museum, again, a two-page letter is sufficient. Organizations that are national, do not have a physical presence, or are cause related, usually require a four-page letter. Organizations such as the Nature Conservancy or the World Wildlife Fund usually require a four-page letter, or longer, to explain what the organization is doing to conserve green spaces or endangered species.

The issue for the organization is to test different letters to see which one works the best for that particular organization.

Copy and Themes

Every direct mail campaign needs an overriding theme. A consistent message that relates to the theme helps readers comprehend what is being proposed and how and why they might want to participate in the cause. Arriving at or creating a theme is one of the fun and challenging parts of formulating a campaign. The theme is what the copy is wrapped around, and it is the glue that holds the copy, the offer, and the message together. An example of complete creative package is shown in exhibit 8.4.

The potential member's most asked question is: "What is in it for me?" Membership prospecting should be promotionally oriented in the copy. Highlight membership benefits first and foremost over the "good" the prospective member will be doing by supporting the organization. Focusing on what's in it for the individual is more important in the acquisition campaign when the prospect is being engaged for the first time. Focus on the mission of the organization is certainly important, but it takes a secondary position in the copy layout.

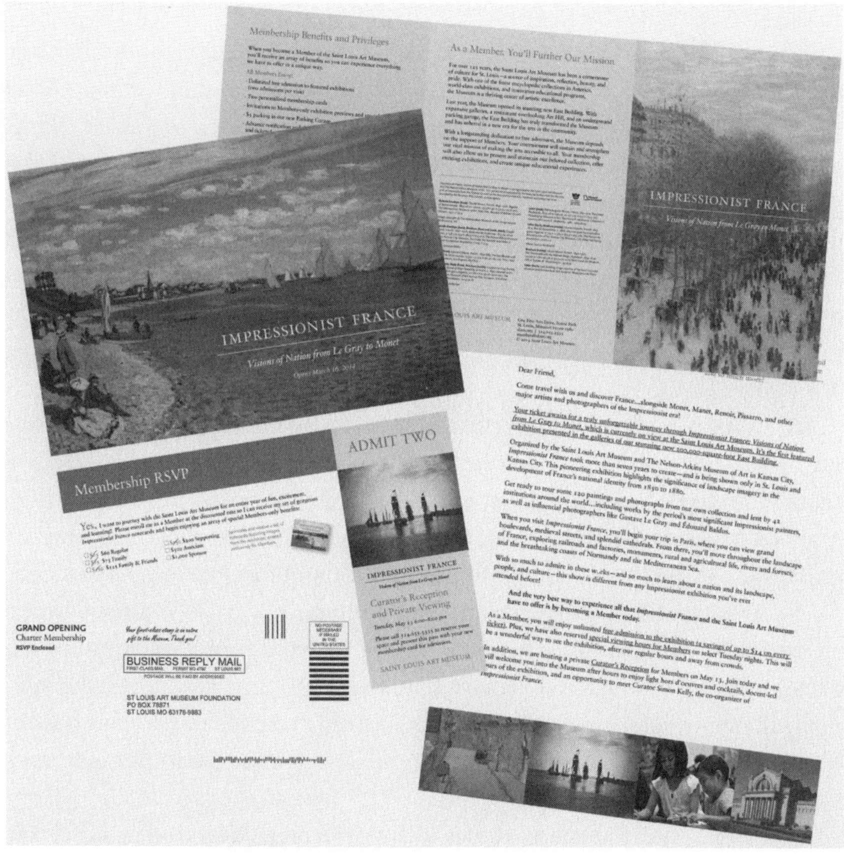

EXHIBIT 8.4

Saint Louis Art Museum—Creative Package

Source: Saint Louis Art Museum. Copyright 2015. All Rights Reserved.

Copy is important in direct mail prospecting for membership. Within the copy of the letter, it is important to appeal to a number of basic human desires such as to be smart, enjoy pleasure, take advantage of special opportunities, save money, save time, or be part of a select group. All of this can be achieved with well-written copy. It is also important to realize that such things as underlining, highlighting, and indenting can draw a reader's eye to important statements.

Other components of the package that make it easy and desirable to respond should also be considered. Perforate pieces that need to be torn out, encourage joining immediately online or responding by phone using a credit card, date the offer to create a sense of urgency, use a "P.S." to highlight an important note, use testimonials from real-life people who are recognizable in the area or region.

It should be noted that direct mail copy is very different from the verbiage used in brochures, proposals, or everyday business communication. Direct mail copy breaks all the rules. There may be incomplete sentences, slang, and "fluffy" copy. To be certain, direct mail copy is not usually part of the repertoire of the president or executive director, or whoever the letter's signer may be. Thus, there is often reluctance by the signer the first time he or she is asked to sign a well-written direct mail letter. In fact, that is the sign of a great direct mail letter designed for membership acquisition purposes.

The Reply Envelope

Including a reply envelope will *always* increase the response rate. In fact, no package should ever be mailed without a return envelope. Without a return envelope, the prospect would have to do too much in order to join. The business reply envelope is not fancy because the post office regulates its graphics. The post office should be consulted about the appropriate barcodes for the organization's particular mailing address. Always have the envelope approved by the post office before printing to avoid problems cropping up after printing. Although not required, it is advisable to print these envelopes in black. Some colors have other colors in their makeup, and certain reds in inks can cause problems with the post office's readers. So do not get fancy here, just print in black.

If possible, use a postage-paid envelope to preclude the barrier of the prospect not having a stamp. There is debate about providing the postage for the return reply. Unless there is money in the budget to test this, it is recommended that the postage-paid BRE (business reply envelope) be supplied, avoiding the possibility that the prospect while paying bills and making donations has one too few stamps and omits the organization.

Membership Consultants, Inc. tested a BRE versus non-BRE for one of its clients, Missouri History Museum, for a direct mail renewal program. The findings were more related to the timing of the responses than to the difference in response rates: Money and memberships arrived more quickly in the BRE group than in the non-postage-paid group. This factor alone saves money for an organization because of the smaller mail quantity that is required for subsequent renewal mailings.

Another option is to use a postage-paid BRE, but print a message on the envelope that states, "Your stamp here will save the organization money." Then, when members use a stamp, the organization can save those stamped envelopes, return them to the post office, and receive a refund. A common misunderstanding is that this refund happens automatically, but it doesn't. The envelopes must be returned to the post office for the refund.

The Response Device

Include all information on the response device that will make processing and servicing a member as simple as possible. The name and address should be printed on the response device so that processing personnel do not have to read handwriting or printing. The list code should be on the response device for easy tracking. Ask the prospective member to include information such as telephone number(s), email address, children's ages, matching gift employers, and any other pertinent information important for the files.

If there is room on the response device, repeat the offer, picture the premium, and list the benefits and categories on the reverse side. Consider listing the categories of membership with the most popular category first, or the category you want people to join. Highlight the category that is a level up from the entry-level category and note that this is the "Best Value!"

After mailing the piece, it is time to track results. Tracking the results allows for future decisions that are based on concrete and objective information. Track the responses by the day and by the week. This will allow the prediction of future campaign results. For instance, sometimes the numbers of responses received within the first ten days after the mailing (starting with the first *heavy* response day) multiplied by two is an indicator of the total number of responses once the campaign is complete. It is important to determine response rate, cost per response, and cost per piece. Then compare the cost per package to the income over the life of the member. Looking at all of these factors helps determine what was successful in a campaign and what changes should be made in upcoming campaigns.

SEASONALITY

Each organization needs to explore and establish its own seasonality in mailing. A library or museum may find that the back-to-school mood in the fall is a prime time of the year, thereby making a direct mail rollout at that time most successful. This would leave the spring or winter for test mailings. On the other hand, a zoo or botanical garden may feel that spring is the best time for a large direct mail campaign with fall being the test time. Each institution is different and testing should be done to determine the most effective mailing time for your organization.

To take full advantage of an organization's seasonality, ideally testing should be conducted in the "off season" so that winning packages and offers can be "rolled out" in larger quantities during that organization's best performing season. Direct mail results may be from 10 to 50 percent higher in the best time of the year for a particular organization. However, other key times in an organization's lifespan can be the exception to the rule of seasonality. For instance, if an organization is celebrating a major anniversary or is opening a new facility in a season that is not its peak season, then that event and the heightened attention and publicity can overcome or surpass its typical seasonal circumstances.

TESTING

Testing is the learning that makes or breaks an organization's productivity in the use of direct mail. Testing is the scientific component that demonstrates what really works and what doesn't in direct mail. The true enemy of a direct mail program is the "gut feeling" that people sometimes impose on a direct mail campaign. Sometimes managers of campaigns or committees will impose what they like or dislike about direct mail on a campaign. To be successful, direct mail campaigns cannot be run on gut feelings or on personal whims, but must be based on industry standards and on testing.

Testing is the systematic and scientific presentation of two or more opposing elements of a direct mail package randomly presented to target audiences under controlled conditions to determine which element of the test will produce the best results. For instance, if an offer is being tested, in this case, the offer of a free tote bag versus a free umbrella, then the remainder of the direct mail package must be identical with the same graphics, the same copy, and the same number of inserts mailed to the same lists that are randomly divided into two groups. The tote bag offer is mailed to one of the randomly selected groups; the umbrella offer is mailed to the other group. The results will speak for themselves. Whichever group produces the most responses, the highest average gift, and, in the end, the lowest cost per dollar raised and the greatest ROI (return on investment) will be the winner. This information can then be applied to the next mailing in the annual cycle of campaigns, the winning element used, and another element tested.

This may be an oversimplification of the testing process, but generally, that is how testing works. Test cells (i.e., a cell is the test group) need to be at least 5,000 pieces in size for a reliable test. That means that for testing the umbrella against the tote bag, at least 5,000 of each offer would need to be mailed. In some cases one of the test cells may produce the higher response rate and the other may produce the higher average gift. The umbrella may cost twice as much as the tote bag. In these cases, all costs of the package and the premium need to be considered. When this is done, it will usually be possible to determine a winner. If the results are inconclusive, repeating the test may be necessary. Verifying the results with a subsequent test is usually advisable.

Other elements that can be tested include:

- Messages or themes: A philanthropic message versus a benefits message
- Package size: A 6" × 9" package versus a #10 envelope package
- A discount offer versus a premium offer
- A plain envelope versus a four-color graphic envelope
- Two-color packages versus four-color packages
- Two-page letter versus four-page letter
- A letter package versus a postcard or self-mailer

In almost every case, it is recommended that an organization conduct its own testing. What has been tested and proven to work for one organization may not be the case for another organization. What has been proven to work for one group at a point in time may need to be retested several years later as the direct mail community changes and other trends may apply.

ANALYSIS

Perhaps the most important part of any campaign is not how much money is collected, but what is learned in the process. The analysis of a campaign is critical, and yet it is the part that is most frequently overlooked. The purpose of every campaign must be to learn as much as possible about list performance, offers, and which package performs best so that the organization can mail smarter the next time. If a full and comprehensive analysis is not conducted after every campaign, then little, if anything, is learned from the campaign to be used in the next one. For instance, if a list performed poorly with respect to response rate, but had a high average gift in one campaign, that list might be deleted from the next campaign if the lists are judged only on response rate.

Some organizations might be married to a particular offer, even though a less expensive offer proves to work just as well in a test of the two offers. The lesson is, don't test what you don't want to change. An organization that delights in its fabulous design that so beautifully depicts what the organization stands for may be reluctant to give up those graphics when a plain white envelope proves to "pull" better (produce better results) than those gorgeous four-color envelopes. Use what is learned to build a foundation on which to build the next campaign. Ongoing testing, analysis, and learning is what makes great direct mailers and separates the professionals from the amateurs.

A complete direct mail report (see table 8.1) usually occurs about sixty to ninety days after a campaign has "dropped" (mailed). This time allows for the full measure of a campaign's response to be received, processed, and tabulated. The data needed to perform a spreadsheet analysis include:

- Number of pieces mailed: In total and by list segment;
- Number of responses: In total and by list segment;
- Amount contributed: In total and by list; and
- Costs: Of creative, printing, processing, mailing, lists, premiums.

With these numbers, a response analysis spreadsheet can be developed. No analysis is complete without a narrative analysis to accompany the spreadsheet. The narrative is needed to point out the subtle nuances that may be missed by those people who are not well versed in the minutiae of direct mail, especially for membership acquisition purposes. Often, individuals who do not have a good working knowledge of direct mail make budget decisions, so

Table 8.1 Sample Direct Mail Productivity and Cost Analysis Matchback Report

List Code	List	Number Mailed	Number of Responses	Response Rate	Revenue	Average Gift	List Cost	Total Cost	Cost per Dollar Raised	Return on Investment	5 Year Revenue
Ac14F-D12	Dropped Members 2012	7,000	227	3.24%	$10,862.00	$47.85	$0.00	$4,760.00	$0.44	$2.28	$17,916.87
Ac14F-D13	Dropped Members 2013	8,000	455	5.69%	$26,491.50	$58.22	$0.00	$5,440.00	$0.21	$4.87	$43,697.73
Ac14F-E1	Education/Classes	394	17	4.31%	$944.00	$55.53	$0.00	$267.92	$0.28	$3.52	$1,557.13
Ac14F-stb13	Single Tickets 2013	1,100	13	1.18%	$990.00	$76.15	$0.00	$748.00	$0.76	$1.32	$1,633.01
Ac14F-stb14	Single Ticket 2014	2,600	37	1.42%	$1,677.00	$45.32	$0.00	$1,677.00	$1.00	$1.00	$2,766.21
Ac14F-P1	Prospect (Friends of Art)	72	2	2.78%	$152.00	$76.00	$0.00	$48.96	$0.32	$3.10	$250.72
Ac14F-t1	Museum of Nat. History	468	10	2.14%	$277.00	$27.70	$0.00	$318.24	$1.15	$0.87	$456.91
Ac14F-t10	Shakespeare	2,070	28	1.35%	$1,903.00	$67.96	$0.00	$1,407.60	$0.74	$1.35	$3,139.00
Ac14F-t11	Park Conservancy	249	3	1.20%	$72.00	$24.00	$0.00	$169.32	$2.35	$0.43	$118.76
Ac14F-t2	Opera	1,100	11	1.00%	$861.00	$78.27	$0.00	$1,677.00	$1.95	$0.51	$1,420.22
Ac14F-t3	Ballet	750	4	0.53%	$162.00	$40.50	$0.00	$162.00	$1.00	$1.00	$267.22
Ac14F-t4	Heard Museum	1,946	43	2.21%	$4,534.00	$105.44	$0.00	$1,323.28	$0.29	$3.43	$7,478.83
Ac14F-t5	Musical Museum	1,828	17	0.93%	$2,466.00	$145.06	$0.00	$1,243.04	$0.50	$1.98	$4,067.67
Ac14F-t6	Art Museum	1,998	26	1.30%	$2,216.00	$85.23	$0.00	$1,358.64	$0.61	$1.63	$3,655.29
Ac14F-t7	Symphony	791	8	1.01%	$1,668.00	$208.50	$0.00	$537.88	$0.32	$3.10	$2,751.37
Ac14F-t8	Zoo *(Households - no presence of children)*	3000	29	0.97%	$1,573.00	$54.24	$0.00	$2,040.00	$1.30	$0.77	$2,594.66
Ac14F-t9	Performing Arts	2,463	23	0.93%	$1,577.00	$68.57	$0.00	$1,674.84	$1.06	$0.94	$2,601.26
Ac14F-M	MULTIS	4,200	64	1.52%	$4,200.00	$65.63	$0.00	$2,856.00	$0.68	$1.47	$6,927.90
AC14-1	Arizona Highways	7,200	76	1.06%	$6,550.50	$86.19	$850.23	$5,746.23	$0.88	$1.14	$10,805.05
AC14-2	Sunset Magazine	6,650	68	1.02%	$6,375.00	$93.75	$680.42	$5,202.42	$0.82	$1.23	$10,515.56
AC14-3	New Yorker	1,846	20	1.08%	$2,116.00	$105.80	$400.15	$1,655.43	$0.78	$1.28	$3,490.34
Total		55,725	1,181	2.12%	$77,667	$65.76	$1,930.80	$40,314	$0.52	$1.93	$128,111.72

the role of the analysis becomes the justification for some rather large expenditures. Direct mail campaign budgets usually rival staff costs as the largest items in the membership department's budget.

Matchback Analysis

Today, with so many ways for people to respond, a matchback analysis is required to get the full picture of a campaign's productivity. A matchback analysis requires a data pull of all transactions from the time of the mail drop date and the next ninety-day period. This total response file is compared to the original mail file. The matches between the two files are considered the full impact of the mailing effort. Even though only a portion of the members responded via mail, the people who joined online, in person, or by phone were all touched by the mailing, which likely influenced their decision to become a member. The matchback analysis will likely produce two times the results as simply running a report with the campaign source code, because source codes are usually not tracked with non-mailed responses. Some matchback analyses have produced five times the mailed, source coded response reports.

DIRECT MAIL USE

There are a variety of uses of direct mail in the membership and development areas of an organization. For the most part the advice given here has been for direct mail acquisition of new members. Mail is also used for renewals and other gifts to an organization. Included here are some general rules for other uses of direct mail for nonprofit membership organizations including renewals and annual or special appeals.

Renewals

Many of the same rules apply for renewal mailings as has been recommended for acquisition. There are, however, a few differences relating to renewals. First, the letter for renewals can be shorter. Because a person has had an experience with the organization, there is less persuading to do, hence a shorter letter. A letter is advised because it does not presume the renewal decision, but kindly asks the current member to consider it. A renewal letter allows for another thank you for past support, something that is always important. A renewal letter also allows an organization to talk about upcoming events and the reasons for renewing the relationship. Some organizations choose to use an invoice format, without a letter, an attempt that presumes the member will renew and just pay the "bill." If there is a question about a campaign like this, it should be tested just as an acquisition package would be tested.

Another element of renewals that can be tested is personalization versus non-personalization. Some organizations with very high renewal rates do not use a personalized renewal package. Timing of the renewal mailings should also be tested. Starting the renewal series ninety days before expiration may be too soon for some organizations; sending the first renewal reminder forty-five days before expiration may be more productive for another organization. The younger the audience, the more immediate the renewal to the expiration date, while older audiences will renew earlier in the renewal cycle.

Annual or Special Appeals

Direct mail can also be used to ask for other gifts to the institution. In fact, direct mail is probably the preferred way to determine whether there is a possibility that a member has the interest and capability to make commitments to an organization beyond the membership commitment. Direct mail is an important technique for the development program, with the membership providing the prospect pool to solicit.

Anticipated Responses

The response rates vary depending on the type of campaign, the history and aggressiveness of a mailer, and the expertise of the staff or consultant conducting the direct mail campaign. Here are some examples of acceptable ranges of response rates per specific type of campaign:

- Acquisition, first time members: 0.5 to 1.2 percent or more. Lowest response rates are seen for non-local organizations, or organizations that are not visitation-based. Highest response rates are seen for zoos or organizations with high admission rates.
- Membership renewal: 10 to 50 percent per renewal mailing; usually at least three renewal mailings are sent for a renewal rate totaling 60 to 75 percent.
- Annual or Special appeal: 5 to 15 percent of the membership solicited, less if to non-affiliated groups (becomes an acquisition campaign). May be as high as 50 to 80 percent if segmented and prior donors are solicited.

- Lapsed member mailings: 1.5 to 8 percent depending on the aggressiveness of pursuing lapsed members; the more aggressive, the lower the response rate.
- Upgrade mailings: 3 to 8 percent to get current members to upgrade their level of membership support (note: half of respondents will renew at the same level rather than upgrading).

MULTICHANNEL ENHANCEMENTS TO DIRECT MAIL

Direct mail is not necessarily a stand-alone method of acquiring, renewing, or appealing to members and donors. Catching people's attention is ever harder today in the fractured media environment. Getting in front of prospects via multiple channels is ever more important. Combining a mailed message with an email touch, online ad, and a social media impression can work to maximize results.

WHAT WORKS AND WHY

With all of the marketing channels and touch points available today to enlist members and get them to renew, upgrade, or give a second gift, how do we know what will work best, and why? Years of experience and industry results demonstrate that direct mail still works and performs with the highest response rates. Direct mail packages (letter, reply device, outer and carrier envelopes, with or without a brochure) work better than postcards. Well-planned and targeted mail campaigns will get more responses than well-planned and executed digital campaigns to the same audiences. But why?

Direct mail experts agree that mail is not restricted by time or space. A direct mail piece can be reviewed repeatedly. With a direct mail package, there is plenty of space to tell the story and many pieces to re-emphasize key points. Emails and banner ads may be much more fleeting. Emails are easier to delete and tend to get lost in an overwhelmed inbox.

An interesting explanation is offered by direct marketing expert Gary Hennerberg in an article in *Target Marketing Magazine* titled "Why Direct Mail Won't Die."[2] In this article, Hennerberg references a *Scientific American* article "The Reading Brain in the Digital Age: Why Paper Still Beats Screens."[3] Research suggests that the brain has been trained and evolved over many years in its ability to process the printed word, and that reading on screens is a new adaptation for the brain. Hence, comprehension is different in these two formats. There are three forms of comprehension: Glance and forget, short-term reading comprehensions, and long-term comprehension. Glance and forget is self-explanatory, short-term comprehension evaporates in few moments or hours, and long-term comprehension can last for hours, days, a few weeks, or perhaps even a lifetime.

Hennerberg describes several methods of direct marketing in terms of comprehension as follows:

- Social Media: Good for building brand and top-of-mind awareness; it is glance and forget unless there are links and clicks to a landing page calling for action.
- Email: Provokes curiosity, and if the reader clicks to a landing page, this action can lead to short-term comprehension. If the email is merely opened, it is more glance and forget.
- Websites and Landing Pages: These are glance and forget if the person searched, happened upon your page, and then abandoned. If there is valuable content and a call to action, there is a shot at short-term comprehension or even long-term comprehension.
- Short or Long Video: Short video is glance and forget unless it prompts and action or opt-in, achieving short-term comprehension. Long videos when viewed in their entirety create short-term comprehension, and if action is taken, long-term comprehension.
- Direct Mail Postcard: Most postcards are glance and forget, but a well-constructed postcard can create short-term comprehension or even long-term comprehension with a strong call to action.
- Direct Mail Package: "The ability to deliver long persuasive copy is the value of direct mail and is why direct mail won't die." Letter packages can be tossed in the trash, and in that case are glance and forget, but when the recipient opens and views the letter, inserts, and storytelling about a cause or organization, at least short-term comprehension is established. With the kind of good convincing copy and creative we all strive to achieve, certainly long-term comprehension and a membership sale are likely.

With this bit of science, and years of experience, these explanations are very good food for thought when trying to understand why direct mail keeps on working, even in the digital age.

SUMMARY

Direct mail is still alive and well and producing the most responses of any channel in use for acquiring, renewing, and upgrading memberships and for converting members to donors. Direct mail is a science with many variables that can be tested and proven. Each use of the mail has its own best practices with respect to lists, package, expected response, and timing. Direct mail can be complemented with digital appeals, but so far, in most cases, cannot be replaced without damaging the membership and donor programs. Direct mail lives! View a variety of full-color membership acquisition direct mail samples and case studies at www.thememembershipbook.com.

NOTES

1. Tom Belford, "New Era Begins in 17 Years," *The Agitator*, February 20, 2014, accessed January 10, 2015, http://www.theagitator.net/online-fundraising/new-era-begins-in-17-years.

2. Gary Hennerberg, "Why Direct Mail Won't Die," *Target Marketing*, May 13, 2015, accessed May 14, 2015, http://www.targetmarketingmag.com/blog/why-direct-mail-won-t-die.

3. Ferris Jabr, "The Reading Brain in the Digital Age: Why Paper Still Beats Screens," *Scientific American*, April 2013, accessed June 8, 2015, http://www.scientificamerican.com/article/the-reading-brain-in-the-digital-age-why-paper-still-beats-screens.

9

Selling Memberships

The Art of On-Site Sales

Timid salesmen have skinny kids.

—Zig Ziglar, American Author, Salesman, and Motivational Speaker

ON-SITE MEMBERSHIP SALES

An on-site membership sale is the face-to-face sale of a membership to an individual visiting an organization's physical site. It can also be the sale of a membership at an organization's off-site event that the organization controls—such as a convention or major event. On-site sales are the most lucrative way to acquire new members; the face-to-face ask is the most personal and compelling. The cost of selling memberships at high traffic times or at special events is usually much less than the revenue, making on-site sales the most cost-effective way to gain new members.

DYNAMICS OF THE SALE

To be successful at on-site sales, the organization must be committed to membership and to the sales efforts. The organization must remove impediments to the sales process. This entails hiring the right people to make the sales, and the expectation of selling in the job description. This means allowing signage to support the sale, offering an incentive for those selling as well as for those buying the membership, and allowing the sales personnel to have first access to the prospects as they approach the entrance to the event or the front door or lobby. Staff and volunteers who sell memberships need training and coaching in the sales process.

ART OF THE SALE

The on-site membership salesperson needs to understand that the customer—a prospective member—is coming with an interest in the organization. The person has the first ingredient needed for the sale: an interest in what is being sold. The other necessary ingredients for a membership sale are for the person to have an experience with the institution (if they are walking in, they are about to have that experience, or they've had it before) and the financial ability to become a member. With the right approach, a salesperson can determine if the visitor has each of these prerequisites to become a member. It is the salesperson's job to find out. "Welcome! Are you here to visit the special exhibit? Have you been here before? Are you a member?" All are good icebreakers to begin the membership conversation.

The artful salesperson quickly develops rapport, figures out family structure or size of the group visiting, and suggests membership as a way to save them money, get them in more quickly, offer a connection to something they have an interest in, etc. The salesperson also offers something of value: free admission, an ongoing offering of involvement and events, a free premium item if they join today, plus the ability to support a worthwhile organization with their membership support.

With this approach, the person will either join or not, but the idea of membership and ongoing involvement has been introduced. Even if the visitor chooses not to join at this time, the door has been opened.

The expectation is that 2 to 4 percent of the people approached will decide to become a member. At high-traffic times, an experienced, well-trained and supported salesperson can expect to sell five to six memberships per hour, sometimes as many as ten memberships per hour.

STAFFING

The staffing of a successful on-site sales effort requires that the person doing the selling wants to be selling. At times, membership sales are added to people's other duties. If the person took a job that did not originally have the sales requirement, that person may be reluctant to do sales. Sales strikes fear in some people, so it is important to staff a sales operation with people who are eager to do sales and able to interact with the public in a proactive way. Sometimes, "sales" is a dirty word to supervisors or leadership. It is important that the process of membership sales be positioned as a way to develop ongoing relationships with members and donors who will help support the organization. Having this vision and understanding is important so that sales are an accepted part of, and seen as critical to, the success of the membership program.

It should be noted that recruiting, hiring, and training people to implement on-site sales is an arduous process. Finding people who will represent an organization in a positive way, are comfortable approaching people and asking for money, and have an aptitude for sales takes great effort. On-site sales is not the type of job that is filled by calling a temporary employment agency. The hiring process is an art in itself. So, too, is the training process. Training includes classroom time to explain the overall role of membership at the institution, what membership has to offer prospective members, learning the benefits and pricing options. Training also involves sales role-playing, modeling the desired behavior for the new team members, and then coaching and shadowing them as they talk to visitors.

People who are successful at the sales process are outgoing, positive, and have a good feeling about what they are selling and who they represent. Good salespeople appreciate being given a goal and are motivated by trying to reach that goal. If multiple salespeople are working side by side at one time, often there will be some friendly competition to see who can sell the most memberships during the shift.

Sales expectations also should be in place for any of the front-of-the-house staff that may interact with visitors. This includes staff working the circulation desk at a library, the admission staff at a museum, a person working at a registration table at an event or conference, a person selling tickets to special venues at a science museum, or anyone working at a gift shop or anywhere people are ready to spend money. Obviously, these employees are hired to do something other than sell memberships as their primary role. But they need to embrace their role in upselling the customer to becoming a member at their point of contact.

These vital staff members need the same training that people hired just to sell memberships receive. Ideally, all staff members need to suggest membership to prospective members when the opportunity arises, and need to be trained to do this.

Employing the help and assistance of staff members who report to other departments is always a challenge. These staff members, and their leaders, have their own goals—to keep lines moving, to sell admission tickets, to maximize retail sales. A membership can be an offering that enhances the purchase a visitor is about to make. It can save money at the gift shop, it can offer them free admission, and it can help the organization have more revenue to provide more of what the member enjoys. So when a staff person is asked to sell memberships for another department, there needs to be perspective: They are helping the visitor when they ask them if they would like to be a member. The staff member is doing the visitor a favor.

Sometimes the sales "staff" is not staff at all, but volunteers. Volunteer membership salespeople can be just as successful as paid staff. Often volunteers have a passion for and knowledge of the organization that rivals or exceeds that of staff. Again, training and goals are needed to guide the volunteers, just as they are for paid staff.

Mechanics of the Sale

The mechanics of the sale are important. In preparation for the sales effort, the benefits to the new member have to be in place. The sales staff needs to understand which benefits are most compelling and will motivate visitors to join. A membership survey is one way to determine favorite benefits and how the membership is used. All of this information is important to be able to prepare for the approach to the prospect.

Offering the prospective member a desirable premium is also a vital part of the sale. A tote bag, an umbrella, or other item that relates to the organization are all good choices for a premium giveaway. These premiums are the takeaway that can tip the scales when someone is weighing the decision of whether to join. Having a tangible item is a complement to the intangible concept of a membership. The new member will feel good walking away with a free item they can use.

Some staff, volunteers, and even members will say that a tote bag will not affect their behavior. However, it is a fact of human nature that behaviors are affected by the offer of something free. What people say and what they do are two different stories. Interesting studies in the power of free are presented in the book *Predictably Irrational* by author Dan Ariely, a behavioral economist and Duke University professor. In a study conducted by Ariely and his colleagues, "customers" were offered a highly prized and exquisitely creamy Lindt truffle for fifteen cents or a good, but plain-tasting Hershey's Kiss for just one cent. Customers compared the price and quality of each, and the results showed that about 73 percent chose the Lindt truffle and 27 percent chose the

Kiss. When the price of both chocolates was decreased by one cent—making the Hershey's Kiss free—suddenly 60 percent of customers (up from 27 percent before) opted for the free Kiss.[1] What is the lesson here? Even though the relative price between the two remained the same, few could resist the allure of free chocolate—even when tempted with a very high-quality, yet very affordable truffle alternative. Free is a powerful motivator.

Equipped with information on compelling reasons for people to join, it is now time to work on an engaging script. Different people will be comfortable with different openings to engage the visitor. Some examples of opening greetings include:

- "Thanks for coming to visit today. Are you a member?"
- "Welcome! Did you come to see the special exhibit today? If so, I would like to make a suggestion that will save you some money today."
- "I see you here at the library pretty often. I would like to suggest you become a Friend of the Library. I can offer you some special benefits if you join now."

Salespeople will develop their own voice and pitch with more experience. In some circumstances, where free admission and free or reduced special exhibition or registration fees are offered, it can be advantageous if the salesperson can "do the math" and show the prospect the financial impact of their decision to join. Having a chart or a "cheat sheet" that illustrates the cost per number of people in their party versus the cost of a membership is a helpful sales tool.

Salespeople should also be armed with examples of benefits offered to members throughout the year. A copy of a newsletter, a listing of events the member will be invited to, or a list of upcoming exhibitions will also demonstrate the year-long value of membership. Finally, being able to give examples of how the membership donation will be spent to support the mission of the organization is also a good selling point to solidify the membership pitch.

NEGATIVE ENVIRONMENTS

Organizations sometimes have expectations of a healthy, robust membership and yet have a climate that is not supportive of membership sales. Impediments to membership sales include some of the following situations:

- Do not allow signage promoting membership or the membership sales efforts.

- Admissions or visitor services staff members who do not embrace or engage in membership sales; membership sales are perceived to be in competition with ticket sales goals.
- Do not allow for special compensation for membership salespeople.
- Do not provide training to front-of-house people who will be conducting sales.

HOW ON-SITE SALES EFFORTS ARE STRUCTURED

Successful on-site sales efforts are best structured by giving the membership department some degree of control of the sales effort. The ideal situation is when the front-of-the-house staff and membership are part of the same department or have the same leadership for both departments. The Museum of Science, Boston has a successful membership program and a very successful on-site sales conversion process. At least part of that organization's success can be attributed to a staffing decision that promoted a long-time membership director to the Associate Vice President of Visitor Services and Membership. This dual role ensures that membership will receive the adequate balance of attention at the point of sale. A similar scenario was established at the Saint Louis Art Museum as it prepared to open a major expansion in 2013. Management and supervision of the admissions desk was aligned with the membership department.

Another pro-membership sales option includes allowing membership personnel to work in a front-of-the-house position. A membership staff person can be assigned to work high-traffic times in the lobby area in advance of the ticket counter, so that membership options can be presented before a visitor purchases a ticket. Positioning a salesperson in this way can relieve the ticketing staff of having the membership discussion at busy times while also being up-front with the membership sales effort.

A third option is to outsource the membership sales process during very high-traffic, high-membership-potential times. For this type of effort to be successful, the team being hired must be well-trained, experienced salespeople who will act as an extension of the organization's own staff. The outsourced staff will be conducting intensive sales of memberships and must have a well-rounded understanding of the organization, its mission, and its membership program. To be successful, the salespeople must share a passion for the organization, just as do staff and volunteers. This outsourced strategy is designed specifically to take full advantage of a busy time with the potential for significant membership sales conversions. Situations that are conducive for this type of solution include grand openings, spring break or holiday crowds, special events, and blockbuster exhibition openings.

A professional, outsourced sales team has been used at a library foundation's popular author events offering preferred seating and autographed books to new members. These professional sales services have resulted in 1,500 memberships for a botanical garden that hosts a popular festival over a three-day period, and 600 memberships were sold at an outdoor sculpture garden that hosts a Mother's Day art fair. Outsourced sales results can be very successful and profitable for the sponsoring organization.

With any of these options, quick membership processing that moves the new members through the door and on to their experience is of utmost importance. At high-volume and high-sales times, it is important to plan special processing considerations. Salespeople's time is valuable—they need to be out selling, not processing the transaction. At a major midwestern museum, during high traffic times such as holidays and spring break, a special processing table is set up to handle the constant flow and line of people who say yes to the membership pitch. The staff of the membership department maintain a table of three processors (one for each salesperson) to keep the flow of sales and processing going. At the Denver Zoo and other venues, instant membership fulfillment is carried out so that the member walks away with a permanent card and useful information about the zoo and membership.

If lines get too long, prospective members will jump out of line and just buy tickets instead of a membership. A members' express line is ideal, if it is a shorter line than the line for the general public. Just make sure the member line is no longer than the other lines to gain access. Ways to streamline the process include having pre-stuffed bags of membership materials, a temporary or permanent membership card, and the membership premiums. These should all be ready to give to the new members.

A special note: Unless an organization has a specially designed, mobile optimized and easy-to-use payment processing app, the assumption that an iPad can be used to handle the on-site sale in a more expeditious manner is not always a safe assumption. Wireless connectivity issues, clunky or extremely long e-commerce forms on the website, and manually keying in information can cause serious problems when a salesperson is attempting to complete a membership sale.

SALES MOTIVATION AND COMPENSATION

Motivating and compensating sales staff is an important ingredient of a successful membership sales effort. Money is the most significant motivator. The best scenario to maximize sales is to compensate the salespeople with financial bonuses based on the number of memberships sold. At some organizations, salespeople are paid from $1 or $2 up to 10 percent of the value of the membership sold, in addition to an hourly wage. This compensation package can make membership sales a financially rewarding and productive job. Some nonprofit organizations have policies or dislike for this for-profit business model; however, this compensation structure works, and works very well.

Other compensation strategies include providing a reward for staff members who meet a predetermined goal. A science center set sales goals for its front-of-the-house staff and then provided a $50 wholesale club gift card to any staff members who met their monthly goal. This bonus was a very motivating offer to a young staff that could buy groceries, gas, or household items with their gift cards. Other bonuses include gift cards to movies, pizzas, or gift shops.

Perhaps less motivating, but still a step in the right direction, is when sales goals are made public with staff on a daily, weekly, or monthly basis and then progress is tracked and reported. If sales goals are met, that situation is celebrated. If they are not met, that situation is also made known and discussed with a focus on why goals were not met and what may need to happen to improve the situation.

EVALUATING SALES SUCCESS

Membership sales are quantifiable. Reporting membership sales data is one of the important aspects of creating and improving a successful sale effort. Tracking sales per day, per hour, for an exhibition run is the first step. Tracking attendance during those same periods is also necessary. Calculating the sales conversion rate divides the number of memberships sold by the visitation number. Visitation totals are paid visitors, not including members, free admissions, or school groups. The goal is to convert 2 to 4 percent of visitors to members. As an example, 100 memberships sold on a day with 5,000 paid visitors equals a sales conversion rate of 2 percent.

An alternative way of calculating sales conversions, used at some organizations, divides the number of membership sales by the attendance (paid, nonmembers, and non-school groups) by the average number of people in a typical party—perhaps two to four. Calculating this way, the 100 membership sold would be divided by (5,000 visitors / two people in the party = 2,500) = 4 percent. Calculated this way, the goal would be a 4 to 8 percent sales conversion rate.

In addition to a conversion rate, sales should be tracked by sales per day and sales per exhibition run. It is important to differentiate between weekdays and weekend sales days and by numbers of days in an exhibition's run.

On-site membership sales will often be the largest source of new members at visitor-based organizations. On-site sales can account for 50 to 60 percent of all new members at these institutions. If on-site sales far exceed these percentages, then not enough is being done to acquire members by other methods, such as direct mail or online. If sales are less than these percentages, then on-site sales may not be getting the emphasis it deserves.

Renewal rates for on-site sales should parallel the first-year renewal rates, typically 25 to 40 percent. Renewal rates of on-site-sold members is usually lower than direct mail acquired members. On-site sales are usually a spur-of-the-moment decision based on a value proposition. A direct mail sale is usually made away from the location, and is often a more considered decision. Accordingly, renewal rates will be higher.

CASE STUDY: SAINT LOUIS ART MUSEUM

The Saint Louis Art Museum offers a good example of an on-site sales program that has evolved over time with several different incarnations over a fifteen-year period. Initially, responsibility for on-site sales rested with the visitor services team that was housed in the marketing department of the museum. The Saint Louis Art Museum is a free museum, with visitors being able to visit the galleries free at any time. The museum hosts special traveling exhibitions two to three times per year, and those exhibitions do require an admission fee of $12 to $14 for adults. The special traveling exhibitions have provided the impetus for membership promotion since free special exhibition admission is a benefit of membership.

With the infrequent nature of the special exhibition schedule, the visitor service staff was neither particularly concerned nor trained to make a significant case for membership. Membership sales on-site were minimal, especially during the non–special exhibition times. With the arrival of new membership leadership, more emphasis was placed on on-site sales at special exhibitions. Since they did not have a supervisory role over the visitor services personnel, and the team was tasked with ticket sales during the special exhibition periods, the membership department made the decision to outsource membership sales and be in control of its own sales destiny.

An experienced, professional team of membership salespeople specifically trained to sell memberships at cultural institutions was hired. This team understood museums and membership. Such assignments should not be staffed with temporary staffing agency personnel; they do not have the necessary depth of knowledge about membership. The professional sales team that was hired became an extension of the museum's staff at high-traffic, high-potential periods, with the same salespeople serving this need for a number of years. These professionally trained salespeople worked weekends and holidays during the traveling exhibition runs. The sales team would greet and talk with visitors about membership, close the sale, and then walk the prospect to the desk for processing.[2] Table 9.1 shows a record of the sales data of a long-term view of the Saint Louis Art Museum's outsourced on-site sales efforts:

Table 9.1 Saint Louis Art Museum Case Study 1999–2013

Year – Exhibit	Days	Memberships Sold	Revenue Raised	Sales per Day
1999 – Masks	3	203	$11,170	67
2003 – German Art Now	14	419	$23,420	30
2004 – Art of the Osage	48	1,092	$60,065	22
2005 – Hero, Hawk and Open Hand	19	271	$15,205	14
2005 – Nature and the Nation	21	472	$28,511	22
2005 – Tombs of UR	27	1,111	$67,617	41
2006 – Impressionist Camera	24	396	$24,272.50	16
2006 – New Ireland	30	540	$34,822	18
2007 – Napoleon	51	2,207	$136,126.50	44
2007 – Waking Dreams	23	603	$39,192	26
2008 – Action Abstraction	31	963	$60,987.50	31
2009 – Ming Dynasty	27	980	$61,310	33
2009 – Japanese Screens	28	491	$32,183.50	17
2010 – Joe Jones	29	659	$41,301	19
2010 – The Mourners	24	310	$21,765	13
2011 – Fiery Pool	35	549	$37,760	16
2011-12 – Monet	54	2,481	$158,544	49
2012 – Orchestrated Visions	25	322	$22,082	13
Winter 2012-13 – Barocci	30	1,017	$78,660	33
	543	**15,086**	**$954,994**	**28**

On-Site Sales Case Study. Saint Louis Art Museum.

In preparation for the grand opening of a new wing to the Museum in 2013, plans were made to transition the reporting structure of the visitor service function. Visitor services became part of the membership director's oversight. Current and new visitor service personnel received intensive membership sales training, tips, and techniques. In addition to ticket sales, the front-of-the-house staff now had full responsibility for selling memberships on a daily basis, during special exhibition times and during totally free visitation times. With the opening of the museum's new east wing, a new parking garage was added with a deep discount for members. The new parking policy gave prospective new members a valuable benefit even when the museum admission was free.

With this new arrangement—a parking benefit, visitor services being totally responsible for sales, and no outsourcing—museum personnel now are able to sell successfully with a conversion rate of 4 to 5 percent of all exhibition attendees during special exhibition timeframes. The sales team is given group goals and monetary incentives are awarded to help them achieve their sales conversion goals.

BLOCKBUSTERS AND ON-SITE SALES

Blockbuster exhibitions can be a combination of both curse and boon for membership. They can be a blessing for on-site membership sales. Blockbuster exhibitions and the sales of memberships during their run can grow membership to new levels. If an organization is prepared to deal with the outcome, it can be the growth that directors and membership manager dream about. Simultaneously, blockbusters can be a curse from a servicing, staffing, and renewal standpoint.

Two case studies of blockbusters and on-site sales are presented here—one at the Desert Botanical Garden in Phoenix and one at the Missouri History Museum. The Desert Botanical Garden hosted two Chihuly exhibitions, one in 2009 and one in 2013–2014. The garden's membership and visitor services departments managed the on-site sales with in-house staff. The second example is that of two back-to-back blockbuster exhibitions hosted by the Missouri History Museum in the mid 2000s that resulted in the doubling of the membership totals thanks to an outsourced on-site sales promotion during the two exhibit runs.

Case Study: Desert Botanical Garden[3]

The membership program at the Desert Botanical Garden had already been in growth mode prior to the first Chihuly exhibition with membership standing at 18,000 member households. The first exhibit was hosted in 2008–2009, just as the economic downturn was hitting Arizona especially hard. This exhibition was the first time the Garden had taken on a presentation of any exhibit of this kind of magnitude. It was *the* exhibit to see in Phoenix that season. Visitation was at an all-time record, and membership expanded by 10,000 members, due in large part to on-site sales. Additional staff were hired and trained. With timed ticketing and access to the exhibit getting more difficult as time passed, a membership was a means to get tickets at a desired time and date and at a discount from the $15 nonmember admission price. Growth in membership was significant and membership totals grew to 28,000. This exhibit and the promotion of membership put the Garden in a totally new position in the Phoenix cultural landscape.

Fast forward four years and the Garden staff made the decision to host *Chihuly in the Garden* once again during the 2013–2014 season with an increased admission price of $22. The Garden had retained 2,078 of the 8,800 members acquired during the previous Chihuly exhibition and increased visibility from the exhibit helped the Garden attract new members even after the show concluded. To prepare for the 2013–2014 exhibit the Garden made significant investments in the facilities, adding a popular dining venue, a new membership kiosk, and expanded parking. Membership again hired and trained staff to be prepared for another onslaught of visitors, and the Garden hosted a new, exciting Chihuly exhibition, this time with its own membership station positioned on the path leading to the Garden entrance, in front of the ticket sales booth. In combination with aggressive direct mail sales, membership again capitalized on this major exhibition, growing to the 40,000 mark.

The Garden's success in on-site sales is a result of very careful hiring and training of the people that represent the Garden and membership sales. In both 2008 and 2013, they held an on-site job fair to recruit seasonal staff for all Garden departments that needed additional staffing for the exhibit. The Garden's guest services and membership sales teams collaborated in all hiring efforts. They focused on customer service and personality in group interviews and further investigated their fit within the team during a second interview.

In 2010, membership sales staff worked to strengthen the relationship between guest services and member services. With increased sales training, group incentives, and goals (such as pizza parties), they matched the 2008–2009 on-site sales during a non-blockbuster year. Maintaining the strong connection between the departments put them in a great position going into the 2013 Chihuly year.

It is obvious from this description that the Garden took great care in vetting and hiring the membership sales people who became the front-line contact with many visitors at the Garden. It was a long and arduous process, but one that was a great success for membership sales and the Garden.

Case Study: Missouri History Museum[4]

The Missouri History Museum curated its own blockbuster exhibition with the *National Bi-Centennial Exhibition of the Lewis and Clark Expedition* in 2004. The U.S. Congress provided funding for the national touring exhibition that opened at the Missouri History Museum in January and ran through Labor Day, before traveling on to other museums nationwide. Membership preparation for this exhibition was extensive and included direct mail, telemarketing, and a major commitment to on-site sales. At the Missouri History Museum, the membership department chose to contract with a firm specializing in on-site membership sales staffing at museums and cultural venues. On-site sales staff was present for all weekends, holidays, and selected weekdays in the summer throughout the nine-month run of the exhibition and for the closing weeks of the exhibition, which were sold out.

This on-site sales engagement had all the necessary ingredients of success—a major exhibition that was garnering massive media attention, an institutional budget for advertising, record attendance, well-trained and experienced sales staff, and total support from the entire institution.

Free admission to the otherwise $12 exhibit, a premium commemorating the exhibit, the availability of a timed ticket even though non-joining visitors may not be guaranteed a ticket at their desired time slot, all combined to make the purchase of a membership a "no-brainer" for the visiting public.

Sales were robust, with 5,931 memberships sold at a cost per dollar raised of $0.32 and sales per hour of six memberships. This and the accompanying direct mail member acquisition efforts allowed the membership to grow from 9,000 members to 18,000 members in the span of one year.[5] Table 9.2 shows the results of the on-site sales effort.

Renewing on-site members who are making a convenience and value decision at the time of their visit takes attention and finesse. In the case of the Missouri History Museum, the Lewis and Clark exhibition was followed up

Table 9.2 Missouri History Museum On-Site Sales

Event	Number of New Members	Total Revenue	Total Hours	Total Expense	Cost Per Dollar Raised	Average Gift	Sales per hour
Lewis & Clark	5,931	$335,660	989.2	$108,494	$0.32	$56.59	6.0
Baseball as America	1,124	$63,160	182.5	$23,019	$0.36	$56.19	6.2

On-Site Sales with Blockbuster Exhibitions Case Study. Missouri History Museum.

with a very popular exhibit *Baseball as America* from the National Baseball Hall of Fame and Museum. Having a blockbuster follow a blockbuster allows for easier renewals or at least easier acquisition of new members to replace non-renewing members.

Both of the cases described here—the Desert Botanical Garden and the Missouri History Museum—employed aggressive efforts to renew the first-year members from their respective blockbuster exhibits. In each case, preemptive renewal phoning was put into place before the regular renewal cycle began. New members were called to see how they were enjoying their memberships. They were engaged in conversation about the exhibition but also about what was coming next at the venues. The call culminated in a suggestion "I see that your membership will be coming up for renewal soon, can I assist you with that today and renew right now on the phone?" As a result, and after the remainder of the full renewal cycle was complete, the Missouri History Museum reached a one-year renewal rate of 40 percent and the Desert Botanical Garden reached 34 percent. At sister institutions in the same market after other popular blockbuster exhibitions, other institutions who did not use these strategies experienced a 10 percent and a 17 percent first-year renewal rate.

STAFFING CONFIGURATION CHOICES

As described in all of these examples, staffing is the key ingredient to success in on-site sales. Staffing decisions are critical when designing or reconfiguring the sales effort at membership organization. Some key considerations for evaluating current practices and making an even greater commitment to on-site sales staffing are presented here.

Current Staffing

If on-site sales are currently taking place and the organization is pleased with results, there is still an opportunity to tweak and improve, if so desired. Tracking sales and comparing to past performance and to industry standards is a way to determine if sales are satisfactory. Track sales by salesperson, compare to peers, and see if all staff members are performing at acceptable levels. If there are improvements that can be made, consider providing additional training. Preparing for a busy season or an upcoming exhibition is the perfect time to add a session to put a focus on sales. Reminders about sales techniques, discussion points, and the math of membership are all topics for a training refresher session.

Goals and Incentives

Goals must be made public and people need to be updated on how they are progressing toward those goals. Incentives are important, and if sales are to be increased significantly, a reward structure needs to be considered. Financial incentives are the most impactful.

If sales with current staff are not satisfactory, examine the issues related to those lagging sales. Does the current staff embrace the role of selling memberships? Does membership have enough influence over existing staff to create a sales turnaround? If the answer is no, then more significant steps need to be taken, including the possibility of retraining, replacing staff, or reconfiguring the reporting structure.

New Staff

Whether replacing existing staff or creating new sales positions, the hiring and on-boarding process for new on-site sales staff is critical. Having a clear job description that delineates expectations and duties is important. Ascertaining comfort levels with selling and working with the public is key. Some form of previous experience in direct sales is preferable. It is even possible to have finalists for the positions take pre-employment tests to determine if the person possesses the desired behavior techniques to be successful at the social, outgoing, and influencing requirements of the job.

Training and on-boarding are important next steps after the hire. Fully orienting the person to the organization, its mission, and the position of membership within the institution is the first step. Ongoing sales training including classroom and on-the-floor sessions with coaching and shadowing are important. Pairing the new people with an adept salesperson will give them a positive, productive coach after whom to model their selling efforts. Finally, tracking their progress, providing feedback, encouragement, and recognition for successful sales efforts will provide them with the support they need to continue.

If the decision is made to hire new staff, in all likelihood that special position should report to the membership manager. A direct reporting situation will be the most beneficial and will require less accommodation than trying to supervise a person who does not report directly to the person counting on the outcome of that person's efforts.

Outsourced Sales

There are times when an organization and its membership team may need a boost that an outside professional sales team can provide. There is a variety of situations that may lead to this decision:

- A need for temporary, part-time staff to supplement existing staff or nonexistent staff;
- A major event such as a grand opening or a blockbuster exhibit; or
- A demonstration of "how to" for existing staff or leadership who may not be buying into the benefits or possibilities of on-site membership sales.

An institution may know that it needs to beef up membership sales, but may be unprepared to add permanent staff to fill this role. As is the case with a one-time event such as a grand opening or reopening, the staffing need may be temporary, with existing staff able to handle the flow during normal traffic times. An organization may also want to have a demonstration of what might be possible, and bringing in a professional, well-trained team of membership salespeople can demonstrate the volume of sales that is possible.

One organization with several very high traffic events throughout the year knew that it was not fully capitalizing on the crowds of visitors from a membership perspective. The organization had been utilizing a team of faithful volunteers, positioned at a membership sales and servicing table in the lobby. But with burgeoning crowds of 5,000 to 10,000 people a day, the membership manager asked the volunteers to take clipboards in hand and greet visitors as they arrived on the plaza in front of admissions. The volunteers, some of them aged, politely declined, preferring the seated positions at their table. The membership manager decided to hire salespeople for the job, but the organization's human resource department would not allow her to hire temporary, part-time staff. Nor would they allow the manager to provide sales bonuses to motivate salespeople. Meeting with this double dose of resistance from volunteers and HR, she turned to an outsourced entity to provide the trained, motivated salespeople who understood membership and the mission of the organization. The result was an expansion from 3,500 more passive on-site sales annually to almost double that amount of 6,500 sales of memberships from on-site sales annually.

SUMMARY

On-site sales is a vital part of any organization's acquisition strategy. With on-site sales providing the largest proportion of new members of all potential sources, it is imperative that membership managers give this topic the consideration and attention that it deserves. Being successful at on-site sales can be the difference between a static program with the same year-over-year sales, and a program that is in the growth mode phase of its development. Even with outsourcing, the cost per dollar raised for on-site sales is lower than all other sources of new members. On-site sales of memberships may have the greatest single impact on a program of any acquisition method.

NOTES

1. Dan Ariely, *Predictably Irrational: The Hidden Forces That Shape Our Decisions*, rev. ed. (New York: HarperPerennial, 2010), 57–58.

2. Membership Consultants, Inc., Saint Louis Art Museum Membership Sales History, 2013.

3. On-Site Sales with a Blockbuster Exhibition Case Study. Desert Botanical Garden. Copyright 2015. All Rights Reserved.

4. On-Site Sales with Blockbuster Exhibitions Case Study. Missouri History Museum. Copyright 2015. All Rights Reserved.

5. Membership Consultants, Inc., Missouri History Museum Blockbuster On-Site Sales, 2004.

10

Marketing the Membership Program

Marketing is too important to be left to the marketing department.

—David Packard, Co-Founder, Hewlett-Packard

MEMBERSHIP'S EVOLVING ROLE

Often membership and marketing are in two distinct departments—with separate reporting structures, separate budgets, and different goals. This can lead to silos, competition for resources, missed opportunities for collaboration, and a lack of data transparency. This is not helpful to membership, and it is a disservice to the institution.

Today, membership needs to be more closely aligned with marketing than ever before. This requires membership to have a seat at the table for strategic conversations regarding the website, advertising planning, and social media. It requires shared goals and access to institutional data. It also means that membership needs to be prepared—and positioned—to take the lead on marketing and communications efforts that directly have an impact on its members, its growth, and its bottom line.

Indeed, membership must take ownership of its own destiny, and proactively advocate for those aspects of the marketing strategy that affect the health of the program. At the end of the day, organizations need to align marketing processes, infrastructure, budgets, and staffing based on meeting the needs of the membership program, not upon how departments are internally structured.

MARKETING ORIENTATION

At its most fundamental level, membership marketing is about motivating consumers—prospective, lapsed, and current members—to take a desired action. However, compared to most consumer products, the decision to become a member is a more complex process. The concept of becoming a member involves not only a transactional value proposition (e.g., money in exchange for benefits), but also deep emotional responses including a sense of community, pride, altruism, and status among other psychological drivers.

In order to be effectively marketed, membership needs to have a *marketing orientation* or, as described in *Strategic Marketing for Nonprofit Organizations*, a "target audience mindset" in which "success will come to that organization that best determines the perceptions, needs, and wants of target markets and continually satisfies them through the design, communication, pricing, and delivery of appropriate and competitively viable value propositions."[1] Thus, a marketing orientation requires implementation of what is commonly referred to as "the marketing mix." As explained in *Principles of Marketing*, the marketing mix is "the set of controllable tactical marketing tools—product, price, place, promotion, people, process and physical evidence—that the firm blends to produce the response it wants in the target market."[2]

In membership, the elements of the marketing mix include the following.

- Product: With membership, the product is a combination of tangible and intangible benefits. Often, the creation and consumption of the membership product is simultaneous, which means that the experience of each product is perishable and unique to the individual. The product also includes the packaging of benefits and naming of membership levels.
- Price: It can be challenging to put a price tag on membership when many of the benefits are intangible. A cost-benefit analysis, conjoint analysis (discussed in the section on market research), and benchmarking can help determine the appropriate cost for membership.
- Place (or distribution): Place includes all of the activities that make the product available to the target audience. In the case of visitation-based organizations, the place may be the library or museum. For others the place may be the member magazine or a nature reserve. For a non–location-based organization, the "place" of distribution may be the annual conference or the organization's website, where benefits are delivered and connections are made.

- Promotion: Promotion includes all of the activities and channels that an organization uses to inform and to encourage prospective members to join, such as on-site signage, the membership desk, direct mail, telemarketing, email marketing, social media, advertising, and the website.
- People: People are incredibly important to the membership experience. The people component of the marketing mix includes everyone who plays a part in the service delivery such as staff and volunteers.
- Process: In membership, process is related to the delivery of member benefits and management of the membership services experience.
- Physical Evidence: The physical evidence includes all of the material cues of the membership, including the facilities, signage, the website, and the presentation of email communications.

Designing Products and Services

A membership program, at its basic levels, is a direct exchange with the member—benefits for the membership dues. The key concept is that of exchange where "target audience members are asked to exchange something they value (e.g. giving up smoking) for something beneficial provided by the nonprofit organization (e.g. becoming part of an anti-tobacco industry cohort)."[3] That is, the member is being asked to incur a cost (i.e., dues) in return for benefits.

In membership, the product is what is presented to the potential member. It includes the benefits, both tangible and intangible. In marketing, there is much written about selecting the right message. The message is how the product is presented to the prospect. If the message is not clear, consumers will not buy—and marketing is, primarily, about buying. Or for nonprofits and membership, it's about joining. There are also messages that create an image of the organization; these are very helpful in persuading potential members that the organization is worthwhile and one that should be supported.

The primary marketing message for membership programs is about the exchange of joining for benefits. The first benefits that are expected and weighed in the mind of a potential member are the tangible ones; those should be first in any message for an institution with tangible benefits. Whether it is admission, a publication, or a discount, this is the easiest and clearest message for a potential member to hear and understand. Messages about the intangibles can be woven throughout those about the tangible ones (e.g., See the award-winning exhibition about Picasso FREE and learn how he influenced other artists!). Or they can be stated separately in another part of the direct mail, brochure, or public service announcement (PSA) (e.g., Your membership helps support our educational programs for the schools.).

Market research gives a basis for what the benefits should be or how the current ones should be changed. For example, when an arts council decided it was time to take a look at benefits, it held focus groups to discuss this issue. The facilitator had the groups discuss the current practice of sending a ticket strip to members, which included tickets to a variety of arts events in the community. Without exception, the focus groups dismissed the ticket strip as too cumbersome, easy to lose in a drawer and, basically never used. When showed a potential membership card to replace the strips, the response was unanimously favorable. The council changed the benefit.

Effective Pricing

Pricing the membership program is a part of the marketing mix. At the lower levels, for the value member, the marketing equation is a direct exchange—benefits for the membership dues. Designing the benefit package is a combination of what the institution is able to offer and what the potential member wants.

The major issue for the institution is making certain that the benefits (tangible and intangible) are commensurate with the price charged. The organization needs to decide what position it wants to take concerning the dues structure. An organization can decide that it wants to be an expensive program and charge a higher fee than others. Or it can position itself within the generally accepted range of other like organizations. Or it can decide that it wants large numbers at a low price. There are examples in all categories.

If the price is low, not much can be offered unless the numbers are enormous. For example, AARP, with dues at $16 per year, can offer a lot with more than thirty-seven million members simply because of the scale of the membership. Not many organizations can do this. Most visitation-based organizations price their membership in line with other like local organizations. If, however, the organization has something for which they can charge a high price to nonmembers, such as a high admission fee, then the organization can charge more for membership than other organizations in the same area. This is particularly true for institutions that attract a large tourist base.

One word of warning: do not ask about the price of membership when conducting a survey. Information about pricing is rarely accurate. If moviegoers are asked about the price of popcorn at the movies, it is always too expensive—but many people buy it. What people want to pay and what they will pay are two different things. Everyone would like to pay less for whatever it is they want to buy; however, if they are really interested, people will pay the price. The best way to determine price is to look at competing programs and the cost of providing benefits, and decide where the organization wants to position itself. If the cost seems to be decreasing the total numbers or total revenue, whichever is more important, then the price can be readjusted to a lower level. As with any part of the program, price can be tested. Test two different offers, determine which works best, and use that pricing structure.

Discounting

While the allure of a heavily promoted cobranded offer (think Groupon or LivingSocial) may be difficult to pass up, this type of deep discounting can quickly erode the price integrity of membership. Moreover, discounting can leave current members who are exposed to the offer feeling as if they have overpaid.

Discount offers tend to attract a value-seeking audience, so renewal rates for this type of pricing strategy are often quite low. Perhaps most damaging is the risk of creating an environment of "discount waiting" among audiences who would have otherwise joined at full price.

Discounting can have another unintended consequence: prompting current members to lapse or postpone renewing until another discount is offered. Experience indicates that while discounting may boost membership numbers in the short term, the long-term impact is depressed renewal rates and lost revenues.

In some cases, a strategic argument could be made for discounting. For instance, offering a discount for a holiday gift membership promotion could help increase membership revenues for year-end and introduce new audiences to the idea of membership. As long as the discount isn't being abused or cannibalizing regular membership sales, then this could be a worthwhile strategy. Most often, however, it is advisable to leverage premiums (whether tangible or intangible) rather than offer a discount.

Delivery

Delivery of the membership program refers to the ability to bring the membership program to the members. For national organizations, this means trying to find ways to bring the membership program to the local level where members live. Museums now consider having satellite locations to serve more of the public, but also to encourage membership for those who do not live near the main location. Of course, technology has offered the ultimate in distribution. Becoming a web member (Met Net) at the Metropolitan Museum of Art allows the member to browse the collections from anywhere in the world. This type of digital access to content is also a new membership opportunity.

For the marketing and the membership program to work effectively and serve the institution, it is necessary to have viable products and services that meet the needs and wants of potential members. Market research is conducted to develop a member profile, help select the target markets, and discover their needs and desires. With this, the membership program can design the offer, price it appropriately, use effective promotional techniques, and provide services where the members want them. When all of this is done well, audiences will respond in kind by joining, renewing, and becoming ever more involved. Having a marketing orientation in the membership program that takes into account all of these efforts will result in a program that meets the needs of the market and motivates people to join. If the membership program is run with marketing in mind, it will thrive.

THE CUSTOMER JOURNEY

In marketing theory, there is a model known as AIDA, or the "purchase funnel." AIDA is an acronym for the various stages within the customer journey (see figure 10.1). The AIDA model "suggests that Awareness leads to Interest, which leads to Desire, which leads to Action."[4]

Awareness is the first stage of any customer journey as it is a prerequisite for all subsequent stages. The Interest stage may be instantaneous (e.g., a visitor may become interested when greeted by a membership sales associate while waiting in line to purchase admission tickets) or it may take several touch points or a life change before the idea of membership becomes of interest (e.g., having young children may create interest in membership at a children's museum). During the Desire stage, there is an emotional connection generated within the mind of the prospective member. This desire creates momentum, and the prospective member begins internalizing the idea of membership, which produces a sense of wanting and ownership. Finally, the Action stage is when the decision to join occurs and the purchase is made.

In membership, there are additional stages in the customer journey, such as renewing, upgrading, giving, and volunteering. As the member's relationship

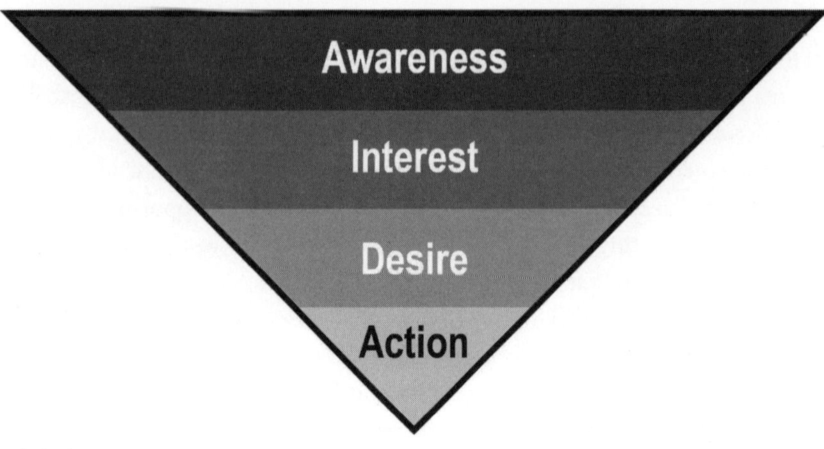

FIGURE 10.1
AIDA Model

with the organization deepens, the member moves further along the customer journey continuum (see figure 10.2). Not all members will progress through all stages, and the membership customer journey does not always follow a linear sequence. That is, members may join, rejoin; upgrade, downgrade; give one year and not the next; and so on.

MULTICHANNEL MARKETING

While the traditional AIDA model simplifies the buying process into a linear funnel, the reality is that the customer journey to become a member is much more complex. This complexity requires a more sophisticated approach to membership marketing. No longer can an organization rely solely on a single marketing activity to drive membership sales. Consumers—prospective, lapsed, and current members—are becoming more difficult to reach due to the ever-multiplying channels they use. This media fragmentation coupled with a surge in technology is ushering in a new era of marketing. Being suc-

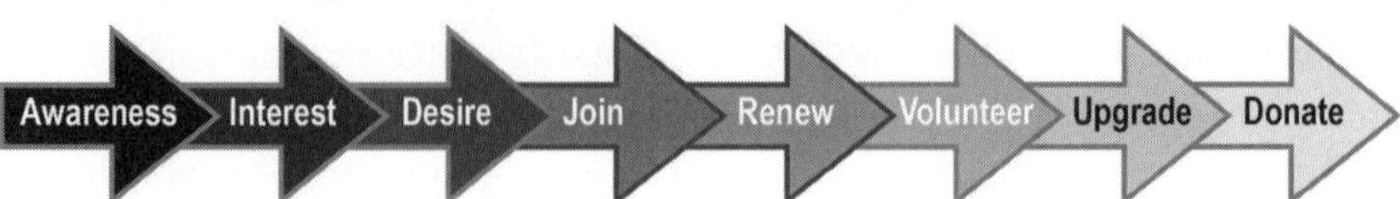

FIGURE 10.2
Membership Customer Journey

cessful in this new, complex environment requires a paradigm shift toward a multichannel approach to marketing the membership program.

The philosophy of multichannel marketing involves integrating multiple channels, or media, to reach prospective members both online and off. These channels may include everything from direct mail and email to social media, digital advertising, media relations, mobile marketing, and so on. Consumers are bombarded with massive amounts of information every day. This information overload makes it extremely difficult for an organization to cut through the clutter and remain top of mind. The power of multichannel marketing comes from a sustained and layered series of touch points. Figure 10.3 provides an overview of the various types of channels that can be utilized to market membership. The ultimate goal of multichannel marketing is to attain enough accumulated impressions to generate top-of-mind awareness when something triggers the impulse to join.

Keys to Success in Multichannel Marketing

Adoption of a multichannel marketing approach increases the likelihood of awareness, and exposes the prospective member to messaging at the moments that most influence their decisions. When strategically integrated, each channel supports the other to raise awareness, create interest, compel desire,

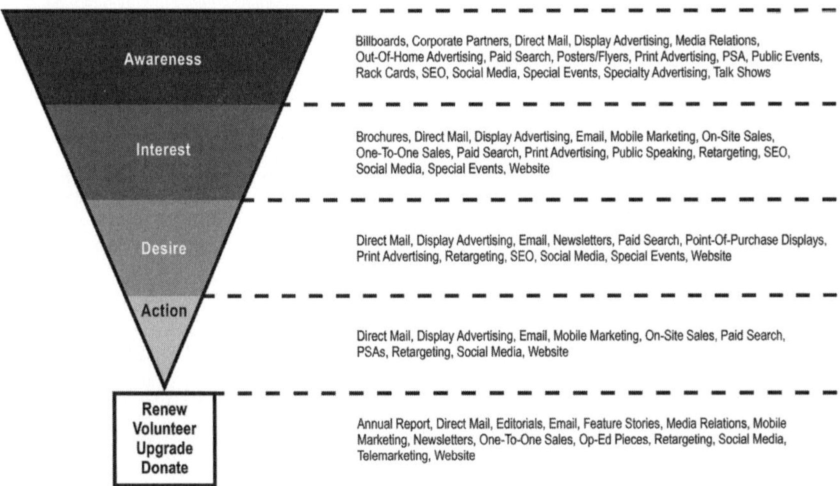

FIGURE 10.3
Marketing Channels

and motivate action. The result is a sustained series of layered touch points that delivers a far greater return on investment than when implemented alone.

There are four key guidelines for successful multichannel marketing. The first is getting the right message in front of the right audience at the right time in the right way. This requires a solid understanding of the target audience. Market research must be conducted to understand target audience motivations, media consumption patterns, technology adoption, and so on to inform the campaign strategy.

The second key to success in multichannel marketing is volume. Volume is the overall quantity of advertising, email, social media content, etc. It is the aggregate number of possible touches someone could be exposed to over the course of the campaign. Volume matters because only a small percentage of the number of potential member prospects reached will have the interest, desire, and financial means to "convert," or respond.

Third, multichannel marketing requires testing and measurement. In order to obtain a holistic view of the campaign performance, it is important to test various aspects of the campaign and to continually adapt the strategy based on the outcomes of those tests. Metrics to gauge success should be established early on and measurement techniques should always be built into the campaign from the outset. Whenever possible, measurement should integrate tracking across the membership database (the customer relationship management system or CRM), website analytics, social channels, email, and e-commerce.

Finally, successful multichannel marketing requires the integration of several channels. Integration does not merely mean use of multiple channels such as direct mail and email. Rather, integration means alignment of strategies by channel, layered and progressive content, and an understanding of how the various channels are going to work together in concert to support the larger campaign goal.

DIRECT VERSUS INDIRECT STRATEGIES

Marketing strategies fall into two main categories, direct and indirect activities. The categories are not mutually exclusive. The direct activities are those that actually "sell" the membership and are used for acquisition, renewal, or upgrading. The indirect activities are those that raise the profile of the membership program, so that when potential members are approached they will join. Indirect marketing is often referred to as image or brand marketing. For those who are already members, image marketing is an affirmation that they belong to a great organization.

The marketing strategy and specific channels used will depend on the type of organization, the geographic boundaries the institution serves, the goals of the campaign, the audience being targeted, and the available budget. An international or national organization may spend more effort and budget on direct mail, for example, while a local visitation-based institution may emphasize on-site membership sales or email.

Direct Channels

Direct channels are those that include a "call to action." They provide the means for a potential member to join. The means may include an enrollment form, a telephone number, an address, or an e-commerce enabled web page. These activities are intended to generate membership sales; their effectiveness is measured by how well they do that.

Direct Mail

Direct mail is still the workhorse of the modern membership marketing campaign. Recent research indicates that not only is direct mail still a significant driver of awareness, but it also yields the highest conversion rate of any channel. And while it may be tempting to think that younger audiences ignore direct mail, the Direct Marketing Association reported in 2014 that young adults (those twenty-four years and younger) are actually among the most direct mail responsive.[5] As digital marketing opportunities continue to emerge, direct mail is evolving alongside the rise of these new technologies. Technological advances like dynamic printing, quick response (QR) codes, and near-field communication are quickly bringing digital and direct mail closer together.

On-Site Sales

This acquisition method has become increasingly popular for visitation-based institutions and for those organizations that hold large events. The cost per dollar raised can be significantly lower than direct mail. Well-trained salespeople become a marketing force. There is nothing better than one person selling to another person. Benefits can be explained, objections overcome, and an emotional appeal made. This can be very effective at those times when there are enough potential members to make promotion financially viable.

Telemarketing

When the word "telemarketing" is mentioned, there is, typically, a less-than-enthusiastic response. Undoubtedly, the mind conjures up images of a huckster selling aluminum siding or worse. The Federal Trade Commission's adoption of strict regulations for telemarketing in the late 1990s coupled with the arrival of caller IDs, mobile phones, decreasing numbers of households with land lines and the do not call list, telemarketing has suffered a considerable setback in its effectiveness as a direct marketing channel. Telemarketing to mobile phones is illegal in most cases without prior consent. Even in the face of these challenges, the phone remains a powerful marketing tool.

For membership programs, telemarketing can be very effective in recapturing long and recent lapsed members, soliciting members for annual or capital campaign gifts, and surveys. The telephone is the next best thing to being there in person. It is particularly good for renewals and for non-fundraising calls that help service the membership relationship. Calling to tell about upcoming events, to thank the member for his or her membership, or to give information about an issue are all positive ways to use telemarketing to communicate about the program. Do not call lists were established by individual states in the late 1990s and early 2000s to restrict the use of phone calls, primarily from commercial entities that did not have a preexisting relationship with the individuals being called. Individuals are allowed to enter their phone numbers into a state-run Do Not Call list that must be honored by telemarketers. Most nonprofit organizations and political campaigns as well as market research calls are exempt from the laws and restrictions. It is best to check with individual state secretary of state offices with respect to these laws.

Advertising

Advertising occurs in a variety of media—print, radio, online, and television among them. Print advertising can take many forms, from ads in national publications to local parents' magazines. The organizations that can afford media placement in national publications tend to be large; however, digital advertising is opening doors to smaller organizations to be able to advertise with major newspapers and magazines via the web. Sometimes local publications will make space available to a local institution either free or at a reduced price. Smaller membership programs rarely have the resources for a substantial amount of print advertising. However, if the institution is advertising for other reasons, such as to increase attendance, then, if appropriate, the membership program can piggyback on the advertising and use it as reinforcement for direct mail or telemarketing, but not as a stand-alone strategy.

Paid television advertising is often too expensive except for the largest of organizations; however, digital "pre-roll" ads (video advertising that is shown before a streaming video) on websites like Hulu and YouTube are allowing institutions of all sizes to take advantage of the viewership shift from cable to streaming TV. Paid radio advertising tends to be less expensive than television, because the audience is smaller. If an organization has done market research and knows the stations that potential members like, radio is a good possibility. The growth of Internet radio such as Pandora and Spotify also offer opportunities for membership promotions. In radio, there needs to be an offer included in the advertising spot so that the potential member is driven to action (e.g., Two free months if you join before December 31!). More likely, especially for visitation-based organizations, is that an exhibition will be advertised with membership mentioned (e.g., Join today and receive free tickets.), or there will be on-site sales to take advantage of the increase in attendance.

Online advertising is just that—advertising shown or "served" to the target audience while he or she is online. Search (pay-per-click or PPC), display, Facebook ads, pre-roll video, and retargeting are all forms of online advertising. Over the past several years, online advertising has become incredibly sophisticated. The emergence of new technologies and software now allow advertisers to target advertising not only based on future search terms and website use, but also based on offline data characteristics, past browsing behavior, and affiliation.

No matter the medium used, the ads must be frequent to be effective. Advertising is not a one-time effort. There are studies of how many times a message must be heard before it moves a person to action—and it is a lot. The concept known as the "effective frequency" is used to describe the number of times a consumer must be exposed to an advertising message before taking the desired action. There is much debate about what the effective frequency is, but most experts in the field of advertising agree it is somewhere between three and twenty times. The takeaway here is that messages are more effective when repeated.

Email Marketing

Email is one of the most powerful, cost-effective, and often underutilized, tools in any multichannel marketing program. Email is (or should be) a one-to-one communications channel, where the recipient receives personalized information based on his or her preferences, behaviors, and needs. In its simplest form, email marketing is a form of direct marketing that involves sending an email message to a particular audience. In membership, email marketing may be used for many purposes, including informing, engaging, promoting, fundraising, advocacy, or selling.

Mobile Marketing

Mobile marketing can take many forms including mobile apps, SMS text messaging, and geo-targeting ads. Membership marketing can take advantage of a whole host of mobile-based marketing strategies from text messages that remind visitors of their member benefit at the gift shop, mobile apps that offer exclusive members-only interactive content, and scavenger hunts to surveys, push notifications, and geo-fenced ads (advertising that can be sent to visitors as they leave the museum based on the GPS location of their mobile device).

With the projected growth in smartphone adoption and tablets in the coming years, the opportunities for mobile as part of the multichannel mix will continue to expand and evolve.

Social Media

Social media has rapidly become a viable and important channel for membership marketing. Contests, promoted posts, lookalike targeting, content stories, and retargeting are all ways organizations can leverage social media for membership promotion.

At visitation-based institutions, visitors most often cite "family and friends" as how they heard about the institution. Social media is the go-to source for this type of word-of-mouth promotion. Social review sites like Yelp and TripAdvisor make it easy for visitors and members to share their experiences. A member who is negative, for whatever reason, will find ways to tell others about it. As we all know, if we have a bad experience, we tell many more people than if we have a positive one. Create positive member experiences, and social media will work for you.

For most nonprofits, social media requires a paradigm shift—in terms of strategy as well as internal processes and staffing. From a strategy standpoint, organizations must transition from a "push" to a "pull" style of marketing. Push marketing is based on one-way messaging (like traditional advertising) whereas a pull style of marketing relies more on engagement, conversation, and content that supports search engine optimization. Moreover, internal processes and staffing must be adjusted in order to support the rise of social media from a membership perspective. This shift requires granting membership staff administrative access to social media properties, discrete budgets for membership-focused social media efforts, and the authority and responsibility to respond to member questions via social media.

Website

The institutional website is a critical component of any multichannel marketing strategy. The website serves as the hub for news updates, member-related information, transaction processing, events and exhibitions, digital assets and collections, and much more. The website should facilitate membership acquisition, upgrades, renewal, and giving. At a minimum, the website should have e-commerce capabilities that allow for joining and renewing online.

PSAs

Public service announcements, or PSAs, are essentially advertisements that are run free of charge on television or radio. PSAs can be effective because they have the potential to reach a large audience. There are some caveats. It can be expensive to produce a well-done PSA that will move someone to action. Because the action needs to be fulfilled immediately, the organization must be able to react when the viewer or listener calls—which can be at any time, day or night. Often the free time that is donated is not during peak or prime hours so there is a lower reach than if the organization were to pay for the ad. PSAs are also good for image building and keeping the membership program top of mind.

One-to-One Sales

Much like on-site sales, this means of marketing the program is inexpensive, personal, and can be very effective. Because it is one-to-one, it does not generate large numbers of members, but those who do join have had a solid introduction to the program.

Brochures

It's hard to find a nonprofit that does not have a brochure. For membership programs there are two issues: first, there should be a membership-specific brochure; second, membership should be mentioned in the organization's general brochure. The membership brochure is a very important marketing tool. It can be used in all membership sales efforts. It is essential to design the membership brochure to be affordable to print and distribute in great quantities.

Corporate Partners

If the organization has a good relationship with any corporations, those companies may be willing to advertise the organization and its membership program in the company's all-employee newsletter. It may be possible to negotiate a corporate membership rate for employees or a company may be willing to pay a portion of the membership fee or offer membership as an employee benefit. This is similar to matching gift programs, some of which will match membership monies.

Newsletters

The organization newsletter should always tout the membership program. Nonmembers who are interested should be encouraged enough by the newsletter to take action to find out how to join. Some newsletters make space for a membership application, especially if the newsletter goes to a large number of nonmembers. Having an application allows members to cut out the application and pass it along to a friend. This type of marketing can be amplified when paired with a special promotional message such as "membership month."

Point of Purchase Displays

At a visitation-based institution, point of purchase displays for membership should be at the ticket booth, in the gift shop, in the restaurant, and anywhere else that is appropriate. Marketing the program where the benefits are immediate, such as at the ticket booth and the gift shop, is effective.

Public Speaking

Anytime anyone speaks on behalf of the organization, there should be a "pitch" for membership and brochures given to the attendees if possible. An enthusiastic speaker who can talk about the benefits and the organization makes membership exciting. This can be an effective way to encourage membership. If an incentive can be used (e.g., Join today and get two free months!) and the audience is large enough, this can be a very cost-effective way to increase membership.

Special Events

At the organization's events, there should be on-site sales with volunteers or staff. If that is not possible, everyone should be offered a membership brochure to take home. An organization might have a members' event where members are encouraged to bring potential members and membership is one of the topics of the event program.

Indirect Channels

These activities put forth the image of the membership program. There is no direct call to action, but there is the intent of making the membership program desirable. Many of these activities are done in conjunction with the institution as a whole.

Out-of-Home Advertising

Billboards, bus wraps, airport signage, and street banners are examples of out-of-home advertising. Visitation-based institutions will usually use billboards and other out-of-home advertising to drive attendance and then have on-site sales for membership. This type of advertising works especially well if the creative and message is coordinated between and among the billboard campaign, direct mail, and email campaigns.

Annual Report

The annual report can be used to tout the successes of the membership program. Membership should always ask for space in the annual report. Numbers, if good and impressive, can be used as well as testimonials about member programs, activities, and services. In organizations with small membership programs, this may be the place to provide recognition by listing members, new members, or those who have upgraded to donor clubs.

Editorials

For organizations with a current public issue message, meet with the newspaper's editorial board to encourage a favorable editorial for the organization that is doing something about the issue. This is a very good way to bring the issue to the attention of the public.

Feature Stories

These stories can be about the organization, about the membership program, or any combination. A group of local institutions might convince a reporter to write an article on the importance of membership to the organizations or on the "business" of membership.

Letters to the Editor/Op-Ed Pieces

If there is an editorial that has relevance to an organization or a membership program, take the opportunity to respond to it. Try to include a reference to the membership program.

Media Relations

News releases are the basis for almost all media relations that relate to print and electronic media. As possible, and appropriate, include an invitation to become a member in releases. This can be done in the body of the release, depending on the subject matter, or it can be included in the boilerplate on all releases.

Posters, Flyers, and Rack Cards

Posters, flyers, and rack cards can be effective if there is a distribution system in place. Designing and printing them is fairly easy and cost can range from inexpensive to very expensive depending on the design, color, and quantity. The issue is delivering them to sites that will take them and making certain that they are, indeed, posted and replenished. They are particularly useful to bring people to an event, a meeting, or other gathering. Membership then becomes an on-site solicitation.

Specialty Advertising

Specialty advertising is the branded promotional items everyone wants. This is the pen, the cap, the tote bag, the mug, etc., all with the organization's logo. Often used as premiums, incentives, and thank-you gifts for membership programs, specialty advertising items are intrinsically a marketing and promotional tool. When people see the item, they are reminded of the wonderful work of the organization. On a per-view cost, they are relatively inexpensive. Cost decreases as quantities increase. For this reason, buying many of an item is preferred. Many organizations produce logo merchandise for sale to members and/or the public; the marketing value of this should not be overlooked.

For member premiums, the items should be exclusively for "members only." Do not sell the specialty items for members to the public; this would take away its "VIP" appeal.

Talk Shows, Live Remote Broadcasts

For membership, target those talk shows that reach the potential membership audience. If the organization has a spokesperson on a show, make certain to remind him or her to mention the membership program, benefits, and how to join. In most instances, talking about membership will be a part of a larger message that the institution wants to impart to an audience. If there are particular talk shows that reach the potential member audience, be proactive in trying to place a spokesperson on those shows. At the Saint Louis Zoo, May was designated as membership month. During that month, multiple marketing opportunities were utilized to focus on membership, including live remote broadcasts from the zoo. Membership and family fun were the focus of the broadcasts, and memberships were a giveaway in on-air contests, elevating the benefits of membership at the zoo.

Public Displays/Events

Sometimes an organization is offered the opportunity to place a display or have a table at an event. There may be many reasons to do this. If membership is the major reason to do it, make certain that the event draws the correct profile for potential members. Have a point of purchase display with the brochure. Consider having a raffle for a free membership to gain other names. If the event does not permit sales, but is rather a display of photos or other objects from the organization, do try to have at least a point of purchase display so that attendees can take the brochure.

BEST PRACTICES IN MULTICHANNEL MARKETING

In order to develop the most effective multichannel marketing strategy, it is important to follow a few best practices. In the *Marketing Workbook for Nonprofit Organizations*, authors Gary Stern and Elana Centor discuss several principles to help nonprofits select an effective combination of marketing channels and tactics.[6]

"Gear materials and techniques to the audience." Make certain that the channels and promotional strategies you choose will reach potential members. For example, if a library is trying to reach a younger audience, buy advertising on the radio stations and websites that reach the appropriate age range, text messaging should be prioritized over email, and pre-roll ads should be placed on key YouTube videos.

"Pick the right mix of techniques—within your budget." The operative words here are mix and budget. Mix is important because not everyone sees, listens, or reacts to the same media. Budget is a concern because every membership program has one. For mix, it is key to decide which of several efforts will be best to reach members or potential members in the most cost-effective way. A small, inexpensive brochure may be the basis of the marketing plan. Added to this might be a social-media-driven awareness campaign. A third effort might be an on-site sales effort. All of these efforts can be carried out with time rather than a lot of money. For an organization with a larger budget, the brochure could be four-color; direct mail may be sent to thousands of households; a robust digital advertising program will drive millions of impressions; and a PSA might be developed for radio and television.

"If it worked, do it again." This rule is true for everything that a membership program does. If direct mail is working, keep doing it. Do not change it because you are bored with it. If you want to try something new, test the new direct mail using the current package as a control. If a special event is successful, keep doing it until the response to it seems to be falling. (Many special events have a life cycle.) Marketing the program must be evaluated on an objective basis (e.g., number of responses), not on someone's whim. Marketing tends to be one area where everyone thinks that he or she is the expert. Know what you are doing and why, and stick to it. Persistence is fundamental.

Other best practices for multichannel marketing include integration, testing, experimentation, and optimization.

Integration

To maximize the effectiveness of any multichannel marketing strategy, there needs to be integration. This means that each channel strategy should support the other. Because an individual will be exposed to the campaign in various ways at various times, it's important that there is consistency in the messaging and creative. This is not to say that the offer, imagery, or strategy must be exactly the same across every channel. In fact, there may be reasons to send different offers out on different channels at different times, or to use different images or messaging themes from one channel to another. The key is to employ a unified approach that delivers a seamless experience to the consumer, even while there are very different tactics being deployed on each channel.

Testing

Testing is critical to optimizing the campaign and maximizing the return on investment (ROI). Testing can take many forms, including A/B testing and multivariant testing.

Experimentation

While the principle of "if it worked, do it again" holds true, it is also important to invest in emerging channels. Without experimentation, the program will never grow. Investing in new strategies provides expanded learning, and quite possibly, uncovering a new technique that could become the most successful component of your campaign. Membership programs that embrace experimentation (and the risks associated with it!) will become the leaders in their space.

Optimization

The most effective marketing campaigns are flexible. With limited dollars, it's important to know which channels are performing and which are falling short. Through the continual process of testing, learning, and adapting, campaigns can be optimized to produce the greatest ROI. Dollars should be reallocated toward higher-performing channels, higher-performing creative should be rolled out to other channels, and so on. Ongoing optimization will ensure that the strategies will become more effective over time.

DEFINING YOUR TARGET AUDIENCE

Before beginning a marketing campaign, it is critical to identify the desired target audience the campaign is intended to reach. In developing a target audience profile, it is helpful to look at your current member profile and create personas for each type of member. Once you have a comprehensive member persona, this information can be used to find lookalike audiences based not only on demographics, but also for indicators such as behaviors, lifestyle, media consumption patterns, and motivational cues.

Who are the audiences and what do they want? How can the organization find out? It can be difficult for membership staff (whether paid or volunteer) to determine what a prospective member wants. The membership manager has preconceived notions based on institutional history, what the institution can afford in terms of time and funding, and his or her own interests. All members are not the same.

Target Markets and Target Audiences

Every organization has one or more target markets for its programs and activities. One or more of these markets may be appropriate for programming, but may not be the right *target audience* for marketing the membership program. For example, a children's museum may want to introduce its programs to elementary school children—clearly the right market for the programs, but obviously not the right target audience for marketing the membership program. The audience(s) in this case would be parents, teachers, grandparents, or all three.

It is essential to understand who the target audience is before jumping into marketing the membership program. If there is a membership program already in place, the first and primary target audience includes those people who are most like the current members. To know what the current members are "like," the membership manager will need to first ascertain the demographic and behavioral characteristics of the members. The data should be collected from a market research project (membership survey) and compiled into a member profile. If the program has been in existence for some time and it is time to add a new market, it will be helpful to gain as much information about that new market and the target audience(s) as possible before developing the marketing strategy. For example, a museum might decide that it would like to attract members who are younger than the typical member. To do this, the membership manager will first need to determine what appeals to this group. The membership program then has to reflect and incorporate the kinds of benefits, services, and events that are of interest to this group. Next the membership manager will need to determine how best to reach this new audience. He or she can conduct a survey, interviews, or focus groups, or research media usage patterns on websites like Pew Research Center (www.pewresearch.org) or Nielsen (www.nielsen.com). Marketing to an audience that is different from the type of member the organization already appeals to takes more than just mailing to a new list. In fact, that kind of mailing rarely works.

If the program is new, gather as much information as possible from similar and comparator organizations to try to determine the characteristics of those most likely to join. If direct mail acquisition is possible, talk with list brokers about the possible lists to use. If the group is starting small, ask friends, relatives, and colleagues who might be interested. Have board members submit lists of potential members.

MARKET RESEARCH: UNCOVERING NEEDS AND WANTS

Determining the target audience's needs and wants is done through research. Most likely in the membership world, market research takes the form of a current and lapsed member survey. Market research is the process by which an organization can determine current, former, and prospective members' needs, wants, and desires—along with a host of other information. Market research is the "set of techniques and principles for systematically collecting, recording, analyzing, and interpreting data to aid marketing decision makers."[7]

Market research is important to a membership program in order to make informed decisions about how the limited resources of time, money, and energy can be expended in the most effective ways. It ensures that institutional decisions are not being made based on assumptions, anecdotes, or past experiences.

It is essential that the organization determine the answers to a number of questions before beginning a market research project. Because of limited time and dollars, the information needs of the study must be determined and prioritized. The first and most important question is what is the goal of the research? Defining the issues to be researched is always the first step. The next set of questions that need to be answered include:

- What information is needed and why?
- Who should be surveyed and why?
- What method should be used? Who will do the research work? and
- What funding is available?

Market research gives two kinds of information: quantitative and qualitative. Quantitative information can be measured, such as demographic information. Qualitative information asks questions like "How do you feel about ___?" and "Why did you visit ___?" This is information that gives perceptions and motivations about why they are members, former members, or visitors. This information can be generalized to a total population, but not with the statistical accuracy of quantitative data.

You can ask about virtually anything. Information can be gathered on benefits, events, the newsletter or other communications tools, member services, exhibits, programs, volunteer opportunities, or messaging concepts.

However, it is important to ask only questions about those areas and issues that can be changed. Ask about the newsletter if redesigning it is a possibility; if a redesign won't happen in the near future, don't ask until a redesign is a possibility. The same is true of benefits, events, educational offerings, and other programs.

Demographic information should always be collected in order to develop a member profile. Include questions about gender, age, education level, income level, and zip code. Age and income are usually asked in terms of ranges. Not everyone will answer, but those who do will give a fair picture of those answering the questions. To assist in developing the marketing strategy, it is helpful to ask about which websites are visited, which radio stations are listened to, which television shows are watched, which newspapers are read, the kinds of magazines subscribed to, and so on. This information can be used in planning acquisition, buying or exchanging lists, knowing where and how to advertise, and determining where to direct public relations.

Research Methodologies

There are a number of ways to obtain the research information. Email surveys, focus groups, and interviews are a few of the methods that membership programs most often use. Other ways of obtaining information can also be helpful in certain situations such as awareness and perceptions studies, conjoint analysis, usability testing, concept testing, and visitor surveys.

Surveys

Purpose: To gather a large amount of data. The data collected can be both quantitative and qualitative. An open-ended section can be included for "other comments." In a membership program, this is the most efficient and can be the least costly of the research methods. Members often take a proprietary interest in their organizations and everyone loves to be asked for their opinion. Who should be surveyed? Current members and former members will give the most direct information relating to the membership program. For visitation-based institutions, visitors can be surveyed. If they are members they can be asked member related questions. If they are not members, they can be asked "why not?" They can also be asked to which other organizations they belong. This information can be used to determine if there is an opportunity to increase the membership program. If a significant number of visitors are members of comparable organizations but not the one they are visiting, there is room for growth. A sample membership survey is available at www.thememberhipbook.com.

Technique: A survey is sent to a sample of the membership. It is also helpful to include a cover letter (for an example of survey invitation copy, visit www.thememberhipbook.com), thank-you gift (e.g., a coupon for organization merchandise, a free ticket for an event) to increase the rate of return. The survey can be mailed or made available online via the website or third-party-hosted platform; a link to the URL can be emailed, posted on social media, or included on a postcard to members for whom no email address is available. Membership surveys can be posted in a "members only" area of the website. Surveys can also be made available to website visitors via a pop-up or to on-site visitors via a postcard with the survey URL.

The telephone is another option for surveying a random sample about the membership program. This method is becoming somewhat more difficult due to the rise of voicemail, caller ID, and people not willing to spend time on the telephone. Fortunately, happy members are often willing to talk about their experience and answer questions. This method can be inexpensive if there is a volunteer corps that can be trained and is willing to do the work. Whether the callers are paid or volunteer, tight supervision is necessary so that the questions are not asked in a way that promotes a bias in the answers. For telephone surveys, respondents may be asked to rate something on a scale of one to seven rather than be asked open-ended questions. The downside is that there may not be enough time to ask as many questions as might be included on a written survey.

A reminder email (or a postcard for those members whose email addresses are not available) should be sent to those who received the survey if the rate of return needs to be increased. Most membership groups can expect a return rate of 15 to 20 percent, far greater than the rate for a for-profit business. The information is then collated and analyzed.

Caution should be used when doing a survey, especially an online survey. With the advent of products like Survey Monkey, people begin to think that they are market research professionals. It is not recommended to survey your own members; as a membership manager, you have a vested interest in the outcome. Questions can be written in a way that can "lead" the responder and sway the outcome of the results—even when not intentional. Membership survey projects are a massive undertaking, and take a significant amount of time to analyze fully. Often, organizations think that they can do this project in-house, only to conduct the survey and then let the responses lay dormant for a lack of time or staff expertise to do a full analysis. When analyzing a survey, managers may not recognize that the results reflect negatively on the programs for which they have been responsible. It is like a doctor examining himself or herself. Market research is best managed by a market research expert.

When performing a membership survey, it is also recommended to include a lapsed member segment to the survey. The survey will be identical to the current member survey but with a change in tense of the survey wording, and with a few additional questions about why the membership was allowed to lapse and about future intentions of joining again. The lapsed member data can be compared to current member data for a better understanding of both groups.

Comprehensive, professional member surveys can be one of the most valuable tools employed by a membership manager. The results will inform literally every decision that is made on behalf of the membership program, in addition to giving staff a deeper and more exact understanding of members' sentiments and motivations. Without such empirical data, managing a membership program is like walking a tightrope blindfolded.

Cost: Costs will be dependent on professional services for the survey design, tabulation, and analysis, on any technical issues or hosting costs that arise with the use of the website or third-party platform, and the number of postcards mailed. If the survey is conducted via telephone, there is the additional expense of the callers.

Time: Surveys can often be accomplished fairly quickly with a deadline for return and a professional firm managing responses, data collection, and the analysis.

Focus Groups

Purpose: A focus group is conducted to generate or to test ideas, creative concepts, and messaging. It is called a focus group because the facilitator "focuses" the discussion on the type of information needed. For membership programs, focus groups are a very good way to test ideas about events, programs, exhibits, or membership benefits. They are also valuable in brainstorming for new ideas about these subjects. For a new program, holding several focus groups to discover what members of similar organizations like about their membership experience would be a productive way to determine what should be included in the new program. It is important to keep in mind the limitations of a focus group. People often behave differently than they think they do or are willing to say in front of a group of strangers. This reality can have an impact on the information obtained from this type of research.

Technique: A randomly selected group of eight to twelve people is brought together for approximately two hours. A script is developed to elicit the information wanted during the session. A professional facilitator leading the group assures objectivity and coverage of the material. Typically, at least three groups are needed to make certain that the information is corroborated. As well, it is possible to convene groups with different characteristics. For example, one group might be longtime members, another first-year members. It is always important to have refreshments available. It is often said that the quality of the information shared in a focus group is directly correlated to the quantity of food provided.

Cost: The cost ranges from very low to very high depending on how much professional help is used. The information is more reliable if professionals conduct the sessions. An organization can also use a professional focus group facility with a special room with one-way glass so that the organization's representatives can watch the group's reactions. If necessary, the sessions can also be videotaped. Often the participants are given a financial incentive to participate. The incentive should be paid out at the end of the focus group. The best practice is to overbook the groups and, if needed, dismiss the extra participants and pay the incentive to each. For affluent audiences such as upper-level members and donors or legislative influencers, a nice lunch is offered in place of a financial incentive.

Time: It can take weeks or months in order to confirm the attendance of a random sample, develop the script, conduct the sessions, and analyze the results.

Exit or Visitor Surveys

Purpose: To gather information from visitors to an institution. This type of survey is particularly useful for information about the visitor's experience. If a visitation-based institution is planning exit surveys, the membership program should be represented by several questions and have input into the demographic information being collected. Because this is typically an all-institution survey, membership needs to select a few very important questions to ask. Remember that a visitor survey is not a membership survey. It is possible, however, to extract member information if enough of the visitors who fill out the survey are members. A visitor survey is not a substitution for a comprehensive membership-only survey.

Technique: A survey form is distributed. It can be completed on location (in which case it needs to be short) or it can be distributed on-site, completed at home, and then returned by mail. While conducting the survey on-site guarantees a completed survey, many people are not willing to extend their stay, especially if visiting with others and particularly if visiting with children. A mail-back survey is far preferable. It allows for more random distribution since even those people in a hurry to leave can participate. If distributed effectively, the return is good. Last but not least, it eliminates any bias that might occur with a live survey-taker.

Cost: The cost depends on staffing the distribution, printing, mailing, and analysis of the surveys. Exit surveys conducted with paid interviewers greatly increases the costs.

Time: It can take several weeks or months depending on survey design, the number of surveys, distribution schedule, and analysis.

In-Depth Interviews

Purpose: This format is used to obtain in-depth qualitative information about the interviewee's perceptions of the membership program. A membership program might use this format if there are major issues that need to be resolved. For example, a professional might be hired to do a study to gauge member reactions in advance of a major benefits change.

Technique: One-on-one interviews usually conducted with a selected group by a professional. It takes the time of the professional and the interviewee. Interviews last from twenty minutes to an hour or more.

Cost: Dependent on professional costs. It is less expensive and tempting to use an organization's volunteers or staff, but the objectivity and candid answers that the organization wants from the interviewee would be lost.

Time: It can take several weeks to gather the information and write the report depending on number of interviews and availability of interviewees.

Mail-Back Surveys Included in a Newsletter or Other Publication

Purpose: To gather information by using an existing communication vehicle. Membership programs want to use this method because it is less expensive than sending a separate survey. This, however, is not a very reliable research effort since participants are not randomly selected. It is also difficult to ensure a significant return or to meet deadlines because many members do not read the newsletter immediately, and some, not at all.

Technique: The mail-back survey is published in the organization's newsletter. Members are asked to fill it out and return it by a deadline.

Cost: The cost includes the design, printing, and analysis of the survey. It becomes an internal accounting matter if a portion of the mailing cost of the newsletter or publication that contains the survey is attributed to the membership department.

Time: Timing depends on the newsletter mailing. There is often a six-to-eight-week lead-time before publishing the newsletter. If this is the case, the survey must be ready, then be inserted and mailed, and responses received. The deadline on the survey should be at least six weeks after the newsletter's mail date. With sometimes unforeseen delays with the newsletter, the survey deadline should give enough time to make certain that it can be returned. It will take four to six weeks after the newsletter is mailed to determine whether enough surveys have been returned for analysis. Thus, if the newsletter is mailed on January 15 bulk rate, allow three weeks for delivery, another three weeks to have returns, and some time in case the mail date isn't met. The survey deadline would be about March 15. Caution is advised, however, as this will only be a survey of the people who read your newsletter, and not a reliable random sample of your entire membership!

Awareness and Perceptions Studies

Purpose: Awareness and perceptions or "Awareness, Attitude, and Usage" studies measure the totality of the general public's or a specific target audience's awareness of, opinions about, and attitudes toward a particular organization. This type of market research helps an organization understand its overall reputation, the quality and appeal of its offering or membership program, and how people feel about various aspects of the experience such as convenience (location, hours, etc.), customer service, and resolution of problems or complaints.

Awareness can be measured in two ways—aided or unaided. Unaided awareness helps an organization understand its position on a top-of-mind basis. For example, a researcher might ask, "When you think of museums in Colorado, which come to mind first?" Aided awareness helps an organization understand the extent to which the general public is familiar with the organization's offering and experience. For example, a researcher might ask, "How familiar are you with the membership program at XYZ museum? Would you say you are very familiar, somewhat familiar, or not familiar?"

Armed with information from this type of study, the organization can take appropriate action to shape its communications and marketing to improve its awareness or address negative perceptions.

Technique: Most often this is a quantitative survey conducted via telephone or online by a professional research firm. Sample sizes are determined up-front in order to obtain enough data to be statistically significant.

Cost: Depends on professional costs. It can be expensive to very expensive depending on the scope of the study.

Time: Six to twelve weeks or more are needed to conduct the fieldwork, analyze the data, and write the report depending on the scope of the project.

Usability Testing

Purpose: Usability testing is a technique used to evaluate a website or mobile app by testing it with actual users. Usability testing can help an organization determine whether users can accomplish certain goals. For example, a museum may want to understand how easily a prospective member can join online. Or if a member is able to access and navigate the digital collection with ease. Or if a particular feature on the mobile app functions as intended.

Technique: In a real or simulated environment, a carefully planned scenario is constructed wherein a person performs a list of tasks with specific objectives in mind. In some cases, the study team observes this process, while in other cases the user performs the test at home and the user's movements, clicks, and comments are tracked and recorded.

Cost: The cost ranges from very little to moderately expensive depending on the type of information needed, and if a professional research firm is used.

Time: Testing time can vary depending on the amount and type of testing needed. Often usability testing can be completed within just a couple of weeks.

Conjoint Analysis

Purpose: Conjoint analysis is a market research method that uses predictive software to statistically test numerous combinations of benefits by quantifying respondent preferences and perceived value. Through this process, conjoint analysis can provide insight into the relative importance of specific benefits in the decision-making process of joining. Because most people are unable to accurately determine the relative importance or value that they place on specific membership benefits, it's very difficult for people to create a combination of preferred benefits from a list of possible options. With conjoint analysis, this task becomes much easier because respondents are presented with combinations of benefits that can be visualized as different "packages." Thus, this type of research can assist in creating membership levels, determining optimal pricing, and developing upgrade strategies.

Technique: A controlled set of possible benefits is presented to the respondent, and he or she is asked to indicate preference by selecting from, ranking, or rating the benefits. Predictive software then quantifies the responses and identifies "preference curves" to show the perceived value of different membership benefits. This type of research can be conducted with both members and nonmembers based on the needs of the study.

Cost: Depends on professional costs. It can be expensive to very expensive depending on the scope of the study.

Time: Six to twelve weeks or more are needed depending on the scope of the project.

Concept Testing

Purpose: The purpose of concept testing is to evaluate and understand audience perceptions and response to creative messaging, visual approaches, or ideas.

Technique: Most often concept testing is qualitative, and is conducted through interviews or focus groups. Participants are shown three or more creative concepts that may include images, ideas, or key messages, and asked for feedback about the concept. This feedback is then synthesized into themes and actionable recommendations are developed from the research.

Cost: The cost ranges from very little to very expensive depending on how much professional help is used. As with other qualitative research methods, the information is more reliable if professionals conduct the study. As with other types of focus groups, a professional facility can be used and participants are given a financial incentive.

Time: Several weeks or months are needed to confirm the attendance of a random sample, develop the creative concepts, and analyze the results.

Use of Professionals

For any of these methods, it is important to talk to a professional in market research to make certain that the methodology has validity for the type of information that is desired. Professionals are particularly helpful in selecting the sample, designing the survey, collating and analyzing the results, and avoiding bias.

The sample needs to be large enough to be statistically valid. It also needs to be selected in a way that makes sense for the information and for the organization. The researcher can also determine the number of surveys needed for the information to be valid. To encourage people to complete a survey, an incentive can be used. A small incentive can help realize a statistically significant return. An incentive can be anything—a coupon that can be printed and used on-site for a discount (e.g., for food, the gift shop, etc.), a promo code that can be redeemed via the web such as a discount code to use in the online store, or a small item such as a bookmark that can be mailed easily. Incentives are also used to ensure focus group attendance—usually money and/or food. Incentives are usually not used for telephone, mail-back, or one-on-one surveys. An incentive to complete a survey can also be an entry into a drawing for a desirable item such as an iPad. At the end of the survey period, the winner would be selected from all eligible survey responses.

The design of the survey will be the key to whether the data are useful or not. It is very difficult to write good, clear questions that elicit the information that is required. If staff or volunteers do the survey design, it is worthwhile to have a market research professional review and edit the questions to ensure there is no bias. The questions should also be tested on a few staff members and volunteers to make certain that they draw out the appropriate kinds of answers. The physical design also needs to be considered so that the data entry is easy to accomplish. No matter who writes the survey, it should look professional; it is reflective of the organization conducting it.

Collating and analyzing the data are projects that should be done by a professional. Between the number of questions and the number of respondents, the data to be entered can be overwhelming. It is also necessary to code open-ended questions so that they can be analyzed. It is a time-consuming task. Special software programs are often used to analyze the data, which a professional research organization will have. With professional tabulation, it is possible to analyze the data in many more dimensions using tab and banner analyses. With this, various questions and answers can be analyzed by and in comparison to a variety of segments. Someone familiar with statistical methods and with significant industry knowledge is best qualified to do the analysis.

One of the downfalls of self-administered surveys by membership managers lies in the time required to fully analyze survey data. Many managers report having conducted an online survey of their members, but that they never had the time to fully analyze it, making the entire effort a waste of time.

Budgeting

Research can range from the very expensive, many thousands of dollars, to a few thousand dollars. There are ways for a membership program to reduce or eliminate the cost. Is there a board member or a member who is a professional market researcher and is willing to donate the services? Is there a board member or member whose company uses a lot of market research and the company he or she uses is willing to do some pro bono work? Is there a local research firm that is willing to do the work pro bono? Is there a local college or university with a business curriculum that would take this on as a class project? Or last, but not least, try negotiating with a professional market research company. Remember that staff or volunteers can always do some of the work, using professionals for those essential tasks that make the research valid.

Using the Information

The point of all research is to make better decisions. The information needs to be used when making decisions about the membership program. The member profile developed from the demographic information becomes an important base for marketing and other institutional programs. If this is the first membership survey (or the first in a very long time), consider a survey two years in a row to establish a baseline of information; then repeat and update the survey approximately every three years.

It is important to use the results as soon as possible. They should be used to inform decisions that are relevant to the information gathered. For example, if benefits were part of the survey, restructure that part of the program. If certain kinds of events bring positive responses, try more of them. Use the demographics to determine where to find potential members. Use the radio, television, and magazine information to place stories and advertise.

Information about members can also be used in the fundraising program. If it is determined that the average age of the membership is older than fifty, this finding signals that a planned giving program would be appropriate. The demographics can also be used in securing corporate sponsorships if the member profile is one that the corporation wants to reach. If a significant portion of the membership watches or listens to a certain station, it is possible to approach that station for in kind media exposure.

Information gleaned from focus groups and member surveys can be helpful in identifying compelling promotional language, marketable benefits, and positioning strategies. And, with the advent of technologies such as marketing automation software and search engine data it is now possible to create unique marketing paths personalized to an individual's behaviors and interests.

If it is appropriate, include an article in the organization newsletter or another communication vehicle so that those who have sent in responses or received the questionnaire will know what has happened with the information. This is also the opportunity to thank them for replying.

THE POWER OF CONSUMER PSYCHOLOGY

There are immense opportunities to leverage the body of research in behavioral economics and consumer psychology to convert more visitors into members in creative and ethical ways. In his influential book, *Predictably Irrational*, behavioral economist Dan Ariely discusses the "predictably irrational" tendencies of consumers when it comes to our buying behavior. These irrational tendencies can affect how prospective members evaluate and make the decision to join. Thus, it is important to ensure that membership is positioned and promoted in the most effective and ethical way.

Everything—from how membership levels are visually presented on the website to the use of premiums—can affect the effectiveness of a membership marketing campaign. Consider the following findings from an experiment conducted by Ariely.

MIT students were presented with three options to subscribe to the *Economist* (see exhibit 10.1). Option A was a "web only" subscription at the very affordable price of $59. The "print only" subscription (option B) and the "print plus web" subscription (option C) were the same price, $125. In the first experiment, sixteen students chose option A and eighty-four chose option C. Nobody chose the middle option.

Ariely then removed the "print only" option and conducted the experiment again. This time, sixty-eight students selected the cheaper "web only" option and only thirty-two students selected the "print plus web" subscription (see exhibit 10.2).

What's going on here? In the second scenario, with only two options, the students had nothing to compare either option to. As it turns out, the introduction of the third option (even though no one selected it) made the "print plus web" subscription look very attractive.[8] Known as "the decoy" effect, this marketing technique can be used to help nudge prospective members toward selecting a particular level of membership (see exhibit 10.3).

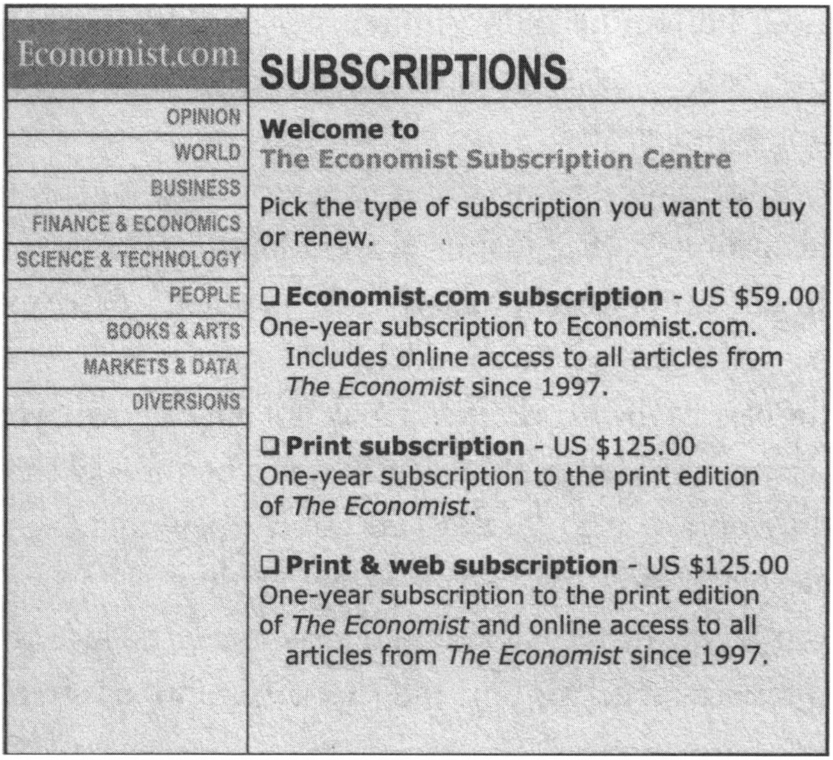

Economist.com

OPINION
WORLD
BUSINESS
FINANCE & ECONOMICS
SCIENCE & TECHNOLOGY
PEOPLE
BOOKS & ARTS
MARKETS & DATA
DIVERSIONS

SUBSCRIPTIONS

Welcome to
The Economist Subscription Centre

Pick the type of subscription you want to buy or renew.

❑ **Economist.com subscription** - US $59.00
One-year subscription to Economist.com. Includes online access to all articles from *The Economist* since 1997.

❑ **Print subscription** - US $125.00
One-year subscription to the print edition of *The Economist*.

❑ **Print & web subscription** - US $125.00
One-year subscription to the print edition of *The Economist* and online access to all articles from *The Economist* since 1997.

EXHIBIT 10.1
The Economist Experiment

Economist.com

OPINION
WORLD
BUSINESS
FINANCE & ECONOMICS
SCIENCE & TECHNOLOGY
PEOPLE
BOOKS & ARTS
MARKETS & DATA
DIVERSIONS

SUBSCRIPTIONS

Welcome to
The Economist Subscription Centre

Pick the type of subscription you want to buy or renew.

❑ **Economist.com subscription** - US $59.00
One-year subscription to Economist.com. Includes online access to all articles from *The Economist* since 1997.
16

❑ **Print subscription** - US $125.00
One-year subscription to the print edition of *The Economist*.
0

❑ **Print & web subscription** - US $125.00
One-year subscription to the print edition of *The Economist* and online access to all articles from *The Economist* since 1997.
84

Economist.com

OPINION
WORLD
BUSINESS
FINANCE & ECONOMICS
SCIENCE & TECHNOLOGY
PEOPLE
BOOKS & ARTS
MARKETS & DATA
DIVERSIONS

SUBSCRIPTIONS

Welcome to
The Economist Subscription Centre

Pick the type of subscription you want to buy or renew.

❑ **Economist.com subscription** - US $59.00
One-year subscription to Economist.com. Includes online access to all articles from *The Economist* since 1997.
68

❑ **Print & web subscription** - US $125.00
One-year subscription to the print edition of *The Economist* and online access to all articles from *The Economist* since 1997.
32

EXHIBIT 10.2
Comparison—The *Economist* Experiment with Decoy

EXHIBIT 10.3
Membership Levels Using the Decoy Effect

Nonprofit organizations can benefit greatly by applying lessons from the fields of behavioral economics and consumer psychology. Some of these learnings include:

1. **Make the membership cost less painful.** Paying for something creates a loss psychologically, and losses are viscerally unpleasant. To combat this feeling of loss, think of ways to reduce buyer pain points at the time of purchase. For example, monthly giving options and discounts for automatically renewing each year can lessen the immediate sting of the up-front cost to join.
2. **Include a default option.** Study after study has found that presenting one option as the default increases the likelihood that it will be chosen. The power of the default option comes from the perception of ownership that is conveyed even before a purchase actually takes place. This sense of ownership translates into a perceived loss if another option is selected instead of the default (see exhibit 10.4).
3. **Use premiums.** Research in the field of behavioral economics shines light on another fundamental truth—people will do crazy things to get something for free.
4. **Don't overwhelm with too many options.** Too many choices can cause buyer paralysis. Psychologist Barry Schwartz argued in his influential book

○ E-Member	$45.00
○ X Member	$75.00
● Contributor	$150.00
○ Patron	$300.00
○ Avant Garde The Next Genereation of Collectors	$500.00
○ Supporter	$600.00
○ Donor Circle Circle Membership	$1,500.00
○ Benefactor Circle Circle Membership	$2,500.00

EXHIBIT 10.4
Default Option

The Paradox of Choice that too much choice can be a bad thing, leading to feelings of unhappiness and avoidance of making a purchase.[9]

5. **Provide immediate gratification.** Consumers like to be rewarded instantaneously for taking a desired action. This reward doesn't need to be complicated—for example, a simple auto-thank-you email with a discount code to "begin taking advantage of your membership benefit right away!" can do the job.
6. **Make benefits comparison easy.** Packaging and promoting membership as a product makes it easier for someone to quickly evaluate and internalize

the benefits of membership. Use tables to make it easier to visually compare different levels.

SUMMARY

To be successful, membership needs to have a marketing orientation, requiring implementation of the marketing mix. Through market research, membership managers can understand audience needs, wants, and perceptions so that informed decisions can be made about how to allocate limited resources. A multichannel approach to marketing ensures that the organization will remain top of mind. Finally, measurement is a critical component of any marketing campaign. Without the proper tracking and attribution, it is impossible to determine what is working and what is not.

NOTES

1. Alan R. Andreasen and Phillip Kotler, *Strategic Marketing for Nonprofit Organizations*, 7th ed. (Upper Saddle River, NJ: Pearson Prentice Hall, 2008), 39.

2. Gary Armstrong, Adam Stewart, Sara Denize, and Phillip Kotler, *Principles of Marketing*, 5th ed. (Frenchs Forest NSW: Pearson Australia, 2012), 58.

3. Andreasen, *Strategic Marketing*, 26.

4. Dhruv Grewal and Michael Levy, *Marketing*, 4th ed. (New York: McGraw-Hill Education, 2015), 378.

5. Direct Marketing Association, "DMA Statistical Fact Book," April 11, 2014, 69.

6. Gary Stern and Elana Centor, *Marketing Workbook for Nonprofit Organizations: Volume 1: Develop the Plan*, 2nd ed. (St. Paul, MN: Amherst H. Wilder Foundation, 2001), 108–9.

7. A. Parasuraman, Dhruv Grewal, and R. Krishnan, *Marketing Research*, 2nd ed. (Boston: Houghton Mifflin, 2007), 9.

8. Dan Ariely, *Predictably Irrational: The Hidden Forces That Shape Our Decisions*, rev. ed. (New York: HarperPerennial, 2010), 4–6.

9. Barry Schwartz, *The Paradox of Choice: Why More Is Less* (New York: HarperCollins, 2004), 147–52.

11

Digital Marketing for Membership

It is not the most intellectual of the species that survives; it is not the strongest that survives; but the species that survives is the one that is able to adapt to and to adjust best to the changing environment in which it finds itself.

—Charles Darwin, English Naturalist and Geologist

The evolution of technology in recent years has ushered in a new era of marketing. The pace at which technology is evolving is staggering. To put things in perspective, consider how long it took the following channels to reach fifty million people.[1]

- Radio—thirty-eight years
- TV—thirteen years
- The Internet—four years
- Facebook—two years

In recent years, technology has become seamlessly integrated into our everyday lives, revolutionizing how we discover, interact with, and consume information. The Pew Research Center found that as of January 2014, 74 percent of online adults use social networking sites,[2] with 47 percent of smartphone owners using social media daily on their mobile device.[3] The reality of our increasingly digital-driven world is forcing nonprofit organizations to adapt, requiring membership to be proactive in building a deeper relationship with technology and marketing than ever before.

According to Gartner's online *IT Glossary*, digital marketing continues to be integrated with multichannel marketing strategies, and includes "addressable branding/advertising, contextual marketing, social marketing and transactional marketing. Digital marketing extends the marketing process through channels such as the Web, video, mobile and social applications, point-of-sale terminals, digital signage and kiosks."[4] And, as the International Chamber of Commerce recently affirmed, this "rapid evolution of digital media has created new opportunities and avenues for advertising and marketing."[5]

Ken Meifert, Vice President, Sponsorship and Development at the National Baseball Hall of Fame and Museum, has shared a compelling insight regarding the importance of digital media in the Hall of Fame's marketing strategy. Meifert says, "Digital is a huge part of our marketing—both for membership and for the Hall of Fame itself. We see it as the future of the Hall of Fame. Being located in Cooperstown, New York with 300,000 visitors, digital is how we can reach that larger worldwide audience that may never actually visit, but who have a passion for baseball. We take the same care in the digital space that we do in the Museum. When looking at digital marketing specifically we use many of the same metrics that are used in direct mail. They are both scientific endeavors." This approach to prioritizing digital marketing exemplifies the mindset of a leading-edge organization.

An investment in digital marketing can support numerous institutional goals including visitation, membership, fundraising, and community engagement. But where to start? One way to think about the impact of digital marketing from a membership perspective is to consider how the total of all online interactions affects the awareness, desire, interest, and actions of an individual. For many organizations, the sheer number of available options is overwhelming. The good news is digital marketing need not be a distressing endeavor. With the right research, objectives, resources, and prioritization, digital media just becomes another tool in the membership manager's toolkit. The bad news? The proliferation of digital media and techniques will only continue to accelerate, making planning and advance resource allocation critical.

PRIORITIZING DIGITAL MARKETING

There is an infinite array of digital media and accompanying strategies. How does an organization decide which channels to use and when? The answer to this question largely depends on the goals, resources, and priorities of the organization. At a minimum, an organization must have an easy-to-use website and e-commerce function. Without this foundation, all other digital marketing efforts will fall short.

With a user-friendly, e-commerce-enabled website, prioritizing digital marketing becomes an exercise in aligning strategies with goals. For example, if a small organization has a goal of increasing engagement among members online, social media may be the best method for achieving this type of objective. Which social media platform to use? That will depend on the demographics of the audience the organization is trying to reach. If the goal is to increase engagement among young adults, Instagram may be a better choice than Facebook. However, if the organization does not yet have an Instagram profile, but does have an existing Facebook page, the organization must decide if resources would be better spent building on the successes of an already established Facebook community. Starting a new social media community from scratch is a challenging effort requiring significant time and resources to gain traction.

A large organization with several thriving social media communities might have a goal of growing its email subscriber list. In this case, a social media contest may provide the fastest path to email capture. Which social media platform to use? Again, this depends on the demographics of the target audience. An organization seeking to sell gift memberships might focus on a layered online advertising campaign that leverages website visitors, current members, and behavioral targeting, whereas another organization with the same goal might choose to use email marketing to sell gift memberships. The difference in strategy will depend on the audience, budget, and goals.

The strategies presented here range from the very basic to the very sophisticated. Proper evaluation and planning are required to determine the organization's current digital capabilities, and to plot a purposeful course forward. In some cases the addition of a single digital strategy may be appropriate—website retargeting, for example. In other cases, a layered approach will be necessary. For example, an organization seeking to sell gift memberships during the busy holiday season may need to invest in several digital channels to be successful such as email, online advertising, and social media.

CREATING A PATH TO MEMBERSHIP

Digital marketing serves to support membership goals in five key ways: (1) by raising awareness, (2) by educating prospective and current members, (3) by capturing data, (4) by keeping the institution top of mind, and (5) by creating an emotional connection to the organization.

Raising Awareness

By capturing attention in a unique, engaging, and memorable way, digital marketing can be leveraged to raise awareness about the organization or a particular cause. For example, a fun, family-friendly photo contest will be shared on Facebook, talked about on a local news segment, and promoted by an influential mommy blogger—all of which help to raise the visibility of the organization beyond the reach of its existing audience, and in a way that would not otherwise be possible without a this type of social media campaign.

Educating Audiences

Digital marketing can create a space to educate and inform audiences about a particular issue or cause as well as the value, benefits, and impact of membership. Consider, for example, how a social-media-driven trivia contest in which the daily questions focus on the museum's collection, preservation efforts, and children's programs could inform audiences in a fun and unexpected way.

Capturing Data

One of the greatest opportunities presented by digital marketing is the ability to track behavior and capture data. For example, an online promotion can help determine which call to action—"Join Now!" versus "Get My Membership"—prompts more clicks or which offer—"Two Extra Months of Membership" versus "Free Tote Bag"—is more compelling? Additionally, digital campaigns can generate a pre-qualified list of membership prospects by capturing one-to-one contact information.

Staying Top of Mind

An important, yet often undervalued benefit of digital marketing is the cumulative effect of the frequent impressions generated by the campaign that help to keep the institution top of mind. That is, even if the person does not enter the photo contest or click on the ad, the repetition of the visual cue alone (i.e., seeing the library's logo and the invitation to join) is a valuable touch point that will remind the individual of the organization, if only subconsciously.

Creating an Emotional Connection

When done well, digital marketing can deepen an individual's emotional connection to the organization. Because digital offers a high-touch, personalized experience, social media, mobile apps, and interactive campaigns provide a unique opportunity to expose audiences to mission messaging, capture personal stories, and build a sense of community.

WEBSITE

For the purposes of this section, website visitors will be referred to as "users" in order to create a distinction between on-site visitors and online visitors.

The institutional website is the hub of any marketing campaign—whether online or off. It is still the place where transactions ultimately occur, and it is the only thing over which the organization has complete and explicit control. Moreover, the website is a conversion engine—that is, the website is a hub for all marketing activity, where emails, advertising, search engines, direct mail, and social media conversations all converge to support the institution's most important goals.

Unfortunately, many nonprofits have fallen behind in recent years, leaving their website outdated, unappealing, and difficult to use. This is problematic for many reasons. First, while social media and mobile apps have skyrocketed in popularity, the website is still the organization's primary brand touch point. As the hub for information, emotional connection, and online conversion, the website is a critical asset in supporting the institution's visitation, fundraising, and membership acquisition and retention goals. Second, the website is also the primary point of e-commerce transactions. In the not-too-distant future, organizations may find that mobile apps, text messaging, and Facebook will rival the website for online shopping, but for now, the website is still the preeminent purveyor of payment processing. Finally, the website is the primary source for search engine results pages. As a prospective member seeks out information related to the organization or its offerings, search engines play a key role in guiding the user to relevant content. Thus, the website supports membership acquisition by providing content that draws users in.

Website Design

As author Steve Krug notes in *Don't Make Me Think*, "People won't use your website if they can't find their way around it."[6] Often, simple adjustments in the user experience across the website and, in particular, within membership web pages can lead to greater engagement, happier users, and improved conversions.

Usability

In website design, the theory of usability is related to the functionality and user experience of the website. The primary objective of usability is to ensure that the site is easy to navigate and intuitive, allowing the user to accomplish his or her goals as quickly and simply as possible. For more information, visit www.usability.gov for a free comprehensive step-by-step guide to website usability.[7]

Accessibility

A well-designed website should provide all users equal access to the content, features, and functionality of the site. To ensure that people with disabilities are able to participate equally on the web, the World Wide Web Consortium (W3C) launched the Web Accessibility Initiative (WAI), which establishes guidelines for accessibility.

Compliance with accessibility guidelines ensures that the website will function properly with hardware and software designed to make the web accessible for people with disabilities. For example, images and multimedia should include equivalent alternative text, or alt text, in the code to allow visually impaired or blind people to access the site content through special text-to-speech software or text-to-Braille hardware. In some cases, adherence to accessibility guidelines may be mandated by law. A complete guide to current accessibility standards is available at www.w3.org/WAI.[8]

Mobile Friendly

In 2015, Google announced an update to its mobile search algorithm giving improved ranking performance to websites that provide searchers with a positive mobile experience.[9] Websites that do not meet Google's definition of mobile friendliness will be penalized and will see a dramatic decline in traffic coming from organic mobile search. Mobile search is defined as search engine queries that originate from a mobile device such as a smartphone or tablet. Why should an organization care about this change? First, according to comScore, mobile devices accounted for 60 percent of all online traffic in 2014.[10] This represents a significant amount of potential website traffic that could be lost if the institutional website is not mobile friendly.

Second, as reported by eMarketer, mobile shoppers accounted for 75.9 percent of all U.S. digital shoppers in 2014,[11] and research from Goldman Sachs notes that by 2018, mobile commerce will equate to roughly $626 billion, rivaling the total amount of e-commerce sales in 2013.[12] As the ubiquity of smartphones continues, mobile commerce will soon overtake desktop purchases. According to the Pew Research report "The Future of Money: Smartphone Swiping in the Mobile Age," consumers are now "increasingly comfortable using their phones to transfer money, purchase goods, and engage in other types of financial transactions."[13] This trend is so pervasive that experts surveyed by the Pew Internet Project and Elon University's Imagining the Internet Center even predicted the end of regular commerce by 2020, with mobile payments becoming the rule rather than the exception.[14]

Design That Influences Behavior

The design of a website—the sum of its imagery, layout, color, navigation, interactivity, content, graphical elements, information architecture, and functionality—affects the user's perception of the organization. Design can either help or hinder the decision-making process. Good design will nudge the user to take a desired action such as watching a video, viewing membership levels, or clicking the join button.

Conversion Optimization

Long form fields, a clunky checkout process, and confusing navigation—individually, these gaps in user experience can be overlooked as minor issues. Over time, however, the cumulative effect of these missteps will have a negative effect on overall conversion rates, resulting in lost membership revenue. The following best practices will help to improve conversion rates and increase revenues from online membership sales.

Landing Pages

Membership landing pages should have clear and concise headlines, a strong call to action, and relevant information. When possible, tailor content based on the user and remove the primary site navigation to avoid unnecessary distractions. In website design, there is a principle known as "above the fold" or the portion of a web page that is visible when a user loads the page in a browser window. It is important to keep the primary messaging and the call to action above the fold, and, if needed, repeat it at the bottom of the page. A benefits comparison chart that quickly communicates the value of membership at different levels can be helpful in highlighting the "most popular" or "best value" level, prompting users to select these options more frequently. Exhibit 11.1 shows an example of a well-designed membership landing page.

Trust Seals

A trust seal is an icon or logo that verifies the security of a website for e-commerce transactions. Exhibit 11.2 provides examples of trust seals such as Norton, McAfee, TRUSTe, and BBB Accredited. A trust seal communicates to website users that a website is legitimate, and that the data being collected are secure. Displaying a trust seal on the website can help users feel safe when providing credit card information online.

Cart Abandonment

Cart abandonment occurs when a user adds a product (e.g., membership) to the shopping cart, but leaves the website before completing the transaction. There are many tactics to mitigate or recapture cart abandonment. First, make it easy for the user to change the order before checking out. Second, offer alternative payment methods such as PayPal. Third, do not require registration to complete a purchase. Instead, provide an option for users to check out as a guest. If the user has moved nearly all the way through the checkout process, but abandons just before completion, an email can be sent with a personalized message and a link to a pre-populated shopping cart containing the item they had selected. Known as an "abandoned cart email," this can be an effective strategy for recovery of the sale. Finally, website retargeting can be used to recapture a lost sale. Website retargeting is an online advertising technique that uses cookie-tracking technology to serve advertising to users based on the web pages they have visited. In this way, an organization can retarget a user who has left the website before completing a purchase with an ad enticing the individual to return and complete the transaction.

Google Analytics and Conversion Goals

Google Analytics is free software that tracks and reports website traffic, user behavior, and referral sources. Google Analytics allows an organization to

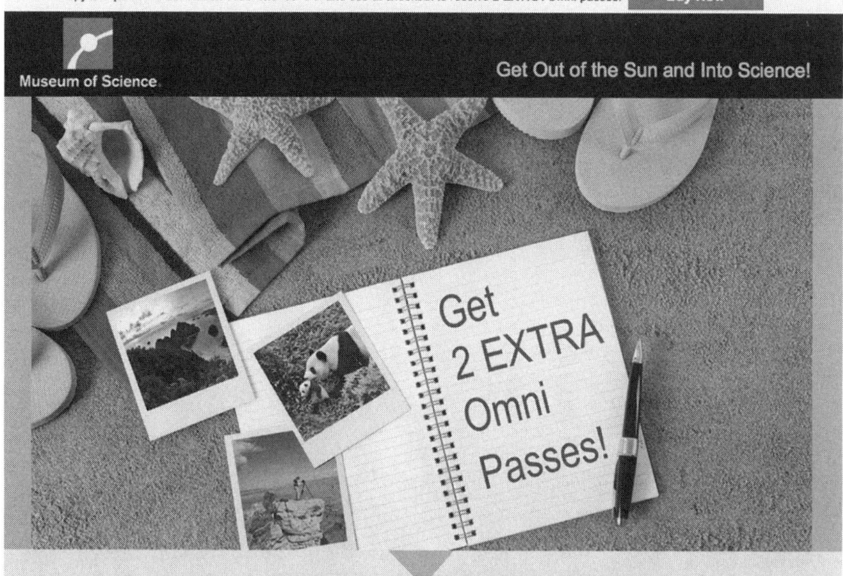

Copy and paste the solicitation code MP1F14 and use at checkout to receive 2 EXTRA Omni passes!
Buy Now
Museum of Science
Get Out of the Sun and Into Science!
Get 2 EXTRA Omni Passes!
Get Your Membership Today!

EXHIBIT 11.1
Sample Membership Landing Page

EXHIBIT 11.2
Examples of Trust Seals

view and analyze the flow of traffic through a website, including membership web pages. This type of information can be helpful in identifying how users discover, consume, and interact with website content. Better understanding of user's online behavior can uncover opportunities to drive more qualified traffic to membership web pages and improve the conversion process.

Google Analytics also includes a measurement feature called "conversion goals." Conversion goals can provide tracking for anything from e-newsletter sign-ups to event registrations and membership sales. As a best practice, membership staff should be involved in determining conversion goals related to membership web pages as well as those activities on the website that directly affect membership sales.

Call to Action

The process of continually improving a website, landing page, or online ad in order to increase the percentage of users who convert (e.g., click on an ad or become a member) is known as conversion optimization. The single most important aspect of conversion optimization is the call to action (also known as CTA). A call to action can be anything from subscribing to an e-newsletter to registering for an event. To be effective, a call to action needs to be clear and unambiguous. For example, "Join Now" is a better call to action than "Submit." Calls to action should be positioned above the fold on landing pages, and should be designed as buttons rather than links.

It is advisable to conduct regular testing to determine the best possible text for a call to action as well as the most effective button color, placement, and size.

A word of caution: Many organizations tend to lump membership and fundraising together on the website. This is not ideal. Members are not necessarily looking to donate and vice versa. Using generic terminology on the website navigation such as "Give," "Support," or "Get Involved," can be confusing to a user who is seeking to "Become a Member" or "Join." Therefore, it is recommended to maintain a distinct and separate link for membership to facilitate better user self-identification.

Pre-Populated Shopping Cart

Whenever possible, create product pages that take users directly to a pre-populated shopping cart with the desired membership level already selected. A pre-populated shopping cart will ensure continuity from advertising or the previous web page, eliminates confusion, and will prevent users from being tempted to downgrade during the checkout process.

Suggestive Selling

Suggestive selling is a technique that introduces an upsell or cross-sell during the purchase process based on the user's current selection. For example, a user who has selected the individual membership level may be offered an opportunity to upgrade to the family level. For suggestive selling to be effective, the recommendation must be personalized and appropriate based on the in-progress transaction.

Privacy and Security

High-profile data breaches at major retailers have heightened consumer privacy concerns. According to the 2015 TRUSTe Consumer Confidence Index, consumer online privacy concerns remain extremely high with 92 percent of Americans worrying to some extent about their privacy online.[15] A survey conducted by the Pew Research Center found that 91 percent of adults "agree" or "strongly agree" that consumers have lost control over how companies collect and use personal information.[16] A privacy policy and compliance with security standards is a requirement of a modern website.

Privacy Policy. The purpose of a privacy policy is to inform and protect users. A privacy statement should be written in straightforward language that is easy to understand. The policy should accurately reflect how the organization collects, uses, and shares information. It is recommended to include an effective date on the privacy statement that is updated whenever changes are made to the policy.

PCI Compliance and SSL

The Payment Card Industry (PCI) Data Security Standards are designed to ensure that organizations that process, store, or transmit credit card information maintain the security of this data. PCI compliance is required for any organization that accepts payment via credit card or debit card. A complete overview of PCI Data Security Standards can be found at https://www.pcisecuritystandards.org/security_standards.[17]

Secure Sockets Layer (SSL) is a security technology that establishes an encrypted link between a web server and a browser. When collecting sensitive data online such as credit card information or social security numbers, an SSL encryption is required.

Member Portal

A member portal is a section of the website customized to the individual member. Accessed by a username and password, the portal allows the member to manage his or her personal profile, membership benefits, and communications preferences. In this way, the member portal supports member servicing. For example, within the portal, a member may be able to manage email communications, update personal contact information, register for events, print out guest passes, renew or upgrade membership, or access members-only online content. When logged in, the member should also be able to shop the online gift store and have the member discount automatically applied to the purchase.

EMAIL

Email marketing is arguably the highest performing digital channel, and it is becoming increasingly sophisticated with the introduction of technologies like marketing automation software. Email marketing can take many forms, including:

Transactional: Automated emails triggered based on an individual's interaction with the organization's website such as buying tickets, becoming a member, or subscribing to an e-newsletter are considered transactional. Transactional emails also include communications such as renewal reminders and confirmation for event registration.

Promotional: Emails that are promotional in nature seek to motivate a specific action by marketing. Examples include promotion of an upcoming event, an offer to upgrade, or an invitation to attend a lecture.

Nurturing: Emails that seek to build a relationship and cultivate a stronger connection to the organization are known as nurturing. Member communications and e-newsletters that contain information such as news, member stories, and updates about upcoming exhibitions are examples of nurturing emails.

Benchmarks

According to research, email subscribers receive an average of 416 commercial emails per month,[18] with nonprofit organizations sending an average of four emails per month.[19]

Table 11.1 shows the expected ranges for open rates, unsubscribe rates, and click-through rates for nonprofits and membership organizations based on data collected by Constant Contact, Silverpop, MailChimp, M+R, NTEN, and Blackbaud.

Data collected by Membership Consultants, Inc. indicates that the majority of membership organizations have email addresses for approximately 70 to 75 percent of their member database, a rate that is growing steadily.[20] The concentration of emails is higher among professional associations and organizations that were founded or have grown up since the advent of email.

The Role of Email in Membership

Email serves many purposes, including driving visitation, marketing special events and programs, and cultivating donors. In membership, email plays a critical role in acquiring new members, supporting member retention, announcing upgrade campaigns and annual appeals, and promoting member

Table 11.1 Email Benchmarks

	Silverpop	Blackbaud	Blackbaud	Constant Contact	Constant Contact	Constant Contact	Constant Contact	Mail Chimp	Mail Chimp	M+R Benchmarks	M+R Benchmarks	
TYPE	*Nonprofits*	*Association & Membership*	*Visitation*	*Art Galleries/ Museums*	*Nonprofit – Arts Organization*	*Nonprofit – Association*	*Nonprofit – Membership Organization*	*Arts and Artists*	*Nonprofit*	*Nonprofit (All)*	*Cultural*	AVERAGE
Gross Open Rate	35.60%	19.99%	20.94%	32.06%	31.97%	29.96%	11.66%	28.05%	25.76%	14.00%	20%	**24.54%**
Unique Open Rate	23.10%	N/A	N/A	N/A	N/A	N/A	N/A	N/A	N/A	N/A	N/A	**23.10%**
Click-Through Rate	2.30%	1.77%	1.13%	7.06%	6.91%	8.47%	7.05%	3.00%	2.97%	1.60%	N/A	**4.23%**
Click-To-Open Rate	10.80%	N/A	N/A	N/A	N/A	N/A	N/A	N/A	N/A	N/A	N/A	**10.80%**
Bounce Rate	N/A	N/A	N/A	9.83%	8.08%	11.89%	3.22%	N/A	N/A	10.00%	N/A	**8.60%**
Hard Bounce Rate	0.064%	N/A	N/A	N/A	N/A	N/A	N/A	0.58%	0.49%	N/A	N/A	**0.38%**
Soft Bounce Rate	N/A	N/A	N/A	N/A	N/A	N/A	N/A	0.80%	0.58%	N/A	N/A	**0.69%**
Unsubscribe Rate	0.060%	N/A	N/A	0.56%	0.49%	0.30%	0.40%	0.27%	0.19%	0.19%	0.19%	**0.29%**

services. In non-visitation organizations, email may be the only conduit to members, putting even more emphasis on the importance of email for membership needs.

Acquisition

In visitation-based organizations, membership's growth is directly tied to its ability to leverage ticket buyer and visitor email lists for membership promotions. The challenge for many visitation-based organizations is capturing contact information from visitors. Moreover, the size of the house list must be large enough to sustain an ongoing membership acquisition strategy. Membership should be regularly represented within institutional e-newsletters, and members should receive tailored e-newsletters that are written with the member in mind. For example, members should not receive an e-newsletter that includes an offer to join. Rather, members should be segmented from the general email list and should receive an e-newsletter that instead offers an opportunity to upgrade. Additionally, members should receive unique communications from the membership department with relevant member-related information such as upcoming preview events, members-only offers, and updates regarding the impact of their support.

Other opportunities may also be available to leverage non-owned lists such as a subscriber list for a local arts or parents' magazine. Often, email marketing to this type of list takes the form of advertising and becomes a sponsored e-blast to the readership.

Another email acquisition strategy is to invest in an expanded email campaign, which allows the organization to send a membership offer to tens of thousands of prospective members. To conduct such an email campaign, an organization will work with a direct marketing vendor to obtain the email list and deploy the campaign in a manner that adheres to CAN-SPAM requirements. By tapping into a vast database of records, an expanded email program can be highly targeted to match up demographics such as age, geography, household income, and presence of children with lifestyle preferences such as hobbies, parenting, and philanthropy in order to identify lookalike recipients based on the current or aspirational member profile. This type of acquisition campaign usually includes repetitive deployments to maximize open and click-through rates.

Gift membership represents another opportunity for email marketing. Gift membership should be marketed at key gift-giving times throughout the year such as the holiday season, Mother's Day, Father's Day, and Grandparents' Day.

Renewals

The renewal process is strengthened with email touch points the month before expiration and the month of expiration as well as thirty and sixty days after expiration. It is important to note that email should be used as an enhancement to the postal mailed renewal cycle—not a replacement. Membership programs that transition to an email-only format for renewal notices tend to see sharp declines in renewal rates and experience difficulty in recapturing large numbers of lost members. Remember that while it is easy to throw away a piece of paper, it is twice as easy to ignore, overlook, or click the delete button on an email.

Upgrade Campaigns and Annual Appeals

Email can serve as an excellent enhancement to support upgrade strategies and annual appeals. Both upgrade campaigns and annual appeals can help an organization identify candidates for donor cultivation.

For upgrade campaigns, email lists for current members should first be segmented by membership level and expiration month. Experience holds that upgrade offers should be tailored to promote two levels above the current membership level, and emails should be sent outside of the normal renewal cycle. That is, members who are due to renew in the spring should be sent an upgrade offer in the fall and vice versa.

Annual appeals should be emailed to all current members to solicit for an additional year-end gift. Annual appeals may also be sent to lapsed members; however, keep in mind that a few will respond to the solicitation expecting that they have renewed their membership.

As with renewals, it is best not to substitute email for direct mail for annual appeals and upgrades. Rather, email should be considered as an added touch point that can increase response rates for these kinds of campaigns. A major benefit of email for annual appeals is the ability to link directly to interactive and supporting online content—a special video message from the executive director, for example.

Member Services

Continued and consistent communication with members is an important part of relationship building and retention efforts. Email should be considered the standard in regular communication with members, and frequent touches throughout the month should be encouraged.

Email Best Practices

Due to continuous advancements in email technologies, ongoing enhancements in digital media integration, Internet Service Provider (ISP) governance, and government regulations, best practices in email marketing will always be a moving target. That said, the following section provides guidelines to ensuring the highest possible performance of email campaigns based on current best practices.

Membership Promotion

Often institutional email policies are too conservative regarding frequency and promotional content. This is not conducive to membership growth. When visitors and website users opt in to receive news and information from the organization, this expectation is inclusive of special offers and promotions related to membership. Generally, it is recommended to send stand-alone promotional membership emails between two and five times per year to the in-house ticket buyer and visitor lists. Excluding membership promotion from such lists represents a critical gap in the institutional marketing strategy that will significantly affect the program's ability to thrive over time.

To ensure that membership is well represented year-round, a shared institutional email calendar should be developed on which promotional membership emails are scheduled. A calendar will also help in crafting membership messaging around relevant events, exhibitions, and high seasons for acquisition.

Segmentation and Personalization

Segmenting lists to tailor messaging is an important aspect of effective email marketing. The days of blasting out the same content to an entire list are long gone. Today's consumers are more sophisticated and there is an expectation not only of timely communication, but also of emails that are relevant and personalized. For example, members should be segmented out from the general e-newsletter list and should instead receive a more tailored e-newsletter with member-specific information.

List-Building Strategies

It is important to develop an intentional strategy to support email capture. List-building strategies are critical to maintaining a healthy email list that can support membership growth. A "give-to-get" model can be an effective method of increasing emails. Give-to-get involves incentivizing visitors and website users to provide their email address in exchange for a small token of appreciation, a freemium (e.g., a white paper or Facebook cover photo), or entry into a drawing for a prize. Admissions and guest services can also be trained and incentivized to ask for email addresses. On-site drawings with entry slips or a digital kiosk in the lobby will help capture email and other contact information from visitors. Additionally, fun, interactive photo booths or postcard kiosks can serve this need in an effective and entertaining way.

Measurement and Optimization

Improving the effectiveness of an email marketing program requires diligent review of several metrics, including open rate, click-through rate, bounce rate, open-to-click rate, and unsubscribe rate.

Often, organizations place too much emphasis on the unsubscribe rate alone without understanding the complete picture. While certainly important, a spike in the unsubscribe rate does not necessarily indicate that there was something wrong with the email content or the frequency of emails. Indeed, such assumptions are often misguided and can lead to fearing anything that might negatively affect the unsubscribe rate.

Best practices from the for-profit sector (based on significant investment in research and testing about what works in email marketing) indicate that it is important to send frequent touches to consumers in order to stay top of mind, establish trust, and deepen engagement. If there are institutional mandates that limit the number of monthly email touches, the organization should periodically evaluate the effectiveness and value of such restrictions. Many times, a review will find that such limitations are arbitrary and not supported by industry research or internal data. Regularly reviewing campaign reporting and experimenting with the frequency of emails can lead to a far more effective strategy than simply limiting the number of email touches.

Finally, resending to non-openers can help identify opportunities for optimizing emails in the future and can also boost engagement rates. There are many reasons why recipients may not have opened the first message. By resending the exact email again, the email will be pushed back to the top of the inbox, prompting some non-openers to open. Other tactics include modifying the subject line and adjusting the timing of the second send in order to increase open rates.

CAN-SPAM Compliance

In 2003, the CAN-SPAM Act was signed into law setting forth the rules for commercial email, giving recipients the right to require that a company stop emailing them, and outlining the penalties incurred for those who violate the law.[21] Email campaigns that are not compliant with CAN-SPAM rules risk damaging the organization's sender reputation score, and can lead to permanent blacklisting of the institution's IP address.

All emails, except transactional emails, are subject to compliance in four primary areas: unsubscribing, content, sending behavior, and list management.

Unsubscribing: All emails must provide a clear and conspicuous way to opt out of future emails, and the organization must honor the unsubscribe request within ten business days.

Content: All emails must include the physical postal address of the organization. Additionally, emails must not use deceptive subject lines that misrepresent the content of the message.

Sending Behavior: The "From," "To," "Reply to," and routing information must accurately identify the organization.

List Management: As a permission-based channel, an individual must opt in to receive email from the organization. Do not buy email addresses, and never sell or transfer email addresses to another list. Use a legitimate email platform that automatically removes hard bounces and unsubscribes from all lists. In email, a hard bounce indicates that there is a permanent reason that the email cannot be delivered to the recipient. Some common reasons for a hard bounce include an error in the email address, a domain name that does not exist, or blocked delivery by the server. On the other hand, when an email platform receives a soft bounce (those emails that are temporarily undeliverable due to server outages or a mailbox that is full, for example) the system attempts to deliver the email for several days. Most providers will eventually classify the email address as a hard bounce if it continues to soft bounce with frequency.

Email Design

Keep designs simple and straightforward with strong calls to action. Many email clients block images by default, so it is important to ensure that the email content can still be conveyed clearly and effectively without images. Embedding images into emails is the primary reason for using HTML, or Hypertext Markup Language. Images should be hosted on a web server and coded into the HTML. This way, images can be downloaded and displayed.

Buttons should be used for primary calls to action in an email whereas links are best for informative or nonessential actions. For example, the call to action "Join Now" would be best formatted as a button. Animated GIFs can also be used to catch the reader's attention and draw the eye toward the call to action.

Emails should be mobile responsive. According to the "U.S. Consumer Device Preference Report," 67 percent of all emails are opened on a mobile device,[22] and 71 percent of U.S. consumers will delete emails immediately if they are not optimized for mobile.[23] To ensure a good user experience and to increase the effectiveness of campaigns, landing pages and e-commerce pages should also be optimized for mobile.

Testing

In digital marketing, there is a technique known as A/B testing, or split testing, in which various design elements, offers, and calls to action can be tested in order to determine which variation produces the best results. A/B testing gets its name from the process of testing two variations of the same design—that is, comparing the results of version "A" to version "B" where A and B are identical except for a single variable such as an image or the placement of a button. As it turns out, email is one of the best channels in which to conduct this type of testing. Opportunities for A/B testing include subject lines, call-to-action language, button color and placement, content ordering and layout, and imagery. Importantly, it is recommended to test only one variable at a time (button color, for example) to ensure valid results.

Email Append

Email appending is the process of taking known member or visitor data such as name and mailing address and matching it against a third-party database to obtain an email address for the record's profile. Before an email address is appended to the organization's database, the individual should be given an opportunity to opt in to receive email communications. To compensate for annual list churn (the percentage of attrition due to unsubscribes, hard bounces, and email abandonment), an email append is recommended for all in-house lists once a year to capture an additional 10 to 30 percent of member and lapsed member email addresses.

Communications Preference Center

A communications preference center allows subscribers to opt in and manage communication preferences such as frequency of emails and subscriptions to various lists. For example, a subscriber may be interested in the educators' e-newsletter, but not in the general monthly e-newsletter, or the subscriber may wish to receive emails from the museum only once a week. By creating an opportunity for recipients to opt out of certain types of lists or messages, it is more likely that he or she will remain subscribed. For CAN-SPAM compliance, there must always be an option to unsubscribe from all future emails.

Member Communications

Regular member communications are important. A contact rate of 24 to 48 times per year via email is healthy and will give members a strong feeling of connection and involvement. Of these communications, three to six should be renewal focused, ten to fifteen should be informational, eight to twelve may be invitations, and six or more may be fundraising related.

At the Museum of Contemporary Art San Diego, members receive three to four emails from the museum per week. This approach to frequent member outreach is refreshing, and represents a modern philosophy of effective email marketing. Even if the member is not able to attend all events or to give an additional gift, simply being invited to participate is a valuable touch point that helps to keep the organization top of mind and the member engaged.

SOCIAL MEDIA

We now understand that the advent of social media has fundamentally changed the way we discover, consume, and interact with news, content, and brands online. The term social media is an umbrella term used to describe any type of web-based software or service that allows users to exchange, discuss, and share ideas, stories, photos, video, and audio. The core differentiation between social media and other digital channels is that social media is inherently participatory. Organizations can leverage social media in numerous ways, including membership acquisition, advocacy, fundraising, and member services.

Types of Social Media

While social media is continuously evolving, there are eight broad categories of social media: (1) Submission Sites, (2) Forums, (3) Media Sharing Sites, (4) Review Sites, (5) Social Networking Sites, (6) Blogs, (7) Microblogging, and (8) Wikis. There are, of course, crossover aspects within each category, and new technologies are continuing to integrate social media into other channels such as mobile apps, text messaging services, and web-enabled devices.

Submission Sites

Submission sites allow users to share content by bookmarking, tagging, voting, and rating. Examples of submission sites include del.icio.us (www.delicious.com), Digg (www.digg.com), and Reddit (www.reddit.com). When an article, website, or offer becomes popular on a submission site, the story will get massive amounts of traffic. Submission sites also provide insight into popular culture by displaying the topics that are trending in real time. For example, the Metropolitan Museum of Art was featured in a post by the online magazine Messy Nessy Chic and received over 4,000 "diggs" (a virtual high five) bumping the story to the top of Digg.com and exposing the article to millions of avid Digg followers.

Forums

Forums were some of the earliest forms of social media, allowing users to connect with people sharing similar interests and participate in discussions. Examples of forums include Google Groups (http://groups.google.com), MacRumors (http://forums.macrumors.com), and Civil War Reenactors (http://www.cwreenactors.com/forum). Forums can be a great way to reach niche audiences and participate in conversations of interest to the organization's stakeholders. Forums are popular for non-visitation organizations as a strong means of communication where members and program managers may rarely get an opportunity for face-to-face interaction.

Media Sharing Sites

Media sharing sites are immensely popular and include social media sites like YouTube (www.youtube.com), Instagram (www.instagram.com), Pinterest (www.pinterest.com), Spotify (www.spotify.com), Vine (www.vine.co), Snapchat (www.snapchat.com), and SlideShare (www.slideshare.com), to name a few. Media sharing sites allow users to share images, video, audio files, presentations, and more. These types of social media sites are an ideal vehicle for rapid content distribution and also offer opportunities for paid advertising promoting membership, events, and upcoming exhibitions.

Review Sites

Sites like Yelp (www.yelp.com), Amazon (www.amazon.com), and Trip Advisor (www.tripadvisor.com) allow users to post reviews and rate organizations, services, books, music, hotels, teachers, museums, and everything in between. Most review sites rely heavily on advertising to generate revenue, offering opportunities to serve advertising to site users. Review sites are quickly becoming a primary channel for customer service. Therefore, it is becoming increasingly important for organizations to frequently monitor reviews, and respond promptly to negative comments in a constructive way.

Social Networking Sites

Social networking sites are the quintessential social media platforms. Facebook (www.facebook.com) and LinkedIn (www.linkedin.com) are examples of social networking sites. Social networking sites provide value to users through connecting people with friends, family, and colleagues. Social networking sites are increasingly becoming centralized streams of content—pushing news, video, photos, and messages directly into the user's feed. As social networking sites continue to monetize their products, advertising and sponsored visibility will become standardized. From a marketing perspective, social networking sites offer immense potential for reaching target audiences online. With sites like Facebook partnering with data aggregation firms, cataloging individuals' online actions, and utilizing technologies like tracking cookies, advertising on social networking sites is sure to become more sophisticated over time.

Blogs

Blogs are a form of social media that allows users to report on news, vent frustrations, voice their opinions, post about vacations, share their poems, or express their ideas on anything about which they may be passionate. Bloggers are now as powerful—and in some cases, more powerful—than traditional journalists. Indeed, journalists today sometimes source news directly from bloggers.

Influential bloggers can be found on any topic. In recent years, the term Mommy Blogger has become synonymous with a woman who has built a following of dedicated readers, and someone who wields significant influence as a publisher of content, reviews, and advice. Bloggers often monetize their blog by selling advertising, promoting products, and negotiating agreements with brands for exposure to the blog's readership. Building a sincere and mutually beneficial relationship with bloggers that have the ear of the institution's target audiences is a worthwhile investment.

Micro-Blogging

Micro-blogging is a messaging service designed to broadcast information to followers in short, public posts. There are hundreds of micro-blogging services worldwide, but the best-known micro-blogging platform is Twitter (www.twitter.com). Twitter is essentially a window to real-time streaming of hundreds of thousands of conversations. Twitter's demographics have been in flux over the past few years, but one thing is certain—Twitter is the place where breaking news happens. Nonprofit organizations can benefit from approaching Twitter as a platform to reach and engage visitors, donors, members, and the media.

Wikis

Wikis are online repositories of information that are user generated, allowing individuals from all over the world to collaborate on, contribute to, and edit entries. The most famous example of a Wiki is Wikipedia (www.wikipedia.org). According to Wikipedia, "all encyclopedic content on Wikipedia must be written from a neutral point of view (NPOV), which means representing fairly, proportionately, and, as far as possible, without bias, all of the significant views that have been published by reliable sources on a topic." The site's terms of service prohibit individuals from editing entries where there is a conflict of interest, and requires contributors to disclose affiliations to the organization such as an employer or client relationship.

Membership Acquisition

Social media can be leveraged to raise awareness and engage audiences on a local, regional, national, or even international level. The three most potent strategies for membership acquisition via social media include contests, advertising, and member-get-a-member campaigns.

Contests

Social-media-driven contests can serve as a valuable lead generation funnel for membership by raising awareness and capturing one-to-one contact information. While it may be easy to discount contests as gimmicky or frivolous, when strategically implemented, contests can connect emotionally with audiences, capturing personal stories and creating a path to membership. Contests are also a valuable PR tool, giving the media relations team a unique and compelling story to pitch journalists and bloggers.

While any kind of social media contest can be fun and engaging—for example, a photo caption contest on the Facebook page or hashtag entries via Twitter—to be effective in supporting membership goals, a contest must meet the following criteria:

- Aligns with the organization's mission;
- Includes a mechanism for capturing personal contact information;
- Reaches new audiences; and
- Exposes prospective members to membership messaging.

When a contest is designed with the above criteria in mind, this type of campaign can reach new audiences, deepen participants' connection to the organization, lay the foundation for future outreach efforts, and grow membership. For case studies, additional resources, and best practices for leveraging social media contests for membership, visit www.themembershipbook.com.

Social Media Advertising

All organizations regardless of annual visitation, type, audience, location, or membership size should evaluate and invest in one or more advertising channels. In recent years, advertising has become more affordable and significantly more targeted, allowing organizations of all sizes to take advantage of paid advertising in order to promote membership, events, exhibitions, and educational programs.

Social media in particular represents an opportunity to reach targeted audiences online with membership messaging. Some platforms like Instagram and Pinterest have recently introduced ads, while others such as YouTube and Facebook have robust and highly sophisticated advertising capabilities. Many social media sites also provide advertising through the Google Display Network or other ad exchanges.

Advocacy

Social media is an invaluable tool in raising awareness and empowering advocates. Two opportunities for leveraging social media for advocacy include online petitions and cause-awareness campaigns.

Petitions

Petitions give supporters an actionable and meaningful opportunity to show their support. Signing an online petition promotes a sense of long-term involvement and helps supporters feel that they are contributing to the cause in a direct and tangible way. Websites like Change.org (www.change.org) offer a simple way for organizations to quickly create and share petitions online. Supporters can follow the progress of the petition, share on their own social media profiles, and be alerted to key milestones or challenges facing the movement.

Cause-Awareness Campaigns

The term "slacktivism" has been used to describe a passive form of online advocacy that makes people feel good, but that does not contribute to the cause in a way that effects real change.

While it's true that many who like a story on their Facebook page or dump a bucket of ice water over their head (as people were encouraged to do as part of an extremely popular social media campaign in 2014 that sought to raise awareness of a disease called amyotrophic lateral sclerosis) will never give a donation or write to their representative in Congress, there is still value in raising awareness and educating audiences about a cause.

Simply creating a space to invite individuals to become more engaged can build momentum—boosting website traffic, Facebook page likes, and media coverage. With the right strategy, a social media campaign can recruit volunteers, spark new partnerships, and generate thousands (or hundreds of thousands) of dollars in donations.

Cause awareness can happen very quickly on social media. Examples of hyper-viral campaigns include the ALS #IceBucketChallenge, #FirstWorld Problems by Water is Life, and the Endangered Song by Smithsonian's National Zoo and Conservation Biology Institute.

Best practices in advocacy campaigns include using hashtags, video, media outreach, and social media toolkits.

Hashtags

A hashtag is a word or phrase preceded by the # symbol (for example, #hashtags). Hashtags originated on Twitter as a way to connect conversations across millions of users and make related tweets searchable. Hashtags are often used to acknowledge and raise awareness about events, causes, emotions, or news. Examples of social cause hashtags include #YesAllWomen, #IceBucketChallenge, #BringBackOurGirls, and #SaveTheTiger.

Hashtags can be used to boost visibility and thread conversations about a cause together across social media platforms. When hashtags go viral, the results can be profound—collective action, innovation, and far-reaching societal and political change. People use hashtags to show solidarity with a cause and to unify many voices under a single declaration. A powerful form of social expression, hashtags provide a way for supporters to convey deep emotions such as empathy, outrage, optimism, respect, and condolences. By connecting conversations together in real time, hashtags provide a live stream of content surrounding a cause or story.

Video

If a picture is worth a thousand words, a video is worth a million. Video is becoming increasingly important as social media platforms and search engines integrate video into feeds and results. When creating videos for social campaigns, keep them short—for best results, two minutes or less in length—and include annotations and hashtags within the video.

Media Outreach

A strong media relations strategy is critical to supporting the goals of an advocacy campaign. Public relations efforts should include a press release, media kit, campaign fact sheet, availability of a spokesperson for interviews, and blogger outreach.

Social Media Toolkit

A social media toolkit is a collection of graphics, videos, statistics, pre-made posts, hashtags, and photos made available to supporters to encourage social media sharing. Exhibit 11.3 shows a social media toolkit created by the Cheetah Conservation Fund with shareable facts, videos, pre-made emails, Facebook cover photos, and Twitter profile pictures to encourage users to share their passion online.[24]

Fundraising

Social media can support fundraising efforts in numerous ways including giving campaigns, crowdfunding, donate buttons, and more.

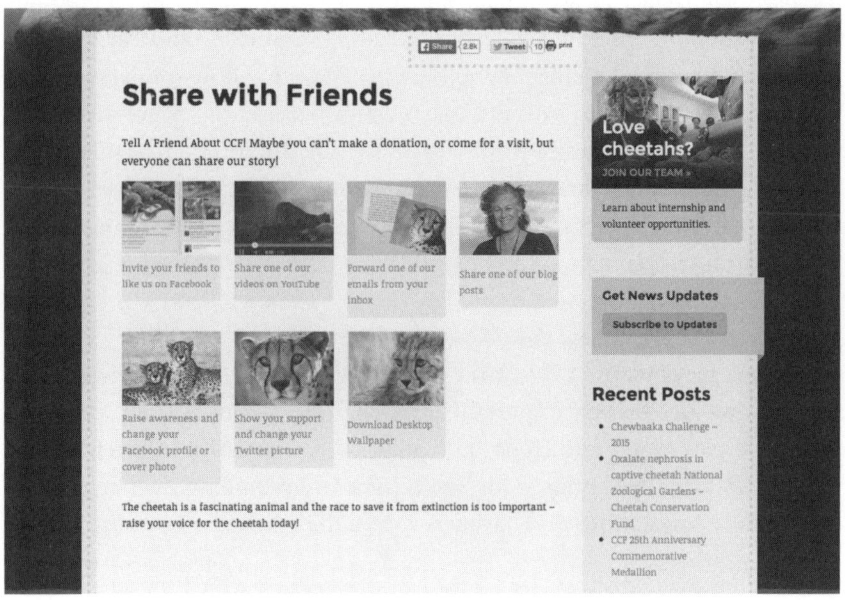

EXHIBIT 11.3
Cheetah Conservation Fund Social Media Toolkit

Giving Tuesday

#GivingTuesday is a global movement dedicated to giving back. Founded in 2012 by New York's 92nd Street Y in partnership with the United Nations Foundation, #GivingTuesday is celebrated on the Tuesday following the American holiday of Thanksgiving and is an opportunity for nonprofits to boost year-end fundraising efforts and raise awareness among new audiences.[25]

Giving Day

In many cities and states across the country, "Giving Day" is hosted by a local community foundation to promote a twenty-four-hour online fundraising competition. Giving Day helps to raise awareness about local nonprofits and provides an opportunity for an organization to reach new members and donors. The Knight Foundation offers information and best practices for planning a successful Giving Day at www.givingdayplaybook.org.[26]

Crowdfunding

Crowdfunding is a way to bring together a group of supporters from all over the world who are passionate about a cause or organization. This type of fundraising can be used as a self-funding mechanism to support special projects, membership goals, and other fundraising initiatives.

Some crowdfunding platforms are free to start a project, while others have varied pricing models to begin a project. The majority of platforms apply a 4 to 5 percent fee to the funds collected as well as a 3 to 5 percent fee for credit card processing. While some platforms follow an "all or nothing model," where the project will only receive funding if 100 percent of the goal is met, others allow projects to keep the money raised, regardless of whether the goal is achieved. Finally, all platforms require a starting and ending time for the crowdfunding to take place. It is important to note that most platforms do not limit to how much a project can raise, thus, projects can continue to accept pledges until time runs out.

Crowdfunding can support a membership program in the following ways:

- Raising Awareness: A well-publicized crowdfunding campaign can generate visibility among new audiences, exposing prospective members to mission messaging and the value of membership.

- Email Capture: Crowdfunding creates an opportunity to collect opt-in email addresses that can be used to market membership.
- Rewards: Membership can be offered as a reward for funders at various levels of support.
- Member Engagement: Crowdfunding provides an opportunity to engage and excite members around a shared goal. Members will be the first to participate and the organization's most vocal promoters of the campaign.

Crowdfunding initiatives are most successful when paired with a project that ties to the mission of the organization, supported by a well-funded and integrated multichannel marketing campaign, and promoted with a professionally produced video that tells the story of the project and mission in a compelling way. For more information about how crowdfunding can support membership, visit www.thememebershipbook.com.

Google for Nonprofits

Through the Google for Nonprofits program, 501(c)(3) designated nonprofits can take advantage of a branded YouTube channel to make it easier for users to join and give.[27] A nonprofit YouTube channel includes a donate button so viewers can contribute to the organization directly from the channel, custom channel branding, video annotations to encourage users to subscribe or visit the website, live streaming, and call-to-action overlays to prompt viewers to donate, sign a petition, or join. For more information on the Google for Nonprofits program, visit www.google.com/nonprofits.

The Future of Social Media Fundraising

Social media fundraising will continue to evolve with a focus on mobile and in-app giving. Examples of this trend include the World Wildlife Fund's "Save the Tiger" tweet-to-give campaign (http://savethetiger.wwf.org.my) and Facebook Donate (an invitation-only program at the time of writing).

Member Services

According to J. D. Power and Associates' 2013 Social Media Benchmark Study^{SM}, 67 percent of consumers have used a brand's social media site for customer service, and younger consumers eighteen to twenty-nine years old are highly likely to use social media for service related interactions (43 percent).[28] Nielsen's "State of Media: Social Media Report" found that 33 percent of users prefer to contact brands using social media rather than the telephone.[29] Perhaps even more telling is that among those who have ever attempted to contact a brand through social media for customer support, 32 percent expect a response within thirty minutes while 42 percent expect a response within sixty minutes, and 57 percent "expect the same response time at night and on weekends as during normal business hours."[30]

These findings may come as a shock to nonprofit organizations that do not have full-time, dedicated staff for managing social media. When members take to social media with questions or concerns, it is crucial that these comments be acknowledged and promptly resolved.

Leading nonprofits have adopted the following best practices regarding social media and member servicing.

Distributed Authorship: Posting responsibility and authority is shared among several departments including membership, marketing, public relations, and guest services.

Social Media Training: Regular training should be conducted for all departments and any staff person, board member, or volunteer who will be engaging on any social media channel on behalf of the organization. Often social media gaffes occur when employees mistakenly post to the organization's social profile rather than their own. Topics should include voice, tone, responding to negative posts, hashtags, and posting etiquette.

Community Guidelines: As with any community, the benefits of bringing people together are occasionally accompanied by inappropriate conduct by a few. Community guidelines address the conduct norms for the organization's social media profile, and clearly state the kinds of behavior that will not be tolerated such as vulgarity, obscenity, hate speech, and personal abuse.

Internal Social Media Policy: An internal communications policy is an important component of an organization's social media strategy. The social media policy should clearly define what constitutes a conflict of interest and outline how employees need to identify their association with the organization. Finally, be sure to cover what content is and is not appropriate to share publicly via social media.

ONLINE ADVERTISING

In his celebrated book, *Confessions of an Advertising Man*, David Ogilvy describes an advertising campaign that successfully increased public awareness of New York's Lincoln Center from 25 to 67 percent and changed perceptions of the center from being "only for wealthier people" to a place "for all the people."[31] Before a person will consider becoming a member, he or she must first have awareness and a positive perception of the organization.

Due to the continued fragmentation of media, nonprofits must adopt multichannel marketing strategies to reach audiences with membership messaging. Even social media—a channel once hailed as the great (free) equalizer of online marketing—is evolving to favor paid media placement. Nonprofits that have not yet embraced online advertising as a necessary component of modern marketing will experience less effective membership campaigns and slower growth as a result.

Online or "digital" advertising includes advertising displayed on any device connected to the web. Digital advertising can be leveraged to raise awareness, drive qualified traffic to the website, and increase membership conversions online. Organizations should be investing in discrete, membership-focused advertising campaigns to support membership acquisition goals online. Opportunities for digital advertising for membership include Facebook advertising, display advertising, search advertising, website retargeting, video advertising, behavioral targeting, direct placement, and mobile advertising.

Facebook Advertising

Beyond "boosting" posts from the page, Facebook offers an incredibly robust advertising module that includes opportunities for CRM retargeting, website retargeting, behavioral targeting, and lookalike audiences. This sophisticated advertising platform allows organizations to reach prospects and lapsed members with tailored membership messaging as well as targeting current members with annual appeal and upgrade ads. Using cookie-tracking technology, organizations can leverage website traffic by retargeting ads to users on Facebook. For example, when someone visits the website, but does not end up becoming a member, a membership ad can be served to the individual the next time he or she is on Facebook. Behavioral and lookalike targeting allows organizations to find audiences that match the current or aspirational member profile on Facebook. Exhibit 11.4 shows examples of Facebook advertising.

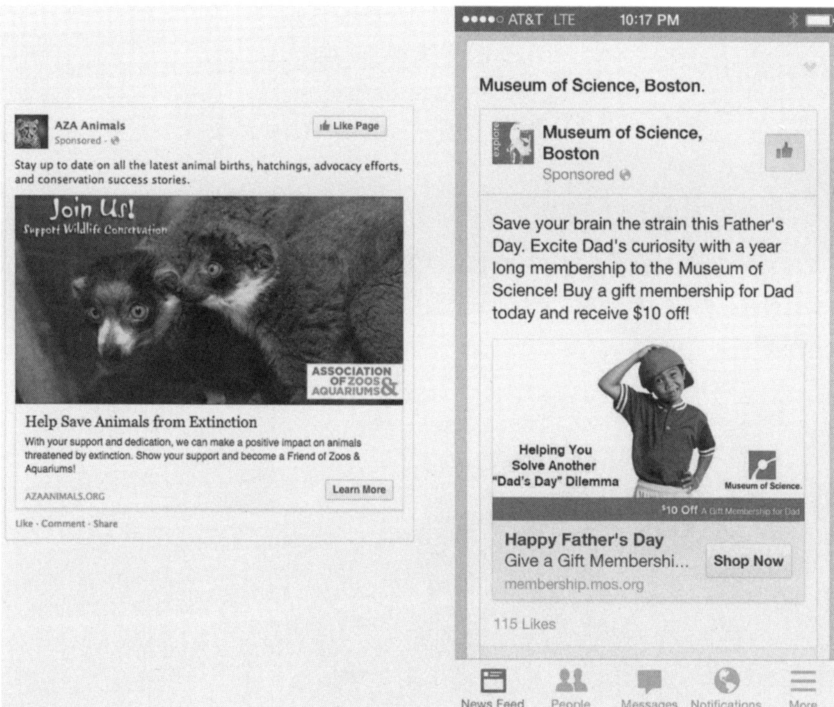

EXHIBIT 11.4
Facebook Advertising

Display Advertising

Display advertising (see exhibit 11.5) includes ad formats such as banners, pop-ups, skyscrapers, interstitials, animated GIFs, and more. Most often display advertising is bought through ad exchanges like the Google Display Network. Campaigns can be structured to target users based on a combination of demographic, geographic, behavioral, contextual, and offline data.

Search Advertising

Every day people turn to Google, Yahoo!, and Bing to help them find information they need. Search advertising taps into the real-time search activities of users to display advertising that is relevant based on a combination of criteria such as keywords, geography, and the type of device used to perform the search. Google's AdWords™ is an example of search advertising (see exhibit 11.6).

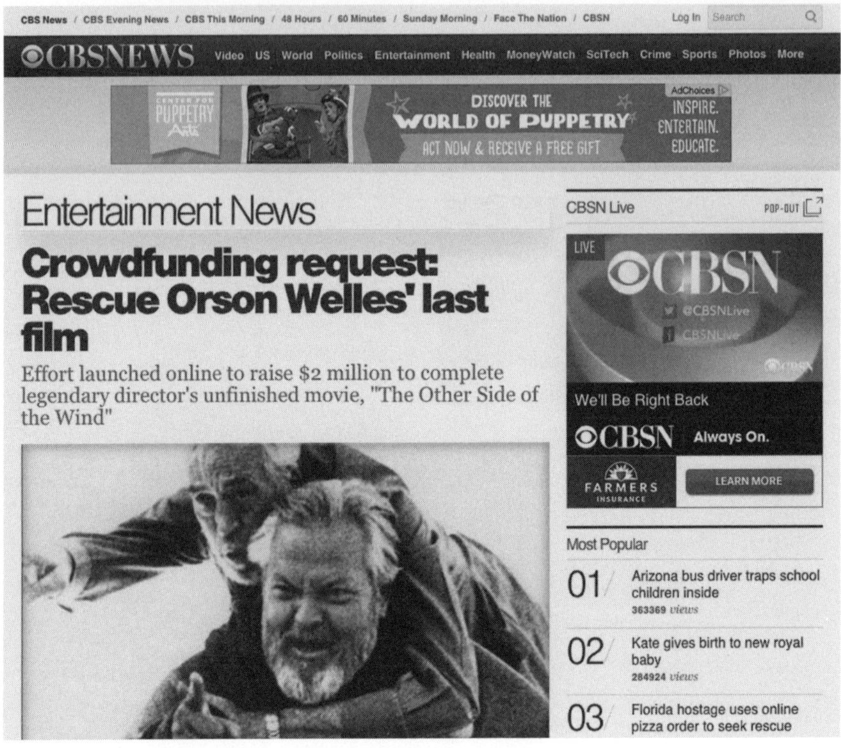

EXHIBIT 11.5
Display Advertising

Website Retargeting

Website retargeting uses cookie technology to serve targeted advertising to people who have visited the organization's website. This type of advertising can have a ten-times-lower cost per acquisition than other forms of advertising because the user is already aware of the institution's brand and offering. This pre-qualification makes website retargeting an efficient place to begin when initiating a membership-focused ad strategy.

Pre-Roll

Pre-roll is a short video ad that plays before or during the loading of online video content. Pre-roll can quickly increase the visibility of the organization with a ten- to thirty-second commercial on popular media sites such as YouTube as well as blogs, websites, and news sites.

Lookalike Targeting

Lookalike targeting is a predictive targeting tactic that allows organizations to reach prospective members who have not visited the website or searched for relevant keywords, but who are nevertheless ideal targets for membership. Working with a qualified marketing agency allows an organization to tap into this type of predictive modeling that is run against 300-plus million user profiles resulting in a small, but very precise audience segment of highly qualified prospects to whom advertising can be targeted.

Behavioral Targeting

By examining prior browsing behavior, behavioral targeting allows an organization to reach prospective members who have searched for specific keywords, visited similar or related websites, or are engaged in relevant content in real time. This type of advertising is extremely effective as it ensures that advertising dollars are focused on the most qualified prospects.

Direct Placement

Direct placement refers to an advertising strategy that is customized based on interest, topic, demographics, lifestyle, and geography. For example, a science museum may be interested in marketing its membership program to the readership of a local mommy blogger who offers opportunities for sponsored content and promotional email blasts to subscribers.

Direct placement may include many types of advertising such as a homepage takeover, premium interest section sponsorship, banner ads and rich media ads, video ads, sponsored social media posts, sponsored editorials, promotional emails, or giveaways.

Mobile Advertising

Mobile advertising includes ads that appear as mobile-optimized text ads, banner ads, videos, or interstitial ads within apps on mobile devices. Mobile ads can be targeted based on geography, device type, and user behavior.

Testing and Optimization

One of the greatest opportunities for digital advertising is the ability to test, refine, and optimize campaigns overtime.

A/B Testing

The technique known as A/B testing, or split testing, allows an organization to test various elements of an ad, including design, offer, and call to action to determine which element produces the best results. A/B testing involves testing two variations of the same design, where version A and B are identical except for a single variable such as the call to action. A/B testing is a simple way to determine which elements of an ad are responsible for driving certain actions. Conducting a split test can provide insight into which aspects of the ad are most compelling. For example, conducting a split test can determine whether a green button generates more clicks than a red button, or whether tickets to a film screening is a more motivating offer than a free umbrella.

Optimization

In advertising, optimization refers to improving the performance of an ad campaign over time. The process for optimizing ads can include adjusting bidding (the means by which online advertising inventory is bought and sold on a per-impression basis), adapting based on geography or keywords, or changing creative to improve performance.

GOOGLE GRANTS

According to a report by the public relations agency Fleishman-Hillard and market research firm Harris Interactive, 89 percent of consumers rely on search engines to seek out information and help make purchase decisions.[32] This represents a significant amount of website traffic being driven by search engines, and Google owns approximately 68 percent of the search engine market.[33] One of the ways Google monetizes its search engine is through advertising known as "paid search." Google's paid search platform is called AdWords™, which displays text-based ads along the top, bottom, and right-hand sidebar of Google's search result pages as sponsored results.

Google Grants is an in-kind sponsorship program offered by Google that provides up to $329 per day (that's $10,000 per month!) in free AdWords™ advertising to 501(c)(3) nonprofits in order to increase visibility and promote their missions within Google's search results.[34] Nonprofit organizations have many goals that can be supported by a Google AdWords™ strategy, including raising awareness, driving traffic to membership landing pages, recruiting volunteers, and fundraising. Exhibit 11.6 shows an example of Google AdWords™.

Few nonprofits realize the full potential of the program due primarily to limitations of time and/or expertise in managing paid search advertising. Search engine marketing is a massive industry, with spending on paid search advertising projected to reach $25.6 billion in the United States in 2015.[35] Without the proper allocation of resources dedicated toward actively managing the AdWords™ account, the institution will not be able to optimize the grants program effectively—leaving unspent dollars on the table and missed opportunities to drive qualified traffic to the website. For more information regarding eligibility, restrictions, and best practices for Google Grants, visit www.themembershipbook.com.

MOBILE MARKETING

The year 2014 was important for digital—it marked the moment in history when the number of mobile users overtook the number of desktop users,[36] and eMarketer forecasts that half of all mobile phone users globally will have smartphones by 2018.[37] The takeaway? Mobile is no longer a trend—it is a critical communications, marketing, and transactional channel.

The Gift of Membership
Gift a Year to the Museum of
Science, Boston. Plus, $10 Off.
membership.mos.org/moms-day-gifts

Give Mom a Membership
Enjoy $10 Off Gift Memberships for
Mom. Unique Gifts That Keep Giving!
membership.mos.org/moms-day-gifts

EXHIBIT 11.6
Google AdWords™

Mobile as an industry has evolved rapidly in a relatively short amount of time, with advances in technology, new social media platforms, and offline integration triggering significant and lasting changes in an organization's ability to reach and engage with audiences of all ages wherever they may be in the world. There are many opportunities for organizations to leverage mobile devices, including raising awareness, nurturing relationships, conducting market research, growing membership, improving renewal rates, supporting annual giving, and providing member servicing. From a membership perspective, there are five main areas where mobile should be evaluated and prioritized in an organization's marketing strategy: (1) mobile websites, (2) mobile messaging, (3) mobile apps, (4) mobile advertising, and (5) near-field communication and beacons.

Mobile Websites

There has been a lot of discussion in the website development community regarding the best way to accomplish designing a website that is user friendly on a mobile device. This conversation typically revolves around three primary design approaches: responsive, adaptive, and mobile-specific. A responsive website is one in which the design automatically responds (or adjusts) to the screen width of the device accessing the website. An adaptive website is designed to reconfigure content or features based on the type of device accessing the content to optimize certain parts of the site for a smartphone or tablet. Finally, a mobile-specific website is a dedicated second website intentionally designed for mobile devices. Typically, a mobile-specific website will have a different URL—m.museum.org, for example. Regardless of the design approach, it is no longer acceptable for an organization not to have a mobile-friendly website. As discussed, in 2015 Google announced that its algorithm would penalize websites in mobile searches that are not mobile friendly—considered by many industry experts to be the search giant's most significant change in years with widespread implications.

Now in its fifth year, the "Adobe Mobile Consumer Survey" provides insight into mobile users' behavior, expectations, and motivations. The report highlights several best practices for ensuring a seamless mobile experience online, including:[38]

- Reducing the number of touch events to complete a transaction;
- Designing for mobile interaction with emphasis on touch-driven controls such as swipe, pinch, and double-tapping;
- Reducing page load time;
- Emphasizing location;
- Ensuring site search and menus are easily accessible; and,
- Optimizing landing pages and e-commerce for mobile transactions.

Mobile Messaging

The mobile messaging landscape is constantly changing with the rapid adoption of so-called over-the-top messaging services such as What'sApp and the continued expansion of mobile messaging with social media platforms, mobile apps, and offline integration. In the United States, the Federal Communications Commission (FCC) regulates mobile marketing. Globally, mobile marketing is governed by each country's telecommunications regulatory authority, and monitored by CTIA—The Wireless Association®, an international nonprofit membership organization representing the wireless communications industry. The CTIA provides best practices for mobile marketing on its website at www.ctia.org. In addition, the Mobile Marketing Association (MMA) offers resources, code of conduct guidelines, and industry research at www.mmaglobal.com.

In 2013, revised rules for the U.S. Telephone Consumer Protection Act, or TCPA, went into effect, with far-reaching implications for mobile marketing.[39] The new TCPA regulations can be found at http://hraunfoss.fcc.gov/edocs_public/attachmatch/FCC-12-21A1.pdf. One of the major updates to these rules is the requirement that an organization have explicit permission (i.e., double opt-in) to send mobile messages. According to the Mobile Marketing Association, double opt-in is the "process of confirming a mobile subscriber's wish to participate in a mobile program by requesting the subscriber to opt-in twice, prior to engaging the subscriber."[40]

The double opt-in process typically occurs as follows. An individual is invited to opt in to receive text messages from the organization by texting a keyword to a "short code" (a five- or six-digit number that is leased from the Common Short Code Administration (www.usshortcodes.com). For example, members may be invited to text PREVIEW (the keyword) to 81732 (the short code) to receive reminders about upcoming member preview events via text. The second opt-in happens when the user receives the first welcome message from the organization. For example, the welcome message might say "Welcome to Museum Member Preview reminders! Reply YES to receive monthly msgs. Reply STOP to end. HELP for info. Msg&Data Rates May Apply." Additionally, subscribers must always be given an opportunity to opt out of all communications, be provided a support contact for help regarding the service, and be informed that participation in the service may entail costs.

For the purposes of membership, messaging primarily falls into two categories: Short Message Service (SMS) and Multimedia Messaging Service (MMS). SMS is a plain text format that has a limit of 160 characters. MMS is a multimedia format that eliminates the character limit and can include images, animated GIFs, videos, or audio clips delivered to the device as an attachment. There are many ways an organization can use mobile messaging for membership, including member services, surveys, annual giving, and contests.

Member Services

According to the Salesforce "Mobile Behavior Report," 54 percent of mobile users report opting in to receive text messages from a brand, and 91 percent of subscribers say receiving text messages from an organization is somewhat or very useful.[41] These findings indicate that SMS text messaging is beginning to gain traction as a hyper-responsive customer service vehicle. For example, a library may offer members a welcome series in which the organization provides a sequence of helpful tips for maximizing benefits in the first year.

Other opportunities for text messaging that support member services include renewal reminders, early ticket sales alerts, event registration, and discount codes for the gift shop or on-site restaurant. Even if the member has opted in to receive text messages once before, it is necessary to receive a double-opt-in with each new service offering. For example, permission to receive renewal notices does not carry over to event registration.

It is also important to be respectful of the time when text messages are sent; many people sleep with their mobile phone near their pillow. To avoid disrupting a sleeping member, it is best not to send any type of text message after 9:00 p.m. or before 11:00 a.m. Finally, organizations should be cautious of abusing text messaging by sending messages too frequently. Typically, text messages should be sent no more than once or twice a month.

Surveys

SMS can be a fast, inexpensive, and effective way to send surveys. The survey length should be much shorter than a traditional online survey. An organization can offer visitors or members an invitation to participate in a mobile survey by opting in via a short code and keyword that will initiate the survey. As with other forms of text messaging programs, explicit permission is required. Importantly, the need for unbiased, statistical data collection and objective analysis of the survey results still applies in a mobile setting.

Mobile Giving

In January 2010, text-to-give became a rapid way to raise urgently needed dollars for the victims of the Haiti earthquake. Since then, mobile giving programs have empowered nonprofits of all sizes and kinds to receive donations via text messaging. According to the Pew Research Center, one in ten U.S. adults has already made a charitable donation via text message.[42]

Most mobile giving programs work one of two ways: by charging the donor's credit card or by applying the donation to the individual's phone bill. Some programs limit donation amounts to $5 or $10 while others offer unlimited donation amounts. There are numerous mobile giving providers such as Give by Cell, Connect2give, mGive, Mobile Commons, and MobileCause to name a few. Typically, a text-to-give program requires a flat fee to initiate the program along with a cost per transaction, and in some cases, there is a monthly service fee.

Like any campaign, mobile giving must be properly marketed to be successful. Begin by promoting the program to members and donors via direct mail and email. Develop signage to raise awareness among visitors. Finally, promote the program on the organization's website and leverage social media to increase support online.

Contests

Mobile offers an excellent opportunity for contests and can help capture visitor contact information. For example, a library might run a text contest asking visitors to share their favorite book for a chance to win tickets to an upcoming lecture. A museum might promote a contest asking visitors to interact with a specific exhibit and provide a keyword to be entered into a drawing for a family membership. A professional association might host a photo contest during a conference to drive traffic to the exhibit hall. With a mobile format, the contest can happen on-site or from anywhere in the world. While the goals of a mobile contest may vary, data capture should always be prioritized so that the organization can add participants to future email and mail campaigns promoting membership.

An excellent example of how to use mobile for membership is History Colorado's mobile scavenger hunt. The contest was designed to raise awareness and promote membership, leading up to the grand opening of its new permanent exhibit *Denver A to Z*. By engaging new audiences, educating participants, and garnering media attention, the contest helped to raise awareness of the center's mission and create a path to membership. View the History Colorado case study as well as resources and best practices for leveraging mobile contests at www.themembershipbook.com.

Mobile Apps

According to a Pew Research Center report, 46 percent of mobile users say their smartphone is something they "couldn't live without,"[43] while a study by comScore noted that 79 percent of smartphone owners use mobile applications (or apps) nearly every day, accounting for seven out of every eight minutes of media consumption on mobile devices.[44] Indeed, apps have become the access point to modern life: games, news, shopping, dining, research, blogging, music, social media, email, banking, travel, movies, file sharing, recipes—the list goes on.

The development environment for mobile apps is constantly changing, and app development can be an expensive proposition. The cost associated with developing an app is related to the complexity of the desired functionality, the platform on which the app is built (e.g., iPhone or Android), the need for APIs (API stands for Application Programming Interface and is a term used to describe intermediary software that allows an application program to communicate with another program or system), the design, and more.

Mobile apps can enhance the on-site experience by providing audio tours, maps, expanded exhibit or educational content, helpful tips, bathroom locators, and so on. Beyond the on-site experience, apps can provide easy access to hours of operation, directions, ticket sales, customer service contacts, virtual tours, and daily event information. Some apps are designed to serve a single purpose such as Cheyenne Mountain Zoo's Sustainable Palm Oil App or the World Wildlife Fund's Snow Globe Charity App.

To support membership effectively, an organization should consider the following features when designing a mobile app:

- Members-only section: An area of the app that offers exclusive content to members.
- Membership messaging: Throughout the app there are often opportunities to promote membership.
- E-commerce: Provide users with an opportunity to join directly from the app.
- Push notifications: This type of alert can include special offers to join.
- Events: An event calendar can highlight members-only events and previews with a link to join.
- Games and activities: Interactive puzzles, word games, photo booths, etc. can provide an educational component as well as an opportunity to capture user contact information.
- Member hotline or concierge: From the mobile app, members can have one-touch access to membership staff.
- Member portal: A member portal can offer members access to their account information, event information and registration, gift shop discount codes, guest passes, and easy renewal and upgrade options.

Mobile Advertising

Much like online advertising, mobile advertising can take many forms—from display and search ads, to in-app ads and geo-fenced offers, advances in mobile technology are opening new doors to reaching prospective members. What sets mobile advertising apart is the integration of location-aware apps and software that can tap into the built-in GPS of a mobile device to deliver timely and relevant advertising based on a person's physical location.

For example, a technology known as geo-fencing allows an organization to place a virtual boundary around its location(s) that can trigger an ad or message to be displayed once a person crosses or nears the perimeter. This type of hyper-local ad offers the opportunity to send a membership promotion to a visitor when he or she enters the museum, steps into the park, or passes by the library. In-app and geo-targeted advertising allows an organization to serve ads to users based on the type of app they are using or their location, respectively. Consider the potential of sending geo-targeted membership ads to visitors waiting in line outside the museum, inviting them to move to the front of the line by becoming a member. This is the power of mobile advertising.

Near-Field Communication and Beacons

Near-field communication, or NFC, uses short-range radio waves via a chip to allow two mobile devices to exchange data by touching the devices together or by bringing them into close proximity. An example of NFC in action is Google Wallet, a money transfer service that enables an individual to use his or her mobile device to pay for products at a point-of-sale terminal by swiping the device over the terminal. Alternatively, beacons are small wireless sensors that transmit data using Bluetooth® Low Energy technology. Beacons broadcast signals that can be received by a compatible device and can also be used to pay for purchases with a mobile device. Both of these technologies require users to activate the technology on their mobile devices, accept location services, and/or opt in to receive notifications.

So what does this all mean for nonprofit organizations? These technologies will soon make the visitor experience truly interactive, allowing visitors to discover more about the artifacts, authors, architects, sculptors, and collections by receiving communications on their mobile devices directly from exhibits, signage, and buildings. Indeed, it appears that NFC and beacons are leapfrogging technologies such as QR codes (at least in North America), allowing institutions to enhance the visitor experience by personalizing content based on the user's location and triggering location-specific notifications. As this technology begins to take hold, it will be critical to incorporate membership into the implementation strategy.

SUMMARY

Social media, mobile, email, and digital channels are expanding at an accelerated pace, as are the opportunities to tap into these evolving technologies for membership. As the media landscape continues to fragment, it will inevitably create new niche markets and open doors to more targeted and personalized marketing strategies. To stay competitive, nonprofits will need to allocate resources toward mobile initiatives, e-commerce optimization, and digital marketing that will grow membership, and, as Ken Meifert says, "reach that larger worldwide audience."

NOTES

1. Sean Bradley, *Win the Game of Googleopoly: Unlocking the Secret Strategy of Search Engines* (Hoboken, NJ: Wiley, 2015), 17.

2. Pew Research Center, "Social Networking Fact Sheet," 2014, accessed April 13, 2015, http://www.pewinternet.org/fact-sheets/social-networking-fact-sheet.

3. "The Digital Consumer," Nielsen, February 2014, accessed March 3, 2015, http://www.nielsen.com/content/dam/corporate/us/en/reports-downloads/2014%20Reports/the-digital-consumer-report-feb-2014.pdf.

4. "Gartner IT Glossary," Gartner, 2015, accessed February 6, 2015, http://www.gartner.com/it-glossary/digital-marketing.

5. International Chamber of Commerce, "Digital Media," accessed February 6, 2015, http://www.iccwbo.org/advocacy-codes-and-rules/areas-of-work/marketing-and-advertising/digital-marketing-communication.

6. Steve Krug, *Don't Make Me Think! A Common Sense Approach to Web Usability*, 2nd ed. (Berkeley, CA: New Riders, 2006), 51.

7. Usability.gov, accessed May 15, 2015, www.usability.gov.

8. Web Accessibility Initiative, accessed May 15, 2015, www.w3.org/WAI.

9. Google, "Finding More Mobile-Friendly Search Results," accessed February 26, 2015, http://googlewebmastercentral.blogspot.com/2015/02/finding-more-mobile-friendly-search.html.

10. Adam Lella and Andrew Lipsman, "The U.S. Mobile App Report," comScore, Inc., August 21, 2014, accessed February 24, 2015, http://www.comscore.com/Insights/Presentations-and-Whitepapers/2014/The-US-Mobile-App-Report.

11. eMarketer, "Mobile's Still Far Behind Desktop for Retail Ecommerce Revenues," February 24, 2014, accessed March 3, 2014, http://www.emarketer.com/Article/Mobiles-Still-Far-Behind-Desktop-Retail-Ecommerce-Revenues/1012100.

12. Alexis Madrigal, "Goldman: There Will Be as Much Mobile Commerce in 2018 as E-Commerce in 2013," *The Atlantic*, March 6, 2014, accessed November 8, 2015, http://www.theatlantic.com/technology/archive/2014/03/goldman-there-will-be-as-much-mobile-commerce-in-2018-as-br-e-commerce-in-2013/284270.

13. Aaron Smith, Janna Quitney Anderson, and Lee Rainie, "The Future of Money: Smartphone Swiping in the Mobile Age," Pew Research Center's Internet & American Life Project, April 17, 2012, accessed March 2, 2015, http://www.pewinternet.org/files/old-media/Files/Reports/2012/PIP_Future_of_Money.pdf.

14. Ibid., 3–7.

15. TRUSTe, "US Consumer Confidence Privacy Index," January 28, 2015, accessed February 18, 2015, https://www.truste.com/resources/privacy-research/us-consumer-confidence-index-2015.

16. Mary Madden, "Public Perceptions of Privacy and Security in the Post-Snowden Era," Pew Research Center, November 12, 2014, accessed January 25, 2015, http://www.pewinternet.org/2014/11/12/public-privacy-perceptions.

17. PCI Security Standards Council, "PCI SSC Data Security Standards Overview," accessed May 12, 2015, https://www.pcisecuritystandards.org/security_standards.

18. Casey Swanton, "How to Lose Customers and Alienate Subscribers," Return Path Blog, October 10, 2013, http://blog.returnpath.com/blog/casey-swanton/how-to-lose-customers-and-alienate-subscribers.

19. Theresa Bugeaud, "M+R Benchmarks Study," M+R, April 22, 2014, accessed April 23, 2015, http://mrbenchmarks.com.

20. Membership Consultants, Inc., "Social Media and Digital," accessed June 8, 2015, http://www.membership-consultants.com/services/social-media-and-digital.

21. Federal Trade Commission, "CAN-SPAM Act: A Compliance Guide for Business," accessed May 17, 2015, https://www.ftc.gov/tips-advice/business-center/guidance/can-spam-act-compliance-guide-business.

22. Movable Ink, "US Consumer Device Preference Report," January 28, 2015, accessed February 14, 2015, https://s3.amazonaws.com/movableink-marketing/Movable+Ink+-+US+Consumer+Device+Preference+Report+-+Q1+2015.pdf.

23. BlueHornet, "Consumer Views of Email Marketing," August 27, 2014, accessed October 23, 2015, http://echo.bluehornet.com/static/bluehornet/resources_downloads/2014-BH-Consumer-Views-Report_02.pdf.

24. Cheetah Conservation Fund, "Share with Friends," accessed May 23, 2015, http://cheetah.org/you-can-help/share-with-friends.

25. #GivingTuesday, "About," accessed April 1, 2015, http://www.givingtuesday.org/about.

26. Knight Foundation, "Giving Day Playbook," accessed May 8, 2015, http://www.givingdayplaybook.org.

27. Google, "Google for Nonprofits," accessed January 4, 2015, http://www.google.com/nonprofits.

28. Jacqueline Anderson, "Social Media Benchmark Study℠," J. D. Power and Associates, February 14, 2013, accessed October 22, 2014, http://www.jdpower.com/press-releases/2013-social-media-benchmark-study.

29. Deirdre Bannon, "State of the Media: The Social Media Report," Nielsen, December 4, 2012, accessed November 1, 2014, http://www.nielsen.com/content/dam/corporate/us/en/reports-downloads/2012-Reports/The-Social-Media-Report-2012.pdf.

30. Jay Baer, "42 Percent of Consumers Complaining in Social Media Expect 60 Minute Response Time," *Convince and Convert*, 2012, accessed November 1, 2014, http://www.convinceandconvert.com/social-media-research/42-percent-of-consumers-complaining-in-social-media-expect-60-minute-response-time.

31. David Ogilvy, *Confessions of an Advertising Man*, 2nd ed. (New York: Scribner, 1989), 42.

32. Fleishman-Hillard International Communications, "Digital Influence Index," January 31, 2012, 10, accessed January 29, 2015, http://cdn.fleishmanhillard.com/wp-content/uploads/2013/06/2012-DII-White-Paper.pdf.

33. comScore, "comScore Releases April 2014 U.S. Search Engine Rankings," May 16, 2014, accessed January 29, 2015, http://www.comscore.com/Insights/Market-Rankings/comScore-Releases-April-2014-US-Search-Engine-Rankings.

34. Google, "Google Ad Grants," 2015, accessed January 15, 2015, http://www.google.com/grants.

35. eMarketer, "Digital Advertisers Focus on Holistic Customer Experience," April 3, 2015, accessed April 16, 2015, http://www.emarketer.com/Article.aspx?R=1012308.

36. Rebecca Murtagh, "Mobile Now Exceeds PC: The Biggest Shift Since the Internet Began," *Search Engine Watch*, July 8, 2014, accessed March 23, 2015, http://searchenginewatch.com/sew/opinion/2353616/mobile-now-exceeds-pc-the-biggest-shift-since-the-internet-began.

37. eMarketer, "Worldwide Smartphone Usage to Grow 25% in 2014," June 11, 2014, accessed May 20, 2015, http://www.emarketer.com/Article/Worldwide-Smartphone-Usage-Grow-25-2014/1010920.

38. Adobe, "Mobile Consumer Survey Results," August 21, 2013, 15, accessed May 16, 2015, http://success.adobe.com/assets/en/downloads/whitepaper/35508_mobile_consumer_survey_results_UE_final-2.pdf.

39. Federal Communications Commission, "Telephone Consumer Protection Act of 1991," 2013, accessed May 27, 2015, http://hraunfoss.fcc.gov/edocs_public/attachmatch/FCC-12-21A1.pdf.

40. Mobile Marketing Association, "MMA Glossary," accessed May 27, 2015, http://www.mmaglobal.com/wiki/double-opt.

41. Salesforce, "Mobile Behavior Report," February 25, 2014, 8, accessed April 3, 2015, http://www.exacttarget.com/sites/exacttarget/files/deliverables/etmc-2014mobilebehaviorreport.pdf.

42. Aaron Smith, "Real Time Charitable Giving," Pew Research Center, January 12, 2012, accessed May 6, 2015, http://www.pewinternet.org/2012/01/12/real-time-charitable-giving.

43. Aaron Smith and Dana Page, "U.S. Smartphone Use in 2015," Pew Research Center, April 1, 2015, 7, accessed April 22, 2015, http://www.pewinternet.org/files/2015/03/PI_Smartphones_0401151.pdf.

44. Lella and Lipsman, "U.S. Mobile App Report."

12

Benchmarking Success in Membership

We still haven't played Madison Square Garden. That's a benchmark.

—*Dan Hawkins, English Rocker of The Darkness*

Benchmarking a program's performance is a way of quantifying the productivity of one aspect of a program relative to that of another's or to an industry standard. Benchmarks become the yardstick by which managers evaluate the effectiveness of their membership marketing efforts.

SELF-BENCHMARKING

Evaluating the success of membership marketing and management practices is critical to the growth of a membership program. Benchmarking is best achieved by comparing a program's performance to similar peer organizations and its own past achievements as well as to a set of aspirational comparators. The first exercise in benchmarking is to gain a historical perspective of how the program has performed in the past. If direct mail response rates of an organization can be viewed over the course of the past five to ten years, a good historical perspective will have been established. Having such a historical perspective is the first step in benchmarking current performance. Table 12.1 provides an example of self-benchmarking.

The next step in benchmarking is to measure a program against its peers and an aspirational comparator set for an external point of reference. However,

Table 12.1 **Self-Benchmarking—Membership History**

	2011	2012	2013	2014
New Members	**802**	**786**	**482**	**925**
Renewed Members	1362	1292	1364	1462
Renewal Rate	63%	60%	66%	79%
Members	2164	2078	1846	2387
Membership Revenues	$206,749	$188,166	$174,688	$176,744
New Members	**802**	**786**	**482**	**925**
Direct Mail	203	245	118	267
On-Site	402	376	174	285
Email	39	13	32	143
Gift	136	127	138	191
Misc.	22	25	20	39
Direct Mail Response Rate	1.02%	1.23%	0.79%	1.34%
On-Site Conversion Rate	0.93%	0.99%	0.76%	0.77%

finding a yardstick to benchmark against is the biggest challenge. Often, it is difficult to obtain data from other programs against which to benchmark, as other organizations may be unwilling or unable to share data. Table 12.2 provides an example of a peer benchmarking study conducted for the Friends of the National Zoo. In this study, the zoo's membership dues and categories were compared to those of similar zoos as well as other Washington, DC, venues.

INDUSTRY BENCHMARKING

There is also value in reviewing the organization's performance compared to the general nonprofit sector. Depending on the type of information an organization is seeking, there may be opportunities to benchmark the institution's performance in areas such as email open rates, online giving, direct mail, and social media activities.

While this type of broad industry benchmarking can be helpful in understanding overall nonprofit trends and gauging critical gaps institutionally, it is important to keep in mind that nonprofit studies are generally not representative of visitation-based and membership-serving organizations. Thus, the membership manager must take the data presented in these reports with a grain of salt and consider the information more as a general guideline rather than as a true benchmark.

Table 12.2 Benchmarking Dues and Admission—Friends of the National Zoo

Friends of the National Zoo		Lincoln Park Zoo	St. Louis Zoo	National Aquarium in Baltimore	Bronx Zoo a.k.a. WCS	Philadelphia Zoo	Admission and Membership Levels	Average	FONZ	Difference
Admission										
Adult	$0.00	$0.00	$0.00	$34.95	$19.95	$20.00	Adult	$12.48	$0.00	100.00%
Senior	$0.00	$0.00	$0.00	$29.95	$17.95	$20.00	Senior	$11.32	$0.00	100.00%
Students	$0.00	$0.00	$0.00	$34.95	$19.95	$20.00	Students	$12.48	$0.00	100.00%
Children	$0.00	$0.00	$0.00	$21.95	$12.95	$18.00	Children	$8.82	$0.00	100.00%
Children (<3)	$0.00	$0.00	$0.00	$0.00	$0.00	$0.00	Children (< 3)	$0.00	$0.00	0.00%
Membership Levels										
			$50.00							
			$60.00				Student/Senior/Grandparent	$55.00	$ –	100.00%
National	$50.00		$5.00				National	$50.00	$50.00	0.00%
Green	$55.00						Green	$0.00	$55.00	100.00%
Basic (Individual)	$60.00	$65.00	$65.00	$75.00	$75.00	$75.00	Individual	$71.00	$60.00	-18.33%
					$119.00					
Dual				$125.00			Dual	$125.00		
Premier (Family)	$80.00	$90.00	$85.00	$175.00	$139.00	$120.00	Family	$121.80	$80.00	-52.25%
		-13%	-6%							
Premier+ (Family +)	$110.00	$175.00	$120.00		$189.00	$160.00	Family Plus	$161.00	$110.00	-46.36%
		-59%	-9%							
			$175.00				Family Plus+ (Keeper)	$175.00	$ –	-100.00%
Patron	$250.00	$365.00	$250.00	$250.00	$275.00	$260.00	Patron	$282.86	$250.00	-13.14%
						$330.00				
Sponsor	$500.00	$500.00	$500.00	$500.00	$525.00	$500.00	Sponsor	$539.29	$500.00	-7.86%
			$750.00							
Benefactor	$1,000.00	$1,000.00	$1,000.00	$1,000.00	$800.00	$1,000.00	Benefactor	$1,100.00	$1,000.00	-10.00%
			$1,500.00		$1,500.00					
		$2,000.00			$1,500.00					
Director's Circle	$2,500.00		$2,500.00	$2,500.00	$2,500.00	$2,500.00	Director's Circle	$2,375.00	$2,500.00	5.00%
		$3,000.00								
Conservation Circle	$5,000.00	$5,000.00	$5,000.00		$5,000.00	$5,000.00	Conservation Circle	$5,000.00	$5,000.00	0.00%
Wildlife Society	$10,000.00	$10,000.00	$10,000.00		$10,000.00	$10,000.00	Wildlife Society	$10,000.00	$10,000.00	0.00%
Champion of Conservation	$25,000.00	$25,000.00	$25,000.00			$25,000.00	Champion of Conservation	$25,000.00	$25,000.00	0.00%

Source: Friends of the National Zoo. Copyright 2015. All Rights Reserved. FONZ levels and rates are based on 2015 and subject to change.

There are several sources available for nonprofit benchmarking:

- *M+R Benchmarks Study* presented in collaboration with the Nonprofit Technology Network provides insight into nonprofit fundraising, website engagement, email marketing, and social media use.
- MailChimp's *Email Marketing Benchmarks* provides statistics related to nonprofit email marketing: www.mailchimp.com/resources/research/email-marketing-benchmarks/.
- Silverpop's *Email Marketing Metrics Benchmark Study* offers insight into nonprofit email marketing statistics and trends.
- Luminate Online's *Benchmark Report* offers data of overall performance and trends in online fundraising.
- *Nonprofit Communications Trends Report* by Nonprofit Marketing Guide provides an overview of trends and statistics on several communications channels including email, direct mail, and social media.
- *Index of National Fundraising Performance* presented by Blackbaud includes revenue and donor trends for participating nonprofits: www.blackbaud.com/nonprofit-resources/national-fundraising-performance-index.
- Blackbaud's *Charitable Giving Report* provides information related to online giving, monthly giving trends, and fundraising broken down by nonprofit size and sector.
- The Association of Fundraising Professionals offers numerous research resources on its website: www.afpnet.org/Audiences/ReportsResearchList.cfm.
- *Nonprofit Content Marketing Benchmark Study* conducted by the Marketing Institute in collaboration with Blackbaud provides information related to trends in nonprofit adoption of social media, email, infographics, blogs, and newsletters.
- *DMA Statistical Factbook* presented by the Direct Marketing Association includes data and statistics regarding direct mail, email, search marketing, social media, and mobile.

Other benchmarking resources include the professional associations that serve an organization's niche market, such as the American Alliance of Museums, American Library Association, Association of Zoos and Aquariums, Association of Science and Technology Centers, American Association of State and Local History, American Society of Association Executives, and the American Public Garden Association.

As noted above, there are also commercial entities that serve these markets such as Blackbaud, Marts and Lundy, the Chronicle of Philanthropy, Giving USA, and many others. The challenge, however, is to find trends and data that apply to a type of organization that is similar and includes the ability to compare to membership trends, not just giving trends. Membership is different from philanthropic giving as a whole. For example, Blackbaud provides giving data and trends in its donorCentric reports by types of organizational relevance. The Arts and Culture segment would apply to museums and libraries. However, some of the organizations tracked in its benchmarking collaborative for museums are large, national institutions like the Smithsonian. So if a small, regional museum were to use this data for comparative benchmarking, the organization would be comparing itself to a large, national, non-local, visitation-based organization. The advice here is to know to whom the program might be comparing itself to ensure appropriate benchmarking.

MEMBERSHIP BENCHMARKING

In late 2008, the United States saw a steep decline in the stock market and unprecedented turmoil in the financial status of the country. Nonprofit organizations were concerned about their programs during this economic downturn. Professionals in the field had never experienced such financially threatening times, and no one knew what to expect in terms of the effect of the decline or the amount of time it might take membership and fundraising programs to rebound.

While the above listed resources are helpful in many respects, these studies do not focus on membership, and are not segmented in useful ways that would provide insight into the trends specifically facing visitation-based institutions. In response to this lack of membership-focused data, Membership Consultants, Inc. initiated a benchmarking survey in 2008 with the aim of providing benchmarking specifically for the membership sector. The *Pulse of Membership* survey has since become the definitive source for membership program benchmarking.

The *Pulse of Membership* surveys membership managers across the United States with an average response rate of 12 to 15 percent. The survey is in-depth, averaging forty questions in length, and provides a historical perspective on many aspects related to membership, including marketing, overall productivity of channels, budgeting, staffing, and salaries.

The following data from the *Pulse of Membership* survey is self-reported by membership organizations, and should be viewed as a foundational component to benchmarking a membership program and understanding the trends facing membership organizations.[1, 2]

Membership Trends

The early years of the *Pulse of Membership* clearly demonstrate the effects of the Great Recession on membership programs across the country. Over time, membership programs have rebounded, with membership totals rising steadily beginning in 2012. Figure 12.1 provides an overview of membership trends year over year beginning in 2009.

Membership Revenue Trends

Membership revenue reports tend to follow the total number of members, as they should. However, sometimes revenue trends slightly outpace membership totals. Increases in dues structures and upgrade campaigns can increase revenues while membership totals remain flat. Figure 12.2 shows trends in membership revenues between 2009 and 2014.

Membership Budget Trends

Membership budgets clearly drive the membership totals and revenues. If budgets decline, eventually membership totals and revenues will as well.

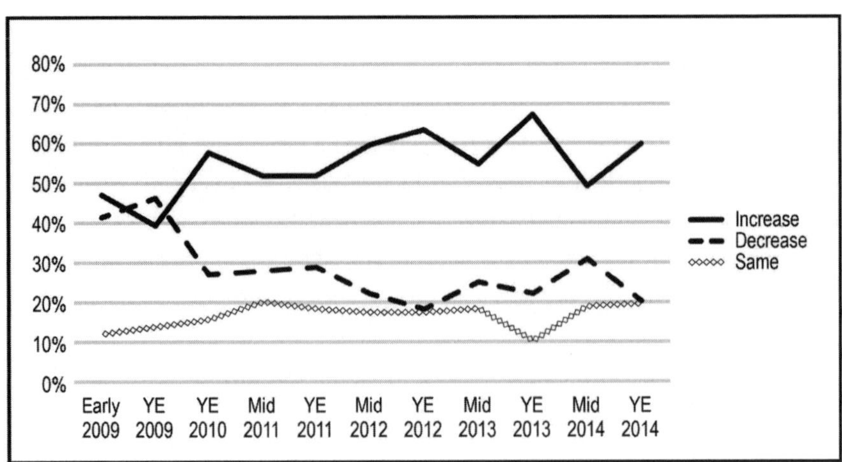

FIGURE 12.1
Membership Trends—Year to Year

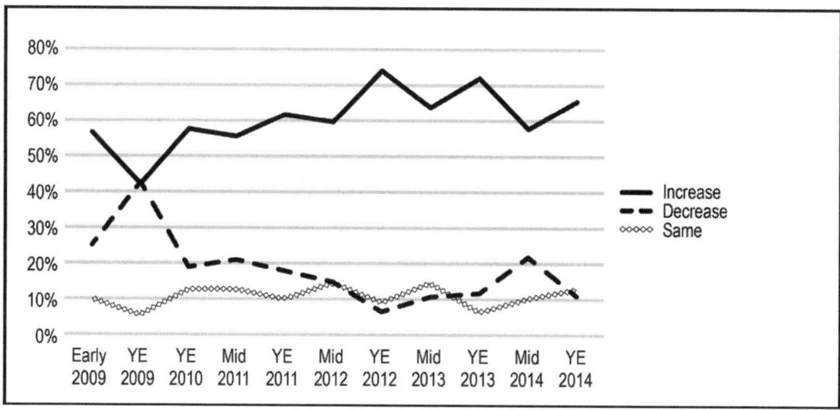

FIGURE 12.2
Membership Revenue

Figure 12.3 shows that outside of the initial 2009 retrenchment, reports of budgets increasing have been growing while reports of budgets decreasing or staying the same have been in the decline.

For the most part, respondents indicated that the 2015 budget will be staying the same as 2014 (45.4 percent), while approximately 30 percent responded that the membership budget would be increasing in 2015 (see figure 12.4).

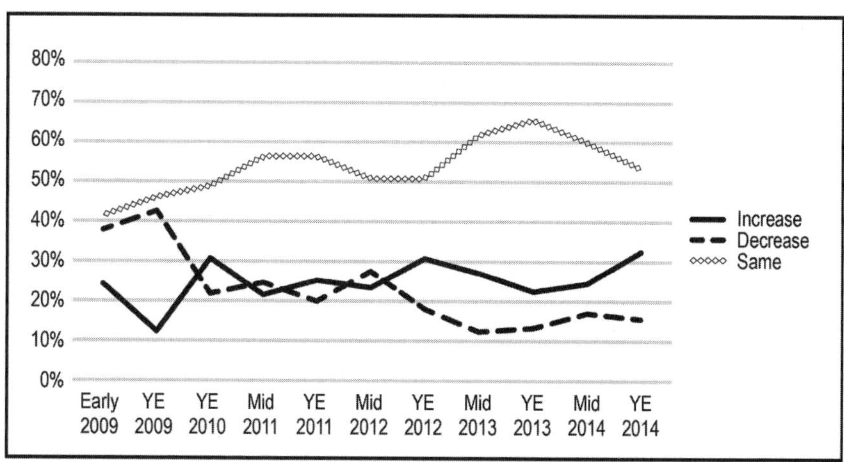

FIGURE 12.3
Membership Budget

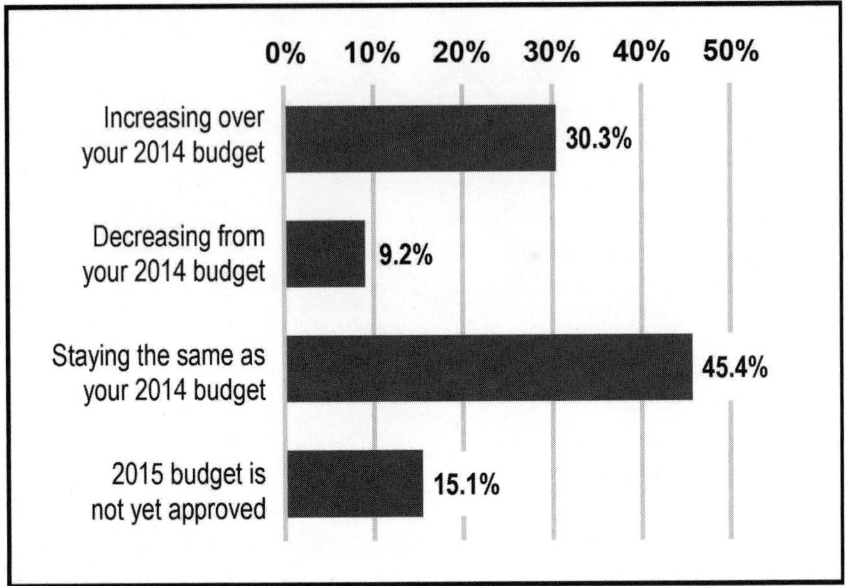

FIGURE 12.4
Is Your 2015 Expenditure Budget . . .

Membership Outlook

Membership outlook is a measure of how membership professionals perceive the overall membership climate. The outlook tends to be more optimistic at the beginning of the year, with a mid-year decline. Also, the trend lines tend to follow general consumer perceptions and stock market performance. Figure 12.5 provides a historical overview of the future outlook as reported by membership managers in the *Pulse of Membership* survey.

Acquisition Trends

Figure 12.6 shows the overall trends in new members acquired. The number of new members acquired has been on the rise with approximately 60 percent of membership managers reporting increases. Only in early 2009 were the reports of new members increasing nearly equal to those reporting decreases in new members.

Figure 12.7 indicates that, of the methods utilized in acquisition, on-site membership sales are the most prevalent source of new members with more than 90 percent reporting using this method. Gift membership promotions

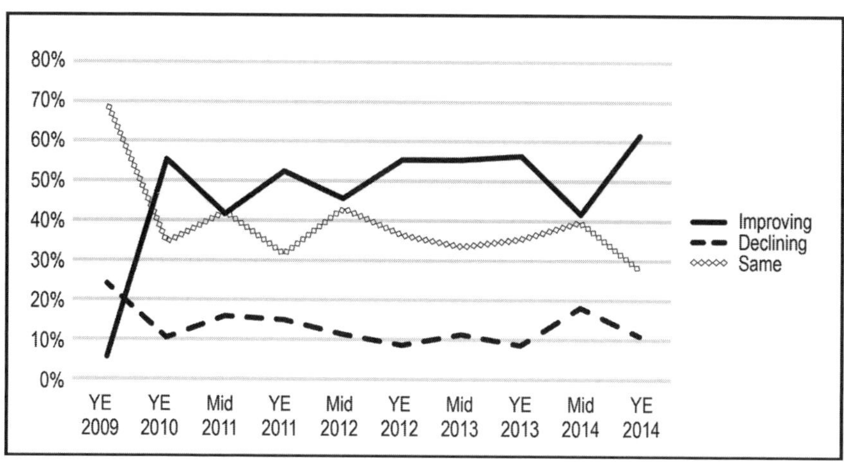

FIGURE 12.5
Membership Outlook

and direct mail are the next most utilized sources of new members. Acquisition from online sources has been on the rise, growing steadily from 50 percent in 2009 to 71 as of year-end 2014.

Renewal Trends

As shown in Figure 12.8, median renewal rates consistently stayed in the mid to upper 60 percent range until 2014 when the median renewal rate

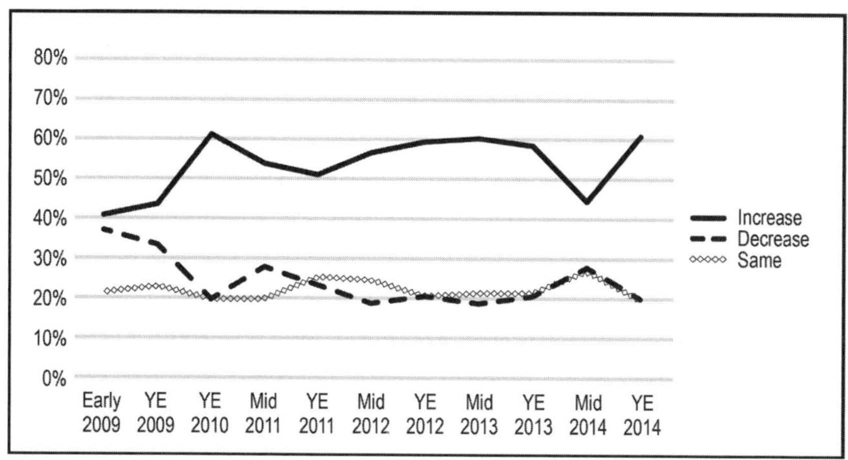

FIGURE 12.6
New Members Acquired

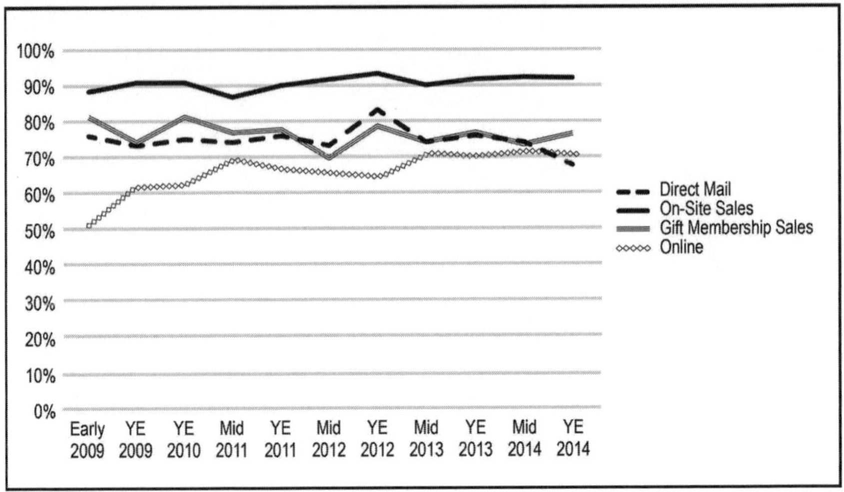

FIGURE 12.7
Membership Trends—Acquisition Sources

jumped into the mid 70 percent range. Consistently, membership managers report that renewal rates are either remaining static or increasing, and only 20 percent of respondents reported declining renewal rates as of year-end 2014.

Figure 12.9 shows the various methods used to renew members. Direct mail is the most used method of renewing members with more than 90 percent reporting usage. Approximately 70 percent of respondents consistently

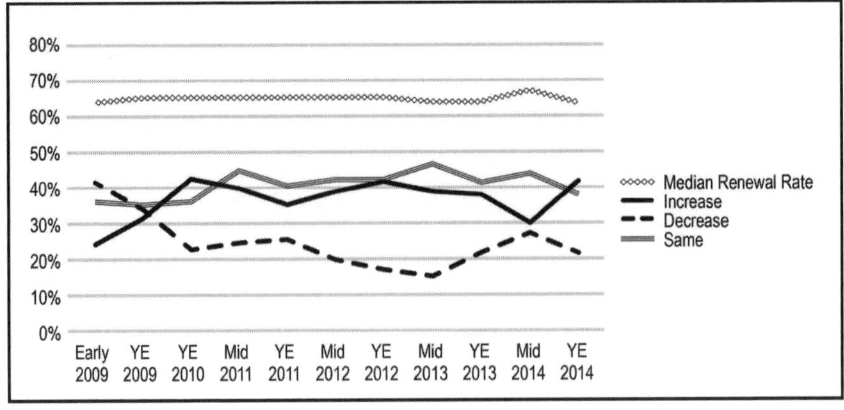

FIGURE 12.8. Renewal Rates

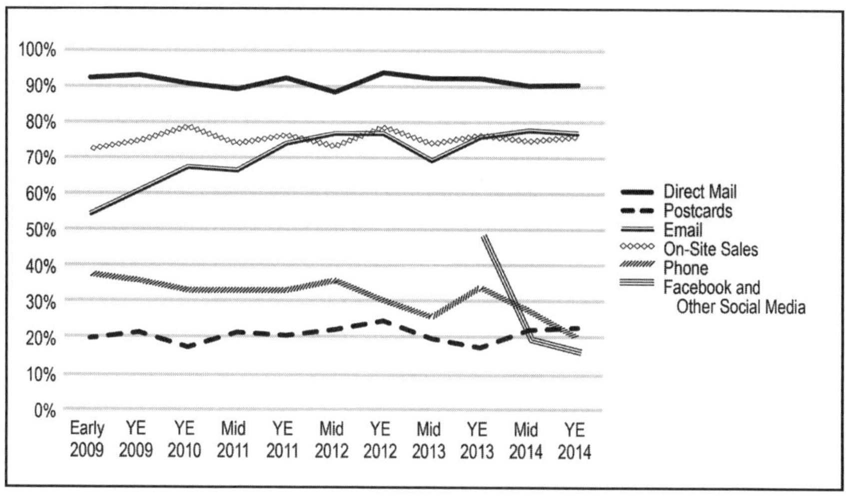

FIGURE 12.9
Methods Utilized to Drive Membership Renewals

use on-site sales, and use of email has grown from 50 percent of respondents in 2009 to 70 percent utilizing this method in 2014. The use of telemarketing as a way to renew members has declined from 40 percent usage to just 20 percent usage. As of this writing, data for use of social media in renewals are too new to determine a trend line for usage.

Social Media and Online Trends

Social media and online advertising are the newest forms of media being used for membership purposes. Membership has typically been the master of its own domain for marketing efforts affecting its destiny. However, in many institutions, social media and online advertising are managed in marketing or another department, and membership may or may not have access or control of its usage to support membership. Indeed, figure 12.10 indicates that fewer than 20 percent of membership managers report a fully active role in the use of social media for membership purposes, and nearly half report having little to no involvement in social media.

Figure 12.11 shows that roughly 70 percent of respondents report that someone in another department manages the institution's social media. As social media continues to become a critical channel in membership acquisition, customer service, renewals, and fundraising, membership's responsibility and

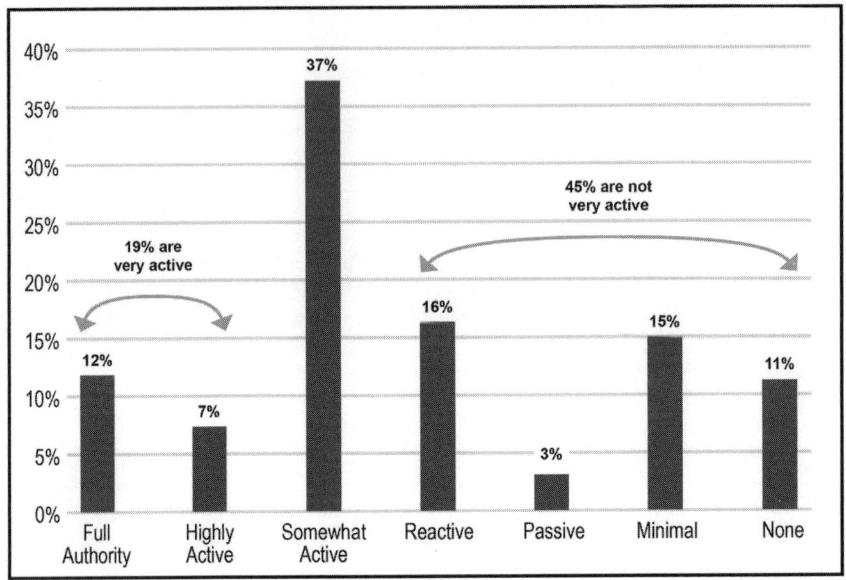

FIGURE 12.10
What Type of Role Does Membership Have in Social Media Content Management?

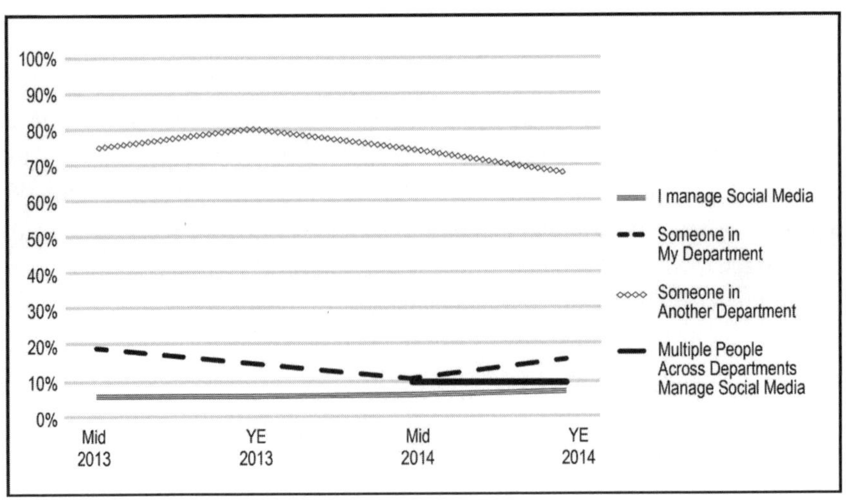

FIGURE 12.11
Who Manages Social Media at Your Organization?

authority in social media will need to expand to leverage this vital channel for membership promotion and to properly service members.

Membership is still finding its way with respect to social media as a way to promote membership and fully engage its audiences online. Figure 12.12 shows the ambivalence and discontent of membership managers with 52 percent indicating dissatisfaction regarding the use of social media from the membership department's perspective.

Figure 12.13 shows the rise of an unfortunate trend in many visitation-based organizations—a policy that limits the number of emails that can be sent to a particular audience within a given month. This type of policy is often arbitrary and misinformed, leading to a less effective communications strategy with members and visitors alike. At year-end 2014, 38 percent of membership managers report having an institutional policy that limits the number of email touches members can receive.

With the growing importance for membership to be proactive in social media, online advertising, and mobile and email marketing, budgeting for digital marketing becomes a critical need. Figure 12.14 indicates an overall lack of preparedness of membership organizations to meet the coming demand of

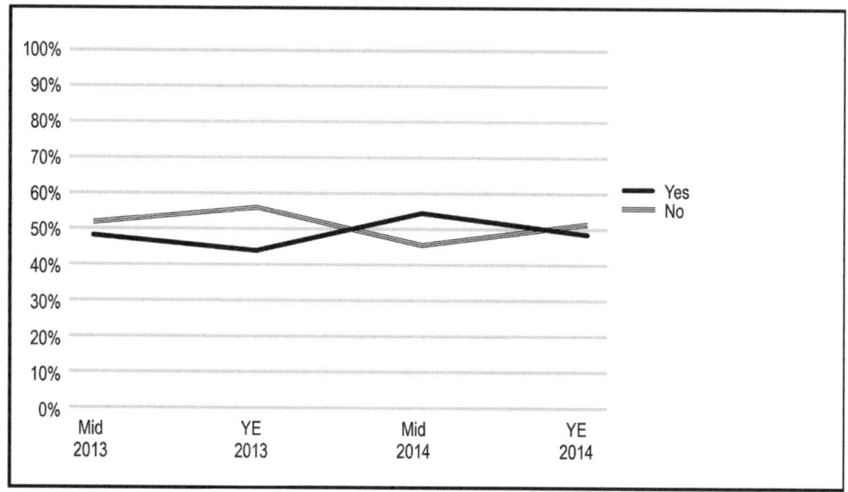

FIGURE 12.12

I Am Satisfied with the Voice or Presence Membership Has in Our Organization's Social Media Plan

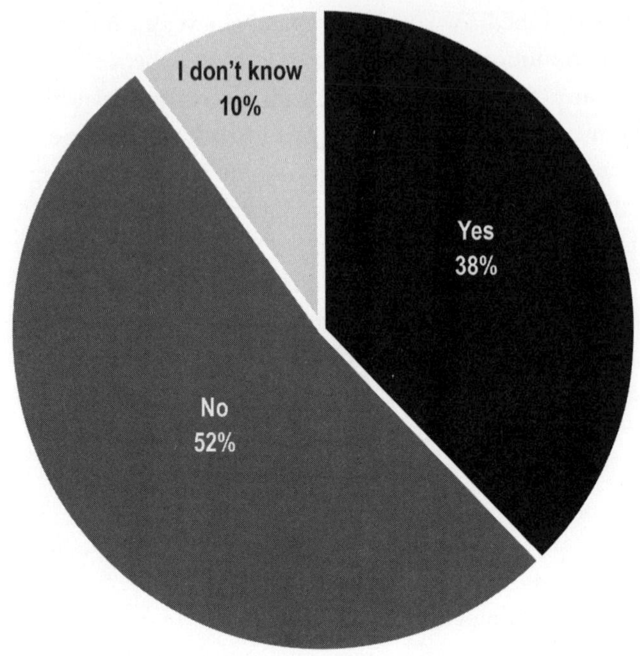

FIGURE 12.13
Does Your Organization Limit the Number of Emails Members Receive?

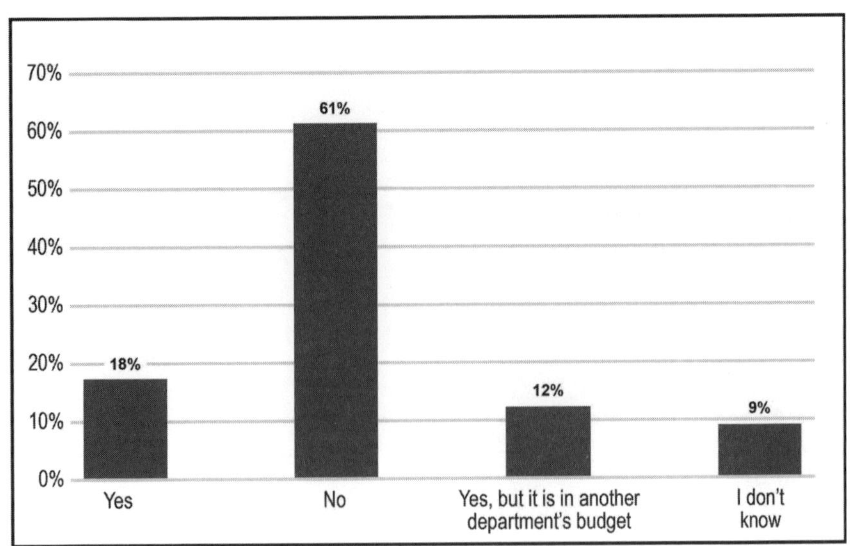

FIGURE 12.14
Does Membership Have a Dedicated Line Item in the Budget for Digital Marketing?

digital marketing with only 30 percent having a dedicated budget for digital marketing initiatives as of year-end 2014.

Organizational Demographics

As shown in Figure 12.15, membership is most often positioned within the development department (47 percent). Equal proportions (16 percent) of respondents indicated that membership is positioned as a free-standing department or as part of the marketing department. However, positioning within the guest or visitor services department has been growing in recent years.

Membership Profession

Fairly consistently, respondents have reported static staffing levels (approximately 70 percent), while roughly 15 percent report decreasing or increasing staffing levels over the past few years (see figure 12.16).

Typically, there must be significant change in the size of a membership program to warrant either adding or decreasing staffing levels. Staffing and membership budgets are often a game of the classic chicken and egg theory—that is, which comes first? The growth that makes bigger budgets and more staff necessary, or bigger staffs and budgets that will position a program for growth? The former is usually the case. However, for organizations that are

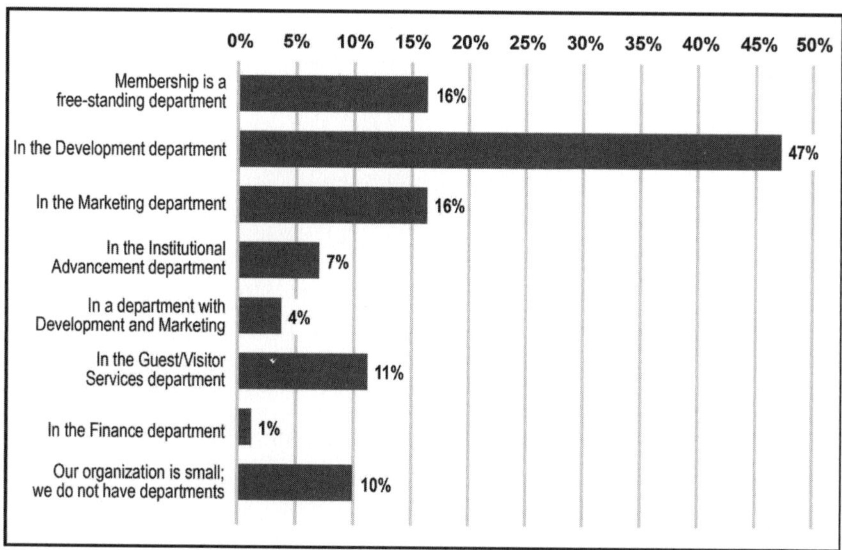

FIGURE 12.15
How Is Membership Positioned in Your Organization?—Check All That Apply

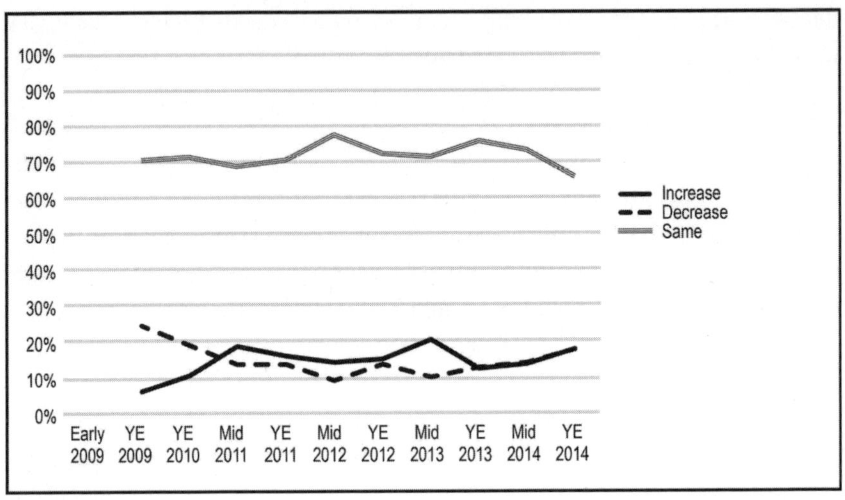

FIGURE 12.16
Staffing Levels

committed to growing or have an upcoming event, grand opening, or major anniversary to plan, the latter may be necessary.

Nearly half of membership managers report having worked in the profession for five years or longer. Increasingly, membership management is perceived as a profession and a position that is worthy of being considered as a career choice, as opposed to a stepping-stone to other positions as it once was. Generally, a longer-term, more strategic staff can lead to a successful membership program. A program with frequent turnover and short tenure of staff can translate into a program with little chance for growth and traction. Figure 12.17 shows the percentage of respondents based on level of tenure.

According to figure 12.18, the majority of membership managers report salaries of between $30,000 and $60,000. Higher salaries are possible when a program is larger or within a major metropolitan area and with roles that have greater responsibility and oversight. Nearly one-quarter of respondents appear to fall into this classification.

KEY PERFORMANCE INDICATORS IN MEMBERSHIP

Key Performance Indicators (KPIs) in membership are industry-benchmarked numbers to compare a program's performance metrics. The KPIs

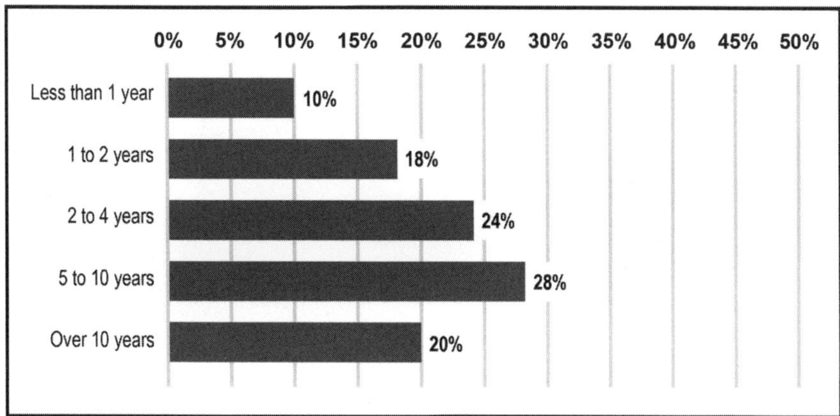

FIGURE 12.17
How Long Have You Served in a Membership Position

provided in figure 12.19 are an acceptable range that performance should fall within for any membership program.

Acquisition

A program's performance can be ascertained by calculating each of the following methods of acquisition to see if the program's metrics fall within the range of acceptable performance.

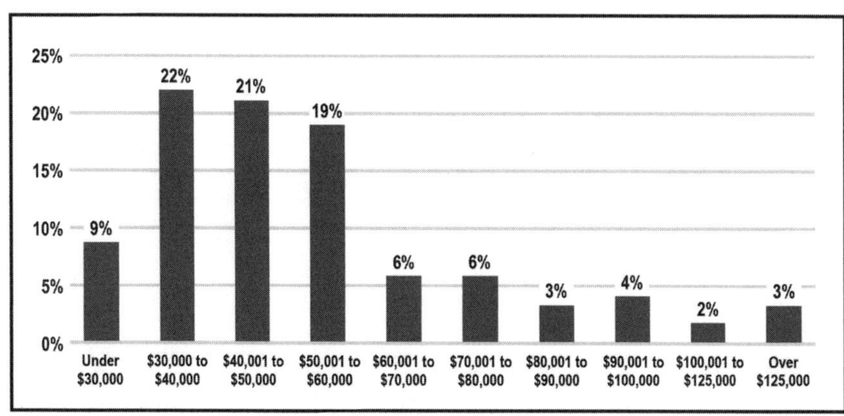

FIGURE 12.18
What Is Your Annual Salary Range?

FIGURE 12.19

Membership Key Performance Indicators

Direct Mail

Response Rates	Visitation-based organizations	0.7% to 2+%
	Non-visitation-based organizations	0.4% to 1%
Average Gift	$5 to $10 above the most popular membership category	
Cost Per Dollar Raised	$0.50 to $1.50	
Return on Investment	$.60 to $2.00+	

On-Site Sales

Conversion Rates	2% to 4%
Sales per Hour	4 to 8, traffic dependent
Average Sale	The amount of the most predominant category

Gift Membership Sales

Volume of Sales	A number equivalent to 5% of overall membership total

Email Campaigns

Email Deliverability Rate	Nonprofit	90%
Gross Open Rate	Arts, Galleries, Museums, Visitation-based	20.00% to 32.06%
	Association & Membership Organization	11.66% to 29.96%
	Nonprofit (All)	14.00% to 35.60%
Click-Through Rate	Arts, Galleries, Museums, Visitation-based	1.13% to 7.06%
	Association & Membership Organization	1.77% to 8.47%
	Nonprofit (All)	1.30% to 2.97%
Bounce Rate	Arts, Galleries, Museums, Visitation-based	8.08% to 9.83%
	Association & Membership Organization	3.22% to 11.89%
	Nonprofit (All)	10%
Unsubscribe Rate	Arts, Galleries, Museums, Visitation-based	0.19% to 0.56%
	Association & Membership Organization	0.30% to 0.40%
	Nonprofit (All)	0.06% to 0.19%

Renewals

Mailed Letter Packages	10% to 30% response per mailing	
Email Reminders	1% to 5% response	
Renewal Rates – Overall	45% to 85%, depending on type of organization	
	Associations	80% to 90+%
	History Museums	75% to 85%
	Art Museums	70% to 80%
	Science Museums	50% to 65%
	Zoos	55% to 65%
	Libraries	70% to 80%
	Children's Museums	40% to 50%

continued...

	Membership Upgrades/Downgrades
Upgrades	With specific upgrade campaign, 5% to 8 % will upgrade
Downgrade	Under normal circumstances, 2% to 4% of members may downgrade annually
Upgrade/Downgrade Ratio	2:1 – Upgrades to downgrades is a healthy scenario

	Lapsed Recapture Campaigns	
Response Rates	For stand-alone recapture campaigns	3% to 5+%
	As part of an acquisition campaign	1.5% to 2.5%
	As part of a telemarketing campaign	10% of the calling pool

	Telemarketing Campaigns	
Lapsed recapture	Contact rate	60%
	Yes rate	12%
	Credit card rate	60% to 80%
	Fulfillment rate for non credit card pledges	50%

Renewals and Lapsed Campaigns

Renewal rates vary by type of organization. A membership program can be compared to the following industry organization types found in figure 12.19. Calculating the percentage of renewing members who upgrade and those who downgrade will provide insight into how a membership program compares to the industry standard shown in figure 12.19.

A program's response rates on lapsed recapture mailings and telemarketing performance can also be compared to the industry benchmarks shown in figure 12.19.

ACTIVITY BENCHMARKING

It is not only important to compare a program's key performance indicators to what is typically expected in the field; it is also necessary to compare the organization's activities to industry expectations for a fully functional program. Developed by Membership Consultants, Inc., the *Making the Grade: Membership Performance Assessment*™ provides a framework by which to measure a program's utilization of industry-accepted methods for marketing a membership program.

The assessment evaluates activity in ten core areas, and can be used to gauge a program's performance and help determine which areas to target for improvement. If all areas in a particular program are rated as an A or B, the membership program will most likely be growing. Exhibit 12.1 can be used to evaluate the program's performance in these core areas.

SUMMARY

Benchmarking is more than finding appropriate comparative data. To leverage benchmarking effectively, an organization must be willing to prioritize investment and activities to support closing the gap in core areas of performance. Benchmarking is not simply documenting static measurements. Rather, true benchmarking focuses on best practices and helps identify trends and opportunities that will have an impact on the membership program. Once the data are collected, the real work begins. Next steps in benchmarking include developing an action plan for key performance indicators, identification of activities for strategic investment of resources and, if necessary, reallocation of staff and budgets to improve underperforming areas.

NOTE

1. Membership Consultants, Inc., "[Webinar Recording] Pulse of Membership Survey Results Year-End 2014," accessed April 21, 2015, http://knowledge.membership-consultants.com/pulse-of-membership-year-end-2014-webinar-recording.

2. Source for Figures 12.1 through 12.19: Pulse of Membership Survey Results Year-End 2014. Copyright © 2015 Membership Consultants, Inc.

EXHIBIT 12.1

Making the Grade Membership Performance Assessment™

Grade	*Membership Acquisition*
A	Have at least 3 well-developed sources of new members Using direct mail as an acquisition tool multiple times a year Using online and social media resources to attract and convert new members Projecting the number of new members expected by month Attracting enough new members to grow the program
B	Tracking new members by source Have at least 2 well-developed sources of new members Consistently attracting enough new members to replace non-renewing members
C	Have multiple sources of new members Have a budget for new member acquisition Sometimes attracting enough new members to replace non-renewing members
D	Relying on only one source of new members Not attracting enough new members to replace non-renewing members
F	Not doing anything to attract new members Waiting for members to join on their own

Grade	*On-Site Sales*
A	Have trained staff working the gate with clipboard in hand Offer regularly scheduled training and rewards for sales staff On-site sales staff reports to Membership Have signage that says "Join Now!"
B	Offer incentives to on-site sales people or admission staff Have signage that says "Join Now!"
C	Encourage on-site sales by admission or museum shop staff Have signage that says "Join Now!"
D	Only a passing interest in getting people to join while visiting
F	No on-site sales efforts

Grade	*Direct Mail Acquisition*
A	Mailing 2 or 3 campaigns per year Evaluating each campaign fully Testing in every mailing
B	Mailing at least 1 time per year
C	Mailing only at times of major exhibitions Will allow for trade of names with like organizations
D	Infrequent use of direct mail Will not allow list trades
F	No use of direct mail

continued...

Grade	*Renewals*
A	Renewal rate of 75% Sending renewal reminders via mail and email — at least 4 touches Asking for renewals on-site if renewal is within 60 days Know program's first year renewal rate
B	Renewal rate of 70–75% Sending more than 3 renewal reminder letters or emails
C	Renewal rate of 60–70% Sending 3 renewal reminders
D	Renewal rate of 50–60% Sending less than 3 renewal reminder letters or emails
F	Renewal rate less than 50% OR Renewal rate unknown Sending only 1 renewal reminder Not sending renewals on regular basis

Grade	*Lapsed Member Recapture*
A	Performing lapsed member appeals by mail, email, and phone
B	Performing lapsed members appeals by 2 of the 3 methods listed above
C	Performing lapsed member appeal by mail (special appeal) or phone
D	Performing lapsed member appeal only in acquisition direct mail program
F	Doing nothing to recapture lapsed members

Grade	*Membership Upgrades*
A	Designing benefits and dues structure to encourage upgrade Performing upgrade specific campaigns via mail and phone or email annually
B	Offering a premium or special offer to encourage upgrade Performing upgrade campaign via mail, phone, or email
C	Suggesting upgrade in the P.S. of a renewal letter
D	Listing all levels of membership on all brochures
F	Never asking for an upgrade Not listing upper levels on brochures and renewal forms

Grade	*Membership Dues*
A	Evaluating cost of membership at every level annually Pricing membership accordingly Have a strategy for regular dues increases Have performed membership surveys/research on benefits, usage, desirability
B	Have increased dues in past 3 years
C	Have increased dues in past 5 years Offering membership at various levels
D	Offering membership at levels less than $50
F	Have not increased dues in last 10 years Offering memberships at $40 or less

continued...

Grade	*Membership Benefits*
A	Surveying membership to determine favorite or most used benefits Benefits offered at key upgrade levels Tracking usage of benefits
B	Multiple benefits at each level
C	Tiered benefits
D	Only one benefit at some levels
F	No benefits listed

Grade	*Digital Marketing*
A	Tracking online sales of memberships Have an online member portal Have a mobile friendly website Communication with members via email 2–3 times per month Prioritizing email capture for both members and visitors Have 70% of members' email addresses Have a social media strategy for membership acquisition Have authority and responsibility to post on Facebook Using online advertising and email marketing for membership acquisition Using marketing automation software to personalize content
B	Encouraging joining and renewing online Have a membership presence on Facebook with regular mentions Sending an e-newsletter monthly Using email marketing for membership acquisition Have 50% of members' email addresses
C	Have a website with a membership landing page and e-commerce capability Sending an e-newsletter quarterly Have less than 30% of members' email addresses
D	Have website but no membership join functionality Not using email for membership acquisition or member communications
F	No website, email, or digital marketing efforts for membership

Grade	*Members as Donors*
A	Asking for non-membership gift more than 1 time per year via mail, phone, email Using segmentation and personalization to suggest gift amounts and upgrades Include email asks with video
B	Asking for non-membership gift more than 1 time per year via mail Supplement mail with online asks
C	Asking for non-membership gift once per year
D	No formal campaign, but have an annual fund pool
F	Do not accept or encourage non-member gifts

13

The Math of Membership

A billion here, a billion there, and sooner or later you're talking about real money!

—*Everett Dirksen, U.S. Senator, Illinois*

Understanding the mathematics of membership is one of the most important aspects of running a membership program, and yet it's often a misunderstood or overlooked part of the program. The math of membership can be as elusive for management staff and board members as it is for the people who run the program on a day-to-day basis. Even the accounting staff of an organization may need an orientation in order to understand the membership numbers. This chapter will end the mystery of the math of membership—once and for all.

THE DEMANDS ON MEMBERSHIP

The organization's management often gives the membership program the directive: "More members," or "More money," or "Make it happen." There is unfortunately little understanding of what it takes to make "more" happen. That lack of understanding makes it difficult for membership managers to attempt to make "more" happen. In the best situations, there will be both institutional and departmental planning, and staff and volunteers will work together to arrive at reasonable goals for the program and understand what has to be done to make it happen.

However, in many cases, membership goals are handed down from above. The board and management will sometimes pluck a number out of the clear blue sky: "Let's get to 20,000 members by our fiftieth anniversary in two years!" is a familiar refrain. These goals might be achievable, but achieving them requires money, a plan, and often, a consultant. At a minimum, aggressive goals require outsourcing of professional direct mail and digital marketing services, and certainly more staff to service the growing numbers of members. All of this costs money, and usually the demand to produce more is not accompanied by more resources.

THE FINANCIAL SIDE OF MEMBERSHIP

Membership managers and their supervisors are always looking for benchmarks by which to compare their program to those in similar organizations. A well-established benchmark in servicing a healthy membership program—one beyond the start-up phase and yet not so massively huge that great economies of scale are in operation—is that it takes one dollar for every two dollars a membership program generates to adequately serve current members, and to do enough marketing to replace non-renewing members and continue growing.

For example, a membership program with 10,000 members and revenues of $900,000 a year would need a budget of about $450,000. If a program is spending less than this 50 percent ratio of budget to revenues and has a program that is operating well and still growing, then a closer examination may be necessary to make sure that there aren't issues that need to be addressed for this level of success to continue. Larger programs will require less than the 50 percent ratio, perhaps a 33 percent ratio of expenses to revenues. For example, a program of 20,000 members may have revenues of $1,900,000 and may have a membership budget of $700,000 (inclusive of all marketing, renewal, and membership department staffing) and have an expense to revenue ratio of 0.35 percent. This is acceptable, as long as the benefits being offered are robust enough to attract and keep members engaged, and there is enough staffing to service the members and their needs. When more revenue is being produced with fewer dollars, it's important to ask a number of questions to make certain that this kind of economic viability can be sustained.

Staffing

Is the program adequately staffed? It takes one data entry person to manage every 7,500 records. The sample program mentioned above (20,000 members) should have three data entry people plus a manager of the database plus the membership manager. A program with too few staff may alienate members at high-volume times with slow response times and delayed membership card processing. Overworked staff can cause low morale and hence grumpy customer service—not a good thing!

Salaries

Are staff members adequately compensated? Often not. Membership positions are frequently entry level and attract young people who have little experience. Good membership managers are hard to find, so keeping them should be key to a successful program. A recent *Pulse of Membership* survey conducted by Membership Consultants found that the median salary for respondents was in the $40,000 to $50,000 range.[1] Too often experienced membership managers leave for a better-paying opportunity. Nothing holds a membership program back more than losing its manager, letting a program remain static while a search ensues, and potentially stagnate while a new person goes through what is usually a one-year learning curve.

Benefits

Are the benefits enough to keep the members engaged? The membership benefits are important, especially in the early years.

Marketing Budget

Next to staff, the marketing budget may be the largest budget item: but is it enough? If the program is to grow, there must be enough money to make it happen. It may be necessary to spend 25 to 50 percent of the budget on the marketing aspects of membership, such as direct mail, on-site sales, digital advertising, telemarketing, special promotions, and the like.

Sometimes organizations spend more than 50 percent of the revenues generated on servicing the membership program. There may be a variety of reasons for that as well, and yet another set of questions that need to be asked.

Size or Tenure

Is the program small or in a start-up phase? If the answer is "yes," then that may explain the high level of expenditures. A start-up program may take several years to break even, perhaps three years. No matter how many members an organization has, it needs a database, someone to run the program, the necessary collateral materials, and a marketing budget. However, with fewer members and revenues to bear the expense, the financial viability of a membership program may not be evident.

Is there an unusual benefit or burden on the program? If so, that costly benefit may be causing an imbalance. Are membership dues too low? If an organization has any dues categories under the $50 level, the cost to serve a member may be approaching what they are raising in dues. Keeping dues at current acceptable rates is important to keep the revenues to run the program high enough to have funds to market the program adequately.

SPEND MONEY TO MAKE MONEY

The most difficult concept for some is that if membership is charged with growing, then it must have money to help it grow. If a program is challenged to bring in 1,000 more members, the membership manager must determine where those members will come from. If all possible channels for acquiring members are being pursued, then a new source of members must be developed, or an existing source supplemented. A 100,000-piece direct mail campaign may be a possible way to acquire those thousand new members. The cost for such a campaign might well be $50,000. Or if on-site membership sales are not being fully implemented, a new staff person may be necessary to concentrate on this activity. If on-site sales are fully maximized, then creating a new weekend event may be necessary to attract enough visitors who can then be converted into members, and that can be costly. Having a budget for online advertising for membership purposes is becoming an increasingly important line item in a membership budget, rather than relying on another department's staff (e.g., marketing) or budget to help promote membership. And with social media quickly becoming a critical new source for acquisition, ensuring that additional budget is available to leverage such opportunities as they arise is a best practice.

Whatever the goal for membership, it is not enough to announce the goal; it is necessary to fund the ways to make that goal a reality.

THE BUDGET NUMBERS

Staffing and marketing are the two largest expenses in a membership budget. In both cases, these line items must increase as the size of a membership program increases. Limiting the staffing budget can result in poor customer service, constant turnover, and probably a static membership program due to membership salaries that are not competitive enough to retain good staff. The marketing budget must be sufficient to attract enough new members to sustain growth in membership or to remain stable from year to year. Depending on the program, these two line items can absorb between 50 and 75 percent of the membership budget.

Counting Members

Counting members sounds easy, but it isn't. Counting has continually confounded many a manager and board member alike. First, members should be counted at the end of a month. Counting members midmonth inflates the numbers and leads to disappointment at the end of the month. Second, fourteen months of members should be included in the totals. The reason for this rule is that it takes several months for the renewals due in any given month to come in (after the three or more notices, and the renewal cycle has run its course). Thus, since renewals for the most recent past two months are still arriving and still in batches waiting to be processed, it is advisable to count these members as current for a sixty-day grace period. This practice is an industry standard and is usually built into the logic of the most prevalent membership database's queries and reports. If an organization were to count only twelve months, then the result would be that many more people would be deleted, only to be added back onto the membership rolls in the next two weeks when they renew with the final notice.

A third reason for counting fourteen months and keeping these members in a semi-current state is for continuity purposes, especially for mailings and communications being sent to current members. For instance, if the current date is March 5 and the membership expired on February 28, chances are the membership is "in process." If a mail file were being prepared on March 5, it would be advisable to include the January and February members in the file, so they don't miss upcoming events or important institutional information. The assumption here is that those members are going to renew, and they shouldn't have a lapse in the flow of communications. For visitation-based institutions, if the member whose expiration date was February visits on March

5, there is no grace period for entry. The member should be asked to renew at that time or he or she does not enter free.

Count members as households, not as individuals. A few organizations have attempted to swell their membership numbers by counting actual people that the membership represents. In other words, they count one family membership as four people, and then multiply the number of households by two or four. This is not typically how memberships are counted and will only confuse the process when trying to link a dollar amount to the number of members, which is how most membership projections are constructed.

Another misunderstanding is the fact that membership totals will go up and down from month to month throughout the year. With seasonality and major marketing efforts during different months or seasons, it is natural that the number will fluctuate if membership totals are compared at the end of each month. Thus, the important comparison is from year to year at each month's end. This is the fair comparison. For example, compare this May's numbers to last May's numbers, not May with April or June. In this comparison, the numbers for this year should always outweigh the numbers for last year in same month comparisons if growth is the objective.

Once an organization has developed good monthly reporting and has done this for some time, there will be annual patterns of membership increases and decreases that are seen seasonally every year. For instance, one botanical garden, with a relatively set pattern of acquisition efforts in the spring and fall, sees the total build through spring to peak by the end of May each year. The totals then decline through the summer (when there are no special promotions), rise again in the fall as new members are added with special events and lapsed members are recaptured with seasonal efforts, and reach another peak by year-end. After tracing the numbers for several years, this pattern became evident. Patterns, individual to the organization, will be seen in those organizations that have consistent, aggressive marketing and management of their membership programs.

It is important for staff and board members to understand these "counting phenomena" so that they have realistic expectations and can make decisions accordingly.

Growth

Growth is one strategy that a membership program can follow. Growth of a membership program is dependent on two factors: renewal rates and the acquisition numbers for new members. Knowing those two numbers makes it possible to predict the future. Generally, it is safe to assume that if there is a certain level of renewals or new members in one year, then it is possible to achieve that level the next year, barring unusual circumstances. If an organization was able to renew 75 percent of the members and attract 3,000 new members in one year, it should be safe to assume the same is possible next year. Using these numbers, table 13.1 below shows the calculations for growth over time for a membership of 10,000 members.

This illustration shows that even with great consistency, something significant must be added to marketing efforts to increase membership totals by more than a few percentage points from year to year. Of course, there is nothing wrong with slow, steady growth. However, the larger a program grows, the more difficult growth becomes, and the more it may cost to acquire additional members. This depends on the organization, the size of the metropolitan area for local groups, and the amount of funding the organization wants to spend on acquisition and renewal efforts. The reality of diminishing returns may apply and it may be time to change the membership strategy from growth to stability and focus on upgrading current members to see revenue growth.

Projections

Constructing membership totals and revenue projections also needs a realistic approach. Often an institution's planning for membership starts with, "We increased membership by five percent last year, let's do the same this year!" Or, "We need more revenue because of decreasing attendance figures, so let's increase the membership revenue expectations to compensate!" This is not the way to plan.

To manage the numbers, it is important to evaluate each source of new members for the previous year. If all is the same—the economy, the number of pieces of direct mail, the number of email and digital campaigns, another

Table 13.1 Growth over Time

	Year 1	Year 2	Year 3	Year 4	Year 5	Year 6
Total members as of January 1	10,000	10,500	10,875	11,158	11,367	11,527
Renewal rate	75%	75%	75%	75%	75%	75%
Renewed members	7,500	7,875	8,158	8,367	8,527	8,642
New members	3,000	3,000	3,000	3,000	3,000	3,000
Members as of December 30th	10,500	10,875	11,158	11,367	11,527	11,642
% growth		3%	3%	2%	1.5%	1%

blockbuster exhibit, the same media attention for the organization, then it is safe to say that the same numbers can probably be achieved again. Not more, the same. If the organization is committed to growing the membership, then more dollars must be added to the budget for new or increased acquisition methods or stronger renewal efforts.

To produce accurate projections, one must start with certain number and percentage calculations:

- The number of new members acquired last year by source and by month;
- The number of members the program expects to attract next year by source and by month;
- The number of members due to renew for the coming year by month;
- The percentage distribution of members by category;
- The dollar value of each membership category;
- The renewal rate; and
- The "flow" of renewals response by mailing (for example, 5 percent of renewals come in from the early bird email, 40 percent of renewals come in on the first renewal mailing, 20 percent come in from the second reminder, etc.).

With these numbers, it is possible to calculate a fairly accurate set of projections, assuming:

- That the number of members acquired is in keeping with what was projected, and that all acquisition efforts planned are actually executed;
- That the projected renewal rate is accurate;
- That the flow of renewals is accurate; and
- That renewals are sent on time every month, without exception.

The sample projections shown in table 13.2 illustrate a typical projection spreadsheet. Note that the exercise begins with new members. Use the history of the program as a rule of what may be possible in the future. If there were 135 memberships via a gift membership program last year, then it is assumed that with a repeat effort, the same result can be expected. However, if a new

Table 13.2 Sample Projections FY15

Projected New Members

PROJECTIONS - New		Jul *2014*	Aug	Sept	Oct	Nov	Dec	Jan	Feb	Mar	Apr	May	Jun *2015*	TOTALS
On-Site Sales		40	40	40	48	48	48	8	20	20	20	40	40	**412**
Acquisition Direct Mail		0	0	500		500	0		500				500	**2,000**
Lapsed Recapture		6	120	6	120	7	10	10	10	120	10	120	15	**554**
Gift Memberships		5	5	5	5	5	80	5	5	5	5	5	5	**135**
Sites		100	100	50	10	5	5	5	5	50	50	100	100	**580**
Website, Emails		30	30	30	30	30	30	30	30	30	30	30	30	**360**
Phone, Mail-in, Other		10	10	10	10	10	10	10	10	10	10	10	10	**120**
Education		5	5	5	5	5	5	5	5	5	5	5	5	**60**
Total New		196	310	646	228	610	188	73	585	240	130	310	705	**4,221**

Projected Renewals

Memberships by Month														
Due to Renew	**% Renew**	552	693	978	543	998	625	445	974	733	928	887	1567	**9,923**
1st Notice	**25%**	138	173	244	136	250	156	111	244	183	232	222	392	**2,481**
2nd Notice	**44%**	243	305	430	239	439	275	196	429	322	408	390	689	**4,366**
3rd Notice	7%	39	49	68	38	70	44	31	68	51	65	62	110	**695**
Total Renewing	**76%**	419	527	743	412	759	475	338	741	557	706	674	1,191	**7,542**

continued...

Projected Total Revenues

	%	Membership Level	Jul *2014*	Aug	Sept	Oct	Nov	Dec	Jan	Feb	Mar	Apr	May	Jun *2015*	TOTALS
Total Members			615	837	1,389	640	1,369	663	411	1,326	797	836	984	1,896	**11,763**
Individual	**36.70%**	**$55**	$12,422	$16,889	$28,037	$12,927	$27,625	$13,380	$8,305	$26,757	$16,085	$16,866	$19,868	$38,267	**$237,427**
Family	**25.00%**	**$75**	$11,539	$15,687.9	$26,043	$12,008	$25,661	$12,429	$7,715	$24,855	$14,941	$15,667	$18,456	$35,546	**$220,547**
History Lover	**31.50%**	**$90**	$17,447	$23,720	$39,378	$18,156	$38,799	$18,792	$11,665	$37,581	$22,591	$23,688	$27,905	$53,746	**$333,468**
Supporter	**1.10%**	**$250**	$1,692	$2,301	$3,820	$1,761	$3,764	$1,823	$1,132	$3,645	$2,191	$2,298	$2,707	$5,213	**$32,347**
Patron	**3.70%**	**$500**	$11,385	$15,479	$25,696	$11,848	$25,319	$12,263	$7,612	$24,524	$14,742	$15,458	$18,210	$35,072	**$217,607**
Director's Circle	**2.00%**	**$1,000**	$12,308	$16,734	$27,780	$12,809	$27,371	$13,257	$8,229	$26,512	$15,937	$16,711	$19,686	$37,916	**$235,251**
Total Revenue	**100.00%**		**$66,794**	**$90,810**	**$150,753**	**$69,509**	**$148,538**	**$71,944**	**$44,658**	**$143,875**	**$86,488**	**$90,687**	**$106,831**	**$205,760**	**$1,276,646**

dimension is added to the repeat effort, then moderately increase the numbers in the gift membership line. Never assume that there will be an automatic 5 or 10 percent increase from year to year unless there is a new effort or an addition to current efforts.

By tracking projections by source and by month, a month-to-month actual analysis is possible. If one source is not performing as was expected, then hopefully another source will be doing better than expected. It is important to be honest and realistic when constructing projections. A heavy dose of optimism or wishful thinking will only cause disappointment a year from now if the numbers are inflated.

Renewals

It is important to look one year ahead. How many people are due to renew in each of the upcoming months for the next year? Start with these monthly numbers when calculating renewals. Then it is necessary to review the last year's flow of renewals. For instance, if there are 1,000 members due to renew in March, the first renewal notices were probably sent out in early February. Determine the overall response by renewal mailing by keeping track of the number of pieces mailed. If that March group of renewals required a second mailing of 600 pieces in March, then the first mailing had a 40 percent response. Likewise, if a third renewal notice quantity of 400 were mailed, then it is evident that another 20 percent of the original group responded to the second mailing. Finally, it is also important to look back occasionally and to find out how many members, by month, have still not renewed. For example, examining the sample month of March several months later shows that there are still 300 who did not renew. With this, it is apparent that the renewal rate for that month is now 70 percent.

RENEWAL MATH AND CASH FLOW

To calculate cash flow accurately from renewals it is important to pay attention to the flow of how members renew. There will be a loyal group of members who renew their memberships the first time they are asked. They respond to the first suggestion of renewing; they renew on the first renewal notice. There are other well-intentioned members who need a little nudge to renew and/or who have a bill-paying schedule that is out of sync with the renewal mailing schedule. These members respond to the second renewal letter. Then there are the procrastinators; they will eventually renew, but only with a lot of reminders, encouragement, and pursuit. These members will renew when they are ready. It is the job of the membership manager to predict when people will renew. While this sounds difficult, it is fairly easy.

Track the percentage of response received from each renewal mailing. To do this, simply track the number of renewal notices sent every month, the first renewal reminders, the second renewal letters, and so on. Armed with these numbers it is possible to find the average rate of response to each letter or email reminder throughout the year. It is important to take an average of the year, since during an organization's high season, renewals may come in more rapidly than during the off-season.

If the first renewal notice is sent two months prior to the expiration month, and elicits a 30 percent response, then plot 30 percent of March's members to arrive in January. Likewise, if the second notice is sent the month before the expiration date and that reminder draws a 20 percent response of the number originally due to renew, then plot 200 of March's 1,000 members due to renew to arrive and be processed in February. To follow this example to its completion, understand that 15 percent of the members will respond in the month that they are due to renew, 10 percent the month after, and another 3 percent even later. Thus, March's members may be spread over the preceding and succeeding months as shown in table 13.3.

March has a renewal rate of 78 percent. However, it is important to understand that 78 percent of March's members do not all renew in March. Hence, March's revenue is a total of new members, plus the renewals that were due from months before and after March.

Once the flow of renewals is determined, and those members renewing during any given month are added to the number of members predicted to join during that same month, it is then time to calculate revenues. Membership programs with graduated dues have a variety of membership levels. It is important to know the percentage of members at each dollar level, and apply those numbers to the total numbers of members processed that month. In this example, if there were 1,000 members projected to be processed during this month, the revenues would be anticipated as shown in table 13.4.

Table 13.3 March Members

	January	February	March	April	May
Due to renew			1,000		
Actually renewed	300	200	150	100	30

Table 13.4 Renewal Revenues

Member Level	Percent of Total Members	Number of 1,000 Members	Dues	Revenues
Regular Member	60%	600 members @	$60	$36,000
Sustaining Member	20%	200 members @	$120	$24,000
Patron Member	14%	140 members @	$250	$35,000
Supporting Member	5%	50 members @	$500	$25,000
Director's Circle	1%	10 members @	$1,000	$10,000
Total monthly revenues				**$130,000**

THE PITFALLS OF PROJECTIONS

No matter how diligent and clever the membership manager is with membership projections, from time to time an inconsistency challenges the numbers and the revenues.

One organization offered "One month free" as an incentive to encourage members to renew on the first renewal notice. It was a fine idea and it seemed to be working. The percentage of members renewing on the first letter increased. In fact, the overall renewal rate increased. But the year-end ramifications of the successful offer were discovered when the revenue projections were not met. After making the offer and giving that free month of membership, the projections did not take into account that a month's worth of revenue had been shifted into the next year.

It is not possible to anticipate everything that might happen in the coming year, but there definitely are occurrences that can affect renewals or people's willingness to join an organization at certain times. One organization found itself in a public relations uproar over the construction of a parking lot (pictured as a "tear down the trees to put up a parking lot" situation) and found members writing angry letters and voting with their renewals, or lack thereof. Another organization found itself in the midst of a natural disaster, massive flooding in the community, which caused a two-month change in its renewal rates; apparently everyone was writing checks for disaster relief rather than to the organization. Yet another organization had problems when a major employer announced it was moving out of the area. The organization had a loss of members who were employed with the company, an unforeseen circumstance that was out of the control of the membership program.

These examples illustrate how the unknown can challenge the best, most accurately determined set of projections.

MEMBERSHIP BENCHMARKS

Everyone is looking for benchmarks to which to compare his or her organization. Every organization is different and will have its own patterns; however, there are some general numbers to measure performance. Each organization should consider its special circumstances when reviewing the benchmarks discussed below.

Renewal Rates

Typically a 65 to 75 percent renewal rate is considered very good. A lower rate of 30 to 40 percent may occur for first-year members. If the organization serves a population that people outgrow (e.g., children's museums), then the renewal rate will be lower. The same will be true of public issue organizations when the issue no longer provokes an intense response.

Renewal rates higher than 80 to 85 percent may happen in professional associations where a member's accreditation or livelihood depends on belonging, and the only way people would not renew is if they die or retire. Alumni and shared experience organizations may also see very high renewal rates, as the members want to continue to belong.

Table 13.5 shows examples of median renewal rates by type of membership organization as reported by respondents to Membership Consultants' *Pulse of Membership* survey.[2]

If renewal rates exceed 85 percent, then an organization must ask itself if it is doing enough to attract new members. A healthy program that is adding

Table 13.5 Median Renewal Rates

Organization Type	Median Renewal Rate
Aquariums	48%
Art Museums	73%
Associations	78%
Botanical Gardens, Arboreta	69%
Children's Museums	45%
History Museums	78%
Libraries	70%
Science Museums	42%
Zoos	50%

Source: Pulse of Membership Survey Results Year-End 2014. Copyright © 2015 Membership Consultants, Inc.

new members at significant rates will find that new members' first-year renewal rates will decrease the overall renewal rate.

DISTRIBUTION OF MEMBERSHIP CATEGORIES

In organizations with graduated dues, typically, the lowest level of membership, the beginning value level, will contain 80 to 85 percent of the total membership. The next higher category will probably be 10 to 12 percent of the total number of members. The support categories, in the $250 to $500 range, will occupy 2 to 5 percent of the total. The highest levels will have a few tenths of a percentage point of the total.

MEMBERSHIP UPGRADES AND DOWNGRADES

If nothing is done to encourage upgrades, then upgrades and downgrades usually cancel each other out. If upgrades are encouraged, then upgrades should outpace downgrades by two to one. An aggressive upgrade program can serve to decrease downgrades. It may be possible, with the right offer, to have 6 to 12 percent of the members who renew upgrade. It is also typical that 3 to 6 percent of those renewing will downgrade their membership levels.

MEMBERSHIP ACQUISITION

Direct Mail

Response rates will range from 0.6 to 1.5 percent. Response rates of less than that suggest problems with the offer, the creative, the lists, the size of the campaign, or the reputation or awareness of the organization. Response rates higher than this are rare, but possible during a time of special circumstances at an organization.

On-Site Membership Sales

The goal, if sales are pursued aggressively, is to convert 2 to 4 percent of the audience into members. There are different ways of calculating the conversion rate of on-site sales efforts. The standard way is to divide the visitation number (minus school groups and members) by the number of memberships sold. This is the calculation method used to arrive at the 2 to 4 percent goal mentioned here. Others use the same visitation number, divide it by the number of people in a typical visiting party for their organization, and then divide that number by the number of memberships sold. This way of calculating will derive a conversion rate that is twice as high as the 2 to 4 percent target rate—resulting in a 4 to 8 percent conversion rate.

Email

Click-through rates for email will generally range anywhere from 1.5 to 8 percent. Response rates (or conversions) for email marketing can range from 1 to 3 percent or more. Email response rates can be negatively affected by many factors such as poor list hygiene, low open rates, an unappealing offer, non-mobile-friendly emails or landing pages, the newness of the list, poor timing of the campaign, or inactive subscribers.

Online Advertising

Click-through rates for online advertising will fall within the following ranges:

- Display: 0.05 to 1.0 percent
- Rich Media: 0.08 to 0.25 percent
- In-Stream Video: 0.6 to 5.9 percent
- Facebook: 0.1 to 2.0 percent
- Search: 1.0 to 7.0 percent
- Mobile: 2.0 to 4.0 percent

Conversion rates for online advertising vary considerably, but can be expected to fall between 5 and 30 percent, depending on the type of campaign. Conversion rates of less than 1 percent suggest problems with the creative, the number of impressions being served, the targeting, low brand awareness, the landing pages, the offer, or the shopping cart.

Average Gift (Membership Sale) by Source

In a direct mail campaign average gifts (or the average membership sale) are usually $5 to $10 higher than the entry-level ask amount or the most popular category, assuming a graduated range of membership opportunities. For people joining on-site, the average gift tends to be the amount of the most popular category, or just a bit less. For online joiners, the average gift is typically right at or just under the most popular category. For lapsed recapture campaigns, the average gift is closer to the lowest category available.

COST PER DOLLAR RAISED

In general, the cost per dollar raised for acquisition is considered successful if it is at $1.00. This would be a break-even proposition for acquisition. In direct mail the cost per dollar raised may be $1.25 to $1.50 and still be in an acceptable range. Overall, if all acquisition sources were combined, the membership marketing program would be considered successful if it operates at that $1.00 cost per dollar raised.

Cost per dollar raised for on-site sales is usually the lowest, since an organization may be using staff that is serving another purpose (admissions staff). To get a true cost per dollar raised in this case, it would be more accurate to consider a portion of that person's salary (30 percent) as a cost for the sales process.

TELEMARKETING

Telemarketing numbers vary greatly depending on whether professional telemarketers are used and the level of expertise. There are a variety of numbers and multipliers used in telemarketing. First there is contact rate. This is how many people are reached for conversation. With the loss of landlines and adoption of caller ID, an expected contact rate would be 60 to 65 percent. The percentage of people who say "yes" will probably be closer to 10 to 15 percent. The next step is determining how donors will fulfill their pledge. Credit card payment is immediate and the desired method. Credit card rates range from 40 to 100 percent. If a donor wants to pay via mail, the fulfillment rate for non-credit card pledges is 30 to 50 percent. In the end, a phone campaign for lapsed member recapture results can look much like the results shown in table 13.6.

BUDGET

For a program of 5,000 to 15,000 members, the membership department's revenues to expenditure ratio will be approximately 2 to 1, or two dollars raised for each dollar spent. For a larger membership program with

Table 13.6 Telemarketing Lapsed Recapture

	Telemarketing	Calculation
Calling pool		10,000
Contact rate	65%	6,500
"Yes" rate	12%	1,430
Credit card rate	60%	858
Non CC pledges	40%	472
Fulfillment rate	50%	236
Total paid		1,094
Average gift		$75
Total raised		$82,050

economies of scale, it may cost $0.25 to $0.35 to raise $1.00 (cost per dollar raised). Marketing the program, including the acquisition budget, will be 25 percent or more of the membership budget. Staffing may occupy a similar proportion.

STAFFING

Staffing levels depend on the number of members. When starting a new program, one person may be able to handle the program until a membership level of 2,000 to 2,500 members is achieved. As the program grows, there will need to be people to manage program strategy and the data issues. Generally, there should be one data entry person for every 7,500 members. In doing the staff calculation, it is important to understand how memberships are coming into the organization. If 60 percent of new members are coming in through the front desk, and the customer service personnel are entering the new members' contact information into the ticketing or database system, then that is a significant amount of data processing done by staff that may be in a different department. If 40 percent of renewals are coming in via the website, and the data is reliable (not a lot of duplicates to check for) then that is a portion of data processing work that does not have to be hand-keyed by membership processing staff. Memberships still have to be batched, checked for accuracy, and reconciled, all of which is a time-consuming job.

When evaluating the right level of staffing for efficient processing, let the amount of time required to get membership cards to the member be the determining factor. If cards cannot get out to new or renewing members in a two-week turnaround time, then more help is needed.

COST BENEFIT ANALYSIS IN MEMBERSHIP

A cost benefit analysis of the membership program's benefit offerings should be done annually. This analysis is helpful for evaluating the cost effectiveness of the benefits and should be used when trying to determine if the benefits or dues structure should be changed. It may also be used to determine the tax-deductibility of upper-level support membership categories.

This analysis requires knowledge of the cost of the benefits and the members' usage of the various benefits. The budget figures should be available from the previous year's budget. Usage may need to be collected from a variety of sources: from membership surveys, from records kept by the gift shop or the admissions desk, or by the finance office of the organization.

There are three methods of evaluating the cost of the benefits program; each measures the benefits package from a different perspective and can be used for different purposes.

Market Value Method

This method measures the market value or the perceived value of the membership benefits. For members who are value oriented, they will consider this number when asking themselves whether they are "getting their money's worth." This number can also be used to promote membership: "Receive $99 worth of benefits for a $50 membership!" This method attaches the fair market value to a benefit, rather than the actual cost to deliver that benefit.

The Actual Cost Method

This method calculates the actual out-of-pocket cost the membership department pays for the benefits. If another department pays for the benefit, there is no "cost" attached to this benefit. Staff costs are not included here. This method is used to evaluate whether a program is spending too much or too little on benefits, and thus, if the organization is offering enough to be attractive to prospective members.

An illustration of the Market Value Method and the Actual Cost Method is included in table 13.7. A fictitious membership program is used to illustrate these methods.

In this example, the $75 membership category has an appropriate market value. The higher the market value, the more attractive the membership will be to the prospective member. However, the actual cost of the delivery of the benefits needs to be in proportion to the category price. It is common for the

Table 13.7 Cost Benefit Analysis

Benefits ($75 Membership Category)	Market Value Method	Actual Cost Method
Free Admission	$48.00	-
Assume $8 admission used by 2 people, 3 times a year.		
Free Parking	$15.00	-
Newsletter (cost of printing, mailing)	-	$8.00
eNewsletter	-	-
Invitations to previews, events	$20.00	$5.00 (printing, mailing)
Attends one preview or event per year		
The "market value" of attending a preview may be compared to an evening's entertainment such as going to a movie: e.g. $10 x 2 people equals $20.		
Membership Card	-	$1.00
Car decal	$0.50	$0.50
Free reciprocal admission	-	-
Ability to participate in travel program	-	-
Behind the scenes tour	-	-
Membership premium	$10.00	$5.00
Total	**$93.50**	**$19.50**

cost of the benefits to be between $12 and $22 for an entry-level membership category in this price range.

Program Cost Method

The final calculation is the program cost method (see table 13.8). This calculation divides the total cost of the program, everything in the membership budget including staffing, by the number of members. This calculation should be no more than half the amount of the entry-level membership category—the most frequently chosen membership category.

This simple calculation divides the total membership budget by the number of members. Membership managers find this to be the easiest and, thus, most used, calculation. It shows the total cost to attract, service, and renew all members. It considers the entire budget, including staff and all administrative charges (except rent and utilities). Again, this number should be no more than half of the amount of the entry-level membership category. This method is used to evaluate the overall cost of the membership program and to ascertain whether the cost of the program is in line with the amount charged for membership.

If the figure reached by dividing the budget amount by the number of members is more than half the most common entry level category, then either too much is being spent to administer the entire membership program, or the entry level category is priced too low.

Table 13.8 Program Cost Method

	Medium-Sized Membership	Large-Sized Membership
Membership budget including publications, salaries, benefits, cost to solicit and serve members	$179,532	$1,090,501
Member households	7,300	52,000
Average cost to service each member household	$24.59	$20.97
Revenue from membership dues	$382,145	$6,198,000
Revenue per member household	$52.35	$119.19
Net revenue	$202,613	$5,107,499
Return on investment	$2.13	$5.68
Cost per dollar raised	$0.47	$0.18

These calculations should be carried out on an annual basis so that a historical perspective for the program can be maintained. It is important to know the costs and values attached to the membership benefits and staffing of the program. Such knowledge and understanding will guide decisions on dues increases, levels of staffing, and decisions on adding or deleting membership benefits.

LIFETIME VALUE OF A MEMBER

With membership it is important to know the lifetime or long-term value of a member. With acquisition costs being high and with the cost to service a member being higher than servicing a donor, it is important to have a long-term view of membership.

To determine the lifetime value (LTV) of a member, perform the calculation shown in table 13.9.

THE MATH OF DIGITAL

Digital marketing comes with its own set of calculations, metrics, and key performance indicators.

Email

Email is the foundation of any successful digital marketing strategy. It is the one-to-one, personalized powerhouse that can boost the overall effective-

Table 13.9 Member Lifetime Value

Data point needed	How to find	Example
Average length of a member	Query database on length of membership Find the median length of membership	5 years
Average gift of a member	Divide total membership revenues by number of members	$100
Donated revenue in addition	Query amount of donations by members Divide by number of members	$20/year to membership
Gift shop purchases	Dollars spent by members in gift shop divided by number of members	$10/year
Program revenues	Dollars of classes and camps by members divided by number of members	$5/year
Capital Campaign	Capital gifts by members divided by number of members	$100
Total Long-term Value		**$775**

ness of direct mail, advertising, and social media efforts. It's important to understand and monitor the performance of email for several reasons. First, measuring the success of each email will provide the information needed to improve the effectiveness of future campaigns. Further, the performance of any given email campaign will directly affect the institution's sender reputation. Sender reputation is associated with the IP address of the organization's email server and is used by Internet Service Providers (ISPs) to filter emails in different ways. Many factors contribute to a negative sender reputation and will directly affect deliverability, including a high bounce rate, illegitimate email addresses, and spam complaints.

Deliverability Rate

Deliverability rate is the number of emails that successfully reach the inbox. This metric considers emails that bounce back due to an incorrect or abandoned email address. It is important to note that the deliverability rate also includes those emails delivered to the junk mail folder or are otherwise automatically filtered into another folder that the recipient may not check often, if at all. The institution's sender reputation directly affects the deliverability of emails.

Open Rate

The number of emails opened compared to the total number of delivered emails is known as the open rate. This percentage helps to gauge the effectiveness of subject lines, subscriber interest levels, and the timeliness of the email campaign. While it may appear that a high open rate correlates with high readership, as a stand-alone metric, open rate is not a very good indicator of engagement.

There are a number of potential issues that can cause an open rate to be skewed. For instance, image blocking can negatively affect open rates. When a subscriber has image blocking turned on in their "email client" or mailbox provider such as Outlook or Gmail, while they can still read the email, unless an image within the email is loaded, the email will not be counted as an opened email. Further complicating the issue is the widespread adoption of the preview pane, which automatically loads images and counts the email as opened even if the subscriber never really looked at the email, thus causing the open rate to be inflated. A declining open rate or a consistently stable open rate paired with a low click-through rate could indicate that emails are not relevant to the audience or that the list has stagnated and emails are largely being ignored by the bulk of subscribers.

Unique Click-Through Rate

According to the Interactive Advertising Bureau (IAB), unique click-through rate or uCTR attempts to answer the question, "How many unique people clicked on a link or multiple links within this email?"[3] uCTR is calculated by dividing the number of unique click-throughs by the number of emails delivered. Thus, uCTR is a good indicator of engagement and relevancy. In some cases, email service providers (e.g., MailChimp, Constant Contact, etc.) may calculate click-through rate differently—as the percentage of link clicks based on the number of opened emails rather than emails delivered.

Click-to-Open Rate

The click-to-open rate or CTOR provides insight into the question, "Of the subscribers who opened the email, how many clicked?" Generally calculated as either the number of unique click-throughs divided by the number of unique opens, or as the total number of click-throughs divided by total email opens, CTOR offers an additional engagement metric to evaluate campaign performance.[4]

Unsubscribe Rate

Calculated as the number of unsubscribe requests divided by the number of emails delivered, the unsubscribe rate is an important metric that gauges whether email lists are being managed properly and if the content being presented is of value to the audience. Unsubscribe rate can also indicate that the frequency of emails needs to be reviewed.

Too often, the unsubscribe rate is held up as the holy grail of email metrics. Anything that risks even a small uptick in unsubscribes is seen as a dire threat to the institution. While a high unsubscribe rate will negatively affect the organization's sender reputation, refusing to experiment with a special promotion or to send an additional email during the week is shortsighted. The reality is that a spike in the unsubscribe rate can indicate more than just that the organization is sending too many emails. For example, a consistently low unsubscribe rate (in the absence of other metrics to the contrary) could indicate that emails are simply being ignored by subscribers. Consider the example of a zoo that had a very low unsubscribe rate for its e-newsletter for many years. When the organization migrated to a new email service provider, the institution found that a large portion of its emails was never making it to the recipient's inbox. The first e-newsletter sent from the new email platform resulted in a significant spike in unsubscribes. The conclusion drawn from this accidental test was that many of the individuals who unsubscribed from that email had already "passively unsubscribed" long ago. The difference was that by using a new email platform, the e-newsletter was delivered into the inboxes of these "psychologically unsubscribed" subscribers, prompting them to actively unsubscribe. People unsubscribe for many reasons—feeling overwhelmed by too much information, kids have aged out of the children's museum, moved to another city, the list goes on. Ultimately, unsubscribe rate is only one piece of the puzzle. To gauge the true efficacy of an email campaign, other metrics must be considered.

Conversion Rate

The conversion rate of an email is the measure of how many people take a specific action beyond clicking a link. Conversion rate is calculated by the number of conversions divided by the number of emails delivered. A conversion can be any type of action. In the case of a membership promotion, joining would be the desired action. For an event, registration might be the goal. With analytics software, it is possible to track the action back to the email that initiated it. For example, an individual might click on a link from a general e-newsletter and then make the decision to become a member after reading about an upcoming exhibition. This membership revenue can be attributed to the particular e-newsletter that generated it.

Google Analytics

Google Analytics is a robust (free!) website analytics tool that allows organizations to track website traffic, conversion goals, page views, referral sources, and much more. Often, Google Analytics administration resides in another department (e.g., IT or Marketing). Regardless of where this authority resides, it is critical for the Membership department to have access to reporting regarding behavior on membership-related web pages. In the best-case scenario, membership will have full administrative access to Google Analytics and will be a collaborative partner in determining conversion goals related to membership. At a minimum, membership should be provided with monthly reports that show page views, referral sources, landing pages, exit rates, keywords, and conversion goals for membership-related pages.

Conversion Goals

In Google Analytics, conversion goals measure desired actions that take place on the website, including joining, registering for an event, or making a purchase in the online store. However, conversion goals need not be revenue related. Goals can take many forms such as e-newsletter signup, social sharing, signing a petition, and watching a video. The key to conversion goals for membership is to establish goals that directly affect or influence growth in the program. For example, a conversion goal could be set up to track when site visitors view the benefits grid or click on a link to learn more about gift membership.

Conversion goals are limited only by creativity. The following is a series of questions that will be helpful in establishing conversion goals for membership on the website.

> What information is most important to track? Does the organization just want general insight into website visitor behavior, or is there a specific action that would be helpful to track?

> What is the expectation of a website visitor's path? If a visitor begins at the homepage, what percentage of visits should result in membership-related page views?

What defines success? Perhaps the definition of success is that once a website visitor views the membership levels, a membership level is selected and a membership transaction is completed. Another definition of success could be simply viewing the membership levels. Success, like beauty, is in the eye of the beholder.

Where are the opportunities for testing and conversion optimization? Would a different button color have an impact on membership sales? What about a default option for the "most popular" membership level—how would that affect online conversions?

Online Advertising

Online advertising can be measured and evaluated in many different ways. The following is an overview of the most meaningful metrics for membership marketing:

Impressions: The number of times an ad is displayed.

Reach: The number of unique people who are exposed to an ad.

Engagement Rate: The percentage of interactions for a rich media ad per impression.

CPM: The cost for every 1,000 impressions.

CTR (Click-through rate): Similar to email marketing, the CTR of an online advertising campaign measures the number of clicks generated per impression.

Cost per Click: The cost the advertiser pays for each click.

Conversion Rate: This is the percentage of clicks that result in the desired action.

Cost per Conversion: The total cost of the campaign or media buy divided by the number of conversions.

Cart Abandonment Rate

Cart abandonment rate measures when a prospective member initiates a membership sale online by starting the checkout process, but leaves before the purchase is completed. The cart abandonment rate is calculated by dividing the number of people who intended to join by the number of people who completed the transaction.

TAX ISSUES IN MEMBERSHIP

The market value method of measuring the value of benefits is the method required by the IRS in determining the tax deductibility of various membership categories. Generally, as of 1997, the IRS ruled that memberships up to the $75 level are totally tax-deductible. Therefore it is no longer necessary to go through this calculation process for the lower levels of membership. Levels of membership above $75 need to consider calculating only the market value of the benefits given to members that are in addition to the benefits given to the $75 level and below. For instance, if a $150-level member receives all the benefits that the $75 member receives, plus a free hardbound publication, the organization needs to determine only the market value of that book. That market value is determined by the sale price of that book if it were sold on the open market. If that item is not sold on the open market, then the cost to produce it may be used.

The exception to the rule on the $75 membership level and below being totally tax deductible is if items are given that cost more than the dollar amount that the IRS determines annually. Currently, that amount is $10.40.[5] For this reason, an organization such as the Smithsonian Institution that gives a subscription to its magazine, priced on the open market at $28, must use the market value to determine the tax-deductible amount of a given membership category. The market value of the benefit given that exceeds the $10.40 amount must be deducted from the amount charged for membership. For instance, if the Smithsonian charges $70 for its Contributing Membership Program, then it must deduct the $28 from the $70 amount for a tax-deductible amount of $42. However, it can also use the lowest published price for a benefit given. *Smithsonian* is sometimes available at the price of $14 in the Publisher's Clearinghouse Sweepstakes. Thus, since that is a published cost in the open marketplace, that number could be used as the portion that is nondeductible.

Other benefits at higher levels must be valued at the market value, not the cost of the benefit. For instance, if a black-tie dinner is used as a benefit of a $1,000 membership category, and a sponsor donates the cost of the catering, the market value of a fine dinner must be used (e.g., $50 per person) rather than the actual cost to the institution, which is $0. On the other hand, if a person joined an organization without the promise of a benefit, and if that person is invited to the dinner and it was not an expectation at the time of the decision to join, then the value of that offering does not have to be included in the calculation of the amount that is tax deductible. In some cases, members may request not to receive benefits. In this case, that request in writing should be maintained in the files to prove that they wanted their entire donation to be tax deductible.

In most cases, the IRS is looking for an organization to make a wholehearted attempt to come to the best possible calculation for its membership program. The calculation described here could serve as that calculation—thus, another reason to calculate it on an annual basis. It is also necessary to inform the members at the time they make the decision to join. Publishing the tax-deductible amount on the response form or on the invitation to join is necessary. Refer to IRS Publication 526 at www.irs.gov for a discussion of tax deductibility issues related to membership programs.

SUMMARY

The math of membership is one of the most important yet often misunderstood or overlooked aspects of managing a program. Renewal rates, response rates, conversion rates, the distribution of membership categories, upgrades/downgrades, cash flow, staffing, and cost per dollar raised are all metrics that the membership manager must understand to make revenue projections accurately. A cost benefit analysis of the program's offerings should be conducted annually to provide insight into the cost effectiveness of the benefits and to determine whether the benefits or dues structure should be changed.

NOTES

1. Membership Consultants, Inc., "[Webinar Recording] Pulse of Membership Survey Results Year-End 2014," accessed April 21, 2015, http://knowledge.membership-consultants.com/pulse-of-membership-year-end-2014-webinar-recording.

2. Ibid.

3. Interactive Advertising Bureau, "Email Campaign Performance Metrics Definitions," 2015, accessed June 1, 2015, http://www.iab.net/guidelines/508676/508905/79176.

4. Ibid.

5. IRS, "Publication 526, Charitable Contributions," accessed June 4, 2015, http://www.irs.gov/pub/irs-pdf/p526.pdf.

14

What's Next in Membership

Change is the law of life. And those who look only to the past or present are certain to miss the future.

—John F. Kennedy, Thirty-Fifth President of the United States

In membership, the one thing you can be certain of is that there will be change. Evolving audiences, new exhibitions, emerging technologies, shifting priorities, changing attitudes—what worked yesterday may not work tomorrow, so it is imperative that membership managers stay current with the trends facing the profession. The coming generational shifts and the emergence of new technologies such as marketing automation, loyalty platforms, and "big data" paired with trends in consumer behavior, monthly giving, and mobile connectivity represent profound opportunities for membership. The question is, are organizations adequately prepared for the wave of change that is on the horizon?

This chapter looks forward to what may happen to the membership program of the future. As this book is being written in 2015, the trends mentioned here are already under way or are being discussed for the future for membership programs. The passage of time will reveal what is true five or ten years from now.

TRADITIONAL CHANNELS CONTINUE TO WORK

Trends for the future can and do include long-term tactics that continue to work and are still relevant. Direct mail, telemarketing, and on-site sales are examples of membership tools that continue to produce for membership programs.

Direct Mail

The reports of direct mail's death have been greatly exaggerated, to paraphrase Mark Twain. As email became the standard in daily communications, many predicted the death of direct mail with certainty, but direct mail is alive and well and continues to be a very viable channel for membership, especially when accompanied by email and digital marketing. List enhancement and modeling allows for more pinpointed targeting of prospects most likely to respond.

Telemarketing

Another tool that is still relevant to membership, especially with renewals and lapsed recapture, is telemarketing. Changes in phone usage, cell phones, vanishing land lines, negative perceptions, and caller ID have all affected the productivity of using the phone to raise funds; however, despite these challenges, the phone still works. Considering that calls are made to current or former members with whom organizations have a relationship, the phone call is still a way to effect a personal one-to-one connection, and that is what membership is all about.

On-Site Sales

Membership control of on-site sales is a trend taking hold within some membership departments. With on-site sales producing such a large percentage of membership sales and revenues, it is understandable why membership programs feel the need to be in control of their own destiny. In some cases, membership and visitor service departments are within the same supervisory reporting structure, allowing the close working relationship that is so important to sales success. In other scenarios, membership hires its own sales staff for on-site sales in admission areas and lobbies. Membership salespeople are well trained, have goals, and play the vital role of being the face of membership. These salespeople are also key to acquiring email addresses and full contact information, and providing immediate membership fulfillment.

MILLENNIALS AND GEN Z

According to population projections by the U.S. Census Bureau, the "Millennial" generation is projected to surpass the Baby Boom generation as the nation's largest living generation,[1] numbering 77 million and comprising roughly one-third of the adult U.S. population.[2] Born between 1977 and 1995, Millennials in the United States will have the largest annual spending power by 2017, estimated at $200 billion annually.[3] They are also the most educated, indebted, optimistic, hyper-connected, nonreligious, underemployed, entrepreneurial, racially and ethnically diverse, and values-driven generation in history—and they are the future lifeblood of every successful membership program.[4]

Millennials share certain generational traits that are important to keep in mind when developing and executing a membership marketing strategy. Described as "digital natives," many studies have noted that Millennials adopt new technologies quickly, expect technology such as websites and apps to work seamlessly, seek instant rewards and recognition, and tend to live their lives via mobile devices. Consider the following statistics related to Millennials' online activities, consumer behavior, and attitudes toward brands:

- Eighty-one percent of Millennials are on Facebook and 55 percent have shared a "selfie."[5]
- Sixty-two percent of Millennials say that if a brand engages with them on social networks, they are more likely to become a loyal customer.[6]
- Eighty-three percent say that they sleep with their smartphones.[7]
- Eighty-seven percent of Millennials use between two and three tech devices at least once on a daily basis.[8]
- Fifty-two percent of Millennials say that they would be interested in monthly giving.[9]
- Eighty-one percent say they value experiences over material items.[10]
- Forty-two percent said they are interested in helping companies develop future products and services.[11]

Millennials have been shaped by major advances in technology, the Great Recession, social media, 9/11, school shootings, streaming media services, the Arab Spring, the 2008 presidential election, and the maker movement. This generation values self-expression, pursues experiences, needs recognition, engages with causes, not organizations, is willing to pay more for products with social impact, trusts online peer reviews over ads, looks for loyalty programs with rewards tailored to their lifestyle, desires exclusivity and the VIP treatment, is influenced by celebrity endorsements, seeks opportunities to co-create products and services, and craves community. This shift will impact everything—how membership benefits are structured, how dues are paid, the involvement of membership in social media and mobile technologies, member communications, messaging, and which marketing channels are used.

Millennials desire a feeling of connectedness with a broader social good. While they prioritize free admission as the number-one benefit of membership, data from IMPACTS, as described in a blog post by author Colleen Dilenschneider, shows that Millennials place higher value on the sense of belonging and positive impact derived from supporting an organization through membership. Indeed, the top five motivations for joining look very different for Millennials than for those thirty-five years old and older. According to the findings, older members prioritize "free admission," followed by "priority access," "members-only functions," "advance notice of upcoming activities," and lastly, "member discounts" whereas Millennial members indicate the primary benefits of membership (in order of importance) as "free admission," "belonging to the organization," supporting the organization," "supporting conservation," and "making a positive impact on the environment."[12]

While the Millennial generation's influence has already begun to shape the next several decades of patronage and membership, organizations must also be preparing for the arrival of Gen Z—those born after 1995—and how this youngest generation will affect the business of nonprofit organizations over the next three to five years. As its generation's formative events have yet to occur, Gen Z is still too young to be defined by shared characteristics. However, clearly this rising generation will have significantly different expectations of brands, causes, community participation, and technology than the generations that preceded them.

To remain relevant in the coming years and meet the demands of the next generation of members, organizations will need to adapt— in terms not only of marketing strategies and technology, but also program offerings, benefits, dues structures, payment options, and communications.

MARKETING AUTOMATION

One of the most impressive and promising technological advances within the membership marketing space over the past few years has been the introduction of marketing automation software. Marketing automation software allows organizations to market more effectively across multiple channels online such as email, social media, and the website by tracking user behavior, tailoring content to the individual, prioritizing pre-qualified audiences, and automating repetitive tasks. As organizations seek to improve the member, visitor, and donor experience through personalized engagement, marketing automation is closing the gap in being able to track online interactions, analyze individual behavior, and tie key activities into the institutional CRM database. The marketing automation marketplace is dynamic and fast changing with many companies vying for market share, including Hubspot, Act-On, Silverpop, Marketo, Eloqua, and Pardot, to name a few.

One way to think of marketing automation is as an enterprise-level system that ties together disparate marketing efforts providing organizations with deep intelligence to understand not only the total impact of aggregated marketing activities, but also to have the capabilities to nurture relationships through personalized content based on an individual's unique behavior. Leveraging customizable algorithms, real-time data inputs, automated workflows, inbound content strategies, and robust analytics, marketing automation provides a 360-degree view of how prospects and members are interacting with membership content online, making CRM data actionable and allowing membership managers to analyze the path that visitors take on the journey to becoming a member, upgrading, or giving to the annual fund. For example, marketing automation can demonstrate how engaging with individuals via social media translates to new members.

The moment has finally arrived to be able to create and deliver personalized content that will appeal to precisely the right people (e.g., prospective members) in the right place (channel) at just the right time (lifecycle stage). For nonprofit organizations, the opportunities for marketing automation are vast: automated renewal email sequences, landing pages with personalized content, tailored upgrade campaigns, dynamic acquisition strategies, social media and digital campaign integration, sentiment analysis (a research technique that aims to determine the overall attitude of a specific subject matter based on the positive, negative, or neutral responses of the online community), donor cultivation, offer and call-to-action testing, shopping cart abandonment recovery, member surveys, lead scoring, event marketing, search engine optimization, quantifying distinct marketing initiatives and channels, automated workflows based on website interactions, new member on-boarding, member modeling, lapsed member recapture, member services, market research, annual fund, gift membership, and more.

Leaders in the cultural and nonprofit space are already adopting marketing automation to reach target audiences more effectively and prove the value of specific marketing activities. By generating new revenue paths for an organization and reducing costs, marketing automation offers an excellent return on the investment required.

LOYALTY PROGRAMS AND FREE MEMBERSHIP

Loyalty programs are becoming increasingly important for organizations to stay top of mind, capture visitor data, drive repeat visits, and grow membership. Loyalty programs work because they incentivize visitors, members, and supporters to engage with the organization on a regular basis whether on-site or online. Loyalty programs support membership by encouraging participants to provide personal information in exchange for rewards.

To be successful, a loyalty program must include several key aspects:

- A simple, quick enrollment process;
- A mechanism for tracking on-site and online activities;
- Ease of use and reward redemption;
- Clearly defined behaviors and the value of each to the organization;
- Highly prized rewards;
- Rewards at every level of participation;
- Exclusive rewards and/or bonus points for members;
- A digital platform that allows participants to track their status;
- Opportunities for progressive data capture;
- Adequate budget for promotion and membership remarketing;
- Integration with social media, website, mobile, gift shop and restaurant purchases, visitation, exhibits, etc.; and
- Ongoing enhancements and new rewards to keep the program fresh and energize participants long-term.

A well-developed loyalty program will be a feeder program for membership, not a detractor. The loyalty program collects contact information, tracks involvement, and sets the stage for membership participation. For example, a free museum that has hundreds to thousands of anonymous visitors annually might leverage a loyalty program to capture visitor contact information to be able to email a membership offer. Another example is a park that many people use without knowing that there is a membership program supporting the upkeep of the grounds. The park might use a loyalty program to track visitors to incentivize and encourage giving based on the amount of time the individual spends in the park.

In recent years, free membership has been heralded as an opportunity to increase access while capturing the highly prized visitor email address and measuring visitor engagement. For example, the Dallas Museum of Art (DMA) was awarded a National Leadership Grant from the Institute of Museum and Library Services (IMLS) of more than $450,000 to support research and expansion of engagement through a free DMA Friends membership program.[13] In addition, DMA received a grant of up to $300,000 from the Meadows Foundation to support the DMA's return to free general admission and concurrent launch of DMA Friends.[14] Through this program, the Dallas Museum of Art is seeking to increase visitation and track engagement by capturing visitor data. The DMA still offers membership (DMA Partners) with levels starting at $100.

While there are certainly valid strategic business reasons for offering free admission or incentives to collect personal contact information and track visitor engagement, promoting "free membership" is a perilous proposition. First, giving away membership for free removes the transaction aspect of the membership equation, thereby devaluing the membership program. Membership is an exchange of dollars for benefits. Without this core exchange, the concept of membership is negated. Second, free membership can be confusing for visitors and members alike; it is difficult to distinguish the difference between a free member and a paying member. Third, free membership often leads to catastrophic losses of membership revenues as people downgrade to the free level. Moreover, if the organization decides to reinstate the paid membership model in the future, recapturing paying members becomes an incredibly expensive and daunting effort. Finally, if the goal of free membership is really to capture visitor email addresses and track visitor engagement, then a loyalty program is far better suited for this objective.

Often the organizations that have instituted a free admission or membership have received a grant or other funding source that helps to underwrite the impending loss of admission and membership revenue. However, if the goal is engagement measurement and data collection, there are myriad opportunities to encourage visitation and capture visitor data that do not undermine the value of membership, including loyalty programs, mobile apps, and near-field communication. In short, the promise of free membership is untested and, given the high risk, such a strategy appears to be shortsighted.

Amy Langfield raised the subject of free admission in the June 1, 2015 edition of *Fortune.*[15] She warns about the revenue impact on an institution. In some cases, free admission has achieved the goal of increasing access. Admissions reportedly accounts for an average of 4 percent of overall revenues at museums. This amount of reduced revenue may be tolerable at some institutions, especially if a funder underwrites the cost of lost admission. However, free admission will certainly reduce the incentive for visitors to become members. Membership revenues typically account for a significant source of revenue, between 10 and 15 percent, at many museums. Thus, it is necessary to weigh the full impact of these "free" options. Free does not necessarily create loyalty, build a membership program, or increase attendance appreciably.[16]

THE EVOLVING SOCIAL MEDIA LANDSCAPE

Facebook has more than 1.39 billion monthly active users; however, the coming years will see a proliferation of smaller, more niche social networking communities. Additionally, younger audiences will continue to adopt newer, smaller platforms such as Snapchat, Instagram, WhatsApp, Vine, Yik Yak, and Kik. Some of the social media sites mentioned as of the time of this writing may not exist in the next three to five years. The key takeaway is that social media is an incredibly dynamic space with an ever-changing landscape. What is true today may not hold true tomorrow.

As social media continues to proliferate, audiences will adopt new platforms at record speeds—requiring nonprofit organizations to evaluate continually the relevance of new sites and apps and to assess their effectiveness in reaching target audiences to meet institutional goals. Regardless of how social media evolves in the coming years, one thing is clear: organizations must embrace new technologies and platforms early. Experimentation will need to become the standard rather than the exception, and budgets and expectations will need to be flexible to accommodate this new approach to membership marketing.

PREDICTIVE ANALYTICS

Data mining. Big Data. Donor intelligence. The sheer amount of data being collected on a daily basis is staggering. Of course, raw data alone are not useful. To be valuable, data need to be investigated, interpreted, and actionable. Data analysis has been around for as long as organizations have been collecting information, but with immeasurable growth in data inflows, we are now entering the proverbial gold rush era of predictive analytics. As defined by Eric Siegel, predictive analytics is "technology that learns from experience (data) to predict the future behavior of individuals in order to drive better business decisions."[17] Examples of predictive modeling include determining the likelihood of a particular individual to click on an ad, open an email, respond to a direct mail solicitation, upgrade, or attend a certain exhibition.

More and more, organizations are turning to data to drive membership and cultivate donors. With the availability of more (and more robust) datasets—both internally and externally—an organization can gain deeper insight into the needs, wants, and motivations of its visitors, members, and donors. In membership, predictive analytics can help identify patterns to improve response rates and reduce costs for direct mail campaigns, increase conversion rates of digital advertising, and boost year-end giving.

MONTHLY GIVING AND AUTO-RENEWAL

Monthly giving provides a reliable, low-cost income stream for nonprofit organizations as well as the international relief and social service organizations that were the pioneers in this field. For many, the ability to give at lower monthly increments to meet their membership level makes joining possible. Moreover, organizations may find that members join at higher levels than they otherwise would if they are able to stretch out their dues over twelve months.

Monthly giving provides a way for younger, cash-strapped Millennials to make a commitment to organizations they are passionate about. For the membership organization, monthly giving provides a steady, ongoing stream of revenue that can give stability to fluctuating cash flow in the seasonal nature of some organizations. It also gives an organization a head start on a higher renewal rate. Monthly giving is at the core of member and donor loyalty. As author Harvey McKinnon describes in *How Monthly Giving Will Build Donor Loyalty, Boost Your Organization's Income, and Increase Financial Stability*, monthly giving programs can help "draw donors closer to your organization" and those donors will keep giving to the organization over a longer period of time.[18] Thanks to public TV and radio, Americans are warming up to the idea of monthly giving that Canada and Europe have embraced for some time.

The first cousin of monthly giving is auto-renewal. This is a once-a-year automatic renewal of a full-year membership. Like monthly giving, automatic renewal is processed through the Federal Reserve's Automated Clearing House (ACH) system or credit card processing. The Museum of Science, Boston has the most robust example of such a program, with 50 percent of its 50,000-plus members file enlisted in an auto-renewal program. Such programs must be managed with a PCI-compliant processing system. CaringHabits.com is a leader in providing the management and processing of monthly giving (the same mechanics needed for auto-renewal) and PCI-compliant processing in the nonprofit space.

LIFETIME VALUE OF MEMBERS

More pressure from institutional leadership, the board of directors, donors, and funders requires greater financial accountability within membership departments. Today, membership managers must be prepared to measure the long-term or lifetime value of a member and demonstrate a strong return on investment for membership marketing efforts.

Lifetime value (LTV) is calculated by determining the median length of membership within a file and then multiplying that number by the average membership donation and other donations and revenues associated with member purchases and donations annually. Matchback analysis and lifetime value can provide insight into the long-term impact of membership on the institution's bottom line. Having the full picture of what a member brings to an institution will help make the case for investment in the membership program.

BLOCKBUSTERS

Blockbuster exhibitions are both a scourge and salvation for a membership program and an institution. Blockbuster exhibitions are characterized by high attendance, high cost to the institution and the visitor, high membership potential, and much attention in mainstream and social media. Everyone loves the revenues, the increased visitation, and the buzz created by a blockbuster exhibition. The downside is that sometimes traveling blockbuster exhibitions may detract from the overall curatorial culture and focus of a particular institution.

Blockbusters can be difficult to manage administratively with many major touring entities taking away control and decision making from the institution and its curators and managers. Exhibition owners can dictate pricing, whether members will be allowed to attend for free, and in some cases, every aspect of the exhibition's presentation. Additionally, blockbuster exhibitions can be a major financial gamble for an institution. The costs to host and present can be staggering. The additional staff time, budget, and institutional resources can be immense. All with no guarantee that the return on the investment or that the visitation outcome will be as positive as it might be portrayed or anticipated. The taxing nature of some major exhibitions can be deleterious to staff, causing exhaustion and turnover.

The returns can also be spectacular. Some exhibitions will put an institution "on the map" by drawing the kind of attention that has never been experienced at that organization. A major exhibition of the blockbuster kind can drive revenues to new heights from admissions, membership, shop sales, and concessions. Memories of such success can leave an afterglow that lasts in the minds of people for years to come.

These myriad circumstances, both positive and negative, have caused some institutions to make future declarations about their intentions with respect to blockbusters. Some major art institutions have declared war on the concept of traveling exhibitions, saying that they are no longer in the blockbuster business, or at least not of the traveling variety. An institution may stage and curate its own major exhibition, choosing to focus instead on its own collection.

The converse of this trend is the adoption of a commitment to make traveling exhibitions with the intention of hitting blockbuster gold an annual endeavor. This is particularly true of the botanical garden world wherein the recent past has seen blockbuster adoption become the latest trend. No longer is the seasonal flower show or Mother Nature's bounty enough to drive dollars, visitation, and membership. The traveling shows of art, light, sculpture, and cultures are a common occurrence among botanical gardens, arboreta, and zoos. Holiday light shows with record off-season attendance give outdoor venues an added boost in typically slower months.

Thus, the trends surrounding blockbusters are proving to be mixed—embraced by some organizations, and faced with policies against blockbusters for others. In either circumstance, these are trends to watch.

THE AGE OF THE CUSTOMER

We are entering what Forrester Research has called "the age of the customer"—a twenty-year cycle in which technology-empowered audiences "know more about your products, your service, your competitors, and pricing than you do."[19]

Much of the opportunity to meet this coming challenge lies in what George Colony, Chairman and CEO of Forrester Research, refers to in his foreword to *The Digital Marketer*, as the four market imperatives that all organizations must be able to adapt to remain relevant. These four market imperatives are (1) transform customer experiences, (2) become digital disruptors, (3) embrace the mobile mind shift, and (4) turn big data into business insights.[20]

From a membership perspective, these market imperatives will play out in the following ways.

Transforming customer experiences. Organizations must be prepared to make substantive investments in improving member, donor, and visitor experiences to build stronger relationships. As Colony notes, this means adopting a "customer obsession," that focuses strategy, energy, and resources on those touch points that increase engagement, streamline processes, and seamlessly integrate technology. Examples of this concept in action include an online member portal, tying visitation and online activity to a loyalty program, mobile-enabled transactions, monthly giving and auto-renewal options, distributed authorship in social media (by which responsibility and authority for social media content is spread across multiple departments), and personalized email communications.

Becoming digital disruptors. Digital marketing is dynamic, powerful, and evolving at an accelerated pace. To stay relevant, membership managers will need to adapt, proactively adopting digital marketing strategies and building deeper relationships with technology and marketing than ever before. In some cases, this will require membership to be the leader in the digital arena—pushing the institution forward to meet the demands and opportunities of the future.

Embracing the mobile mind shift. Mobile is no longer a trend; it is a way of life. Integrated within every facet of our work and personal lives, mobile technology is now a foundational channel in reaching and engaging visitors, members, and donors. Organizations will need to be prepared to embrace mobile marketing fully in order to keep up with consumer expectations. Opportunities for membership to leverage mobile include SMS text messaging, mobile apps, mobile-friendly websites, and on-site engagement such as interactive exhibits, loyalty activities, near-field communication, and geo-fencing.

Turning big data into business insights. Membership in the coming years will emphasize not just data collection, but data insights. Advances in the field such as marketing automation, predictive analytics, multivariate testing, and real-time optimization will drive efficiencies in membership marketing, allowing for more sophisticated and higher performing campaigns. Membership managers must be prepared to advocate for membership, proactively identifying new technologies and services that will reduce costs, improve the member experience, increase renewal rates, and generate new revenue streams.

As digital strategies become more and more integrated with other channels—both online and off—membership departments will need to work collaboratively across the organization to execute initiatives that span multiple institutional roles. To illustrate the point, consider the online membership sale. Who should own the process of optimizing the checkout function?

- Marketing may think that because the checkout function falls under the umbrella of the website, the marketing department controls changes and upgrades to the checkout process.
- IT may feel that because e-commerce is tied to the structural integrity of the website, requiring technical integration with various databases, the programming aspect alone puts optimization of the checkout squarely in the domain of IT.
- Clearly, the growth of the membership program is directly impacted by the clunky, antiquated checkout function that doesn't offer a prospective member a simple, no-hassle way to join. Should the membership department have full authority to improve the checkout process to meet its online sales goals?

Thus, there are many potential stakeholders who have an interest in the online checkout function. Often these distinct departments have unbalanced needs when it comes to the e-commerce capabilities of the organization, or worse, entirely disjointed goals and priorities. If marketing is rewarded solely for driving admissions, where is the incentive to prioritize online membership sales? If IT's priorities are focused around the new POS implementation, when will membership's needs be addressed? Unfortunately, the result of such interdepartmental issues manifest in abandoned shopping carts and lost membership revenue.

By emphasizing common goals, nonprofits can create an opportunity for shared conversations about the impact and value of membership to the institution. There needs to be a direct incentive and shared goals across departments that make membership a priority for all. When marketing, IT, guest services, and development are all invested in the growth and sustainability of the membership program, the institution wins.

The bottom line is that prospective members do not care why the checkout process is not more user friendly; they will just give up. This new reality is forcing organizations to break down silos, end territorial job functions, and rethink departmental goals to focus on customers—specifically, the visitors, members, and donors who will provide financial stability to the organization in the future. As a result, membership is changing. Membership is becoming more responsive, more innovative—evolving into a collaborative, market-focused, data-driven machine.

The landscape of the modern nonprofit organization is evolving rapidly, requiring membership departments to move at warp speed to keep up with new technologies and trends in consumer behavior. It is vital that membership managers stay ahead of the curve. The success of tomorrow's membership program will depend on the adeptness and adaptability of today's membership manager. So, here's to you—the fearless leader who will embrace the coming challenge with optimism and excitement, forever seeking the opportunity that inevitably comes with change.

SUMMARY

The future of membership is a mixture of both old and new. Certain channels and strategies will remain viable and a necessary part of the marketing mix. The continued relevance of direct mail, telemarketing, and on-site sales anchors successful membership programs in a secure, time-tested way. Future strategies need to focus on younger audiences, which will create a new reality for membership. What Millennials and Gen Z expect, how they engage with organizations, and their motivations will dictate the next evolution in membership. These new, younger patrons will lead the way in the ever-changing digital landscape. Expectations of involvement, experiences, and personalized communications will define how the next generation of members engages with an organization. How an organization responds and adapts to this coming change will ultimately define the future of its membership.

NOTES

1. Richard Fry, "This Year, Millennials Will Overtake Baby Boomers," Pew Research Center, January 16, 2015, accessed February 9, 2015, http://www.pewresearch.org/fact-tank/2015/01/16/this-year-millennials-will-overtake-baby-boomers.

2. Nielsen, "Millennials—Breaking the Myths," 2014, accessed February 9, 2015, http://www.nielsen.com/content/dam/corporate/us/en/reports-downloads/2014%20Reports/nielsen-millennial-report-feb-2014.pdf.

3. Micah Solomon, "The Millennial Customer Has $200 Billion to Spend (But Wants a New Style of Customer Service)," *Forbes*, January 21, 2015, accessed February 9, 2015, http://www.forbes.com/sites/micahsolomon/2015/01/21/the-millennial-customer-has-arrived-has-200-billion-to-spend-and-wants-a-new-style-of-customer-service.

4. Scott Keeter and Paul Taylor, "The Millennials," Pew Research Center, December 10, 2009, accessed February 9, 2015, http://www.pewresearch.org/2009/12/10/the-millennials.

5. Pew Research Center, "Millennials in Adulthood," March 7, 2014, accessed February 9, 2015, http://www.pewsocialtrends.org/2014/03/07/millennials-in-adulthood.

6. *Elite Daily*, "Millennial Consumer Trends," 14, accessed February 9, 2015, http://cdn29.elitedaily.com/wp-content/uploads/2015/01/2015_EliteDaily_MillennialSurvey3.pdf.

7. Nielsen, "Millennials—Breaking the Myths."

8. *Elite Daily*, "Millennial Consumer Trends," 12.

9. Case Foundation, "Millennial Impact Report," 2013, 6, accessed February 9, 2015, http://casefoundation.org/wp-content/uploads/2014/11/MillennialImpactReport-2014.pdf.

10. Will Palley, "Data Point: Constantly Connected Millennials Crave Sensory Experiences," *JWT Intelligence*, January 25, 2013, accessed February 9, 2015, http://www.jwtintelligence.com/2013/01/data-point-constantly-connected-millennials-crave-sensory-experiences/#axzz3dBAtuWLw.

11. *Elite Daily*, "Millennial Consumer Trends," 14.

12. Colleen Dilenschneider, "How Generation Y Is Changing Museum and Nonprofit Structures," *Know Your Own Bone*, October 30, 2012, accessed May 4, 2015, http://colleendilen.com/2012/10/30/how-gen-y-will-change-museum-and-nonprofit-membership-structures-data.

13. Dallas Museum of Art, "Dallas Museum of Art Receives Institute of Museum and Library Services Grant," accessed March 14, 2015, https://www.dma.org/press-release/dallas-museum-art-receives-institute-museum-and-library-services-grant.

14. Dallas Museum of Art, "Dallas Museum of Art Announces Grant from the Meadows Foundation to Support Free General Admission and DMA Friends," accessed March 14, 2015, https://www.dma.org/press-release/dallas-museum-art-announces-grant-meadows-foundation-support-free-general-admission.

15. Amy Langfield, "Art Museums Find Going Free Comes with a Cost," *Fortune*, June 1, 2015, accessed June 2, 2015, http://fortune.com/2015/06/01/free-museums.

16. Colleen Dilenschneider, "Admission Pricing is Not an Affordable Access Program (Fast Fact Video)," *Know Your Own Bone*, September 16, 2015, accessed September 16, 2015, http://colleendilen.com/2015/09/16/admission-pricing-is-not-an-affordable-access-program-fast-fact-video/.

17. Eric Siegel, *Predictive Analytics: The Power to Predict Who Will Click, Buy, Lie, or Die* (Hoboken, NJ: Wiley, 2013), 11.

18. Harvey McKinnon, *Hidden Gold: How Monthly Giving Will Build Donor Loyalty, Boost Your Organization's Income, and Increase Financial Stability* (Chicago: Bonus Books, 1999), 10.

19. David M. Cooperstein, "Competitive Strategy in the Age of the Customer," Forrester Research, October 2013, 5, accessed December 22, 2015, http://solutions.forrester.com/Global/FileLib/Reports/Competitive_Strategy-CMO-2013.pdf.

20. George Colony, Foreword to *The Digital Marketer*, by Larry Weber and Lisa Leslie Henderson (Hoboken, NJ: Wiley, 2014). x.

Appendix A

Planning Worksheet: Acquisition

DETERMINE STRATEGY ______________________________

____

OBJECTIVE 1. ______________________________

____

ACTION PLANS

a. ______________________________

b. ______________________________

c. ______________________________

d. ______________________________

OBJECTIVE 2. ______________________________

____

ACTION PLANS

a. ______________________________

b. ______________________________

c. ______________________________

d. ______________________________

OBJECTIVE 3. ______________________________

____

ACTION PLANS

a. ______________________________

b. ______________________________

c. ______________________________

d. ______________________________

Appendix B

Planning Worksheet: Renewals / Current Members / Lapsed Members

DETERMINE STRATEGY ______________________________

____

____

OBJECTIVE 1. ______________________________

____

ACTION PLANS a. ______________________________

b. ______________________________

c. ______________________________

d. ______________________________

OBJECTIVE 2. ______________________________

____

ACTION PLANS a. ______________________________

b. ______________________________

c. ______________________________

d. ______________________________

OBJECTIVE 3. ______________________________

____

ACTION PLANS a. ______________________________

b. ______________________________

c. ______________________________

d. ______________________________

Appendix C

Planning Worksheet: Upgrades

DETERMINE STRATEGY ______________________________

____

____

OBJECTIVE 1. ______________________________

____

ACTION PLANS a. ______________________________

b. ______________________________

c. ______________________________

d. ______________________________

OBJECTIVE 2. ______________________________

____

ACTION PLANS a. ______________________________

b. ______________________________

c. ______________________________

d. ______________________________

OBJECTIVE 3. ______________________________

____

ACTION PLANS a. ______________________________

b. ______________________________

c. ______________________________

d. ______________________________

Appendix D

Planning Worksheet: Events

DETERMINE STRATEGY ______________________________

____

____

OBJECTIVE 1. ______________________________

____

ACTION PLANS a. ______________________________

b. ______________________________

c. ______________________________

d. ______________________________

OBJECTIVE 2. ______________________________

____

ACTION PLANS a. ______________________________

b. ______________________________

c. ______________________________

d. ______________________________

OBJECTIVE 3. ______________________________

____

ACTION PLANS a. ______________________________

b. ______________________________

c. ______________________________

d. ______________________________

Appendix E

Planning Worksheet: Record Keeping

DETERMINE STRATEGY ____________________

____

OBJECTIVE 1. ____________________

____

ACTION PLANS a. ____________________

b. ____________________

c. ____________________

d. ____________________

OBJECTIVE 2. ____________________

____

ACTION PLANS a. ____________________

b. ____________________

c. ____________________

d. ____________________

OBJECTIVE 3. ____________________

____

ACTION PLANS a. ____________________

b. ____________________

c. ____________________

d. ____________________

Appendix F

List Trade Agreement with Mailing Organization

The Mailing Organization is requesting a membership mailing list exchange with your organization to be used in its upcoming membership acquisition direct mail campaign. We are requesting usage of your list for our upcoming expected mail date of **February 23, 2015**.

______ **Yes**, we agree to participate in one list exchange with the Mailing Organization.
Our comma separated file and record layout will be provided by **Wednesday, February 4, 2015**.

We are sending ________ quantity of names.

______ **No**, we are not interested in participating at this time, but you may contact for future mailings.

______ **No**, we are not interested; please do not request our participation for future mailings.

Both trading organizations agree to the following:

* Organizations participating in the list exchange agree to ensure confidentiality and security of the lists.

* Membership data will be sent directly to a 3rd-party mail house. None of the information contained on the list may be copied, entered, or appended to any borrowing institution's files. Only prospects responding directly to the mailer may be entered into the mailer's permanent database.

* No telephone and/or email contact will be made.

* The source of the list will not be divulged. Codes imprinted in the mailing cannot reveal its source, including abbreviations or initials of the organization.

Names will be merged with other lists before mailing and duplicates will be purged. The resulting list is then processed to comply with current U.S. postal regulations.

Please send your file to **third-party@mailhouse.org**. Please label your list with your org's name and Mailing Organization. Please send list in Excel spreadsheet or ASCII comma delimited format, *preferably with these fields*:

Preferred Salutation / First Name / Last Name / Street Address 1 / Address 2/ City / State / Zip

To receive the Mailing Organization list, please contact Membership Manager, at (xxx) xxx-xxxx or by email: **membership@mailingorganization.org**.

Please sign to indicate your agreement to the above list exchange guidelines. A copy bearing both signatures will be returned to you.

Approved:

______________	______________	______________
Name	Trading Organization	Date
______________	______________	______________
Name	Mailing Organization	Date

Appendix G

Membership Case Studies

NATIONAL BASEBALL HALL OF FAME AND MUSEUM[1]

National Reach—Focused Growth—Digital Adoption

In 2001

This is an excellent example of how a program can develop from 3,000 members and net income of $7,000 to one of 13,000 members and net income of $314,000 in three years by doing some very basic things. The National Baseball Hall of Fame has also incorporated significant use of its website.

In 2015

Growth to 32,000 members utilizing direct mail, on-site sales and a commitment to digital marketing in a very robust way. The Hall of Fame's membership program is now generating more than $2,000,000 annually in support of the Museum's mission.

History

1980–1997 The Hall of Fame Fan Club

Single level of membership
Averaged 2,500–3,500 members annually
Limited on-site presence for membership
Limited direct mail

One letter renewal, with a renewal rate of 60 percent
Three-week turnaround for new members and renewals
Revenue of $102,000
Net of $6,800

1998 Re-launched as Friends of the Hall of Fame
Graduated tiers of membership
Limited on-site presence
Limited direct mail
Non-secure Web presence
One letter renewal, rate 55 percent
3,441 enrolled
Three-week turnaround for new members and renewals
Revenue of $189,000
Net of $112,000

1999 Friends of the Hall of Fame
Graduated tiers of membership
Limited on-site presence
Limited direct mail
Non-secure Web presence
4,899 enrolled
Three-week turnaround for new members and renewals
Revenue of $342,000
Net of $223,000

2000 Increased Profile
New marketing materials
Member activities
Increased on-site presence
Direct mail acquisition
Three letter renewal sequence
Secure Web presence
Fulfillment turnaround 48 hours or less
Revenue of $625,000
Net of $314,000
Increase from 4,800 to 13,000 members

Major focus on premiums
Premiums selected for rapid fulfillment
Fulfillment in 48 Hours
Welcome letter, membership card, gift message combined—mails immediately upon processing
Premiums follow ASAP
Currently fulfill in-house
Early Adoption of Online Membership Activity

Promotions for Hall of Fame now directed toward having people visit the website rather than visiting Cooperstown
April 2000—150,000 Web visitors, with 110 members enrolled
April 2001—191,000 Web visitors, with 110 members enrolled
May 2001—launch of direct email program

Knowledge based e-newsletter

Content and Mission driven

Can opt-out

Custom offers

Full tracking of click through activity

Fast Forward to 2015
32,000 members from all 50 states
Still committed to direct mail and on-site sales, while aggressively pursuing all online and digital channels
Direct mail of 200,000 annually from a high of 400,000 in the early and mid-2000s
On-Site sales account for 5,000 to 6,000 memberships annually
Museum Box Office operations were moved to Development and Membership Department with a major focus on training staff in sales
Renewal rate of 75 percent; first year renewal rate of 35 percent—a series of 4 email reminders and 7 mailed packages
Major focus on email, website traffic analysis, content testing for monetization purposes
Drives 20 percent of membership sales activity online

Has emails for 85 percent of members; total email universe is 100,000

BBHOF historically had healthy gift shop with catalog sales that helped drive membership. Now, catalog has given way to online gift shop sales with membership driving sales rather than the reverse as in the past. Members buy more and spend more than other audiences.

Staff size of processors—Database Manager and 3 FT processors plus 5 or 6 seasonal processors during summer

120,000 Facebook followers; voting contests on Facebook; Facebook strategy is to drive website traffic

Utilize Twitter and Instagram in addition to Facebook

Utilize website and Facebook retargeting

Membership revenues of $2,200,000 and net income of more than $1,000,000

Ken Meifert is the Vice President, Sponsorship and Development, at the National Baseball Hall of Fame and Museum. Ken has risen through the ranks from Membership Manager to his current position. With a 14 year involvement in membership, the program has had the care and consistency needed to grow the program in terms of size and sophistication.

Courtesy of the National Baseball Hall of Fame and Museum, Cooperstown, New York.

DESERT BOTANICAL GARDEN[2]

Phoenix, AZ

Large Organization Significant Growth; Exhibit Driven

Grew from 18,000 (2008) to 40,000 (2015)

2008

Program had grown from 12,000 in 2003

Use of direct mail to acquire and to recapture

Renewal rate of 60 percent

2009

Hosted first major Chihuly glass sculpture exhibition

Grew from 18,000 to 28,000 members

Utilized direct mail and on-site sales

Very strong visitation

This popular exhibition helped DBG grow at a time when the economy caused other organizations to experience membership declines

2010

Created stronger training program for admissions staff and volunteers

Increased on-site capture rate from 3.75 percent in 2009 to 5.9 percent in 2010

2013–2014

Garden hosts second *Chihuly in the Garden* exhibition

Grew to 40,000 members

Aggressive direct mail and on-site sales

Attracted 1,894 members from direct mail

Attracted 10,868 members from on-site sales

Garden invested heavily in site improvements from 2009 to 2013—new restaurant, membership kiosk and enlarged parking amenities

2014–2015

Launched effort to increase first year renewal rate, after major blockbuster exhibition

Performed a First Year Member Pre-Emptive telemarketing campaign—achieved a 31.42 percent first year renewal rate compared to an average of 25 percent for first year

65,000 Facebook followers

ST. LOUIS COUNTY LIBRARY FOUNDATION[3]

Small Membership—Steady Growth

1,350 Members in 2015

Increased from 400 members in 2009

Hosts one of the most successful schedule of author events in the country—80 to 90 events per year, with an average of 200 attendees per event, but as high as 1,000 attendees

Membership built primarily from in-house solicitations and monthly mailings

Memberships sold on-site at author events

Priority seating at author events is most coveted benefit
Free featured book at upper level membership purchase

Added direct mail acquisition campaigns in 2012—two campaigns annually of 5,000 and 10,000 quantity
Much personal service and attention paid to members
Membership revenues help fund literacy and children's programs
Foundation has 173 Facebook followers; Library has 10,000 Facebook followers

ABRAHAM LINCOLN PRESIDENTIAL LIBRARY AND MUSEUM[4]

Rapid Growth—Plateau—Rejuvenated

2005

Museum and Library open
Missed opportunity at grand opening
Only 450 members after 1.5 million visitors in the first year and a half
Program had only one time admission benefit
Dues too high
Membership not promoted in any meaningful way

2007—2009

2 years after opening, new foundation begins to focus on membership
Professional membership plan developed
Membership marketing begins with direct mail
On-site sales begins, professionally trained
Membership grows to 6,000 members in time for Lincoln Bicentennial in 2009

2010–2014

Membership in maintenance mode
On-site sales continue with 300 new members added per month, enough to maintain, but not grow
Direct mail is curtailed
Membership at 5,500

2015

Library and Museum plan for tenth anniversary
and Sesquicentennial of Lincoln's death
Retraining and refocus of on-site sales
Membership grows to 7,000
22,000 Facebook followers

FRIENDS OF THE SAN FRANCISCO LIBRARY[5]

Solid Program—Maintenance Mode

Friends of the San Francisco Public Library is an independent 501(c)3 organization that supports the San Francisco Public Library, a major urban library system.

Friends has been in existence for 54 years, since 1961

3,800 Members: Renewal Rate of 70 percent

3,733 Friends Facebook followers and 1,563 Friends Twitter followers

(15,000 Facebook followers for the SF Public Library)

Two Big Book Sales are major fundraising events every year; Friends host and manage with 800 volunteers.

IMBIBE is another popular annual event; food and beverage donated; Scheduled in several branches each year.

Promotion of the Big Book Sales includes 50 bus shelter ads, 500 Posters, 1 billboard

On-site sales at Book Sale; early entry to Book Sale is most popular benefit.

Use direct mail, list trades, mailing 10,000 pieces

In 2014, Friends raised $4,039,679 annually, expense budget of $3,473,450

Staff 17; over 800 volunteers

An overview of all that the Friends of the Library does for the San Francisco Library system is available at http://www.friendssfpl.org/?About_Friends

SAINT LOUIS ART MUSEUM[6]

Growth—A Grand Opening

Opened a new wing 2013, the first expansion in 50 years

During construction and partial closure, membership dipped to 9,500 in the summer of 2010, five months after the groundbreaking for the new East Wing

A free museum, but with admission fees charged for major traveling exhibitions

With the opening of the new East Wing, a new parking garage and visitor service counter added

Visitor Services becomes part of Membership team, a change from when it had reported to Marketing. And with that transition, also moved from outsourced on-site sales to in-house team

Program employs use of direct mail for each major exhibition; has historically performed 1 or 2 campaigns a year for past 30 years

During special exhibitions, on-site sales team has a 4 to 5 percent on-site sales conversion of people attending the exhibition. (As a free museum other than special paid exhibitions, with these robust free attendance numbers, overall membership conversion of total attendance is 1 percent.)

Membership has grown to approximately 16,000 since grand opening of East Wing and the return of a robust exhibition and programming schedule

No significant adoption of digital campaigns for membership to date

Has 38,000 Facebook followers

NOTES

1. Case Study of the National Baseball Hall of Fame and Museum. Ken Meifert, Vice President of Sponsorship and Development at the National Baseball Hall of Fame and Museum. Copyright 2015. All Rights Reserved.

2. Large Organization Significant Growth; Exhibit Driven Statistics. Desert Botanical Garden. Copyright 2015. All Rights Reserved.

3. Small Organization Steady Growth Statistics. St. Louis County Library Foundation. Copyright 2015. All Rights Reserved.

4. Source: Abraham Lincoln Presidential Library and Museum. Copyright 2015. All Rights Reserved.

5. Solid Program—Maintenance Mode Case Study. Friends of the San Francisco Library. Copyright 2015. All Rights Reserved.

6. Grand Opening Growth. Saint Louis Art Museum. Copyright 2015. All Rights Reserved.

Glossary

A/B Testing: Also known as split testing, a process of running a simultaneous experiment between two variables to determine which receives better results.

Above the Fold: The visible portion of a web page when the page first loads in a browser window.

Acquisition: The process of asking prospects to join the organization's membership.

AIDA: An acronym for the various stages within the customer journey including Awareness, Interest, Desire, and Action.

Algorithm: A set of programmed rules used by a search engine or social media platform to determine the relevance of results and stories.

Ask: The solicitation of a gift; sometimes refers to the amount of the gift.

Average Gift: The calculation of the total amount of revenue generated divided by the number of respondents.

Beacons: Small wireless sensors that use Bluetooth® connections to transmit data or prompts directly to a mobile device.

Behavioral Targeting: An online advertising technique that uses a combination of software and data to target web users based on previous actions.

Benefits: The tangible or intangible items that are offered in exchange for joining the organization.

Bounce Rate: The percentage of emails that are undeliverable.

BRE: Abbreviation for business reply envelope, often included with a membership solicitation for the potential member to use to return the membership form. It can be printed with or without postage included.
Button: Any type of graphical element embedded on a web page, ad, or email that prompts the user to take a particular action.
Call to Action (CTA): A statement or instruction used in advertising, email marketing, and online media that explains to a user how to respond to a promotion, offer, or invitation.
Cart Abandonment: The act of not completing an online transaction.
Click-Through Rate (CTR): The frequency of interactions for an email, ad, or landing page as a percentage of the number of emails sent, ad impressions, or views.
Conjoint Analysis: A statistical market research method that uses predictive software to test numerous combinations of benefits by quantifying respondent preferences and perceived value.
Conversion: Any measurable activity such as purchase, clicks, email sign-ups, or downloads.
Conversion Optimization: The process of improving the experience of a website or landing page with the goal of increasing the percentage of visitors who take a desired action.
Conversion Rate: The measure of desired actions taken as compared to the click-through rate (CTR).
Cookie: A small piece of data automatically sent from a website and stored in a user's computer or mobile device that identifies the user's browser, making the user recognizable as he or she browses online or returns to a website.
Cost per Acquisition (CPA): The price to obtain a new member.
Cost per Dollar Raised (CPDR): The amount of money required to raise $1 in donations.
Crowdfunding: The practice of raising money for a project or initiative by collecting small monetary contributions from a large number of people, typically online.
Customer Relationship Management (CRM): A database that supports management of member, donor, and visitor interactions with the organization using software to organize, automate, and log sales, renewals, marketing, customer service, and cultivation activities.
Dedupe: See deduplication.

Deduplication: The merging of mailing lists for the purpose of eliminating the duplicates. Also known as merge/purge processing.
Deployment: The launch and management of an email campaign.
Domain: The unique URL of a website, e.g. www.xyzmuseum.org.
Downgrade: A member who chooses to decrease his or her membership level.
Drop: When a campaign mails from the post office; or a particular mailing.
Dues: The amount paid for a membership. Sometimes called the donation, gift, or contribution for the membership.
Email Append: The practice of taking known member or visitor data such as first name, last name, and postal address and matching this information to a third-party database to add an email address.
First-Year Member: A person who has joined within the last twelve months.
Five-Year Income: What a campaign produces financially if the five-year life of a member is taken into consideration.
Flat Dues: A structure that offers dues at one level. See graduated dues.
Fulfillment: The act of generating and distributing the appropriate information and benefits to a member who joins or renews.
Geo-fencing: Software that uses the global positioning system (GPS) of a mobile device to define geographical boundaries.
Geotargeting: The process of serving ads to users based on the global positioning system (GPS) of a mobile device.
GIF (Graphics Interchange Format): A format for storing digital images and short animations.
Google Analytics: A free service that tracks and reports website traffic, user behavior, and conversions.
Graduated Dues: A structure that has multiple levels of dues. See flat dues.
Hard Bounce: An email that is permanently undeliverable.
Hashtags: A word or phrase preceded by the # symbol used within a social media post to identify a keyword or topic and facilitate search results.
HTML: Abbreviation for Hypertext Markup Language, a set of commands used by web browsers to display content to users.
Incentive: A gift that is offered to encourage joining or renewing. Used interchangeably with premium.
Internet Service Provider (ISP): A company that supplies Internet connectivity to a user.

Interstitial: Full-screen ad that cover the interface of the host application or web page.
IP Address: The numerical identification assigned to a user's computer on a network.
Keyword: Terms or phrases used by search engines to return relevant content or ads based on a user's query.
Kill File: The file of names of those who do not want to receive direct mail or telemarketing from the organization. Also called a suppression file.
Landing Page: The screen where a user is taken upon clicking on a hyperlink within a website, email, or ad.
Lapsed Member: A member who has not renewed within a specified period, usually two or three years.
Lifetime Value: The monetary value of a member over the time of his or her membership.
Lockbox: A service from a bank or other company that receives the member's enrollment form, opens the letter, deposits the check, and sends a report to the institution.
Marketing Automation: Software designed to integrate data tracking, customize content, and mechanize processes such as segmentation, workflows, and campaign management.
Matchback Analysis: The process of comparing an original mail or email file to a list of all transactions during a campaign period to calculate the full impact of a campaign.
Member Portal: A password-protected website or section of a website that offers resources, personalized services, exclusive content, and information to members.
Membership: The belonging to an organization or institution that involves receiving benefits in exchange for dues or other commitment.
Merge/Purge: The consolidation of mailing lists for the purpose of eliminating the duplicates. Also known as deduplication or deduping.
Multichannel Marketing: The practice of using several media simultaneously to reach an audience such as email, advertising, direct mail, etc.
Multis: Names that appear in duplicate when all mailing lists are merged and before duplicates are removed.
Multivariate Testing: A technique used to determine which combination of variables performs best out of all the possible combinations.
Multi-Year Member: A member who has renewed at least once.

Near-Field Communication (NFC): Short-range wireless technology that enables smartphones and other devices to establish radio communication through touch or proximity.
Open Rate: The percentage of people who view an email based on the total number of emails delivered.
Open-to-Click Rate: The number of unique interactions with an email divided by the total number of unique views expressed as a percentage.
Pay per Click (PPC): An advertising management system that allows advertisers to bid for placement and interactions of paid search results.
PCI Compliance: Abbreviation for the Payment Card Industry Data Security Standards, a set of requirements designed to ensure that organizations that process, store, and transmit credit card information maintain a secure environment.
Pixel: See Retargeting.
Premium: See incentive.
Pre-Roll: Streaming ads that show before or while an online video is loading.
Pull: The productivity of a direct mail campaign; the response a direct mail campaign generates.
Renewal: The process of asking members to continue their membership; a member who has made the commitment to continue.
Renewal Rate: The rate at which members continue their membership.
Response Rate: The number mailed in a direct mail campaign divided by the number of responses.
Retargeting: A cookie-based technology that uses a JavaScript code called a pixel to assign an anonymous tag to a user in order to serve him or her advertising online.
Retention: The practice of keeping of members.
Return on Investment (ROI): The yield on the money spent on a campaign or the amount that will be returned to the organization for every dollar spent; the amount raised divided by the cost.
Rich Media: An umbrella term to describe online advertising formats that use interactive and audiovisual elements to provide a more engaging experience for the user.
Rollout: The mailing of a large number of direct mail appeals after testing with a smaller quantity.
SCF: Abbreviation for Sectional Center Facility, the first three digits of a zip code; a reference to the postal handling facility; used when ordering lists for direct mail.

Search Engine Optimization (SEO): The process of improving a website's position or ranking within organic results displayed by companies like Google or Bing in an effort to maximize traffic to the site.
Seed: The practice of adding an internal email address or postal address to a campaign to receive a sample. Also known as seeding.
Serve: The delivery of an online ad to an end user's computer or mobile device by an advertising management system.
Soft Bounce: An email that is temporarily undeliverable.
Split Testing: See A/B Testing.
SSL: Abbreviation for Secure Sockets Layer, a security technology that ensures data exchanged between a server and browser remains private by encrypting the communication.
Stewardship: The actions taken to make certain that the member's gift is properly spent and accounted for.
Subdomain: An additional word or phrase that precedes the primary URL to display different web content (e.g., join.xyzmuseum.org).
Suggestive Selling: A technique used to offer complimentary products or an upgraded membership during the sales process.
Support Member: A member who elects a dues or donation level that is clearly more than the perceived economic benefit of the membership. See value member.
Suppression File: The file of names of those who do not want to receive direct mail or telemarketing from the organization. Also called a kill file.
Trust Seal: A designation mark that verifies to users that a website is legitimate.
Unsubscribe: A request from a user who no longer wishes to receive email from an organization.
Upgrade: A member who chooses to increase his or her membership level.
URL: Uniform resource locator; the unique name that allows a computer user to access a resource.
Usability: A measure of the quality of a user's experience when interacting with website content or services.
Value Member: A member who elects a dues or donation level that provides the tangible benefits that are of interest. The perceived value of the membership is equivalent to or more than the dues contributed. The donation made may or may not include financial support for the institution; however, the motivation to join is in the benefits. In an organization with graduated dues, the first several levels will usually be value levels. See support member.

Index

About the Authors

Patricia Rich is a founder of EMD Consulting Group and has consulted throughout the country and overseas on fundraising, membership, planning, search, and nonprofit management issues for all types of organizations. She has been the president/CEO of the Arts and Education Council of Greater St. Louis and the director of planning and development at the Missouri Botanical Garden, being responsible for all phases of fundraising, membership, and strategic planning, which she has taught at the University of Missouri–St. Louis.

Dana S. Hines is the president and CEO of Membership Consultants, Inc. Dana founded Membership Consultants in 1987 and has served over 500 membership organizations nationally, providing membership audits and strategic plans, direct mail, and multichannel campaigns to acquire, renew, upgrade, and convert members to donors. Dana and Membership Consultants have been leaders in the membership arena, serving clients such as the National Baseball Hall of Fame, Museum of Science Boston, Desert Botanical Garden, Phoenix Zoo, History Colorado and Forest Park Forever. Dana served as a membership manager for the Missouri Botanical Garden prior to her membership consulting career.

Rosie Siemer is the founder and CEO of FIVESEED, a digital marketing agency and interactive design studio delivering integrated online marketing, social media, and mobile solutions for visitor-serving organizations, education, associations, and nonprofits. Rosie has consulted for leading institutions across the United States including the Museum of Science Boston, History Colorado, Phoenix Zoo, Museum of Contemporary Art San Diego, University of Nebraska, Colorado Center for Nursing Excellence, and the Association of Zoos and Aquariums. Rosie serves on the Board of Directors at the World Trade Center Denver, and is an instructor at the Rocky Mountain World Trade Center Institute on the topics of international social media and mobile marketing.